Irish History
FOR
DUMMIES®
2ND EDITION

By Mike Cronin

WILEY

A John Wiley and Sons, Ltd, Publication

Irish History For Dummies®, 2nd Edition

Published by
John Wiley & Sons, Ltd
The Atrium
Southern Gate
Chichester
West Sussex
PO19 8SQ
England

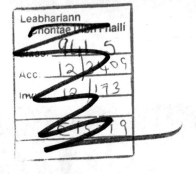

E-mail (for orders and customer service enquires): cs-books@wiley.co.uk

Visit our Home Page on www.wiley.com

WILEY

Irish History
FOR
DUMMIES®
2ND EDITION

About the Author

Mike Cronin studied history at the University of Kent and at Oxford, and has taught history to university students for the past fifteen years. He has published widely on the history of Ireland, and also on the history of sport. His books include a history of sport and nationalism in Ireland, a jointly authored history of St Patrick's Day celebrations around the world, and a general history of Ireland. He is currently the Academic Director at Boston College's Centre for Irish Programmes in Dublin, and is researching the history of major public spectacles and festivals in twentieth century Ireland.

Author's Acknowledgments

Over the years I have taught many university students who knew no Irish history and had no Irish heritage. This was a challenging and fascinating process as it forced me to rethink my teaching of Irish history from the beginning. Much of what appears in this book, and the ways that different periods of Irish history are explained, emerge from the challenges laid down to me by my students over the years. To all of them, for their patience and their interest, I offer my thanks.

I would also like to acknowledge the work of two important people at Wiley: Alison Yates who first came to me with the idea for this book, and Rachael Chilvers who worked long and hard in making sure that everything was done properly. The efforts of the development editor, Tracy Barr, the copy editor, Martin Key, and the technical editor, Neil Fleming, are much appreciated, and all made incisive and valuable comments that have improved the text. For the new edition, I have to thank Mike Baker and Simon Bell for holding my hand and going through this all again.

My colleagues at the Centre for Irish Programmes at Boston College were, as always, a mine of useful information and a source of support, and in Dublin, Thea Gilien graciously allowed Dummies to interfere with the work of the office. For his help (again) with the Irish language, and his general enthusiasm for life, I'd like to thank Brian Ó Conchubhair. At home, my family, Moynagh, Ellen and Samson, were as joyful as always, and their love and support invaluable in everything I do. Anything that is amiss with the book is all my fault, and all the wonderful people listed above are blameless!

Publisher's Acknowledgments

We're proud of this book; please send us your comments through our Dummies online registration form located at www.dummies.com/register/.

Some of the people who helped bring this book to market include the following:

Commissioning, Editorial, and Media Development

Project Editor: Simon Bell,
    (Previous Edition: Rachael Chilvers)

Commissioning Editor: Mike Baker,
    (Previous Edition: Alison Yates)

Assistant Editor: Ben Kemble

Copy Editor: Martin Key

Technical Editor: Dr N.C. Fleming, Queen's University, Belfast

Publisher: David Palmer

Production Manager: Daniel Mersey

Cover Photos: © CORBIS: Brooks Kraft, Bettmann, Hutton-Deutsch Collection, Reuters; Hulton Archive/Getty Images; The Irish Image Collection

Cartoons: Rich Tennant (www.the5thwave.com)

Composition Services

Project Coordinator: Kristie Rees

Layout and Graphics: Carl Byers, Joyce Haughey, Corrie Socolovitch, Kim Tabor

Proofreader: Laura Albert

Indexer: Claudia Bourbeau

Contents at a Glance

Table of Contents

· ·

Part III: The Invading English Kings: The Fourteenth and Fifteenth Centuries 109

Chapter 8: The Scottish-Irish Rebellion and Its Aftermath........111

Chapter 9: From Richard II to Henry IV: More Turmoil in Ireland ...127

Introduction

· ·

*W*hen I first travelled to Ireland to do some research, I was amazed by the reaction of the people I talked to. After I had explained what I was doing, I was half expecting people to nod politely and then run off to watch paint dry because that would be more interesting than talking about Irish history. What I found instead was a country full of people who were passionate and excited about their history and wanted to talk and talk and talk about it. Every person had their own story. This could be about a family member who had been involved in or witnessed a great moment in history, or the story of the local area and the events that had unfolded there. And these were great stories. They weren't boring facts recited without any humour or excitement, but tales that brought the events of the past to life.

I quickly realised that in Ireland, unlike any other country I had ever visited, history was alive and well and everyone seemed to own it and have their version of it. True, it wasn't always accurate and if the stories I heard are to be believed, then the General Post Office in Easter 1916 (see Chapter 21) was the busiest place in the world as everyone's grandfather, uncle, aunt, and cousin seems to have been there. In a way the accuracy of these tales doesn't really matter. They show that everyone wants to be involved in the story of their country. Not everyone can be centre stage, but we can twist the past a little bit to make sure that our relatives had at least a walk-on role. History in Ireland is everywhere. It's in people's heads, it's in the architecture and the landscape, it's on television, and it's always causing rows in bars across the land. In some parts of Ireland history has been made into tourist attractions, in Northern Ireland historical conflicts are still being politically fought out, and across the island history is being made every day. For this new edition of the book, I've taken the story bang up to date, and added some extra information from recent years to help you learn more about Ireland.

About This Book

While you've been standing in the bookshop or searching online before you bought this book you would have noticed one thing: there are lots and lots of books about Irish history out there. So what's different about this one? Well, unlike the others it doesn't presume any prior knowledge about Ireland and things Irish. Most other books are also very dense with endless pages of text that don't offer much fun or any distractions along the way. Also, many of the books out there concentrate on specific bits of Irish history – Ireland in the nineteenth century, Ireland before, after or during the famine, Ireland since yesterday, or even Ireland before time began. That's not to criticise any of these books, most of them are very good, but they are date-specific. What's offered here is one big, entertaining sweep of Irish history. The story takes us from the first people arriving in Ireland, right to the present. The journey is a long one but there's lots to see on the way and loads of interesting Irish people to meet.

One big question we've got to deal with from the outset is to define what we are dealing with in this book. What does 'Ireland' actually mean? Well, this book looks at Ireland in several different ways. At one level this is simply a book about the history of the island of Ireland. All of it, from Malin Head in the north, to Mizen Head in the south. But Ireland, like any other country, isn't an island (well it clearly is an actual island, but you know what I mean. Its history isn't one of isolation). As well as taking in the history of Ireland, the book also deals with all those external forces and countries that had an impact of Irish history: England and Britain, America, France, and so on. We'll also take a look at how Ireland influenced the rest of the world, and how, in the twentieth century the two bits of Ireland (the Irish Republic and Northern Ireland) got on with each other.

Of course, the big issues in history are contentious. People worry whether or not history as it's told is true, and whether or not the whole thing is biased one way or the other. Well, my answers to those questions are simple. First of all the truth . . . what I've tried to do here is to tell the story as it happened and without bias. Remember, Irish history is very contentious and both the nationalist and unionist communities have their own version of the past. However, there are lots of interesting things in history that weren't strictly true and have become part of the whole folklore and mystery of Irish history. We can't simply ignore these tales, so they are included here but with an explanation. As to the whole question of bias, this is a tough one. We all have our opinions, and I am sure you'll have yours. Make up your own mind as you go along, and if you don't agree, that's great. History is made up of rows and fights, so our disagreements just fit into a long and noble tradition.

Conventions Used in This Book

The way that this book is put together has been planned to entertain and inform you. You will find a lot of detail and a whole host of icons that explain different bits and pieces along the way.

Sidebars (text that is enclosed in a shaded grey box) are pieces of information that are interesting. They're not central to the story however. You can either skip them altogether, save them for later, or read them with the general text. They're just there to help you understand the joys of Irish history in its entirety. The same is true for text next to the Technical Stuff icon. It's there for your information, and will give you the inner detail. But the material isn't necessary for your understanding of the topic. Again, skip it if you want. This isn't homework, and no one will know.

Foolish Assumptions

Obviously I don't know you (so hello, nice to meet you), and I had to make some assumptions about the kind of person who'd want to read this book. As a result I'm assuming that you're a really great person and that:

✔ You're interested in Ireland because you've got some Irish blood in you, are visiting the place for the first time, or have seen it on the news and wanted to know more.

✔ Maybe you know a bit of Irish history, but find it all very confusing figuring out who's who and what's what.

✔ Perhaps you did learn some Irish history at school but it's all gone a little hazy since then.

✔ You know about Irish things from listening to other people and just want to know more.

✔ Or you recognise a good story when you see one.

How This Book Is Organised

This book has been put together so that you can go from beginning to end or, if you fancy it, jump from topic to topic. To make getting round the book, and the history of Ireland, easier I've divided the book into parts (there's seven of them). Each part relates to a specific period in Irish history, and contains a series of chapters with information about that era. The sections in the book, as well as the kind of material you'll find in them, are listed below.

Part 1: The Snakes Leave Ireland

In Irish history there is no Christopher Columbus or Captain Cook. Ireland was never discovered you see, it simply emerged one day from under the glaciers of the last ice age. It sat there unnoticed and unloved for a while until people from Scotland started taking holidays there, and liked it so much that they decided to stay. The first settlers were a fairly simple people and restricted themselves to a bit of hunting and gathering. It gets interesting once the Stone Age starts and people start building big tombs, and then, later still, things get even more interesting when the Celts and the first Gaelic people arrive. Men start throwing their weight around and get to be king of various bits and pieces of Ireland, and a system of rule begins to emerge. The period closes with the arrival of the most famous Irishman of all – St Patrick. Not only does his life end up being celebrated by green beer around the world, but he also brings Christianity to Ireland and chases away all the snakes (or so they say).

Part 11: The Normans Are Coming! The Twelfth and Thirteenth Centuries

Ireland got very used to being invaded during this period of history. Whether it was the landscape, the beauty of the monasteries, or the weather, Ireland certainly seemed to be able to attract a whole string of people who wanted to visit the place and take over. First to arrive were the Vikings. Initially they were happy to content themselves with a little bit of plundering, but eventually they decided to settle – they even started up a small town called Dublin. The Irish kings seemed fairly powerless to do anything about the Vikings, and let themselves be walked all over for a few decades. Eventually they got their act together and convinced the Vikings to go home. Problem was that the Normans got involved in Irish politics and they came invading too. It was the start of centuries of constant interaction between Ireland and the people from across the Irish Sea.

Part 111: The Invading English Kings: The Fourteenth and Fifteenth Centuries

Once the Normans had paved the way, the English got a taste for Ireland and seemed reluctant to leave. The constant problem for the English was that the Irish were a troublesome lot, and wouldn't quietly accept being ruled by an English king. They were constantly plotting and causing all kinds of problems. Also, they always seemed happy to make friends with anyone, such as the Scots or the French, whom the English hated. During these two centuries Ireland was a fairly unsettled place, and successive English kings struggled to know what to do. At various times they poured troops into Ireland to try and suppress the country, or else they stuck their heads in the sand and tried to ignore it. They also tried to control the Irish by laws which were supposed to make them more English. The problem was that many of the English who settled in Ireland liked it so much they started speaking Irish, marrying Irish girls, and becoming like the natives.

Part IV: Religious Wars and Family Feuds: The Sixteenth and Seventeenth Centuries

As well as being invaded, religion became one of the great themes of Irish history. Since the time of St Patrick all had been straightforward. Ireland and England, despite their differences, both accepted that the Pope was a really important guy, and in things God-related they all took their orders from Rome. In the sixteenth century however it all went pear-shaped. Henry VIII decided he didn't like his wife anymore, and tried to get a divorce. The Pope wouldn't let him, so Henry went off in a huff and set up his own Church. Protestantism was born. Ireland didn't take to the change in religion well, and resisted the new religion, preferring instead to keep its priests and their links with Rome. England tried to change Ireland by sending over Protestant settlers by a process of plantation, but that simply set up two separate communities who deeply distrusted each other. In the end, it all came down to a royal war between Protestant King William and Catholic King James at the Battle of the Boyne. William won, and the last hope of a Catholic on the English throne disappeared.

Part V: Catholic and Protestant: The Eighteenth and Nineteenth Centuries

Ireland and Britain struggled to find a way to get on during the eighteenth and nineteenth centuries. The British were a bit paranoid. They saw Ireland as a troublesome, backward place that was still dominated by Catholicism. This was a real pain as Britain was busy trying to build an Empire and see off annoying European enemies such as the French. The real problem was that the Irish, in search of some level of independence, encouraged the French to help them in a rebellion in 1798. The whole period saw an upswing in demands for some form of liberty for Ireland. At first, and spearheaded by

Daniel O'Connell, these demands were just for religious freedom. But in the second half of the nineteenth century they changed into political demands for national freedom. Also during this period the Great Famine of 1846–51 struck. It killed countless thousands and encouraged a million more to emigrate. This was the beginning of the large scale Irish diaspora and they would have a major impact wherever they went.

Part VI: Divided in Two: Life from the 1880s

By the end of the nineteenth century many people in Ireland were sick and tired of British rule and wanted to do something about it. The first big movement was a cultural one that convinced Irish people to embrace their own culture. If they wanted to be truly Irish they had to stop adopting British habits. The Cultural Revival, as it was called, encouraged people to speak Irish, read Irish plays and novels, and play Irish games. There'd be no more cricket for the Irish. The success of the Cultural Revival found an echo in politics, and demands for Home Rule (political freedom from Britain) increased. It was all looking good for Ireland until a million Germans heaved into view and started the First World War. The War fractured politics in Ireland, and led to the rise of Sinn Fein and the IRA. They fought a war against the British and won a partial freedom for Ireland in 1922. Partitioned Ireland (Northern Ireland as part of Britain and the Republic of Ireland as a separate state) was always an uncomfortable fit, and the whole thing exploded into violence in the 1960s. The Troubles in Northern Ireland lasted for over three decades and were violent and bloody. Fortunately it now looks like they may be all behind us. While the Irish Republic enjoyed a brief boom, in the form of the Celtic Tiger, it is sadly once more a place of economic depression and outward migration.

Part VII: The Part of Tens

This bit of the book is intended to give you a whole load of information and some gems of knowledge that will allow you to impress friends, family, and strangers alike. They'll tell you what the most important events were in Irish history, explain which are the most important Irish documents, and also give you a list of the ten great things that the Irish have given the world (the ejector seat for example). There's also a list of Irish people who deserve to be better known, and for those of you who decide to visit Ireland, a list of places that you simply must see. Remember, it's a personal list of mine, so feel free to add some of your own.

Icons Used in This Book

Obviously there's loads of history in this book, and a mass of information for you. But history isn't just about facts and figures, and famous people. As you'll see when you read the book there's loads more. Throughout the text there are a series of icons that will give you extra information, settle some arguments, and get you thinking about how history has affected the present.

Great stories abound in Irish history, but there's always a thin line between fact and fiction. This icon means that we'll check out whether or not some stories in Irish history are really true.

What happened in the past continues to affect the future. This icon highlights how historical events are still shaping life in Ireland today.

One thing that historians love more than history is a good old-fashioned punch-up. Irish historians have been particularly prone to disagreeing with each other, and this icon will highlight different interpretations of Irish history that have been put forward.

This icon highlights certain points that are important in making sense of what's coming up.

You can skip these bits, but they're there to assist you understand some of the more complex points and give you additional information.

Where to Go from Here

In an old Irish joke, a tourist is lost and stops to ask a local directions. The local scratches his head, thinks for a brief moment and then tells the tourist: 'Well, if I wanted to go there, I wouldn't start from here.' The sentiment is a good guide for this book. There is no right way of reading this book, and no right place to start from. You can do the traditional thing and begin at the beginning and finish at the end or, alternatively, you can just dive in where you fancy. If you want to know about the Famine, then go to chapter 18, but equally if St Patrick takes your fancy, then start at chapter 4. All the parts and all the chapters have been written so they can be read in isolation. Wherever you choose to start, enjoy it and enjoy Ireland and its history.

Part I
The Snakes Leave Ireland

In this part . . .

Ireland, or what would come to be known as Ireland, lay under a sheet of ice for a very long time, and not much happened. But then finally, as the ice melted, people started visiting Ireland from Britain. Some of them liked it so much that they decided to stay. These first people figured out how to grow crops, set up some of Ireland's first towns, and brought some life to the place.

The first Gaelic people arrived during this time, and started making Ireland truly distinct. They had their own language and started a system of ruling through kings that would dominate for centuries. Also, one of the most famous Irishmen ever came to the island: St Patrick. He brought Christianity with him and transformed the Irish into religious people. It was a big step because it made Ireland one of the most cultured places in Europe at the time.

Chapter 1

No Man Is an Ireland

Most of us know bits and pieces of Irish history. When we drink green beer or go parading on 17 March for example, most of us know the celebration is about St Patrick, and has something to do with snakes and the shamrock. But how much do we know about the ways in which this day became so important to Ireland and the Irish around the world? And what about the troubles in Northern Ireland? We know that the troubles involve Catholics and Protestants, and that the IRA (Irish Republican Army) has been in the middle of it all, but how did the troubles actually come about? And there's some fourteen centuries of history between the arrival of St Patrick and the troubles!

Then there's the people. Most of us can name a few famous Irish people – Brian Boru, for example, or Michael Collins – but Irish history goes beyond these well-known names. In fact, Irish history has a cast of millions, a nearly endless list of characters who have inhabited the island over the centuries. Ireland has given the world some of the smartest people in the arts and literature, some great musicians and dancers as well as a host of committed politicians and religious leaders. These people have been joined by various invaders and visitors as well, making things even more interesting.

Irish history is not just the story of the great and powerful. The story also includes the people who died over the centuries from famine and disease, the millions who sailed off and settled in new homes across the globe, the workmen who built canals, roads, and railways in Britain, America, Canada, and elsewhere and the priests and nuns who did missionary work in the developing world. We don't know many of these people as they never got to be well-known, but they're all part of this story.

I'm Irish – But Who Isn't?

Probably like lots of you reading this book I have Irish ancestors (but don't worry if you haven't got any, it's not compulsory). The remarkable thing about the Irish is how successful they have been getting around the world. There's a long history of comings and goings in Ireland, and understanding these patterns of arrival and departure help explain why everyone seems have some Irish in them.

Arrivals

As you'll see when you start reading the other chapters, Ireland was a favourite place for various different peoples to invade. These invasions had a real effect on who the Irish were as everyone eventually got on so well they started mingling and mixing. The following sections discuss who these new arrivals were.

Celts

Although not the first to arrive, the Celts were the original major influx of foreigners. The Celts brought a new language to Ireland, as well as the most up to date forms of metal work and, by contemporary standards, a network of trading connections that spread onto the continent. The last wave of the Celts were Gaelic people, and it was they, especially in language terms, that made the people in Ireland distinctly Irish. You can read more about the Celts in Chapter 2.

Vikings

Coming from Norway and other places in Scandinavia, the Vikings had a big impact on Ireland. They set up trading routes with fellow Vikings in Europe, and although not much loved by the Irish, whom they kept attacking and killing, the Vikings did establish many of Ireland's main towns and cities.

The Vikings, also known as the Norse, did what all the invaders did – they started mixing with and marrying the Irish. Rather than forcing their culture on Ireland, or eventually going home, the Vikings got integrated into Irish society. Historians talk about the Hiberno-Norse tribes of Ireland. These were a mix of the Irish (Hiberno) and Viking (Norse). Such interactions meant that the Irish kept getting diluted and changed over the centuries. For more about the Viking influence in Ireland, sail to Chapter 5.

Normans

Arriving at the end of the twelfth century the Normans made the most critical intervention in Irish history. They had taken over England after winning the Battle of Hastings in 1066 and, by contemporary standards, had fairly clear ideas about how things should be run. They were initially invited into Ireland to help settle a local squabble, but liked it so much they stayed! They also followed the tradition of inter-marrying and adapting Irish habits (and, after they adapted to Ireland, became known as the Irish-Normans) so that as the years went by their fellow Normans sometimes struggled to recognise them. By deciding to stay, the Normans linked together the histories of Ireland and England for centuries to come. You'll find out more about them in Chapter 7.

English

When did the Normans become English? Well, without a long detour into the history of England and the early Middle Ages, the simple answer (and a bit of a fudge) is sometime in the thirteenth century. What is important is that the English, and particularly their monarchs, started thinking of themselves as distinct from their Norman (or more specifically French) origins. In fact they really started hating the French and began fighting with them constantly. In Ireland the emergence of a clearly defined and distinct England, as opposed to something that was still Norman, meant that the English just struggled to recognise anyone in the Emerald Isle. The Irish had always been a bit of a mystery, but the Irish-Norman crossbreeds were equally alien. English kings, such as Henry II, Richard the Lionheart and King John, eventually sent armies to Ireland, and started an influx of English people to Ireland. For more about the English involvement with Ireland, have a look at Chapter 9.

Planters

After the Reformation (see Chapter 11) there was a need to make Ireland loyal to the new religion of Protestantism. The Irish, being Catholic, had resisted the whole idea. Rather than spend any more time trying to convince them of the virtues of the new product, Elizabeth I decided to send in her own people. A process of plantation began. What this meant was that the Crown gave big chunks of land to any Protestants who were prepared to go and settle Catholic Ireland and sort it out. It was a brave move. It resulted in a new breed of English (and Scottish) migrants to Ireland. They were devout Protestants and saw their job in Ireland as a religious mission. Plant yourself in Chapter 13 to find out more.

Spaniards and Frenchmen

Tales have always been told about dark-haired and dark-skinned Irish people who were the descendants of ship-wrecked Spanish sailors, but these stories seem a bit far fetched. The Spanish got involved in Ireland during the English-Spanish Wars of the Elizabethan era, and clearly bits of the Armada did end up crashing into Ireland. Some of these sailors probably did decide to settle and inter-marry but it's doubtful that their genes were so powerful that their features are still showing up in children today. As well as the Spanish, the French also got involved in Irish politics at various times after their own revolution in 1789. A few French fleets and invading forces arrived in Ireland (always unsuccessfully) but the fact is that they landed (see Chapter 15).

New Irish

Ireland had always been seen as a place, certainly since the eighteenth century, that you left. However, in recent decades, what with wars in other parts of the world, and the booming Irish economy, more and more people have decided to make Ireland their home. Since the 1990s Ireland has witnessed an influx of new people. So when you're in Ireland don't be surprised when your barman or waitress is from China, Eastern Europe, Australia, or South Africa. The new Irish are making the whole country, and especially Dublin, a multicultural place.

Departures

One of the most important stories in Irish history isn't really about Ireland at all. It's about the people who left. By the end of the twentieth century between 70 and 90 million people around the world were estimated to be able to claim an Irish ancestry. For an island that doesn't even house six million people, that's an impressive diaspora.

Irish people started leaving early on. Some of the first emigrants were travelling monks, and they were followed by people who joined the British army and helped establish the British Empire and a host of people who travelled across the Irish Sea in search of work.

The Irish in Britain

For all the antagonism between Britain and Ireland, the Irish were a key component in the success of the British. The Irish provided workers for British factories during the industrial revolution, and built the country's canals and railways. They were soldiers in the British armies that went to the four corners of the world, and also travelled the Empire as teachers, civil servants, missionaries, and engineers. In both the World Wars of the twentieth century the Irish joined up in huge numbers, sacrificed their lives, and were a key component in ensuring victory.

In the seventeenth and eighteenth centuries it was famine that drove people out of Ireland. Also, the world had got bigger, and places as far away as America and Australia were open for business and ready to receive the Irish. In the second half of the nineteenth century the population of Ireland leaked like a sieve, with hundreds of thousands of them packing their bags and leaving. In the twentieth century it was little better. Economic downturns in the 1920s, 1950s, and 1980s convinced whole new generations to try their luck someplace else. The fighting in Northern Ireland from the 1960s also persuaded many people that their future lay out of Ireland.

The Irish that left remained very loyal to their homeland. Over the centuries many of them would return, or would encourage their descendants to do so. The rate of return has been especially marked since the boom of the 1990s and the availability of highly-skilled jobs in information technology and finance. Also, many companies that have located their businesses in Ireland have directors and executives with an Irish heritage. While their decisions to locate their companies in Ireland undoubtedly had a solid business rationale, one also has to reckon that their choice was also driven by a romantic attachment to the old country.

The story of emigration is, at one level, thoroughly depressing. People left their homes because of poverty, and often died in transit. Once in their new homes many were forced to do awful jobs, found solace at the bottom of a glass, or else died in the kind of poverty that they were supposed to be escaping. It's the stuff that fills the song books of many an Irish singer, but the story of emigration was also one of great success. Without the Irish the world would have been very different. They played a key role in making countries such as America and Australia successful, they proved themselves very good at business and politics, created some of the world's greatest art, literature, and music of their time, and sent money back to Ireland to keep people afloat there.

So Much History in Such a Small Place

Ireland's not a big place. Cut it out of the pages of an atlas and place it on somewhere like America, Australia, or Canada, and it just gets swallowed up. Yet, as the old saying goes, size isn't everything. For a small place, Ireland has had a huge impact on the world, and a lot of things have happened on the island. The following sections discuss the main themes of Irish history, each of which had a large hand in the historical events throughout the ages and in shaping the Ireland of today.

Ireland and the land across the Irish Sea

Britain and Ireland, like Tweedledum and Tweedledee, are inseparable. Clearly the history of Ireland can't be split off from the history of Britain. The events in Ireland and Britain constantly have an impact on each other. Sometimes it was for the good but, more often than not, someone suffered. Britain involved itself politically with the affairs of Ireland from the twelfth century. Economically the two places were closely linked, and it was Irish immigrants to Britain that became a central part of the workforce during the industrial revolution. In the early twentieth century the British and Irish fought a war over whether Ireland should be independent, and since the 1960s the British have been involved in the troubles in Northern Ireland.

Religion

Often blamed for everything, the impact of religion on Ireland has been huge. From the arrival of St Patrick and the advent of Christianity, the Irish have been a very religious people. The picture was made more complex with the invention of Protestantism and its difficult relationship with Catholicism. Lots of murders and martyrs came out of that battle. Despite all the other aspects of its history that have been important, the impact of religion on the island has been most long lasting. Whether it was the suppression of old religions such as Druidism, the introduction of Christianity, the struggles over the reformation or the religious component of the troubles in Northern Ireland, religion has been central to the story of Ireland.

The two religions had an important bearing on the kinds of countries that the Republic of Ireland and Northern Ireland became in the twentieth century, and still are today.

Today both the Republic of Ireland and Northern Ireland have laws that protect the free observance of any religion as desired by the individual. Clearly though, the two states have favoured Catholicism and Protestantism respectively. In the Republic, the teachings of the Church were very powerful, and laws relating to social issues such as divorce, abortion, and contraception have been political hot potatoes in recent decades. Officially the Church and State are separate in both the Republic and the North, but as most people still have strong religious affiliations, many laws are still more in tune with Church teachings than they would be elsewhere in Europe.

Land

In the John B. Keane play, *The Field* (there was a film of the same title), a man kills another over the ownership of a small patch of land. It's a powerful play, and captures well one of the dominant themes in Irish history – who owns the land?

Ireland was, until well into the late twentieth century, an agricultural and rural country. People traditionally made their living from the land. The problem was that other people (landlords) owned it, and the ordinary Irish farmer couldn't afford to buy it. The Irish were removed from the ownership of the land in the centuries before the late 1800s, and this was deliberately done so that the Irish could not have access to power of wealth. The control of land, as we'll see, was an important way of controlling the power balance in Ireland and also an attempt to enforce Protestant beliefs on an unwilling Irish population.

You'll see this issue crop up time and time again in the book, so remember – while the Englishman's home might be his castle, for the Irishman it's a nice green field he can call his own.

Famine

Irish history is littered with episodes of famine when bad weather and disease led to near total crop failures. Over the centuries millions died, and famine appears constantly as one of the great tragedies of Irish history.

Out of all these famines, one of the greatest tragedies of Irish history was the Great Famine of 1845–51. If the famines had been numbered like Hollywood sequels, it may well have been 'Famine 28: the Return of the Hunger'. Nevertheless, this famine was important for a number of reasons:

- ✔ It led to the mass emigration of the Irish around the world.
- ✔ The famine was blamed on the British, and this led to resentment towards them.
- ✔ The deaths of so many people illustrated how the Irish economy and infrastructure was in a terrible state.
- ✔ It led, in the second half of the nineteenth century, to demands for land reforms and eventually to the widespread support for Irish independence.

Emigration

In response to famine, as well as a lack of economic opportunity and political upheaval, the Irish emigrated like no one else in history. But the mid-nineteenth century emigration was nothing new. People from Ireland were instrumental in the early settlement of America. Even earlier, and in response to political defeats, Irish nobles had left Ireland for Europe in the early seventeenth century. Irish missionaries had also been central in the spread of Christianity across Europe in the eighth and ninth centuries. So, as you can see, the Irish have always been travelers, and that's why we find their descendants across the globe.

Self-determination

A constant recurring theme of Irish History is the wish of the Irish just to be left alone (unless they needed external help against the British at which point they often turned to the French or Spanish). They desired, campaigned for, and fought wars in support of the ideal that everybody else would scarper and leave them to run their own country the way they wanted to. Prior to the nineteenth century the Irish were most concerned with preserving their Catholic religion and the control of the land. This is why they so opposed the British who they believed wanted to take over the land and force Protestantism on them. In the late nineteenth century this tradition of resistance manifested itself as a nationalism that took up arms in the cause of an independent Ireland.

The idea of self-determination has lots of different expressions, and over the centuries various leaders have emerged with different ideas of how it can be achieved. Leaders include:

- ✔ Brian Boru (see Chapter 5) was a great Irish leader. Credited with throwing the Vikings out of Ireland, he's a good example of the early Irish leader. His main aim was to keep invaders away from Ireland.

- ✔ Hugh O'Neill (see Chapter 12) wasn't very fond of Queen Elizabeth I and her rule over Ireland. He encouraged a rebellion across Ireland and managed to get the Spanish involved too. His aim was to drive the English out of Ireland, and he nearly managed it. He lost in the end though, but he demonstrates well the spirit of successive Irish nobles who tried to take on the English.

- ✔ Daniel O'Connell (see Chapter 16) is seen as one of the great Irish leaders. He was a firm believer in combining constitutional politics with mass popular support. He mobilised the Irish people in a campaign against anti-Catholic legislation and was successful. He considered Ireland as a Catholic nation, and one that should have had a level of independence from Britain.

- ✔ Eamon de Valera (see Chapter 22) rebelled against the British in 1916, and was one of the main figureheads of the period of revolution. He firmly believed that Ireland should be an independent Republic, but had to settle for less. He encapsulates the ideology of political independence that dominated Ireland in the first half of the twentieth century.

Culture

Where would the world be without the Irish contribution to culture? And when I say culture, I don't simply mean the clever stuff such as Samuel Beckett plays, I mean all culture: dance, song, music, sport, literature, drama, language, singing, and so on. Without the Irish there'd be no Riverdance, no traditional Irish jigs, no U2, no Bloomsday, no hurling, and no *The Importance of Being Earnest* (Oscar Wilde was born in Dublin and educated at Trinity College, Dublin).

Remember, despite all these modern manifestations of Irish culture, the tradition of skill, artistry, and innovation goes way back. The National Museum in Dublin is full of stunning Celtic metal work and jewellery, while Trinity College houses the world's finest collection of illuminated manuscripts that were created by highly skilled monks in Irish monasteries. Ireland also has a rich oral tradition, and an amazing language. But it's not all insular: Irish culture is also the product of external forces. The successive raiders and invaders, be they Viking or Norman, all contributed their own cultures, and this made Ireland ever more innovative.

Living History

Molly Malone wheeled her wheelbarrow through the streets wide and narrow trying to sell dodgy shellfish to an unsuspecting Dublin public. Whether anyone got sick off of her wares isn't clear, but she is forever immortalised in bronze on Nassau Street, Dublin. Every day I walk past her, and every day poor old Molly is being climbed over and photographed. What Molly does prove is that Irish history is everywhere. From the famine memorials in far flung places like Boston, to the statue of Carson on the drive up to Northern Ireland's parliament at Stormont, Irish history has been commemorated in paint, stone, and bronze. Battle sites are still there to see, ancient buildings have been preserved, pints of Guinness can be drunk anywhere in the world, and St Patrick's Day is celebrated annually from Lagos to Limerick. Irish history, and its legacy, is alive and well and appearing somewhere near you.

Throughout the book there are details of the ways in which Irish history has been commemorated. You'll find these useful in explaining various statues and commemorative events, but hopefully they will also get you thinking. As you walk round your neighbourhood, or when you visit Ireland, take a look at what's around you. Wherever you are you'll always find a little bit of Irish history that someone has remembered and commemorated. And if you think you live in a town where there is no Irish history, no statues, Guinness, or Paddy's Day parade, then simply pick up the phone book. Look under O, and you'll find an O'Kelly or an O'Sullivan: in your town – they're the living legacy of Irish history. They may not realise it themselves, but without Ireland and its history, they wouldn't be there.

Ireland Today

Ireland is an island set off the west coast of Britain, and sits in the Atlantic as the last stop between Europe and America. It's home to some 5.7 million people. But it's not one country, but two. Of the 32 counties that make up Ireland, the six in the north-east are Northern Ireland, which is formally part of the United Kingdom (so it's British). The other 26 counties form the Republic of Ireland, which is a separate state ruled from a parliament (the Dáil) in Dublin. Northern Ireland's population is 1.7 million, while some 4 million live in the Republic.

Both parts of Ireland are members of the European Union, but only Northern Ireland, as part of the United Kingdom, is a member of NATO. The Republic of Ireland has a traditional policy of neutrality. There are two working languages in Ireland: English and Irish. According to a recent survey, 1.5 million people in Ireland declared themselves as Irish speakers, of which 340,000 used Irish every day. Officially the Republic of Ireland is a bi-lingual state so all signposts and official documents have to be in both Irish and English. In the Gaeltacht areas (those where Irish is the first language), all place names and road signs are in Irish only. From January 2007 Irish will be recognised as an official language of the European Union.

There are two main religious denominations in Ireland: Catholicism and Protestantism. In Northern Ireland 86 per cent of the population sees itself as having a religion. Of these 53 per cent were Protestant and 44 per cent Catholic. In the Republic of Ireland 92 per cent of the population belongs to the Roman Catholic Church and only 5 per cent are Protestant. Both parts of Ireland have seen an increase in the number of people from other religions largely as a result of inward migration since the 1990s.

And for the record, the people in the Irish Republic do their shopping with euros, while those in Northern Ireland spend British pounds. The flag of the Republic is the Irish tricolour and in Northern Ireland it's the Union Jack. In the former they all stand to attention for the national anthem, *Amhrán na bhFiann* (*A Soldier's Song*) and in the latter it's for *God Save the Queen*.

Chapter 2

The First People Arrive

The first people started living in Ireland around 7000 BC, and trying to imagine what the country looked like, and what these people got up to, is difficult. But a series of archaeological remains that were left behind give us some clues as well as the large number of neat artefacts that are now housed in various museums around the country.

This chapter is going to piece together these early centuries of Irish life, and look at the way in which those years changed the country. The big event, sometime around 300 BC, was the arrival of the Celts and, by contemporary standards, they really modernised the country.

As well as explaining what the Celts got up to, the chapter outlines their great contributions to Irish life, from metalwork to motorway building. An important fact to remember is that early Ireland avoided a Roman invasion. While many parts of Europe were controlled by the Romans, they never bothered with Ireland. This had an impact and Ireland missed out on great innovations such as aqueducts, baths, amphitheatres, and gladiators.

Anyone There? Early Settlers

Ireland was, like most of Europe, freezing cold for a long time. During the last ice age, Ireland sat quietly under a glacier, and nothing much happened. The whole place looked like the Antarctic and was covered by a big sheet of ice. Finally though the sun started shining, the ice melted and some people arrived.

Hunters and gatherers

The first great period of human civilisation in Ireland goes under the name of the Mesolithic age, and covers the years from around 8000 BC until 4500 BC. In this mere 3,500 years, the population of Ireland probably never amounted to more than a few thousand people.

These first settlers probably came to Ireland, to modern day County Antrim, across the sea from Scotland and lived life as hunter-gatherers (killing animals and collecting berries). It's also thought that some people would have been able to walk to Ireland as fluctuating sea levels allowed for the occasional appearance of land bridges between Britain and Ireland. Archaeologists have found several sites belonging to these first people including:

- ✔ Mount Sandel in County Derry where the remains of Mesolithic huts and charcoal from cooking fires were found.
- ✔ Woodpark in County Sligo
- ✔ Around the Shannon estuary where several Mesolithic age tools made from flint were found.
- ✔ Lough Boora in County Offaly
- ✔ The Curran in County Antrim

What this distribution, as well as a series of settlements in Munster, shows is that the hunter-gathering Irish got around the place. The pattern shows that settlements were mainly near the coast or else near inland waterways demonstrating that these ancient Irish were people who were lovers of the boat.

Hunter-gathering wasn't a stable way of life. No great towns and cities grew up. The middle of Ireland remained frozen for a long time, and once the ice melted the land was covered in a dense forest. What the hunter-gatherers wanted was to sail down the coast, set up a small camp, and live a quiet, subsistence lifestyle. As long as there were enough birds and animals to eat, and nuts and berries to live off (sounds like a forerunner of the Atkins diet), they were happy.

Because these people didn't build big settlements, and lived a foraging lifestyle, we don't know that much about them. Their dwellings probably consisted of small round structures made from saplings, which were covered with animal skins for shelter. The tools these people used were made from flint. They lived in small groups, comprising no more than fifteen people, and their success depended on their ability to work as a group to ensure a supply of food. Because of their dependence on nature for their food, their lives would have been deeply affected by the movements of the sun and the moon and the passing of the seasons. It is likely that their sense of belief would have been based around the ideas of cosmology and mythology because they lived so close to nature.

New (Stone) Age farmers

The next important period in Irish life only lasted a mere two thousand years. The Neolithic Age, or the Stone Age to the rest of us, lasted from 4500 BC until 2500 BC.

The population grew slowly during the Neolithic era as the people became more settled and developed an agricultural system that could sustain them. There were some contacts with sea-borne traders from Britain and Europe, and these contacts helped the coastal settlements develop even further. During this period, the population of Ireland probably peaked at around 100,000.

Cultural advances

The Stone Age was an important period of transition in Irish life. Rather than living in small groups and relying on hunting and gathering, the Irish, in contemporary terms, modernised. They began using new technologies, and fundamentally altered the way in which they provided themselves with food. What then were the important features of Ireland at this time?

- ✔ **The residents of Ireland stopped running around gathering nuts and berries and figured out the basics of farming.** Agriculture was *the* big step forward during Ireland's Neolithic period. Somewhere around 4500 BC, goats, sheep. and cattle were imported into Ireland, along with cereal crops. As a consequence Ireland became a much more settled place. While people were still at the mercy of the weather, disease, and other natural inconveniences, they had the opportunity to raise their own livestock and grow their own crops. The development of basic agriculture also meant that the residents of Ireland stopped wandering about so much, and began building dwellings on more permanent sites.

- ✔ **Rather than chomping away at food with no regard for manners, the Stone Age also ushered in the age of pottery** – which meant that the Irish figured out some basic table manners. These pots were of a very basic design and made by coiling lines of clay round and round to make the pot. These were hardened in a fire, and some were even given basic forms of decoration. They had all kinds of uses whether as a lamp (fat was placed in the pot and set alight) or as storage for food.

✔ **Best of all, these early people got their heads round the use of stone.**
By chipping away at it they could make stone tools and weapons. By
using the rock porcellanite, rather than the old flint, the Irish could
make more impressive and useful tools such as axes and digging tools.
This allowed them to clear trees and make better land available for farming, and also have tools that were better for working the soil.

Clearly lots of new things happened in Ireland during this period. Many historians and archaeologists used to think that this was because there was an
influx of a new population into Ireland who brought new skills and ideas with
them. More recent evidence suggests that there was no major invasion or
immigration during these centuries, and that the population who were already
in Ireland just figured it out for themselves.

These developments might sound a bit basic, and in some ways they were. But
the rest of the world was not developing particularly quickly. Although certain
regions were showing innovation – Egyptians began building pyramids about
2700 BC, and folks in England began working on Stonehenge in 1860 BC –
Ireland wasn't doing too badly on the development front.

Big burial mounds

The greatest legacy of the Stone Age Irish was their megalithic monuments:
huge tombs that were built across large parts of the country, many of which
are still standing today.

When the early Irish died, they went through a complex burial process. Their
remains were buried (although many of them were cremated) in stone tombs.
To help the dead on their journey they were buried along with pottery, weapons, foodstuffs, and jewellery. These tombs also served as temples for the
population.

Booleying

Sounds like some obscure word from the dic-
tionary, and indeed it is. Whether or not the
Stone Age Irish realised that they were booleying, they were. And they did it very well.
Basically booleying means moving cows from
the fertile lowlands, where they spent the
winter, to higher areas in the spring when the
new grass began to grow. This meant that they
could use the lowlands for crops. It doesn't
sound that exciting, but booleying was cutting-
edge stuff, and marks the Stone Age Irish out as
agricultural innovators. By feeding their cattle
so well the Irish were also able to use them for
the production of butter and cheese. The Irish
dairy industry had begun!

Archaeologists know of about 1,200 tombs that the Stone Age Irish built, although they don't really know for sure who was buried in them. So while the Irish of this period weren't as clever as the Flintstones or the people that built the pyramids, they certainly managed to put together some important structures. The tombs can be divided into four types:

- ✔ **Court Tombs:** The oldest design of them all. Court tombs were mainly built in the north of Ireland where the earliest populations settled. Nowadays the remains look like piles of rocks, but at the time these sealed tombs with courtyard entrances were very cleverly constructed.

- ✔ **Passage Tombs:** Not many of these were made, and even fewer of them still remain. But for most visitors to Ireland today, the Passage Tombs seem the most impressive. The best known of these tombs is the one at Newgrange, which was built around 3200 BC. Passage Tombs were a particular favourite of the Irish for about 700 years and they demonstrate that the Irish had figured out astronomy: The passages were aligned with the stars.

- ✔ **Portal Tombs:** These are the most basic of the four types – the flat pack, do-it-yourself variety of Stone Age burial sites. Portal Tombs are most common in the north and south-east, and were simple constructions in the dolmen style (only three stones needed!).

- ✔ **Wedge Tombs:** There are loads of these across Ireland, and they were the most common structure built. They are also the last in the Stone Age period to be put together and are centred around a wedge-shaped entrance to the burial chamber.

Buildings and Bracelets: The Bronze Age

The period of the Stone Age gave Ireland some of its great archaeological remains (see the preceding section). Sadly, the Stone Age couldn't last. Basically everyone got fed up of chipping away at things with pieces of stone and moved on to the smart new technology: metal. So the Stone Age was replaced by the new and exciting Bronze Age, and Ireland became a place where beautiful jewellery and metalwork were made.

Whilst stones had been good for Ireland, metal, in the form of bronze, was even better. Metalworking began in about 2500 BC, and the Bronze Age lasted until about 700 BC.

Newgrange

Now a World Heritage site, Newgrange is the most impressive of the Stone Age burial sites in Ireland. It's still a vital stop on any tourist itinerary and a wonder to see. Given the intricacies of the site, you have to kick yourself and remember that the Irish got Newgrange together 600 years before the Pyramids, and nearly a thousand years before the English figured out Stonehenge. The site is huge and is centred around a buried Passage Tomb. It is intricately decorated, and at the winter solstice the sun shines directly along the full length of the tomb lighting an underground chamber. Smart guys these Stone Age Irish.

Newgrange isn't the only such passage tomb. Other important ones are built at the Boyne, Loughcrew, Carrowkeel, and Carrowmore.

Life in Bronze Age Ireland

Bronze age people lived in houses that were made of timber, and covered with wattle and daub walls. Thatched roofs, made from reeds, were added to ensure that everyone stayed dry. They cleared more and more of the forest areas, and expanded their agricultural operations by using the land for grazing animals and growing cereal crops. They were more efficient than their predecessors because they were able to use bronze to make even stronger tools and weapons to work with. They even figured out cooking! The Bronze Age people are known to have placed a trough of water next to a fire, in which they heated large rocks. When the rocks were hot, they were thrown into the water which became hot enough to cook meat in. Its reckoned that by using this method Bronze Age people would have been able to get the water to boiling point in around thirty minutes, in which they would then be able to cook meat.

Bronze Age metalworking

How did Ireland get to be a Bronze Age country? Its biggest advantage was a supply of natural resources in the form of copper, a major ingredient in the manufacture of bronze. There were many copper mines in the south-west of Ireland, and the first mining began on Ross Island, County Kerry.

The Irish had so much copper that it became a major exporter. The Irish metalworkers probably only used about one per cent of the total output of the Irish mines: the rest went overseas. Tin, which was the other major component of bronze manufacture was imported from Cornwall, across the water in England.

So what was all this bronze used for?

- The Irish made lots of tools and weapons from the bronze. This was much stronger than anything that had been used before, and was worked into axes and daggers. Weapons and tools were made by making a mould in stone, into which molten bronze would then be poured. This allowed the Irish of the time to make the same weapon or tool time and time again.

- Another major improvement in table manners was made with the widespread manufacture of drinking vessels.

- Music came to Ireland, or rather the early metal wind instrument did, in the form of brass horns and trumpets.

- With one eye on looking good, and showing off their wealth, the Irish also used bronze to make a whole range of jewellery.

As Ireland also had a plentiful supply of natural gold, as well as copper, the skills of the metalworkers were put to use in making some of the best jewellery and ornaments made from precious metals that were available anywhere in Europe. Irish metalworkers were famed for their torques (twisted metal bracelets and necklaces) as well as their earrings, horse tackle, and sun disks.

All this jewellery had religious significance that came from the intricate designs and patterns that were used, and demonstrated how advanced the Irish were in such metalworking. The presence of such jewellery, especially that which was made in gold, suggests that there were some people in Bronze Age society who were better off or more powerful: an early form of aristocracy.

Because of their skill, and the abundance of natural resources, Ireland led the way in the production of jewellery and ornaments during the Bronze Age. More gold products have been found in Ireland dating from the Bronze Age than anywhere else in Europe. Go into the National Museum in Dublin, and you'll see exhibit after exhibit that demonstrates just how good the Irish were at this kind of work.

Then Comes the Iron Age – and the First Celts

The Iron Age arrived in Ireland sometime around 700 BC. With their close links across the Irish Sea, and the steady flow of trade in and out of Ireland, it's likely that the Irish population would have figured out the Iron Age for themselves. As it was, they didn't have to. Why? Because some fresh visitors arrived in Ireland about 700 BC. These iron weapon-wielding invaders were known as the Celts, and they would dominate Irish life for the next few hundred years (you can read more about the Celts and their impact on Ireland in the next section).

The population in Ireland, although it numbered maybe only 200,000 in total, had been evolving for a few centuries. Prior to the Celts there had been no major influx of a new population.

The first Celts arrived in Ireland in around 700 BC. They emerged from continental Europe, travelled through Britain and finally made their way to Ireland. They must have been a scary sight. They spoke a different language, looked different, and came armed with some serious weaponry.

Basically there were four different sets of Celtic invaders: the Priteni, the Bolgic, the Lagin, and the Goidels, or Gaels. Each of these groups, once they had established themselves, intermingled with each other and also with the Irish. They had a dramatic effect and even got the Irish speaking differently. The following sections describe the influence that the Priteni, the Bolgic, and the Lagin had on the native Irish in more detail. For details of the Gaelic influence, head to the section 'Celts Go Gaelic … But No Romans Arrive' later in this chapter.

The Priteni

The Priteni arrived in Ireland in 700 BC. This group seemed to have been successful in establishing itself in Ulster and Leinster. Their time in charge was short lived however, and they were replaced two centuries later by another wave of Celtic invaders, the Bolgic. The Priteni's only real significance is that they arrived in Ireland. They settled areas that could support them, but did not, it appears, aggressively displace the people that were already living in Ireland.

Taking over half of Ireland: The Bolgic

The Bolgic pitched up in about 500 BC. When they arrived, they took over from the Priteni as the dominant people. Like their predecessors they had travelled through Europe, settled in Britain, and then made the short crossing to Ireland. Everywhere they went they took over, and the story was the same in Ireland.

The Priteni had been successful in settling parts of Ulster and Leinster, but it was the Bolgic people that managed to take over half of Ireland for themselves.

The Bolgic people came in four varieties or tribes, and these took control of separate bits of Ireland:

- The Uluti were most successful in the northern part of the country. In fact, the name Ulster derives from them. They established their capital in modern day Navan.
- The Darini and Robogdii jointly occupied Antrim and North Down, and also had extensive interests across the water in Scotland.
- The Iverni controlled most of Munster.
- The Ebdani were a smaller concern than most of the others, and lived on the east coast of Ireland. Whilst some people claim that this tribe lived on a patch of land that would eventually be known as Dublin this is very unlikely. Dublin would have to wait for the Vikings before being founded (see Chapter 5).

Although the evidence about them is patchy, the Bolgic appear to have been quite successful in taking over and controlling pretty much half of Ireland, and certainly had Ulster and Munster in their hands.

And then the second half: The Laginians

The Celts were never ones to let things stagnate, and the constant stream of Celtic peoples from Europe continued unabated. The next group to arrive, in about 300 BC, were the Laginians. They had their origins in Brittany and later branches of the family were set up in Cornwall and Scotland. But the group that came to Ireland came direct from Brittany.

They obviously had a problem though. Ireland wasn't virgin territory and the people there had seen the Celts before. It was a land where previous Celtic invaders had made their home, and it was doubtful that they'd want to share with these new arrivals.

The Laginian invaders had two choices: look for a patch of land that previous Celts had ignored, or get into the messy process of fighting it out. They settled on the first option, and largely tried to avoid fighting the Bolgic people.

Leaving Brittany the Laginians headed for the west coast of Ireland, and the region of Connacht. They ignored Munster and Ulster, knowing that their Celtic predecessors were happily dug in and wouldn't give up without a fight.

Dún Aengus

When the Laginians won their battle in Connacht, the defeated Bolgic people scattered. They seem to have sought refuge on the islands off the west coast of Ireland. Here they built a series of impressive forts at Dún Aengus and Dún Conor on the Aran Islands, and at Dún Balor on Tory Island. Dún Aengus is by far the most impressive and still draws thousands of visitors today. Perched on the westerly cliffs of Inishmore, the largest of the Aran Islands, the fort is some 100 metres above the sea. It is a breathtaking place, and looks directly out over the Atlantic. Peering out from the fort the modern visitor knows, unlike the Celtic residents, that the next stop is America, some 48,000 kilometres (3,000 miles) away.

There was a Bolgic presence in Connacht, although it wasn't huge, and the Laginians did take them on. A battle was fought in Sligo at Moytura, and the Laginian king, Cairbre, led his forces to victory.

With the Laginian success in Connacht, and also in Leinster, the island of Ireland was divided between themselves and the Bolgic tribes, who controlled Munster and Ulster. About this time the concept of the four provinces of Ireland emerged, and the country was divided into four areas: Ulster, Leinster, Munster, and Connacht. The meeting point for the four provinces, the middle of the country, was at the Hill of Uisneach. So, what the Celts had achieved (allowing for shifts in the exact lines of the borders over the years) was a division of Ireland into four provinces that still exists today.

The whole period of the Celtic settlement of Ireland brought one important change. Previously the Irish lived in small groups, and while there were undoubtedly local power structures in place, the exact nature of these remains unclear. The Celts, as they spread across the country and settled the land, developed clear power structures. By the later Celtic period these had evolved into a system of local rule by a king. There were some 100 or 200 kings spread across Ireland, all of whom ruled over their local tribe. These kings built themselves royal sites that attested to their wealth and power such as Navan Fort in County Armagh, Dún Ailinne in County Kildare, and the monuments at the Hill of Tara in County Meath. The structures for basic governance that the Celts put in place would remain largely unchanged until the time of the Norman invasion of Ireland in the twelfth century.

Iron Age advancements

It might seem churlish to argue that one metal was better than another, but iron was much stronger than bronze. Because of its strength, iron was much better as a metal to fashion tools and weapons from, and allowed for advanced forms of building and fortifications to take place. It also revolutionised agriculture because bronze, for all its beauty, wasn't really strong enough to make robust agricultural implements. As such, iron had a real impact on Irish society. Tools could be used for a variety of jobs, and wouldn't bend and break regularly. That had been the critical problem with bronze – it wasn't reliable enough. With iron, as long as the tool was kept sharp, one implement could be used for a variety of jobs time and time again. Iron made everything from digging a hole to chopping down a tree more efficient.

Celts Go Gaelic

The final Celtic invading force that emerged in about 100 BC changed Ireland more profoundly than all their predecessors. These Celts came from Gaul (present-day France).

There were two big groups in the final Celtic invasion. They went under the collective name of the Goidelic or Gaelic people. The two branches were:

✔ **The Connachta,** who entered Ireland along the river Boyne, and travelled inland. They defeated everyone they encountered along the way, and finally got as far as Tara, where they beat the local Bolgic king. They were able to defeat everyone as they were better fighters, had more experience in the battlefield, and had a better sense of military tactics. The Connachta carved a new territory out for themselves, which was bordered by the Liffey and the Boyne and became the fifth province of Ireland (which no longer exists), known as Meath (now just a county). They also journeyed west and took Connacht (which was named after them) and also suppressed Leinster.

✔ **The Eoganachta,** who came to the south-west of Ireland. Rather than finding a place for themselves, the Eoganachta worked through the lands that had previously been occupied by the Bolgics. As well as defeating them militarily, there was some Celtic brotherly love, for the Eoganachta and Bolgic peoples got together and ruled Munster together.

By the end of the fourth century the Gaelic conquest of Ireland was nearly complete. They had three of the old provinces under their control (Connacht, Leinster, and Munster) and had opened up a new one (Meath). The only place that resisted the Gaels was Ulster which was still dominated by the Bolgics. Ulster would resist for quite a while and didn't finally fall until the fifth century (see Chapter 3).

Minding P's and Q's: A new tongue

The Irish who were settled in Ireland before the Celts arrived spoke a non-Indo-European language. Consequently the Irish were still chatting away to each other in a language that had not been influenced by developments else-where in Europe. The Celts – or one group of them anyway – changed all that.

The Priteni, the Bolgic, and the Laginians (discussed in the earlier sections) spoke a Brittonic, or what linguists have labelled the P-Celtic tongue, the language traditionally found in southern Britain and France after the period of Celtic invasion. Yet the Irish used a Goidelic or Q-Celtic language. So where did the Q-Celtic language come from?

The Q-Celtic language of the Irish was brought in by the Gaels. Unlike the earlier Celts, the Gaels spoke a Q-Celtic language. Q-Celtic languages gave us modern Irish, Scots Gallic, and Manx. The language is the one often collectively referred to as Gaelic.

The complexity of the language situation shows how the experience of Celtic invasion and interaction was different in Ireland and Britain. The Gael's Q-Celtic language turned the Irish away from the old P-Celtic form, and, in the future, would further separate them from the inhabitants of Britain.

Houses and settlements

As well as taking over, and bringing a new language, the Gaels did lots of other neat stuff that brought a degree of modernisation to Ireland, including:

- ✔ **Houses:** The Gaels loved round things, and so their houses were round. They were of a wooden construction with thatched roofs, all enclosed with piles of earth or dry-stone walls. It might not sound like a centrally heated dream home, but this was house building of the first order.

- ✔ **Lakeside homes:** One of the clever innovations of the Gaels was to build houses in the middle of lakes. They were built on artificial islands (known as *crannogs*) which allowed for greater protection from attack. Living by the water is also a pleasant experience.

- ✔ **Towns:** Not what we'd understand as a modern town, but by Gaelic standards many of their settlements were large. They supported their own population through agriculture, and housed all the requirements of modern life. These were small farming units built within a circular enclosure to protect the residents and their livestock from cattle raids. The houses were wooden framed, and covered with wattle and daub walls.

Slige: The Gaelic motorway

As well as houses, the Gaels also started to work on the problem of transport. They weren't happy spending days and weeks trying to get their chariots across rough, open countryside, and so they decided to do something about it. They also wanted to get from town to town quickly. The motorway was born.

These first motorways emerged as a practical response to a specific Irish problem: the bog. How would the Gaels get their heavy chariots over acres of boggy land? The solution which, in part would have been inspired by their knowledge of Roman technology, was to fell trees and lay them across the bogs. The trees made a roadway that would then take the weight of the chariot. Ingenious!

The design was refined and a series of roads emerged. The base was a bed of birch or larch, and over this was laid split beams from oak trees. These were pinned in place by oak pegs, and thus the Gaels created the motorway.

By 100 BC a series of great roads was in place. The east coast was the most important trading centre for the Gaels, and the roads probably radiated out from there. Each road was wide enough to allow two chariots to pass each other by, and the roads, known by the name *slige*, went out from the east coast to Waterford, the Shannon estuary, Galway Bay, and Sligo. Known by their Irish names – slige Dála, slige Asail, and slige Midlúachra – these roads formed the three high roads of Ireland.

Why the Romans Never Made It

While the Gaelic population of Ireland was busy building houses and motorways, a new force had emerged in Europe. The Roman Republic had been going for a good while by the time the Gaels arrived in Ireland, and by 55 BC Julius Caesar had turned his attention to Britain. If the Romans followed most other European invaders, then Ireland would be next in line. Bolstering the chance of invasion was the fact that there was no love lost between the Romans and the Celts because they had been fighting with each other across Europe during the whole period of Roman expansion . Ireland would have been a natural place for the Romans to attack to teach the Celts another lesson. But Rome never invaded Ireland. For details of why the Romans never invaded, and their thoughts on the Irish, see Chapter 3.

Interaction with the Romans was not simply a question of whether or not a country was invaded. There was a long tradition of Ireland trading with the Romans, and many men had travelled out of Ireland to take their chances (and earn a living) fighting with Roman legions in Europe. Although the Romans never invaded Ireland, they knew it was there, and the Irish were fully aware of the power and importance of the Roman Empire.

The real reason why Ireland probably avoided the Romans was the situation in Britain. By the time the Romans arrived in Britain they had been conquering places for years. They knew better than to dash in, run the flag up a pole and call the place home. They knew that for any invasion to be successful there had to be complete suppression of the locals. Until that had been achieved, there was no point in moving on to the next venue.

The Romans feared that if they moved on Ireland before they had fully conquered Britain, the Picts (a troublesome British tribe) would take advantage and make life difficult for them in Britain. Also, they had heard terrible stories about the violent, uncultured and possibly cannibalistic Irish, that they just didn't fancy it.

Chapter 3
The Early Irish Kings

*O*ne of the great historical periods was that of the Roman Empire. The Romans managed to conquer large swathes of Europe, and everywhere they went they took their roads, aqueducts, amphitheatres, coinage, and a whole host of other neat stuff.

In the Monty Python film, *The Life of Brian*, a character asks 'What have the Romans ever done for us?' In the context of Ireland it's a fair question. As this chapter explains, the Romans never invaded Ireland (although it seems likely they visited). As a result Ireland never underwent the modernisation that the Romans enforced on everyone else.

Without a Roman invasion, for which the Irish were probably very grateful, the Irish were left to their own devices. During this early period, the first Irish kings appeared. Their stories are an appealing mix of fact, myth, and legend. In this same period the Irish developed their first form of writing. This chapter takes a look at what the Irish got up to in the absence of the guiding hand of Rome, and how they developed their own system of rule.

The Romans: They Came, They Saw, and They Didn't Bother

The Romans first took a look at England in 55 BC, didn't fancy it very much and went away again. They came back a year later and landed. The Romans were never really sure whether or not they really wanted to be in England, and certainly didn't seem to have enjoyed it much. But stay they did.

Once in England, the Romans, like all good visitors, started exploring. They had a look at Scotland, played around with it for a while, and decided they didn't like the look of it either. Hadrian even built a wall to keep the Scots out. Before the wall was built though, the Roman leader, Agricola, went to Scotland, stood on the western coast, and looked across the water at a land in the distance. He didn't know what it was – just a chunk of land – but it was Ireland.

To invade or not

Like someone deciding whether or not to buy a house, Agricola weighed up the pros (might make a nice port to make travel to Gaul easy), and the cons (too much effort), and pondered the question: Invade Ireland or not?

By the time Agricola was looking at the Irish coast, weighing things up, the Romans had been in Britain long enough to know that it was hard work being there. The weather wasn't great, the locals didn't like them much, and they were a long way from home.

The question was whether or not Ireland would yield anything useful. If it was just another cold, wet place where the natives were barbaric – like Britain – then there was no real point, either strategic or economic, in invading.

Shortly after Julius Caesar had invaded Britain, one writer, a supposedly clever man who knew a few things, confidently wrote that the Irish 'think it decent to eat up their dead parents'. Not a nice image, and there's no real evidence that the early Irish did actually feast on dead Mum's leg or the lifeless head of dear old Dad. But it does demonstrate that the Romans (the force of civilisation) saw the Irish as barbaric (and best avoided).

And so Agricola had his answer: Leave Ireland to the Irish.

Only one legion required

The Romans gave the world a lot. Having been so successful getting across Europe and building an empire they were definitely confident of their own abilities.

Agricola got to meet a minor Irish king who had been exiled from his own country. They chatted about Ireland, and whether or not invasion would be practical. With all the confidence that a Roman could muster, Agricola declared that Ireland could be taken by using just one legion of Roman soldiers. This meant that Agricola was reckoning he could take Ireland with a force of approximately 4,000 men. Now the Romans were good, but were they really that good?

Anyway, Agricola got cold feet and lost interest, and the one legion theory was never tested.

Rome's impact on Ireland

Once the Romans had decided not to invade Ireland – sighs of relief all round – the important question remains: Did the Roman Empire have any effect on Ireland at all?

In a word, yes.

The Romans stayed in Britain for a few centuries and they undoubtedly traded with the Irish who lived on the eastern seaboard. These exchanges made the Irish aware of Roman technology, and introduced them to new ideas such as coinage and all the clever things that the Romans were doing with metalwork.

Encouraged by the Romans, some Irish also chose to leave home and set up new bases in Roman Britain. Irish colonies appeared in south-west Wales, in north Wales and in Devon and Cornwall.

So, all in all, although the Romans never landed on Irish soil in the form of an invading army, they definitely had an effect on Ireland.

The Rise of the Irish Kings

So the Romans chose not to invade Ireland and spent their time making changes to Britain instead. But what was happening in Ireland at this time?

A bit of fighting, actually. Although we, unlike the Romans, wouldn't call the Irish barbaric, Ireland was a bit of a messy place. Different tribes and groups established themselves in charge of their local areas. Occasionally one particular group or another would decide to expand beyond its boundaries, which would lead, as you might expect, to conflict with the neighbours. Tribal rules dictated matters such as succession, but beyond the tribal boundaries there were no real rules. Strength and power often were the deciding factor: if you wanted your neighbour's land or his cows, and your forces were bigger and stronger, then you could have what you wanted. As a result power in Ireland was always a balancing act. Neighbouring kings had to be mindful of what the other kings were up to, and would form alliances to protect themselves.

Out of this environment rose some of the great Irish kings, rulers who would build settlements, organise the farming of the land, oversee law and order (or what passed for it), and ensure that everyone was, as far as you could be in these early days, happy and content. The main thing was to avoid instability and war. It was better to broker local deals to keep the peace than charge into battle. These kings were very sophisticated diplomats.

Drumanagh

Some fifteen miles north of Dublin lies Drumanagh. At this spot archaeologists found Roman brooches, as well as Roman coins from the reigns of the Emperors Titus, Trajan, and Hadrian. Some people believe that this proves all the historians have been wrong, and that the Romans landed in Ireland and set up this coastal fort in preparation for an invasion. In the mid 1990s this became a big story in the newspapers but the historians and archaeologists remain sceptical. There was a good deal of trade between the east coast of Ireland and the Romans in Britain and the historians argue that what was found in Drumanagh (and elsewhere in Ireland) isn't evidence of a Roman presence in Ireland, but simply the bits and pieces that traders had brought back with them after doing business in Britain.

For these early years of Irish life, we don't have a solid history to work from. While there are bits and pieces of evidence, and material that archaeologists have been able to examine, we don't have a big archive of official documents. Historians have had to rely on poems, stories, and legends that were handed down orally and then written up much later. For example, the oldest source for the story of Tuathal (introduced in the next section) is a ninth century poem by Mael Mura of Othain. In other words, what we know about Tuathal comes from the pen of a man who lived some 700 years later.

Two cheers for Tuathal, the first true Irish king

One of the first great Kings to emerge in Ireland was Tuathal, who is said to have ruled over Ireland in the first or second century.

As the story goes, Tuathal was the son of Fiacha Finnfolaidh, a High King (the most powerful man in Ireland). The other kings from Ireland's four provinces didn't care much for Fiacha, and rose up against him. Finnfolaidh was overthrown, his sons, including Tuathal, were sent into exile, and Éllim, the King of Ulster, was promoted to High King.

According to legend, God wasn't too happy about Éllim taking over as High King. To punish Ireland for giving Éllim the top job, God made Ireland suffer a significant famine. Whether the famine of this story was real or not is difficult to say. Famines were not uncommon during this time. And whether God brought down the famine because he was annoyed over Éllim's appointment . . . well, that's for you to decide, but the early Irish were very superstitious and looked for divine explanations to understand the hardships that befell them.

Clearly Tuathal was not going to sit around in exile while someone else did his Dad's old job, so he decided to go back to Ireland and fight.

Tuathal was about 25 when he came back to Ireland with his brothers, Fiacha Cassán and Findmall, and an army of 600 men. Landing at Malahide (just north of modern day Dublin), they marched across Ireland to Tara (the traditional place of power), and defeated Éllim in battle.

After having seen off Éllim, Tuathal and his band of men worked their way around Ireland and also beat the other provincial kings. He then assembled all the Kings and the Irish nobility at Tara, and made them swear their allegiance to him and accept him as their High King.

Once in charge, Tuathal established Meath as his home (the area around Tara) and fortified the main settlement.

Arranged marriages and political problems

Leinster was a bit of a tricky area for Tuathal. It was nearby to his own stomping ground, and the Leinster Kings had a tradition of being quite powerful.

The King of Leinster at the time went by the name Eochaid Ainchenn. By way of making a friendly agreement with him, Tuathal agreed that Eochaid could marry one of his daughters (marrying off your children is a common theme in early Irish history – see it again in Chapter 7).

But there was a sticking point. Eochaid married Dairine, but he really fancied her sister Fithir. To try and get the daughter he wanted, Eochaid told Tuathal that Dairine was dead. Tuathal allowed him to marry Fithir. All looked to be alright until Fithir met Dairine, who wasn't dead after all. The two women were said to have died of shame.

Now, we all know how protective fathers are of their daughters, and this chain of events was bound to produce a response. Eochaid was in big trouble.

Cows, cows, lots of cows

Tuathal could have done lots of things to make Eochaid suffer for the way he treated the girls (he could have been killed). Tuathal decided instead to hit him where it really hurt – in his pocket.

Eochaid, and the whole of the kingdom of Leinster, was made to pay Tuathal a Boru Laigen: a cattle tribute. This was in the days before cash transactions became the norm, and cows were essentially a form of currency. For the pain he had caused Tuathal, Eochaid was forced to hand over 15,000 each of cows, hogs, bed coverings, cauldrons for beer, slave women, and maids. To seal the feeling of guilt, Eochaid also had to hand over his own daughter to Tuathal.

Such were the ways in early Ireland: cross a man and you had to pay him off, big time, in cows.

He's so cool: Finn Mac Cool

The next great figure in Irish history after Tuathal was Finn Mac Cool (or more correctly, Fionn mac Cumhail) who ruled over Ireland at some point during the third century AD. His name has been passed down through Irish history and his story mixes fact with legend.

According to the historical account, Finn was born to Cumhal, the leader of the fianna (the military elite charged with protecting the High King), and his wife Muirne. According to legend, his birth was a little more dramatic than that. It's said that Fin Mac Cool's father, Cumhal, had asked Muirne's father, Tadg, for her hand in marriage. But Tadg said no, so Cumhal abducted her. Tadg was understandably annoyed and appealed to the High King of the time, Conn, for help. They caught up with Cumhal and killed him. Problem was that Muirne was already pregnant. Dad was a bit annoyed about this and ordered his people to burn Muirne (so much for fatherly devotion). Lucky for Muirne, Conn wouldn't allow this and placed her somewhere safe until the boy was born.

Once Finn was born, Muirne left her son, and this is the last we know of her. She handed him over to the care of Bodhmall (his auntie and a druid priestess) and a warrior woman, Liath Luochra. Interesting choice of parents it has to be said, but ones that instilled in Finn a respect of traditional ways and the ability to fight.

The following sections share a few legends associated with Finn Mac Cool.

The tales of Finn are important as they mix together history and legend. They also provide Ireland with a series of heroic stories that allow the Irish to look back on their history with pride (see Chapter 20 for details of the cultural revival). The stories are also important as they show how Ireland was a place apart. It did not have the order of the Roman Empire, but existed as a separate and distinct country: a special and magical place.

Sucking the salmon of knowledge

As a boy Finn was sent to the poet Finneces to study. Finneces had spent ages trying to catch the salmon of knowledge (anyone who ate this fish would have all the knowledge in the world). Finneces caught it and asked Finn to cook it for him. Sadly Finn burnt his finger on the fish and instinctively sucked his burning thumb. In the process he swallowed some of the salmon and now knew everything. Smart boy!

Finn: Arthur in disguise?

While people are aware of the story of Finn, he's not as well-known as King Arthur. The King Arthur story, and his merry knights of the Round Table, has inspired a whole tourist industry and countless Hollywood films – there's even been a Disney version. Some people argue that Finn was the original inspiration for the King Arthur story, but that the Irish version was all a bit dark, chaotic, and unchristian. So, remember next time you're off to a fancy dress party as King Arthur, maybe you should be dressed as Finn.

Taking over the fianna

Finn's Dad had been the head man in the fianna. Obviously Finn wanted to get back the post, but how to do it? It is told that the fianna had a real problem with a fire-breathing fairy called Aillen. He was a nasty piece of work and used to burn the royal palace down every year. Finn came to Tara with a bag of magical weapons (a gift from Dad), and managed to kill the fiery fairy. All the fianna recognised his strength and cunning and so he was put in charge.

My deer Mrs Finn

Finn met and fell in love with his wife Sadbh one day while out in the woods. The problem was that she was a deer (a druid had turned her into one). Rather than kill the deer, Finn recognised her as human and spared her. She turned back into a lovely woman and Finn married her after which she fell pregnant. Crossed druids aren't happy though, and the bad druid turned Sadbh back into a deer, and she promptly vanished. While he never found the Mrs again, Finn did eventually find his son, a boy called Oisín.

We get the story of Finn from the Fenian cycle, one of the great texts of Irish myth. All the detail of Finn's life and the weird and wonderful things that happen to him were reputed to have been narrated by his son Oisín. Without him, we wouldn't know about Finn.

Niall of the Nine Hostages

One of the last great figures before the arrival of Christianity in Ireland (see Chapter 4) was Niall of the Nine Hostages (Niall Noigíallach).

Like the story of Finn and others, the history of Niall comes to us from texts written much later such as the Roll of Kings in *Lebor Gabála Erenn*. As ever the story is a mix of legend and factual information.

Niall started life at the top. He was the son of the High King Eochaid Mugmedon and Cairenn, the daughter of the King of Britain. Despite his auspicious beginnings, life wasn't easy for Niall, who had to prove himself strong and smart enough to be king.

Rescuing Mum

Niall's early life was a contest because his mum, Cairenn, was the second wife of King Eochaid (Kings could have more than one wife). Eochaid's first wife, Mongfind, didn't like Cairenn and made her do lots of hard labour around the place. To keep her son safe from Mongfind, Cairenn fostered Niall out to a poet, Torna, who brought him up.

Obviously the mother–son bond is a strong one, and Niall returned home as an adult to rescue Cairenn from the clutches of Mongfind.

Kissing his way to the top

One question was on everyone's mind: Who would succeed Eochaid, the High King, when he died? Eochaid couldn't make up his mind, so he set the local druid the task of deciding. The druid devised a contest.

He locked Niall and his three half-brothers into a burning forge and gave each the task of saving what they could. Whoever rescued the best piece of equipment would become heir to the throne. Niall emerged with the anvil, and the druid proclaimed him the winner, and therefore the heir. (For the record, the other brothers came out with a sledgehammer, bellows, weapons, and a bundle of wood.)

Sadly for Niall, Mongfind refused to accept the decision and a new contest was devised. This time, the brothers had to find water. They discovered a well that was guarded by an ugly old hag, who demanded a kiss in exchange for the water. Two of the half-brothers refused outright, while the other offered the old woman a peck on the cheek. Only Niall did the job properly with a full-on-lips smacker of a kiss. The old woman turned into a beautiful woman who revealed herself as the sovereignty of Ireland. She was so pleased with Niall's kiss, she made him King.

Taking hostages

As King (or even High King), you had to ensure that everyone underneath you in the pecking order stayed loyal to you and caused no problems. To do this, hostages were routinely taken. Here's how the system worked: To ensure someone's loyalty you would demand that they send a close relative to live with you; this person became your hostage. So long as everyone behaved, you took good care of the hostage, often treating them like members of your own family. If there was any trouble though, you could threaten him or her as a way of forcing the transgressors back into line. If threats didn't do the trick, you killed your hostage.

Niall's name, Niall of the Nine Hostages, came from his use of this system. It's reckoned that he took hostages from each of the five Irish provinces, and then one from the Scots, Saxons, Britons, and French. The five provinces were Ulster, Connacht, Leinster, Munster, and Meath (in more modern times Meath was swallowed up and became part of Leinster). By having his nine hostages, Niall ensured that everyone he did business with behaved themselves.

Day-tripping to attack Britain

Niall was a regular visitor to Britain. The place had gone to the dogs since the Romans had left, and Niall found it easy to attack the various British tribes that had taken over.

He made a series of raids on Britain, and regularly plundered the place, bringing home all kinds of goodies. On one such trip he took away a young boy, whom he thought would make a useful slave. The boy would become a central part of Irish history: he was the boy who would grow up to become St Patrick. To find out about St Patrick's influence on Ireland, head to Chapter 4.

Niall's legacy

Niall is an important figure in Irish history because of the reach of his power. He worked outside Ireland as well as in it and showed what High Kings could do if they were powerful enough. Everyone that succeeded him would aspire to the level of control that he had managed.

Niall was a descendant of the Uí Néill dynasty. By becoming such a powerful High King, ruling over Ireland and intermarrying with other royal families in Ireland, the Uí Néills became a dominant force in Irish history. For centuries after Niall's death, the majority of the High Kings of Ireland would come from the Uí Néill family tree. All the stories that surround Niall are important – they demonstrated to his successors, and the general public, how great the dynasty was and the amazing things that the Uí Néill predecessors had done. By being so heroic, and having so many great stories told about him, Niall set the standard for his successors.

Ogham Is the Word: The First Irish Texts

One of the signs of any established civilisation is its eager support for the written word. The Irish are famed for their story telling abilities, and their oral traditions. The Gaelic people who had settled in Ireland (see

Chapter 2) had brought with them a flourishing oral culture, but also a basic written form. The world of Finn and Niall was also one in which Ireland's first written language appeared and flourished. This is important as it recorded, albeit in basic terms, the ways in which the Irish lived at the time and the kind of world that they occupied. It also helps bridge the gap between all the folklore that surrounds the great men of this period, and real history.

So, how do you have writing when you don't have pens and papers? Originally Gaelic text was probably inscribed into wood, but by the fifth and sixth century in Ireland text was being carved into stone.

The Ogham texts that appear carved in stone are found across Ireland (315 examples are still out there). Many of the texts were carved into standing stones, and functioned as either memorials to the dead or else as territorial markers.

So, what did Ogham look like and how did you read it? Well, you didn't begin at the top left-hand side of the stone and read it left to right. Oh no, you read it by beginning at the bottom left-hand side, and worked your way upwards. When you hit the top, you then read downwards along the next column of characters. There were twenty five characters in the Ogham alphabet. Into the stone was cut a long vertical line. By putting further lines across, or next to the vertical, letters could be formed. For example, the letter 'a' was formed by putting one horizontal line through the vertical line.

Confused? Well, you probably are! The main thing to remember here is that this was an important step. Okay, so it doesn't quite equal the invention of the internet or the printing press, but the Ogham alphabet was a big move forward for Ireland, making it officially a literary country!

Chapter 4

Snakes Alive! Christianity Comes to Ireland

• •

In This Chapter

▶ What St Patrick did for Ireland

▶ The arrival of Christianity

▶ Ireland's Monasteries and the export of religion

▶ How the Kings of Ireland coped with God

• •

*W*e all know about St Patrick . . . he's the one who chased away the snakes, did clever things with the shamrock and gave us one of the biggest party days of the year. Well all that is kind of true, but St Patrick did much more than give us 17 March as an excuse to drink green beer.

During his lifetime – most people accept that was some time during the fifth century – St Patrick travelled across Ireland and Europe. He was very important for bringing Christianity to the Irish, whose religion, up until that time, was polytheistic. He also established the first monasteries that would grow in number in the second half of the sixth century and sustain Christianity during the Dark Ages.

Without St Patrick, Ireland wouldn't have become the country it did. The next few pages explore the religious beliefs in Ireland before he arrived, the man himself, how he converted an entire country (almost), and the impact that this new-fangled religion had on Irish customs and culture. After reading this chapter, you'll be able to sort out fact from fiction (and know what happened to all those snakes).

Holy Tree Huggers! The Druids

Before Christianity the religion that people followed in Ireland was organised by the Druids. It was the same religion that ancient tribes followed in Britain during the same period. The Church didn't like the Druids as they saw them as pagans who based their religion on myths and superstitions rather than a belief in a Christian God. The Druids in Ireland were quite powerful as the kings of Ireland listened to them. They took all kinds of advice from the Druids: what day to start a battle, when to sow crops, and even whether getting married was the right thing to do. But what did the Druids believe in?

Druid beliefs

The Druids were basically early hippies – although very smart ones. Their whole system of belief was based on the wonder of nature. They were very much in touch with the earth and their own feelings.

The Druids were effectively the priests of their religion. They were well educated, usually literate and had an excellent grasp of matters environmental and astrological. The Druids used nature to see into the future by reading signs. They would have a look at how the rain fell, which way the birds were flying and how the leaves changed colour, and process all this information so that they could give advice. As everyone firmly believed that the Druids could predict the future, and tell people what course of action was best for them, everyone listened very intently to what the Druids had to say. Especially as they also believed in sacrifices and dabbled in magic – you wouldn't want to upset your local Druid!

Living in Pagan Ireland

Druidism was based around an appreciation of nature's forces. There were two types of power that were important: Brí (a power that could be developed) and Bua (a power that is gained or lost depending on the actions of the individual). Sounds complex; so how does this actually work?

Brí was linked to the basic nature of a place and is a higher power than Bua. It was to be found in hills, cliffs and other natural features of the landscape. Places with a high Brí power, for example the Hill of Tara, were instilled with great importance by the Irish.

Bua was linked with what actually happened in a specific place. For example, if a battle was fought in any given place, then the power of the Bua of that place would be affected depending on the result, and whether the event was positive or negative.

The two forces were linked together by the Druids and the Irish people lived their lives based on these ideas. If a King wanted to gain additional force for a battle or a seat of power, he would combine a Brí location with the actual happening, the Bua. By doing this he would hope to gain an advantage as the two forces would combine.

What this meant in practice was that the Irish were very aware of their surroundings and of the forces of nature. They would not begin any major undertaking without reference to a Druid, who could tell them which of the natural forces they could use best.

Another important idea in Druid Ireland concerned the dead. The Druids had a well-developed sense of the Otherworld. This was a place where the dead would go. At the moment of death a person would begin a journey. For the Irish the first part of the journey was through a nothing zone, such a dark passage, a fog or mist and so on. If they managed this part of the journey they would arrive in the Otherworld, a parallel universe where they would spend eternity.

While the Christians dismissed all this as pagan gobbledygook, for the Irish it worked. The pagan forms of religion such as Druidism gave them a model for how they would live their lives, and the essential guidance they needed to make decisions. Given the wild landscape that they lived in, and the powerful forces of nature they were surrounded by, it probably all seemed perfectly logical.

Knocking on Heaven's Door: Enter St Patrick

One thing is for sure, St Patrick wasn't a mythical character. There is enough evidence in the form of written accounts to show that St Patrick did move among the Irish and convert them to Christianity. But obviously we don't have a full account of his life, and some gaps remain.

Patrick: the early years

It seems that Patrick was born around the year 389, and that he was probably Welsh and went by the name of Sucat. He was raised as a Christian, and was loyal to the Roman Empire, which controlled most of Europe at the time.

Reasonably well-off, the young Sucat should have probably had a nice quiet life, but he was kidnapped – by the Irish – when he was sixteen.

Carried off by his Irish kidnappers, Patrick found himself in modern county Antrim (although some say Connacht). Like all slaves, for that is what he was, Patrick was put to work, and found himself tending sheep on a lonely hillside. He did this for six years.

It's not recorded whether Patrick was any good at tending sheep, or if he enjoyed the experience. One thing is clear though. Being stuck out on a mountain with only sheep for company gave the young Patrick time to think about things. He started getting visions of a religious nature, and thought more and more about God and Christianity. His visions convinced him that his days tending sheep must come to an end and that he had to escape.

Not only was Patrick looking to escape slavery, he also wanted to get away from Irish religious beliefs. At the time the Irish had avoided Roman occupation and so had not taken to Christianity. They believed in Druidism (refer to the earlier section 'Holy Tree Huggers! The Druids'), a belief system that Patrick found offensive. He believed that Christianity was the only true religion, and it was to free the Irish from Druidism and convert them to Christianity that would make him return years later.

Patrick fled the mountainside, and travelled to the coast. Here he got passage on a ship bound for Europe. According to one legend the boat was carrying a cargo of Irish wolf hounds, but Patrick's reaction to another period of confinement with animals isn't recorded.

Holidaying in Europe

After a few years sitting on a mountain looking after some sheep, what's a young man to do? Why head off to a monastery, of course. And that's just what Patrick did. His first stop was St Martin's monastery in Tours. From there he went on to the island sanctuary of Lérins. The time he spent in these secluded religious orders gave Patrick the time to think about his new religious devotion and begin planning for the future.

At the same time, the great bishop, St Germain, had begun working in Auxerre. Germain was known for his great learning and his charitable works with the poor. Wanting to learn everything he could, Patrick travelled to Auxerre and placed himself in the hands of St Germain. It was there that he entered the priesthood.

A brief sojourn in Britain

About the time that Patrick was devoting himself to good works and St Germain, Britain was having a few problems. Christianity had been established in Britain, but people were getting very confused. They started combining some of the old Druid ideas with those of the Christian Church. One theory that gained much popularity in Britain was that of pelagianism. Basically this was a belief that there was no such thing as original sin, but that humans had responsibility for their own morals and their salvation. The omission of the idea of original sin was offensive to the Church and they saw it as a heresy.

The Church felt that it was losing control of the British because of these heretical ideas, and that they might all be won over to paganism. St Germain was given the job of going over to Britain to sort everyone out, and he asked Patrick to join him.

In Britain Patrick did a great job, and started winning people back to the Christian Church. He was spotted as a mover and shaker, and the big promotion wasn't long in coming.

Then back to Ireland

The Church had long had their eye on Ireland as a country that was ripe for conversion. In 431 Pope St Celestine had sent a chap called Palladius over to do the job, but Palladius found the Irish too scary and failed. Ireland stood out as a place that was resisting Christianity. The Pope needed the right man to do the job: someone who knew the Irish and didn't find their warring ways too frightening.

St Germain suggested to the Pope that Patrick was the man for the job of converting the Irish, and sent him to Rome for the job interview. Patrick passed with flying colours, and was given a whole bunch of important religious relics to travel back to Ireland with. It was also at the job interview that he got the name Patrick. The old name of Sucat was got rid of, and the Pope gave him the name of Patritius – Patrick to you and me.

By the time he landed on Irish soil once more (reckoned to be in the year 433) Patrick had been away for a long time.

Patrick spent the rest of his life – nearly 60 years (he died around 492 at over 100 years old) – in Ireland spreading the word.

Christianity Comes to Ireland

Patrick landed in Ireland in Wicklow, and proceeded north. He reckoned that his most pressing work lay ahead of him in modern Ulster. He chose Ulster because it was the area he knew best from his days looking out for the sheep. Also, the kings in Ulster would be most willing to accept the Christian ideas as paganism was weakest there. Once in Meath he met up with an Irish chief who had already converted to Christianity, one Dichu, and he was able to give Patrick a barn to use as a Church. The mission had begun.

Although Christian missionaries had been in Ireland before, the Irish had proved largely resistant. They preferred the old ways of Druidism and ancient beliefs rather than this new fangled organised religion coming out of Rome. For this reason, Patrick had a huge job ahead of him.

Ireland wasn't a carefully planned out suburb that would allow Patrick to go from door to door and proselytise in Irish living-rooms. It was a wild and often dangerous place, where Christianity was viewed as something entirely foreign: a dangerous new idea from overseas. Patrick had to convince the people and their rulers that Christianity was the true way to salvation, and that if they chose to stay with their old pagan beliefs their soul would be in trouble when they died. And in doing so, he had to avoid upsetting anyone – particularly the Irish kings – or else death or exile would be the result.

Still, he did have a few things going for him:

- ✔ **A small band of Christian converts already existed in Ireland:** Patrick wasn't totally alone in his endeavours. He had a small network of previous converts he could work with. The visit of Palladius was undoubtedly a failure when compared to the work Patrick would do but it's clear that he had some local successes in Leinster. These early converts would have been great supporters of Patrick's mission.

- ✔ **He spoke the people's language:** The language of Ireland at the time was Gaelic. Although Patrick originally hailed from Wales, he learned the Irish tongue during his years as an Irish slave. Now, years later, as Patrick sought to convert the Irish, he was able to talk to them directly in their own language, unlike many other missionaries who had problems in making themselves understood.

- ✔ **He was fervent but humble.** Patrick was not one for a life of luxury. He shunned all forms of wealth, preferring instead to live his life in a rough hair shirt, and sleeping on bare rock. Patrick also spent a lot of time in personal prayer.

> ✔ **He clearly wasn't greedy.** While the Irish kings may have had to be convinced about the value of the religion that Patrick was promoting, they were reassured by the fact that he wasn't looking to invade, start wars or take over. This lack of aggression would have won him friends.

Tackling the five kingdoms

The organisational structures of Ireland in these early centuries were quite messy. This wasn't a modern country with a central administration, but a chaotic mix of small kingdoms, religious institutions and lots of wild countryside in between.

Between the fifth and eighth centuries half of Ireland was uninhabited. Much of the land was as good as useless – not even good enough to provide grazing for animals. All told, Ireland was a pretty inhospitable place. The population was small, and very spread out.

The basic structure of Ireland during this period was as follows:

> ✔ At the top level Ireland was divided into five kingdoms or provinces, known as the five fifths of Ireland. These were: Ulster, Meath, Leinster, Munster and Connacht, but they weren't always stable and didn't always have a single king.
>
> ✔ At the bottom level were the *tuath* or peoples, ruled over by a single *rí* or king.
>
> ✔ Between the five kingdoms and the *tuath* were a whole series of local agreements.
>
> ✔ A king may accept that there was someone locally who was more powerful. The stronger king, the *ruire*, would be accepted as an overlord. These deals went all the way from the local level to the provincial.

All this sounds very ordered, like some form of modern management pyramid, but it wasn't that simple. There were regular wars, battles and periods of infighting that made the whole structure very unstable. It was in this heady mix of kings that Christianity had to find a place.

With the arrival of St Patrick, the kings of Ireland had to really start thinking hard about Christianity and its God. Prior to Patrick, they had relied on old pagan ways and didn't have to worry too much about Christianity. Patrick and his descendants changed that. It took time for many of the kings to accept Christianity, but the monks were persistent.

St Patrick's great achievement, according to the record books, is that he brought Christianity to Ireland. Well, sort of. He was very successful in that he was starting from almost nothing and he did gain plenty of converts. He was particularly successful in winning over the kings. He knew how power worked. Once the kings told their people to put away their Druids and accept the new God, then the people followed.

So how did Patrick win over everyone? Did he simply go around telling everyone how great Christianity was, or did he have some smarter selling techniques up his sleeve?

Telling stories

Patrick had to explain the Holy Trinity – the idea of a three-part but single God – to the Irish. In an age before PowerPoint presentations or training videos, he had to be innovative. According to legend, he picked up the shamrock, and used its leaves to explain to the Irish the mystery of the Holy Trinity. He showed that, linked together perfectly in one stem of the plant, there were three leaves, one each for the Father, the Son and the Holy Spirit.

Whether or not this visual lesson worked for the Irish is unclear. One thing that is for sure is that the plant survived as a living embodiment of Ireland's patron saint, and it's still worn all round the world – whether as a freshly picked plant or a plastic blow up inflatable – to celebrate the work of St Patrick.

Showing off relics

If there's one thing you need when you're doing a difficult job, it's authority. Patrick's authority came from the Pope, Celestine, as he was the one who told Patrick to go to Ireland. To let people know how important Patrick was, and the power that he had, Celestine also gave him a load of relics and spiritual gifts to help him on his way. The relics are recorded as being those taken from the bodies of St Peter and St Paul. These Patrick bought to Ireland, or so the story goes, and he showed them off everywhere he went.

Performing miracles

One of the most well-known miracles attributed to St Patrick is his freeing Ireland of snakes. According to legend, Patrick stood with his staff and banished the snakes from Ireland.

The snake-banishment miracle is the most lasting and fascinating of all the stories relating to St Patrick and his time in Ireland. Some claim that he performed an actual miracle, ridding the island of the pesky creatures with divine help. Others say that the story is metaphorical, that the snakes represent the pagan religions that Patrick drove out of Ireland. (In paganism, the serpent, or snake, is a common symbol. If Patrick drove out the snakes, he was really driving out the pagans and the whole thing acted as a quick story demonstrating the victory of Patrick's Christian mission in Ireland.) Still others (namely scientists) have argued that Ireland was separated from the rest of continental Europe at the end of the last Ice Age, and because snakes can't swim, no snakes ever arrived in Ireland (or New Zealand for that matter), and the St Patrick story is a load of old blarney.

Participating in (and subtly changing) pagan rituals

The main mission of Patrick was to convert the pagan Irish to the ways of the Christian Church. One of the problems with the pagan religions, or so it was argued, was that they were full of superstitious mumbo-jumbo. That said, Patrick knew that to win over his audience he had to wow them. To do that he indulged in a bit of miracle working. The aim was to challenge the pagan forces (those that were bad) with Christian ones (those that were good). By winning the day through his miracle works, Patrick would have shown the Irish that his way was the best way.

- ✔ **Lighting the Paschal fire on the hill of Slane.** Easter eve was a traditional pagan celebration that marked the coming of spring. Tradition dictated that the first fire had to be lit by the king, as any other fires being lit would upset the work of the Druids. Patrick lit his first at Slane, as a direct challenge to the Druids, and then the forces of Christianity and Druidism battled it out. Patrick was arrested and brought in front of the king, Laoghaire, to explain himself. Patrick was able to explain himself so well that he won over the king, and was given permission to make converts among Laoghaire's people. Patrick had got his first big royal scalp.

- ✔ **The overthrow of a famous traditional idol called Cenn Cruaich.** This idol had been worshipped across county Cavan. This was a stone idol that was supposed to represent the force of paganism. The image of Cenn Cruaich was said to be so powerful when people saw it, that it filled their hearts and held them to the pagan way. Patrick believed that such images held the Irish in fear, and prevented them from accepting Christianity. He engaged in a bit of vandalism, and destroyed the stone by pushing it to the floor where it broke. By doing this he freed people's hearts from paganism, and won them over to his way of thinking. Patrick was able to demonstrate to the people that nothing bad (warts, boils, famine or sudden death) happened to them if they rejected the pagan way.

Setting up churches

Patrick established churches across the country, notably in Connacht and Ulster. He also set up Armagh as the place of his bishopric.

St Patrick's purgatory

Patrick often retreated from public life to reconnect with God through periods of solitude. One of his favoured places of retreat was the island of Lough Derg. The island is now home to St Patrick's Purgatory and a regular place of pilgrimage. People travel from across the world to pray there. The season runs from 1 June to 15 August, and pilgrims spend three days there. They are allowed one simple meal a day, and fast the rest of the time. While on the island they pray constantly and perform nine stations of the cross in bare feet.

Consecrating bishops

During his time in Ireland, Patrick consecrated 350 bishops. These men were the future of the Church in Ireland and ensured that Patrick's work would continue after him.

Patrick's contribution in a nutshell

The real importance of St Patrick in Irish history is that he managed to establish Christianity in Ireland on a solid footing. And by becoming Christian, Ireland moved closer to Europe than it had ever been before. No more was it a distant place of unruly, pagan tribes, but was now connected through a common Church.

But Patrick's influence continued well beyond his death because of the Churches and monasteries he set up across Ireland. These institutions had a huge impact on Irish life in successive centuries. You can read more about them in the section 'Christian Ireland'.

Finally, by living such an interesting life, and becoming Ireland's patron saint, Patrick gave us 17 March as a day of celebration. It's actually the day he 'fell asleep' – died in other words. Now one of the biggest global annual parties, St Patrick's Day is a lasting testament to the man and his work.

Christian Ireland

After the death of Patrick, and all his hard work, the Church had to make its own way. It wasn't easy. Ireland was divided into a network of self-ruling *tuatha* (peoples), who were ruled over by a *ri* (king) who was in charge.

Some of these *tuatha* welcomed the Church, others just weren't interested and preferred the old ways. But Christianity didn't die with Patrick. He had established a following for the Church, and had introduced enough people to the religious life who could continue his work. Where Patrick had won kings over to Christianity, they stayed loyal. Those areas that stayed immune from the charms of Christianity, especially in the West of Ireland, were those areas where Patrick himself had struggled.

During the fifth and sixth centuries the Church started to win most people over to Christianity, and a period of steady growth and expansion began. The followers of Patrick were very important in this, as they continued to work as missionaries across the length and breadth of Ireland spreading the word. Church officials met the Irish half way and adapted to their way of thinking and accepted some of their customs, and as a result most of the Irish accepted Christianity. Rather than enforcing the strict beliefs of the Church, the Christian missionaries allowed the teachings of the Church to be adapted to local conditions. So long as the kings were loyal to the Church, that was the main thing. If they indulged in a bit of paganism on the side, no worry.

The influence of the monasteries

In the second half of the sixth century, monasteries began appearing across Ireland. These communities of monks were important places of learning and worship, and also provided a link between the community and the Church.

The monasteries emerged because of an impulse for religiously-minded men to escape from the real world. They wanted time by themselves, and started living as hermits. In many cases these hermits developed a popular following, and these groups often formed the basis of the monastery.

One of the first famous monasteries was established by Enda. Enda was born in Meath, and had been a military man until his sister St Fanchea convinced him that he should give his life to God. Enda founded his first monastery in Ireland on the Aran Islands, and his followers would spread out and set up ten further monasteries in his name. He had many disciples who would be key figures in Irish religious life, such as Colum Cille, Brendan of Clonterf, Ciaran of Clonmacnois, and Finnian of Clonard.

The big three monasteries, and the most famous, appeared during the sixth century: Clonard, Clonmacnois, and Clonfert. These became famous as the leading educational monasteries that trained Irish men (and foreigners) to be brilliant scribes, artists, and thinkers. These were the religious equivalents of the Ivy League Colleges: only the best and brightest went there, and once trained, they went round the world to spread the word.

Having his bell rung

One of St Patrick's greatest periods of retreat took place on a 1,200 metres high mountain in County Mayo: Croagh Patrick. The story goes that Patrick went up the mountain as he was told to by his guardian angel. He is said to have spent forty days there living in a small cave. The aim of the trip was to gain a special blessing for the people of Ireland. But it wasn't that simple. All the forces of evil that opposed the Christian mission gathered on the mountain in the forms of hideous birds. The battle between good and evil was a long drawn out affair, but eventually Patrick was able to scatter the flocks of evil birds and cast them into the ocean. It's said that he rang his bell, the St Patrick's Bell, as his moment of victory approached, and that its ring was heard across Ireland. It brought peace and joy everywhere it was heard.

Saints and scholars

When we think of monks we think of guys in brown robes, sandals, and shaved heads who kept themselves busy gardening and brewing beer or mead. Some of that's probably true, but the real impact of the Irish monastic system was the brain power that was harnessed. It's not for nothing that Ireland became known as the land of Saints and Scholars.

A monk named Finnian developed one of the most important and lasting themes in Irish monastic life: a concentration of intellectual life alongside the religious. In other words, monks became the smartest guys around during this period, and the monasteries were the universities. People went there to learn, to hone their skills, and to carry on their research. Although much of the output of the monasteries was destroyed in later political upheavals, these guys did an enormous amount of work and produced some of the most beautiful books ever made.

The Irish monasteries had several learning functions:

- They welcomed people into the monastery who wanted to learn from the resident monks.
- The teaching of the scriptures in the Irish monasteries was the best in the world.
- The monks of the time were recognised as some of the best people at writing and speaking Latin.
- The monasteries in Ireland advanced a rational and reasoned approach to understanding the Bible that had previously been lacking.

✔ As well as all their religious work, the monks loved history. They were among the first people to start researching and writing a history of Ireland.

✔ The monks celebrated God in many ways, but they were the best at doing so through poetry and song.

The Great Books

One thing that the monasteries are famed for, more than anything else, were their illuminated manuscripts. These were works of technical and artistic brilliance that are still a wonder to look at today. The manuscripts were illustrated copies of the gospels. These were the days before the printing press, and everything had to be done by hand. It demanded literacy and great skill. The manuscripts were revered and highly prized items, of great religious significance.

Illuminated manuscripts were team efforts and took years to be completed. This was not simply a drawing and writing exercise. The monks who executed works like the Book of Kells had been in training for years. The materials they used were of the highest quality and would have cost a lot to buy. The books were not only of the Rolls-Royce standard for sixth century publishing, they were deliberately designed to celebrate God in the most perfect way.

The monks that wrote and drew the pages in the illuminated texts were not the only ones that contributed to these manuscripts. The monasteries were the homes of some of the greatest metal workers, sculptors, and bookbinders of the period. All this artistic skill produced the climate that allowed these books to happen.

The main books of the period that are still around today are:

✔ **The Book of Durrow.** Made in the seventh century, and now housed in Trinity College, Dublin, it is the oldest complete illuminated gospel in existence.

✔ **The Book of Kells.** Produced in the early ninth century, this is the granddaddy of them all. Still on display, again at Trinity College, the Book of Kells contains the four gospels of of the Bible in Latin and still pulls in the crowds. It's the best example of an illuminated manuscript anywhere in the world.

✔ **Book of Armagh.** Dating from the eighth century, and one of the oldest Gaelic scripts (that is, it's written in Old Irish), the book contains works about St Patrick, as well as portions of the New Testament. It has been identified as being the work of predominantly one scribing monk named Ferdomnach and, like the others, is also held in Trinity.

Monk-y business, Part I: On a mission round Ireland

One of the great ideas that the religious men of Ireland took up was that of the *peregrination*. Basically it was religious backpacking. Rather than staying at home in the safe confines of the monastery, the idea was to go wandering about by yourself and in doing so have a meaningful relationship with God.

Quite often such journeys took these men overseas, but they also took domestic journeys. On their travels these men would not only sort out their own relationship with God, but also spread the word as they went. They were God's door-to-door salesmen and were really important in spreading Christianity in Ireland and abroad.

All the monks who had trained with Enda on the Aran Islands were famous for travelling about Ireland. Without Colum Cille, Brendan, and the rest of them, God might have never made it off the islands. Brendan of Clonterf was so famous his life was the subject of a book, *Navigatio sancti Brendani* – the Voyage of St Brendan to the English-speaking amongst us.

Monk-y business, Part II: Taking God farther afield

The really brave men of the peregrination (travelling monks) were those who made it off the island of Ireland and struck out for Britain and Europe. The two most famous guys who managed this were Colum Cille and Columbanus.

Men like Colum and Columbanus, and a host of other travelling Irish monks, were very important in spreading the Irish monastery model across Europe. Without the Irish it's doubtful that Christianity would have been so well established on the continent by the end of the eighth century.

Colum Cille

Starting life as a minor noble, Colum trained as a monk with Finnian of Clonard and was responsible for founding several monasteries in Ireland, such as the one in Derry in 546 and Durrow a decade later. He suffered from wanderlust, and in 561 left Ireland behind and set sail.

One reason for Colum's travels was supposedly his part in mass murder. Some claim that he had copied a psalter (a translation of the Psalms) which, it was ruled, belonged to someone else. All hell broke loose and his family leapt to his protection: basically a simmering feud started that led to a localised war. At the ensuing battle of Cúl Dreimne, lots of people were killed, and everyone blamed Colum. The story goes that his travels out of Ireland were the penance that he had to serve for getting everyone killed. Seems like a reasonable plea bargain.

Colum Cille left Ireland for Scotland where he established a monastery on the island of Iona. It became one of the great monasteries and in later years the followers of Colum would travel back to Ireland, and throughout Scotland and England, eventually setting up some ninety or more places of worship on the Ionian model.

A Saint called Kevin

One of the great religious men of this period, and a home-based one at that, was St Kevin. He was born in 498 and went originally by the Irish name Coemgen. Kevin studied for many years, and eventually made it to the status of monk. A very religious man he became a hermit at Hollywood in County Wicklow. Kevin was perfectly happy by himself, praying and talking to God, and he spent seven years as a hermit, eating nettles and enjoying the solitude, but people were fascinated by him and kept dropping by.

Kevin was credited with lots of miracles. Kevin was known as a man of great patience. It's said that a blackbird laid an egg in his hand. Rather than disturb the egg, Kevin didn't move until the baby bird hatched. In another story Kevin fed a group of harvesters with meat and ale as they had no provisions. After they had eaten he asked the men to fill their tankards with water and collect the bones from their meal. Lo and behold, an entire new meal of meat and ale appeared. And these are just two of a whole series of miracles that Kevin conducted! Whether or not they happened is anyone's guess.

Kevin eventually realised that all these people wouldn't leave him alone, so he decided the best plan was to set them up in a monastery so that they might leave him alone. He set up the monastery at Glendalough and put himself in charge as abbot. It all went swimmingly and attracted lots of devout people who were prepared to join him. The monastery grew rapidly and eventually formed the basis of a whole town. Kevin died, reputedly at the ripe old age of 120, and his monastery continued in existence until it was attacked and vandalised in 1398. Kevin was canonised in 1903.

Although Kevin is long dead, and the monastery was dissolved by the English in 1539, Glendalough remains a constant attraction for visitors and pilgrims. Nestled in the hills of County Wicklow, the remains of the sixth century monastery are still impressive. Not only can you see the round tower that was built to defend the monastery, but also the remains of the Church and a whole selection of stone crosses. If you're prepared for a bit of walking it's also possible to see St Kevin's bed where he reputedly spent all his years as a hermit avoiding the crowds.

Columbanus

Another man from a good background, Columbanus decided to go backpacking round Europe. He was hugely influential, and he established a series of monasteries across Europe and as far away as Bobbio in Italy. The order in monasteries set up by Columbanus was all rather strict, and worship centred around the idea of penance. Despite the harsh conditions, it was popular at the time, and some fifty monasteries followed his model.

The King–Church connection

How would the Irish kings react to having these missionary monks telling them what they should and shouldn't believe in?

In the seventh and eighth centuries the Church in Ireland prospered because it had the support of various kings across the country. Without these local patrons, and their muscle, the Church would have struggled. The authority of the Church stemmed directly from the power of its support, and the sheer number of monasteries in Ireland is testament to the way in which Irish kings took to the new religion. The monks were on a mission to convert Ireland, but without the patronage of the kings they would not have succeeded.

As the various kings – big and small – across Ireland began to accept Christianity and actively support monasteries and other religious establishments in their kingdoms, they changed the country.

Key examples of the King–Church relationship could be found in:

- **Armagh:** claiming a special bond with St Patrick, the church in Armagh had the support of the ruling Uí Néill dynasty and became the most important church of the period.
- **Kildare:** championing the life of St Brigid, the Kildare church had the support of the local Uí Dúnlainge dynasty. As their patrons were not as powerful as the Uí Néill's, the Kildare church had to accept a secondary position to Armagh.

Unfortunately, the Church sometimes got caught up in the fights between different kings. For the Church to survive it had to have the support of the local, and ideally, most powerful king. With his support the life (and buildings) of the Church would be protected. Because of this, church life took on a political dynamic and the Church became closely allied to different kingships.

Forget Christian kindness! This is war!

Although finding God and accepting Christianity had undoubtedly improved life in Ireland, it didn't put an end to the struggles between the different kings. The country was still made up of a patchwork of small kingdoms that struggled with each other for some kind of local and regional authority and power. Ireland had, in the main, become a Christian country, and supported some of the most important religious establishments in Europe at the time. But a belief in God and support for the Church didn't mean that the competing kings of Ireland loved each other unreservedly. Local politics and power struggles were still more important than any belief in religion. The arrival of Christianity brought a specific brand of religion to Ireland. It did not radically alter the existing power structures, nor did it bring peace, love, and harmony.

Ireland at this time was a fairly basic society. There were no national structures, and although there was a legal system in place, this relied on military might and honour to enforce it. There was no police force or civil service. The measure of wealth and the unit of currency was the cow and all issues of honour and power were settled according to the number of cows which any king owned. Alternatively a female slave could be used as currency, with one slave being equal to six cows.

There were many rows and bust ups before the end of the eighth century. During this time the main struggles were:

- ✔ 604: The joint High Kings of Tara are assassinated by their enemies.

- ✔ 637: Congal Claen, a disposed prince, lands in County Down with an army of mercenaries in an attempt to challenge the Uí Néill's. He is defeated at the battle of Moira.

- ✔ 722: Fergal, king of Tara, invades Leinster to collect tribute owed to him. Defeated in battle, he is killed along with a large number of his men.

- ✔ 738: To avenge his father's death, Aéd, son of Fergal, fights in Leinster, but this time the men from Tara win.

- ✔ 743: Domnall Mide leads an army against Aéd, wins the battle, and takes the overkingship of the Uí Néill's.

Lots of other scraps and battles took place beside these, but they give you a flavour of the way Ireland was going. Family feuds go on for years, no one seems to forget a grudge, and successive generations always seem intent on avenging something or other.

Despite the growing influence of Christianity, all this violence made Ireland a quite unstable place, and also meant that no central authority developed. The Irish were not united. Sure, some kings were more powerful than others, but there were always alliances being made and broken, battles won and lost that made the overall picture unclear.

Part II

The Normans Are Coming! The Twelfth and Thirteenth Centuries

The 5th Wave   By Rich Tennant

THE NORMANS INVADE IRELAND

In this part . . .

Ireland and invasion – the two words went together very well in the twelfth and thirteenth centuries. The Vikings enjoyed plundering and pillaging their way through whole areas of Europe, and Ireland didn't escape their attentions. It wasn't all doom and gloom though. The Vikings did do some important things, like settling on the banks of the River Liffey and calling the place Dublin. But the Irish didn't care for them much. The Viking presence had the important result of making the Irish kings think about working together.

Once the Vikings had finally gone however, the Irish simply couldn't find any stability in their own system of ruling each other, and pulled in an outsider. They invited the Normans. Problem was, once the Normans had arrived, they wouldn't leave, thereby changing Ireland forever.

Chapter 5

The Vikings Arrive First

In This Chapter

▶ The first Viking Invaders arrive in Ireland

▶ Dublin is founded

▶ Irish and Viking infighting

▶ Brian Boru: The first great Irish king

The history of Ireland is dominated by stories of the Norman invasion and periods of British rule (discussed in Chapters 6 and 7), but these folks weren't the first invaders. The people who arrived first with aggressive intentions were the Vikings.

The whole period of Viking incursions into Ireland really unsettled everyone. The Vikings challenged the system of rule that had been established by the Irish kings, and also caused problems for the smooth running of the Church in Ireland. The Vikings weren't all longships, big beards, helmets, and pillaging, however. They made real contributions to Irish life and changed the ways in which the country had traditionally been governed. Nevertheless, the Irish wanted them gone and eventually managed to boot them out. In the midst of all this chaos, one of the great Irish kings – Brian Boru – emerged to claim Ireland for himself.

This chapter looks at what drew the Vikings to Ireland in the first place, where they set up camp, and their most important legacy – the founding of Dublin. It also outlines the important facts (and a few legends) surrounding Brian Boru, the great Irish king who managed, at least for a short time, to bring all of Ireland together.

The Men from Scandinavia

The first recorded visit of the Vikings – big fellows from Norway – off the Irish coast was in 795. The visit wasn't exactly friendly. The Vikings weren't in Ireland to look at the weather and enjoy the landscape; they wanted to take things home. They were in Ireland to do some looting.

The pattern of attack

In 795, the Viking raiders turned up at Rathlin Island off the coast of Antrim. They plundered and burned the local church, and then went home. This brief visit set a pattern that was to go on for years.

The Vikings, although well organised, weren't an invading force from another nation. They were mostly working on a freelance basis, and whatever profits they took from the Irish excursions were for themselves. Initially there was no agenda to settle Ireland or to have a permanent Viking presence there. Simply they wanted to arrive, plunder, maybe kill a few people, and then go home.

Although the Viking raids, and certainly the threat of them, must have been a real pain for the Irish, they weren't initially that frequent. By the 830s the recorded Viking attack rate was only one every year. The following list highlights some of the more notable raids:

- ✓ 795: Vikings attack Iona, Rathlin, Inishmurray, and Inishbofin.
- ✓ 802: Vikings attack Iona (again).
- ✓ 824: Vikings raid Skellig Michael, capture the hermit Étgal, and starve him to death.
- ✓ 837: Fleets of Vikings go inland on the River Liffey and the Boyne.

This pattern of occasional appearances changed in 837 when the Vikings started arriving in large numbers. Sixty ships appeared that year on the Boyne and on the Liffey rivers. In 840 they spent the whole winter on Lough Neagh, and in 841 started establishing permanent fortified bases around the country.

The Vikings attacked quickly and ferociously so the Irish didn't really have much chance against the new visitors, but they put up a fight nonetheless. Although they had quite a few failures, the Irish did have some successes:

- ✓ 812: The King of Eóganacht, Locha Léin, defeats the Vikings.
- ✓ 825: The Irish defeat the Vikings at Ulaid (but lose a battle with them at Osraige).
- ✓ 835: The Irish defeat the Vikings at Derry.
- ✓ 845: The Irish King of Meath captures and drowns the leader of the Vikings, Turgesius.

By 848–9, the Vikings begin losing a series of engagements against the Irish, and the first period of Viking invasion came to an end. But they would be back!

In itself the Viking arrival was annoying, but at least there was the hope that they might get bored and go home. The real problems began when the Irish started working with the Vikings. Some sections of Irish society made deals with the Vikings, and worked with them to attack Irish opponents. These Viking–Irish alliances made the Vikings a permanent feature in the Irish political landscape, and destabilised the delicate balance of power that existed between the different Irish kings.

Looting the Church

The great attraction for the Vikings was the wealth of the Irish Church. The Irish Church had become increasingly famous, and stories of its riches had spread far and wide.

Churches and monasteries were particular favourites of the Vikings. Not because they wanted to visit and marvel at the beauty of these places and say a few prayers, but because they wanted the loot that was inside. Although the monks tried to protect themselves by building high walls and towers, these fortifications were no protection against the marauding Vikings. Unfortunately, the end result was more than just the loss of a little wealth:

- ✔ During the period of Viking attacks, many monasteries, such as the one at Nendrum in Strangford Lough, disappeared forever when they were abandoned after Viking attack. The buildings were destroyed, countless monks murdered and the survivors forced to flee to a new home in a more fortified monastery.

- ✔ The men from Scandinavia weren't conducive to the quiet reflective lifestyle of your average monk. With the Vikings causing havoc in Ireland the amount of manuscript illumination undertaken in the monasteries declined sharply.

The Book of Kells and other great illuminated manuscripts that you see in the museums today were made either before or after the Vikings arrived.

Founding Dublin (and you thought it was Irish)

Dear Old Dublin . . . home of Guinness, and Molly Malone, much loved by Swift and Yeats, a real Irish city. Well, no actually . . . it's a Viking town. When a large Viking fleet set up its winter home on the Liffey in 837, it was perhaps inevitable that they would try to establish something permanent. By the 840s records talk of Viking buildings and fortifications appearing, and the name Duiblinn begins appearing. So yes, it's the Vikings that started the city, and put its first buildings together.

Once established, the new 'city' of Duiblinn started to grow quickly (well, quickly by Viking standards). In the 850s Dublin had its first kings: Amláib (Olaf the White), a Norwegian, and Ímar (Ivar the Boneless), a Dane. Once in charge the White and the Boneless brought a large number of captives from Viking incursions into northern Britain to Dublin, and used them as labour. For the rest of the ninth century Dublin functioned as the most important, and only permanent, Viking trading place in Ireland.

In the tenth century Dublin continued to grow. Along with York, in Britain, Dublin became the most important of the Viking's westerly trading ports. By 953 the value of trading across the Irish Sea through Dublin became apparent when the city began minting its first coins. From its small origins, Dublin had grown to such a size that it had developed a cash-based economy.

One of the great burdens of twenty-first century life is paying tax on our earnings. Although much disliked, the tax system does mark us out as thoroughly modern people and formally marks the relationship between citizen and state. Well, modern it might be, but Viking Dublin also had a tax system. In 989 the householders of Dublin had to pay a gold tax to the local authorities. From coinage to a tax system in a mere forty years – how quickly Viking Dublin progressed!

The Irish Get Their Own Back

Having moved from occasional incursions for the purpose of theft, to establishing a permanent residency, the Viking presence in Ireland had, by the mid-ninth century, become a fact of life. As the Vikings settled and built permanent residences and fortifications, they actually became prone to attack. Whereas before, no one knew where they were until the longships appeared into view, now everyone knew where they were. Viking towns and settlements could be attacked by the Irish who didn't want them around the place. As the ninth century wore on, the Irish did well against the Vikings. Communities of Vikings were attacked in Meath, Kildare, and Cork, and hundreds of Vikings were killed by the Irish. In 849, the Viking settlement at Dublin was even attacked and plundered, but not occupied.

To further complicate matters, a new dimension arrived in the middle of the ninth century: Vikings from Denmark. It all got very confusing very quickly. The Irish hated the Vikings (both old and new) and attacked them. The old

Vikings, who had been in Ireland for years, hated the Danish Vikings and attacked them. The newly arrived Danish Vikings, who just wanted a piece of the action, attacked everybody.

The longer any invading force is present in a country, the more they mix with the local population. By the time the Danish Vikings arrived, a good deal of cultural assimilation had taken place between the original Viking invaders and the locals. Marriages between the Irish and Vikings were not uncommon, and there were plenty of children around who were evidence of close Viking–Irish relationships. Also, many of the Vikings had taken to Christianity, and became closer to the locals that way. That's not to say it was all joy and peacefulness – the locals were still very suspicious of the Vikings. It was only in Dublin, and other Viking strongholds that real intermixing took place.

Ireland became an increasingly bloody place as the Irish and Vikings fought it out. The Irish began winning battles, and eventually the Viking settlements at Wexford, Youghal, Limerick, and Waterford (which had originally been founded during the 840s) were all defeated. At last the Irish were getting their own back on the Vikings.

Then, in 902 the Irish kings of Brega and Leinster combined and attacked the Vikings of Dublin. The defeat was the final one (for a while) of the Vikings in Ireland. Their settlement in Dublin was destroyed, and they were forced to set sail and leave the Irish in peace.

After their great victory against the Vikings in Dublin, the Irish returned to a tranquil life, and all was well with the world. Well, for a few years at least!

The Return of the Vikings

Everybody in Europe had got a bit sick of the Vikings and their marauding nature. By the start of the tenth century many parts of Europe were too well-organised and well-defended to allow Viking incursions. What the Vikings needed was a poorly defended and chaotic place that would allow them to land, do their pillaging, and not put up too much of a fight. Oh, sounds like Ireland's worth a visit (again).

The Vikings roared their way back into Ireland in 914, and this time didn't mess about. They landed in large numbers and their first major act, in 915, was to attack Munster. One account at the time recorded 'immense floods and countless sea-vomitings of ships, so that there was not a harbour nor port nor strongpoint in Munster without a Danish or foreign fleet'. In other words, there were lots of Vikings around!

Contemporary Viking Tourism

The Vikings may have left Dublin long ago, but their legacy lives on. In the National Museum of Ireland there is a permanent exhibition dedicated to the Viking period in Irish history. Visitors can see Viking artefacts, and learn about how these early Dublin residents lived their lives. There is even a model of a Viking house which you get to walk through. To get some 'real' Viking action it's also possible to take a city tour of Dublin on board a Second World War amphibious landing craft. It tours the city's main attractions and even goes onto the water of the Grand Canal Basin. All this is done under the careful guidance of your driver – a Viking! As you walk round the city don't be surprised when endless tourists wearing Viking hats start screaming at you.

The Irish response to this new invading force was to no avail. The King of Tara, in the name of Irish unity, threw his lot in with the Munstermen, but he too was defeated by the Viking forces. More defeats followed. The King of Leinster was killed in a battle against the Vikings at Leixlip, and when the King of Tara tried to attack the Viking stronghold of Dublin he too was killed. The Irish were really struggling. The presence of the Vikings was forcing them to defend themselves and enter battles they'd probably rather not fight. All the chaos meant that traditional power balances were upset, the farming calendar was thrown out, and the young men of Ireland were dying in battle. The return of the Vikings simply destabilised everything all over again.

The Vikings were doing well against their Irish enemies, but they felt that Britain offered greater riches. In the 920s and 930s the Dublin Vikings concentrated not on winning Ireland, but on taking over the richer town of York in Britain. As a result, their power base in Ireland began reducing, until they only really controlled the area around Dublin.

Irish kings regroup

One of the reasons the Vikings had been successful in Ireland was because the Irish were so divided. By the tenth century the Irish kings had begun realising that while they were divided they stood little chance of resisting any invader. The years of Viking incursions changed things, and the Irish started thinking more collectively. The Viking years are important as they taught the Irish that division could only lead to weakness. If they got together they could defeat troublesome newcomers like the Vikings and rule Ireland more effectively.

So now, with the Vikings back in Ireland, the Irish had to either respond or allow themselves to become Nordic. They chose to resist and another period of struggle between the Irish and the Vikings began. Here are some of the main dates in this second wave of Viking visits:

- ✔ 914: The Vikings return to Munster, and seize Waterford.
- ✔ 917: They return to Dublin, and begin the life of Cork city.
- ✔ 921: Viking fleets appear on Lough Foyle, and attacks on Armagh follow.
- ✔ 922: The city of Limerick is founded. Viking fleets take control of all the main waterways in Ireland.
- ✔ 937: The leader of the Dublin Vikings, Olaf, son of Godfrid, is defeated in battle in England.
- ✔ 950: End of second period of Viking invasions.

The second period of Viking invasions was no less damaging to Ireland than the first. What had changed however was that the interaction between the Vikings and the different Irish kings had increased, and that the trading ports established by the Vikings, such as Waterford, survived their departure.

Two cultures become one

To say that the Vikings arrived in Ireland one day and finally left years later, never to return, is much too simplistic a way of describing what happened. History just isn't that straightforward. The Vikings were in Ireland, on and off, for the best part of a century and a half. While they were mostly self-interested (what kind of invader isn't?), they did form alliances with the Irish and begin mixing with them. There were regular incidences of Irish–Viking marriages, and many offspring resulted from these unions.

Once the Vikings had begun inter-marrying with the Irish, and making political deals with them, they became part of the landscape. Their beliefs began to follow the way of Christianity and their language became Irish rather than Norse.

The longer they were away from home, the more they could be seen as Irish, rather than specifically Viking. They were as unfamiliar to later Viking raiders as the Irish were themselves. In essence, the Vikings became Irish.

An important factor to bear in mind is that, during the Viking assimilation into Ireland, the Norsemen became more involved in Irish culture. However, the different Viking settlements often worked separately and formed alliances dependant on their own specific circumstances. Consider this example.

The Viking New Towns

The second wave of Viking invasions led to the foundation of a town on the banks of the River Lee, namely modern Cork city. During the two periods of Viking invasions, many of the main modern towns and cities of Ireland were founded.

The main towns and cities that have clear Viking origins are Cork, Dublin, Limerick, Wexford, and Waterford. The legacy of the Viking incursion into Ireland is clear in many place names. Experts acknowledge that upwards of 50 names or terms for landscapes or settings were borrowed from Norse and used when the Vikings named their new homes (for example, Leixlip, Howth, and Wicklow all come from Norse).

Mathgamain, King of Cashel, and leader of the Munster dynasty of Dál Cais, was throwing his weight around in the second half of the tenth century. In an attempt to control him, his enemies sought the help of the Limerick Vikings. Despite their power, the Vikings were no match for Mathgamain, who defeated them at the battle of Saloghead. Wary of any future animosity from Limerick, Mathgamain himself sought Viking allies. He made a pact with the Vikings of Waterford, and they supported him until his death in 976.

In addition to showing how the goals of Viking settlements could be at cross purposes, it also demonstrates how Irish kings such as Mathgamian would fight one Viking group one year, and form an alliance with a different group later on.

All invaders or immigrants eventually assimilate and adapt the traditions and customs of their new home – a fact that is important in Irish history. In the same way that some of the Vikings settled in Ireland and became, to all intents and purposes, Irish, so would later invaders and settlers such as the Normans and the English. As the invaders became more Irish than Norse – or English or Norman – all kinds of problems developed. Ireland was often settled forcibly, and when these settlers turned to Irish ways rather than promoting the values of their former home, they were seen as traitors. This becomes a big issue with the Normans (see Chapter 7) and the English (see Chapter 9). But remember, this assimilation isn't just a one way process. All invaders brought with them new technologies (such as new forms of housing, weaponry, and shipping), as well as cultural and linguistic forms. The Irish took on board many of the things that were brought into their country, and as a result all the invaders had an important legacy.

Big Brian Boru

The story of Brian Boru is one of legend – part fact, part myth.

According to legend, Brian was the brave man and fearless leader who brought together a small Irish force and managed to expel the Vikings from Ireland. In doing so he permanently rid the country of the terrible Vikings and ensured that Ireland would continue as a Christian country and not be driven towards some horrible paganism. It's a great story, but reality is far more complex.

The rise of a legend

The Ireland before Brian's rule was adjusting to the fact of the Viking incursions, and many of the kingships across Ireland were in a state of transition as families attempted to reclaim their traditional authority over their local area. Brian's brother Mathgamain had taken control of Munster in 964 after he defeated a rival king, Mael Muad. Three years later, Mathgamain was supposed to be having a peaceful meeting with Mael Muad to straighten things out, but Mael seized him and killed him. Brian succeeded his brother as King of Munster, and obviously had a score to settle.

Not a lot is known about Brian Boru. He was born into the family of the Munster kings, and brought up to be a fighter. His family had often fought against the Vikings of Limerick but also traded with them. Brian had gained an appreciation of the importance of naval warfare from the Vikings, and this would serve him well later in life. He was born to be a military leader.

Although Brian was vicious and brutal in his attacks, he was forgiving in the peace. After killing Mael Muad, Brian allowed Muad's son, Cain, to retain his father's kingdom; he also gave Cain his own daughter, Sadhbh, as a wife. Cain duly remained loyal to Brian, his father in law, for the rest of his life.

During the latter half of the tenth century (976–82, to be exact), Brian established himself as King of Munster. In 976 he inherited his brother's title, and by 982, driven by the desire to avenge the death of his brother, he had defeated all his opposing kings in the Munster area. With his superior army, his skill in the battlefield, and his use of naval warfare, Brian proved much stronger than any of his local opponents. He even managed to defeat the Irish/Viking people of Limerick and their allies. The capture of Limerick demonstrated once more the strength of Brian, but also his humanity: although he killed the ruler of Limerick and his son, he did not destroy the town and allowed the Irish/Viking population to remain living there so long as they swore their allegiance to him.

In 996 Brian secured the submission of Leinster by mounting a major invasion and threatening all the local kings with murder and mayhem unless they submitted to him. They all saw sense in making a deal, and agreed to accept Brian as their king.

By 988, Brian had raided Meath to impose his authority over the kings there, and then turned his sights to the lands of the High King, Mael Sechnaill. Mael, for his part, didn't take too kindly to Brian's attention, and turned right back and attacked Munster. Mael was Brian's main opponent. As the man who held the title of High King, Mael was supposedly the most powerful (and richest) man in Ireland. But Brian wanted to be High King also. To achieve that he would have to win the submission of Mael. It would be a long and bloody process before one of them emerged victorious.

The Irish kings get together

Dublin in the latter part of the tenth century was a very prosperous city. It made its wealth from trading with traders from across Europe and because of its place as an important port. Clearly such wealth was attractive to any Irish king who fancied a bit of action. Although you might expect that it was Brian Boru who took a fancy to Dublin, it was actually Mael Sechnaill, the High King, who saw the advantage of Dublin as a place to plunder. He had taken Dublin in battle in 980 and had captured it again a year later. He won the submission of the leaders of Dublin, and left them to run their own affairs.

In 995, Mael returned to Dublin, forcing the local leaders to submit again, and plundering it of its wealth. While such tactics kept Mael in booty, it also brought him to the attention of Brian. If Brian was going to be a real contender for the High King title, he couldn't have his opponent walking in and out of Ireland's most important and wealthiest city at will. Brian would have to convince Mael that he was the stronger of the two.

Many city populations had become a dilution of the Viking and Irish peoples. Historians refer to these combined people as the Hiberno-Norse (Hiberno being Irish people with the Norse being the Viking). By the later decades of the tenth century many of the original Viking settlements such as Limerick and Dublin could be considered to be Hiberno-Norse controlled.

By 997, Mael realised that Brian was too strong for him (especially after Brian had so easily won the submission of Leinster) and he struck a deal. At a meeting at Clonfert, Brian and Mael agreed to divide the country: Mael would control the northern half of Ireland (Meath, Connacht, and Ulster), Brian the southern half (Munster and Leinster). Mael, although doing well out of the deal, accepted that he was in the secondary position because Brian's military forces were far stronger. Mael had to take what he could and hope that Brian wouldn't turn on him.

Initially it all went swimmingly, and the two accepted the peace. They even went up against the Hiberno-Norse of Dublin together for a spot of plundering in 998. And all seemed well in Ireland. But human nature being what it is – and with two such large egos involved – the peace wouldn't last.

The kings fall out

In 999, there was a revolt in Leinster which was backed by the Hiberno-Norse of Dublin who were sick to death of Brian throwing his weight about. It was a key turning point and fractured the fragile peace that existed between Mael and Brian. Mael hadn't been directly involved in the revolt, but such uprisings demonstrated to Brian that opponents (whoever they were) were a headache.

The revolt in Leinster was a real annoyance to Brian. He crushed the rebellion at Glenn Máma, and in the process it was estimated that 4,000 were killed in battle.

Mael Mordha, the King of Leinster, and Sitric, the King of Dublin, were forced to accept Brian as their over-king, but again Brian also offered reconciliation. He gave Sitric one of his daughters as a wife, and in turn (at least according to legend) took Sitric's mother as his own wife.

With Leinster and Dublin his, it was obvious that Brian would be unable to resist the penultimate piece of the country that he didn't control: Mael's Meath.

In 1000, Brian invaded Mael's kingdom. Despite the occasional victory, Mael had no answer for Brian's forces. In 1002, he surrendered his title and Brian was the undisputed High King of Ireland.

Brian Boru, the High King

So this High King title sounds great, but what did it actually mean? In theory all the kings of Ireland, from the smallest to the largest, had accepted Brian as their over-king, and were supposed to pay him tribute (protection money) and let him throw his weight around. In some ways the spirit of the title High King is similar to that of playground bully: you're the biggest and no one dare stand up to you. But of course it wasn't that simple. The problems that Brian faced were:

- ✔ Ireland was a big place, and Brian couldn't control everybody. It was inevitable he would face some local opposition.

- ✔ Brian couldn't bring about stability and complete acceptance of his High Kingship – there was always some local squabble challenging his authority.

- ✔ Despite claiming the title of High King, Brian had never actually imposed his will on the kings of Ulster. They would always be a threat unless he could suppress them.

- ✔ The Hiberno-Norse communities were always a law unto themselves, and Brian had to make regular deals with them to keep them quiet.

As you can imagine, these problems were difficult to manage. All that Brian could do was to make deals, threaten people when necessary, and hope that everyone behaved themselves. It was a tough job being High King.

Attacking Ulster

Brian finally decided that if he was going to have complete control of Ireland, he had to squash the kings of Ulster. He brought together a force of men from Munster, Connacht, Leinster, Meath, and Dublin, and set about attacking Ulster. In 1003 and 1004, he tried to win Ulster on the battle field, but failed.

Brian switched tactics in 1005. Rather than beating the Ulster kings into submission, he decided to court the support of the Church in Armagh. Looking to religious leaders to secure a political victory may seem a bit odd, but the Irish religious institutions were very powerful during the tenth and early eleventh centuries, and the most important place in the whole of Ireland was the Church at Armagh. Once the bishops in Armagh recognised and supported a leader, that leader had the religious stamp of authority behind him. Brian gave the bishops in Armagh twenty-two ounces of gold to win them over and declared that it would be the religious capital of Ireland. By confirming Armagh as the most important place in Christian Ireland, Brian got the Church behind him, and this approval gave him a further stamp of authority.

If Brian could not attain what he wanted militarily then he knew that he could attain it through the Church. Therefore Brian spent a week at Armagh, recognised the Church's authority, and started giving the Church money. The Church loved all the attention and gave Brian its backing.

With the support of the Church, Brian found life in Ulster slightly easier. He managed to extract hostages and tributes from all but one of the Ulster kings by 1008. He was nearly there!

The thorns in his side were the Cenél Conaill in the west of Ulster. He fought against them yearly, until 1011, when he had really had enough. This time he sent in ships and an army, and the Cenél Conaill had no chance. Brian had won the day, and taken control, so far as he really could, of the whole of Ireland.

Brian's last stand

Like any playground bully, Brian wasn't a popular man. His fellow kings across Ireland were jealous of the power he had over them and they were constantly on the lookout for a reason to challenge his authority. Three years after he had finally won over Ulster, Brian found himself facing these challenges:

In 1012, Flaithbertach, an Uí Néill king in the north, decides to take control of the area for himself, and fights a successful series of battles that wins Ulster back from forces loyal to Brian. Then in 1013 he advances south and marches towards Meath.

At the same time as Flaithbertach is causing trouble in the south, the Hiberno-Norse of Dublin feel rebellious and decide to challenge Brian's authority too. In response, Brian lays siege to Dublin but is unsuccessful and has to retreat. Sitric, the King of Dublin, knows that Brian will be back. To bolster his own forces, in 1014, Sitric seeks the support of Vikings on the Isle of Man and the Orkneys. Brian, aware of the danger, gathers his own forces for the big battle ahead. He even gets his old enemy Mael Sechlainn to help him, but Mael deserts him before the battle starts and goes home.

Although the High King technically had all kinds of power over everyone in Ireland, it was only really enforceable through military strength. If Brian ducked a fight, his days as High King would be over. He had to meet all challengers and see them off if he wanted to retain the title.

On 23 April one of the best known Irish battles was fought at Clontarf, north of Dublin. It was an evenly matched battle, and one that lasted a whole day. Brian's forces won the day, and his High Kingship was intact. But a lot of good that did him because, sadly for Brian, he was killed by a retreating Norseman. The days of Brian Boru, the High King, were over.

Chapter 6

Irish vs. Norman Invaders...
But Who's in Charge?

In This Chapter

▶ Trying to become High King

▶ Creating a more powerful church

▶ Making friends with the Normans

▶ The Normans arrive

When High King Brian Boru was killed in The Battle of Clontarf (see Chapter 5) Ireland was left without the one man who was powerful enough to demand the respect of all the other kings in the country.

People did try – everyone was desperate to elevate themselves to the position of High King – but they simply weren't powerful or scary enough. That meant that there were decades of infighting, and lots of Irish people died in the constant squabbling. But they didn't keep the fight within the family. The Irish had a tradition of inviting outsiders to join them in their struggles, and in the second half of the twelfth century they did it again. This time was different, however, because the invited party – the Normans – quite liked the idea of being in Ireland and weren't content to simply turn up, fight a battle for an ally, and leave again. They wanted a piece of the action long-term.

This chapter looks at life in Ireland in the eleventh and twelfth centuries and explores why no one was big and tough enough to effectively fill Brian Boru's shoes. You'll also find out why and how the Normans arrived, and understand how they set about interfering in Irish life.

Realities of Irish Kingship: A Royal Pain

The kings discussed in the following sections of this chapter were regional kings who aspired to unite all of Ireland under their own leadership. As you read about their trials and travails, keep in mind that they had to deal with these realities of Irish politics:

✔ Having control of one of the provinces of Ireland was an impressive feat. A certain degree of political know-how was required as well as a good sized army and the ability to win over people and institutions (such as the Church) that were locally powerful. To make a strike outside of one's own province and start demanding that neighbouring kings accept you, took a whole heap more effort, political savvy, and firepower. Few had the skills or strength necessary.

✔ Because the Irish kings had no formal system of inheritance, the question of who would take over was all a bit messy. And even if there was a smooth succession of a title, the authority connected to it would only cover the immediate family kingship. The new king would have to get on his horse, and travel round Ireland and try and win over everybody else again.

✔ Irish kings during this period were realists. If they had a stronger king coming onto their patch, and they didn't have the strength to beat them, they'd make some kind of arrangement to keep themselves in power locally. The whole thing was a game. You hung around, waiting for alliances to rise and fall, and always looked after number one.

✔ Ulster was always the biggest challenge to anyone who wanted to be High King. It was a distant and remote place with hard terrain that made it difficult to attack. Also, the Ulster kings had a fearsome reputation as fighters and weren't easy to defeat.

The Kingly Contenders, Round 1: The Munster Men

Being High King, the most powerful man in the whole of Ireland, was an attractive job. Okay, so it came with some drawbacks, as Brian Boru had discovered. People didn't particularly like being ruled over by a big bully, and they kept trying to topple you. In Brian's case, his opponents went so far as to kill him – always a blow to the old career prospects. But for all the drawbacks, and the fact that whoever took the title of High King would always be opposed, it's the title that lots of the kings in Ireland aspired to.

Think of it like being the heavyweight champion of the world. You get to be famous, all the girls love you and, if you play your cards right, you get to be very rich. But there's always a contender out there who fancies your crown. This is what life was like in eleventh century Ireland. The title holder was dead, and a series of contenders battled and to take the crown of the High King.

Donnchad (Brian Boru's son)

Immediately after the death of Brian Boru, his son Donnchad succeeded him. As head of the Dál Cais lineage, Donnchad should have been very powerful, but he faced internal opposition from his own half-brother, Tadg. Rather than meekly accept the rise of Donnchad, Tadg resisted, and kept rising up against him. In the best spirit of family harmony, Donnchad did the only thing that he could with his difficult half-brother: he had him killed.

By 1025, Donnchad, having dispatched Tadg, was the undisputed King of Munster. This was a million miles from the power of High King that his father had.

Donnchad struggled to impose himself on the rest of Ireland, and eventually lost control of his own back yard in Munster. Despite calling himself King of Ireland, everyone ignored Donnchad's claims, and by 1059 he was so powerless that he had to face the ignominy of submitting to the King of Connacht. It all got to be too much, and in 1063 he quit.

Rather than battle on any more, Donnchad decided that the game was up and went into retirement. Before saying 'Ta-ta' for good, however, Donnchad looked for a successor.

There were various kings trying to climb the greasy pole at this point. The two most important were:

- Diarmait, member of the Uí Chennselaig dynasty and, from 1042, King of Leinster. He worked closely with the old Hiberno-Norse families, and even declared himself King of Dublin.
- Turlough O Brien, King of Munster, and nephew of Donnchad. He accepted initially that his position was weak, and kept his head down. Rather than battling the rising star of Diarmait, he chose to work with him and accept his dominance.

He handed the kingship of Munster over to his nephew Turlough. (Turlough was the son of Tadg, the brother that Donnchad had killed years before.) But that didn't really settle things down, because Diarmait had his own big plans.

Diarmait

Diarmait, King of Leinster, had big plans. He quickly became the most powerful king in the southern half of Ireland, and attacked Meath. He dreamt of taking over Connacht, and in 1067 he tried to win it. Sadly for him it all went pear-shaped and he was repelled. In 1072 he was killed in battle while trying to take new lands in the north.

Although Diarmait's life was relatively short and sweet, he had, in a way, been successful. He had never really cracked the High King business though, and certainly never won over Connacht or Ulster. When he died it was recorded that he was the *King of Ireland with opposition*. It's an important title that acknowledged his successes, but stressed that he had failed to make it all the way to High King status.

Turlough (Donnchad's brother)

With Diarmait dead and buried, there was a renewed shuffling of the pack. Who would now emerge as the most powerful king? Would they go all the way and be High King, or would they only make it to the status of King of Ireland with opposition?

The next contender was Turlough. With Diarmait dead, Turlough, Tadg's son and Donnchad's nephew, spent a couple of minutes mourning and then did what any friend would do: He invaded Diarmait's home territory.

By the end of 1073, Turlough had control of Leinster, Dublin, and Meath, and a province that Diarmait had never managed to hook – Connacht. Ulster, however, remained beyond his reach. Although Turlough never managed to actually capture it, the Ulster kings did occasionally call on him in Munster and ask for his help in settling local struggles.

For all his success, Turlough had a hard time of it. He had to invade everywhere to convince the other kings to submit to him, and this all took time, money, and effort. While he was away banging the heads of other kings together, there was always the risk that someone would try to undermine him at home.

Turlough died in 1086. He was recorded in the annals as the King of Ireland. Okay, so he hadn't made it as far as High King because of failing to take Ulster, but he had got further than Diarmait: officially he had no opposition. Turlough was so well-thought of about the place that Pope Gregory VII called him the 'magnificent king and noble King of Ireland'. Praise indeed!

Muirchertach (Turlough's son)

With Turlough six feet under, the thorny issue of succession came to the fore again. The problem was that he had three sons: Muirchertach, Diarmait, and Tadg. Rather than play favourites, Turlough left the whole thing unclear and left the three sons to fight it out between themselves. Although his son Muirchertach was eventually successful in taking over Munster, the province that he won was severely weakened. Rather than taking over the powerful kingdom his father had built up, the years of brotherly infighting had left Munster weakened. To make matters worse, many of the other kings around the country saw their opportunity and decided to strike while Munster was weakened.

Leinster and Connacht initially ignored Muirchertach and withdrew the submission they had made to his father. And the northerner, Domnall Mac Lochlainn of Ulster decided that Munster was so weak he chose to travel down and force Muirchertach to submit to him in 1090.

But Muirchertach was made of sterner stuff. The next few years of his life would be a real roller-coaster. He demonstrated what could be done if you put your mind to it, found out how impossible a place Ulster was to force a submission from, and experienced the problems of having a brother who was a pain in the neck. The highlights of Muirchertach's life were:

- ✔ 1092: He invades Connacht and puts them all back in their place.

- ✔ 1093: Back in Connacht again – they had decided they could go it alone. Not a chance, and Muirchertach put them in their place: again!

- ✔ 1094: Expels the King of Dublin and kills the King of Meath. Puts his own people in charge.

- ✔ 1095–6: Decides to take on Domnall Mac Lochlainn in Ulster. Brings forces from Munster, Connacht, Meath, and Leinster (it's an all-Ireland match), but still can't defeat Mac Lochlainn.

- ✔ 1114: His brother Diarmait, who has been a pain for years, kicks him off the throne.

- ✔ 1115: Rallies against his brother, briefly retakes the throne, but is thrown off it again a year later.

- ✔ 1116: Poor old Muirchertach has seen enough. He enters a monastery to see out his last days.

The life story of Muirchertach is a long and arduous one. Although he, like many before him, failed to win over Ulster he managed to get his Kingship status to one where he ruled over Ireland, but with opposition. He had shown, as his forefathers before him, that success depended on huge military resources, a degree of luck, and the support of local elites. While the system had not taken Muirchertach to the level of High King, he had begun to establish a national network of local kings to whom he had given power. This was the first step to a national system of political institutions that would allow someone, potentially, to become High King.

The Legacy of the Munster Kings

What then was the legacy of Muirchertach and his fellow Munster kings, Donnchad and Turlough? They had achieved much, and become very powerful. They oversaw a series of initiatives that would continue the transformation of Ireland. These included:

- ✔ The Munster kings, as with others in Ireland, became increasingly aware of the power of the Church and of the new Norman rulers in England. Rather than simply ignore these new forces they accepted their presence, and this enhanced the standing and their strength.

- ✔ Muirchertach used marriage as a political tool. He married his daughters off to leading English nobles as a way of cementing political alliances. This gave the Munster kings such as Muirchertach additional political and military support – with the English in the family, he had their tacit support.

- ✔ Rather than using traditional seats of power, such as the old Munster town of Kincora, the kings based themselves in the towns that had been established and fortified by the Vikings, such as Limerick and Waterford. Such towns were built to withstand the force of modern warfare – it was better to be based in a strong, fortified town, than living out in the open.

- ✔ The Munster kings were especially keen on invading, visiting, and controlling Dublin. As a result they gave Dublin renewed political prominence, increased its prestige as a trading port, and effectively established it as the capital of the country.

The Contenders, Round 2

With the death of Muirchertach, it was time for some new kids on the block. Without a strong leadership Munster slipped in significance. There was space in the political structures of Ireland for someone else to see if they could dominate. This shift in focus from province to province wasn't unusual and is a common feature of Irish history: no one province dominated the centuries.

Turlough O Connor

One of the first contenders to the throne emerged from the west of Ireland. His name was Turlough, but this time he was an O Connor. The O Connor family had become increasingly powerful in Connacht, and kept eyeing the opportunities that were available elsewhere in Ireland. Although Turlough's attempt at becoming High King was a failure, his son would claim the title.

When you wish upon a cross

There's one great story about Turlough O Connor. It was believed at the time that a very special piece of wood had arrived in Ireland, namely a piece of the cross on which Jesus had been crucified. Turlough got hold of it, and had it enshrined into the cross of Cong (a thirty-inch high cross, now in the National Museum of Ireland, that's reputed to be the finest example of such metalwork from this period). In an act of wish-making, he made a prayer on this holy relic that he'd be made King of Ireland.

Turlough O Connor began his quest for the big title by attacking and gaining control of Munster. He divided it into two and set up his own kings on the two thrones there. He then used the same strategy in Meath: dividing the province into four separate parts and putting lesser, but friendly, kings on the throne. In Leinster and Dublin, once he had them under his control, he put his son on the throne.

In Leinster, he had a bit of a problem. Dermot Mac Murrough, another great name of this period, should have become King of Leinster, but lost out when Turlough placed his son in the job. Dermot turfed him out and eventually came to an agreement with Turlough: Turlough would allow Dermot to have the kingship of eastern Leinster so long as he behaved.

Like many before him he'd failed to get control of Ulster, and had only managed to control everywhere else by brute force and through puppet kings. Men like Dermot had been placated, but always remained a threat.

And then in 1156 Turlough O Connor died.

Upon his the death, the main forces in Ireland were:

- Rory O Connor, successor of Turlough, and King of Connacht.
- Muirchertach Mac Lochlainn of Ulster.
- Dermot Mac Murrough of Leinster.
- Tiernan O Rourke of Breffny (part of Munster).

These families, with their aspiring kings, liked nothing better than attacking each other, making threats and generally intimidating each other and anyone else who got in the way. Well, you can probably see where this discussion is going.

Squaring off: The fight for supremacy

In the 1150s, Mac Lochlainn of Ulster and Mac Murrough of Leinster formed an alliance, although the former was definitely the more powerful one in the relationship. They attacked Connacht and forced O Connor to submit. In the face of the alliance that had attacked him, O Connor had no choice but to form a partnership with O Rourke.

The result? Ireland's largest royal families had divided themselves into two blocks. The new game would be Ulster and Leinster versus Connacht and Breffny.

Mac Lochlainn believed that he had done enough to claim the title of King of All Ireland, and used that title. To underpin his self-proclaimed power he granted land to the Church in Newry and began controlling, as far as he could, land distribution. This process was underpinned by the use of charters and seals and suggests that Mac Lochlainn was developing a legal style authority for his kingship.

With the two-way split that had developed in Irish royal affairs, conflict was bound to follow. And it did with great force. The series of battles and squabbles that took place between the two groups is quite complex, but here goes.

In 1165, O Connor and O Rourke, recognising that Mac Lochlainn was busy with a local power struggle back in Ulster, quickly invaded Meath and took Dublin.

To announce the taking over of a town, the invader would offer a *tuarustul*. Effectively this was a payment to ensure loyalty in the future and make sure there were no hard feelings between the newly conquered townsfolk and the victorious invaders. When Mac Lochlainn had taken Dublin in 1154, he gave a tuarustul of 1,500 cows. O Connor bettered it in 1166 by giving Dublin 4,000 cows. The city was awash with cows, but happy to accept the payment and swear loyalty to the new ruler in town.

After their success in Dublin, and refreshed with additional forces, the O Connor–O Rourke alliance swept through Leinster, Connacht, and West Ulster. Assisting the rise of O Connor still further, his bitter rival Mac Lochlainn was killed in an unrelated battle in Ulster. So the battles for control of Ireland in the second half of the twelfth century were finally over. Here's how it fell out:

- ✔ **The O Connor–O Rourke alliance triumphed.** O Connor proclaimed himself High King and was accepted as such. Having ridden on his coat tails, O Rourke was in a great position now that his mate was in charge.

> ✔ **The Mac Lochlainn–Mac Murrough alliance was in tatters:** Mac Lochlainn was dead, and Mac Murrough was in real trouble. Anybody with a grudge against Mac Murrough dived in and attacked him.

Of course, the end is never the end in battles for control. Although defeated, poor old Dermot Mac Murrough, friendless and unloved, had no choice but to leave Ireland and sail off to Bristol in 1166. But don't feel too sorry for him. He eventually made new friends in England: the Normans.

Rory: At last, a High King

Once Mac Lochlainn had died, and Mac Murrough was banished, Rory O Connor, son of Turlough O Connor of Connacht, was in pole position. He called all the kings of Ireland together at Athlone and they accepted him as High King. As a reward for their acceptance of him, he did what all great leaders do: He started charging them tax. He then brought the clergy together, and got them to accept him as head honcho. In 1168 he presided over the great festival of Aonach Tailteann (a big summer festival that would eventually be revived in 1924 – see Chapter 22).

Rory was the first all powerful High King, and unlike Brian Boru, he stayed alive long enough to enjoy it. He had no opponents in Ireland, but sadly he would be the last of the High Kings. The Normans were coming.

Bout's Over: Enter the Normans

So what do you do if you've been soundly defeated and run out of your own home? Especially when Rory O Connor is happily journeying round Ireland being heralded by everyone as the High King?

Mac Murrough had two options after leaving Ireland: Accept defeat and never return to Ireland, or find someone who was an even bigger bully than Rory O Connor and try and get them to come and fight on his side. As you can imagine, Mac Murrough chose option two.

Once in Bristol, Mac Murrough went to see a friend who told him that his best bet was to get the King of England on his side. So Mac Murrough sailed off to France, where he found Henry II, and asked him for his help.

Henry agreed to the request and gave Mac Murrough a royal seal of approval for his mission of retaking his land in Ireland. With Henry's authority behind him, Mac Murrough could recruit English soldiers to help him in Ireland. Which he did with quite a degree of success.

With the humiliation of Mac Murrough that culminated in his exile, he became a loose cannon. He stopped playing by the messy Irish rules (refer to the earlier section 'Realities of Irish Kingship: A Royal Pain' for the problems with these rules), and instead looked for the support of a far stronger foreign power. His actions would have consequences that he probably never anticipated.

One of the key figures that agreed to help Mac Murrough was Richard fitz Gilbert, the Earl of Pembroke. He was of Norman stock, and would go down in history by his other name: Strongbow. Alongside Strongbow a whole group of other Normans offered to assist Mac Murrough, and Irish history took another major turn.

While Mac Murrough's mission to retake his land in Ireland had the English royal seal of approval, this probably wouldn't have been enough to motivate anyone but the most ardent supporter of the English Crown. The men who followed Mac Murrough to Ireland went along for one main reason: to get rich. Ireland was a virgin land as far as the Normans were concerned. For them, acquiring land in Ireland added to their power and prestige. At least that's what they hoped.

Early skirmishes

With the approval of Henry II and the Normans behind him, Mac Murrough began his lengthy attempt to retake Ireland. Events moved quickly and, frankly, weren't too kind to Mac Murrough:

- 1167: Mac Murrough returns to Ireland with a small force, but is defeated by O Connor and O Rourke.

- 1169: Norman mercenaries from England land in County Wexford. They take Waterford and Ossory. Mac Murrough's fortunes start looking up. But then Mac Murrough challenges O Connor and O Rourke again and loses. This time they force him to submit and promise that he'll bring no more foreigners in. To seal this deal, Mac Murrough hands over his son as a hostage to O Connor.

    Mac Murrough was defeated so quickly because some of his English mercenaries, as is the habit of mercenaries, decided that the pay was better on the other side and deserted him.

These events showed just how confident O Connor was. He didn't seem to fear Mac Murrough, even when backed by the foreigners from England, and obviously didn't really see Norman involvement in Ireland as a serious threat. History proved him wrong.

Strongbow settles in

In the summer of 1170, the English earl Strongbow made his move. He brought with him an army of 1,000 men and 200 knights (they also had armour and archers – things that the Irish just weren't up to speed with). They were the most technologically advanced army of their time. This was like pitting Stone Age man against the crew of the Star Ship Enterprise: no contest.

By September 1170 Strongbow and his forces had taken control of Dublin. This was a hugely important step and had ramifications for the future (see chapter 7). The main points were:

- ✔ A modern and well-armed Norman force was in Ireland and they weren't going away in a hurry. This was an invading army not a mercenary force.

- ✔ The power of O Connor as High King was over. He couldn't defeat Strongbow, and the idea of an Irish King ruling with consensus disappeared for good.

- ✔ Strongbow's successes alarmed Henry II. While he had sanctioned Mac Murrough recruiting troops to assist him get his land back, that didn't mean organising an army that might challenge his own authority in England.

Bottom line: Ireland's days of running its own affairs were over. After the fall of Dublin to Strongbow in 1170 it would take until 1922 (see chapter 21) before the city would again rule its own affairs and not take its orders from England.

The Power of the Church

While all these Irish kings were banging their heads together and trying to outdo one another, one national institution was blossoming: the Church. Muirchertach and the other Munster kings had, like Brian Boru before them, accepted that Armagh was the most important and powerful seat of the Church in Ireland. What they agreed was that where they had royal authority, Armagh would have Church authority in the same regions.

During the twelfth century the Church in Ireland organised itself and, as a result, its power increased. Church power became inseparable from the power of the Kings. Without the backing of the Church, any King who had national aspirations would fail. Equally, the Church needed the military and political support of the Kings to ensure its own authority across the land.

Growing more connected

Two major shifts took place in the Irish Church in the twelfth century. The first, at the beginning of the century, and driven by the appointment of the first papal legate to Ireland in 1101, was a momentous act. It vested papal authority in one man in Ireland, and gave him the power to enact reforms on the Irish Church. This had the effect of reorganising the Church in Ireland and moving it closer to the home of all Church authority: the Vatican.

Church councils

Two big gatherings formally changed the way that the Church was run in Ireland. The first, the Council of Cashel in 1101, ensured that the administration of the Irish Church was brought in line with the rest of Europe. The changes meant that the Church would be free of secular taxation, that priests would be celibate, and that the right of sanctuary would be honoured. The second, at Rath Breasail in 1111, was even more important as it reorganised the Church geographically. Under the new rules the Church would:

- Be divided into two provincial organisations: one in the south, one in the north.
- Cashel would be the seat of power for the south, Armagh for the north.
- Each province would be divided into twelve dioceses with clear boundaries. Many of these are still in existence to this day.

The changes were important as they established the Church in Ireland on a clear organisational footing, and gave it a greater authority over everyone – even the kings. However, Ireland was still, for most of the twelfth century, a fairly remote place, and the Church there still remained remote from the day to day authority of the Vatican.

The second big twelfth-century change for the Church was the Norman invasion that would mark a real turning point. It made the Church an even more powerful body. While the Church had close relationships with the Irish kings in the twelfth century, it had often ignored rules and regulations coming out of the Vatican. This annoyed the Pope who had asked Henry II to invade Ireland to bring the Irish Church into line. The arrival of the Normans ended the isolation of the Irish Church, and brought it closer to the European Church system. After the Normans had landed and the Vatican directed the Church more clearly, Ireland stopped being such a remote and isolated place.

The Church established itself as an important power-broker in the twelfth century. It wasn't a perfect body though. The main reforms during this period were:

- ✔ An acceptance of the authority of the Vatican, and a greater willingness to accept rules and ideas emerging from Rome. Prior to this period the Church in Ireland had often been remote from central Vatican authority.

- ✔ Closer relationships with the Archbishop of Canterbury and the power of the Church in England. The Church in England was keenly supported by the Normans (in fact, England had been invaded with the support of the Pope).

- ✔ The link between Canterbury and Ireland was formalised in 1072 when the Archbishop, Lanfranc, claimed authority over Ireland.

- ✔ A continuation of the monastic system which flourished with the support and patronage of various Irish kings.

- ✔ An increase in the number of Irish people, especially the kings and their supporters, who were making pilgrimages to Rome. This allowed them to feel closer to the Church and more in tune with its wishes.

Many of these reforms were successful, but others were ignored on the ground. After all, people had been worshipping their own way for years – a bunch of Normans and some new rules from the Vatican weren't going to change the habits of a lifetime. For all their faults though, the reforms did allow the Church a degree of stability and continuity. The Church was able, with support from various Irish Kings, the Vatican, and the Archbishop of Canterbury to work largely unhindered by the power struggles between the different Irish monarchies.

A growing, and ever more organised Church, would naturally be an important power-broker in Ireland. Not only did the Church have religious authority over the Irish – it received its orders and power from God in the human form of the Pope – but it also had an increasing power because of its links to the Normans. The Church, although having to work with the kings of Ireland, in many ways had more powerful allies than the kings did.

The Church in Ireland, like many people, wasn't overly fond of the new Norman arrivals. However, the Papal authority of the King of England wasn't to be disputed. The Church of Ireland had done well during the twelfth century, and had been one of the main important national institutions. With the arrival of the Normans, the significance of the Church increased.

Chapter 7

Boy Meets Gael: The Norman-Irish Alliance

. . . .

In This Chapter

▶ Meeting the Irish

▶ Marrying the Irish

▶ Threatening the English Crown from Ireland

▶ Forcing the English Way on Ireland

▶ Meeting the Irish Parliament for the first time

. . . .

With the arrival of Strongbow the Normans had landed in Ireland, and showed no signs of leaving. (See Chapter 6 for more on Strongbow. His real name was Richard fitz Gilbert, and he was the Earl of Pembroke. He was of Norman stock, and had been invited to fight in Ireland by Dermot Mac Murrough, who wanted help in winning his lands back in Leinster. Strongbow accepted the invite, arrived in Ireland in 1170, and changed Irish history forever.) The Norman presence in Ireland made everything very complex.

As the Normans integrated into Irish life, they changed Ireland quite dramatically, and also became a thorn in the side of the English Crown. The problem was, were the Normans who had invaded Ireland loyal to England, or were they mixing with the Irish so quickly that they were aligning themselves with the troublesome Irish monarchies? It was all very confusing.

To try and sort out the Irish, and their Norman allies, the English kings had to start involving themselves with Ireland in a way that had previously been unimaginable. Not only did they have to intervene by sending in big beefy soldiers to sort the whole mess out, they also tried to get the Irish behaving in an English manner and accepting the rule of law and order.

All the good intentions of the English (well, if they were good intentions) floundered, as we'll see, because the Irish just didn't like being told what to do.

Strongbow: Making Political and Personal Hay

Strongbow had been brought to Ireland by Dermot Mac Murrough specifically to fight on his behalf. The hope was that Strongbow would prove so powerful (especially with all his modern military gadgets), that he'd win the battles he had to fight easily.

This turned out to be the case. But what was in it for Strongbow? No matter how persuasive Dermot Mac Murrough might have been in selling an idea, he still had to give something to the man from Wales. And remember, this wasn't simply a case of Strongbow slapping on some armour and coming over to Ireland. He had to gather a force together, get boats organised to take everyone to Ireland, and pay all the bills. In the event, Strongbow had to borrow the money that would get him and his men to Ireland. So what did MacMurrough offer? This:

✔ **A pretty girl:** Lure number one for Strongbow was the love of a good woman. Well, he hoped it'd be love as he had never met the woman in question. When Mac Murrough came looking for help from Strongbow he had to offer his daughter, Aoife, as part of the deal. The day after Strongbow had helped Mac Murrough take Waterford he got his prize. In August 1170 the happy couple tied the knot to scenes of great celebration.

It may seem a bit harsh, by modern standards, to offer your daughter to a complete stranger in return for his military muscle, but this was the twelfth century. Marriages were often used to cement political agreements, and kept everyone loyal, in the longer term, to the agreement.

✔ **Some cold, hard cash:** As lovely as Aoife was, it seems unlikely that Strongbow was motivated solely by the promise of marriage. This wasn't some tale of gallant knights and damsels in distress, but the brutally realistic politics of twelfth century Ireland. Dermot Mac Murrough was, in principle, a rich man. Although he had been turfed out of Ireland by the High King O Connor (see Chapter 6), if he could reclaim his former territory he'd be wealthy again.

Strongbow came to Ireland specifically to get a piece of the action. If he was successful in returning Mac Murrough to his throne, he'd get the girl and the cash. It was a high risk venture. Win the battles and get the prize, lose and go home with nothing (or more likely, get killed in battle).

✔ **A title and some land:** Mac Murrough had agreed with Strongbow that if he got him his lands back then the rewards would be twofold. First off Strongbow would get some loot and some land, and then, when Mac Murrough died, he'd inherit the lot and the title of King of Leinster.

Fighting the good fight

If you go out into the market place, like Mac Murrough did, looking for hired muscle, then you have to hope they do their job. Especially when you've promised them your daughter and your kingdom as a reward.

Strongbow was up to the task. He quickly took Waterford, where he was married, and then moved on to Dublin. Working with forces that were supportive of Mac Murrough, and using the superior fire power of the Normans, there was no stopping Strongbow. He and his forces moved quickly through Ossory, Meath, and Breffney and all the kings there submitted.

For the High King O Connor, all looked pretty bleak. Fortunately for him the winter of 1170 was fairly grim, and the invading army decided to take a break and spend the cold months in the safety of Leinster.

As modern as Strongbow's fighting techniques were, Ireland was still a difficult place to move fighting men, with all that they required, around the country. Winters were also fairly bleak, and not a good time to be fighting the locals who knew their way around and were more suited to the poor conditions. Safer to stop over somewhere and start fighting again in the spring.

Before Strongbow could get started again, things changed when, in May 1171, his father-in-law died. Dermot Mac Murrough had lived long enough to see his kingdom back in his own hands, but wouldn't have the joy of finally defeating O Connor. Strongbow was now King of Leinster, as agreed in the original deal that had brought him to Ireland.

So Strongbow had a decision to make: settle for what he had or take the battle to O Connor as he had planned. He also needed to consider what to do about his own King in England, Henry II, who was keeping his beady eye on Strongbow.

Claiming his kingdom

With his shiny new crown on his now royal head, Strongbow was in a potentially powerful position. But clearly the locals weren't going to roll over and take this cuckoo in the nest lying down.

Although Strongbow was technically superior to his Irish enemies, and had the kingship of Leinster, he was still an outsider and faced by some serious enemies, namely O Connor, the former High King and the people in Leinster who were less than enamoured with their new Norman king.

In the early summer of 1171, these enemies took action. When various factions in Leinster rebelled against their new king – a foreigner in charge wasn't the future that they wanted – O Connor saw his chance, and marched on Dublin.

So there Strongbow sat: besieged in Dublin, with all his enemies sitting outside the walls waiting for him to either submit or starve to death. In desperation, Strongbow offered O Connor a deal: He, Strongbow, would accept O Connor as his lord (a big deal considering Strongbow had a king of his own in England – Henry), and in return O Connor would let Strongbow retain control of Leinster and his title and lift the siege, with no one getting hurt.

O Connor said no, and made a counter offer: He offered Strongbow control of Dublin, Waterford, and Wexford and nothing else. The result: stalemate.

Strongbow decided there was nothing for it but to fight. With his troops he stormed out of Dublin, and caught the Irish having a wash and brush up in the Liffey (seriously: O Connor was bathing when his enemy rode into view). The Irish were defeated, and Strongbow ruled the roost once more.

O Connor went home with his tail between his still-wet legs, and Strongbow then had to face a bigger threat: Henry II.

King Henry Comes to Ireland

When Dermot Mac Murrough had travelled to see Henry II and ask him for his help in recapturing his lands from O Connor, Henry had supported the idea (refer to Chapter 6). Clearly letting a few of his subjects, men like Strongbow, have a bit of an adventure in Ireland was fine. What Henry didn't envisage was that the men Mac Murrough recruited would get so involved in Irish affairs or politics.

Strongbow was a real thorn in Henry II's side and Ireland a real concern. Here's why:

✔ **Henry didn't like Strongbow to start with.** Here he was, swanking about in Ireland, marrying princesses and calling himself the King of Leinster.

Henry II had come to the throne in 1154. He succeeded Stephen, who had, in 1135, succeeded Henry I. The problem in that little lineage was that Stephen wasn't the direct descendant of Henry I. Henry I had wanted his daughter, Matilda, to take the throne when he died. There was a civil war to settle the succession, which Stephen won, and so he ended up on the throne. Stephen had no children, and agreed, so long as he could stay on as King till he died, that Henry I's grandson Henry (whose mother was daughter Matilda) would take over. Why I am telling you all this? It's important in the Irish context because Strongbow's father had taken the side of Stephen in the civil war. As a result Henry II wasn't Strongbow's greatest fan, and any funny business in Ireland would instantly raise suspicions.

✔ **Henry didn't trust Strongbow's allegiance.** Strongbow had a big army at his disposal, and seemed to be setting up Ireland as an alternative kingdom which might one day challenge England. Ireland could easily be used as a launching pad for a campaign aimed at toppling Henry.

✔ **This situation was the first real interaction between Ireland and the English Crown, and no one was quite sure which way the Irish kings might jump.** If Strongbow defied Henry, the Irish kings might very well back Strongbow, despite their not-so-distant acrimony; or work against both of them.

✔ **Henry, in December 1170, had the Archbishop of Canterbury murdered.** He had real problems at home as a result, and Ireland was just one more distraction he didn't need.

It was time for Henry to act. He demanded that all his subjects, including Strongbow, return immediately from Ireland or else they would lose all their lands and titles. Strongbow politely ignored him.

Henry decides to invade but doesn't

Clearly Strongbow's decision to ignore the call from Henry II to come home was a snub to his King. The fact that Dermot Mac Murrough had also died and Strongbow seemed stronger, made the situation all the more pressing.

Henry amasses his forces

Henry had a real problem: He wasn't simply going up against some local Irish annoyance, but one of his own. The reason Strongbow had been so successful in Ireland was because he had employed the latest modern military technology. If Henry wanted to beat him, he'd have to be well-organised and heavily armed.

Henry took most of 1171 to put his army together. It was so large that 400 ships were needed to move everything across the Irish Sea. He had to take with him the men he needed, all the animals, as well as enough supplies to last them. This was like packing for the biggest ever family summer holiday.

Strongbow capitulates

Strongbow, fresh from his victory over O Connor, as well as his survival of the siege of Dublin, was fully aware of Henry's plans. While it was easy to ignore a letter from the King demanding that you go home, it would have been stupid to pretend that Henry wasn't serious about invading. Strongbow capitulated.

He travelled back to England and met with Henry II in Gloucester. Rather than being mean about the whole thing and having Strongbow killed or thrown into a dark dungeon somewhere, Henry decided to listen to him. The terms they agreed were:

- Strongbow would say he was very sorry.
- Despite all the annoyance that he had caused, Strongbow swore his allegiance to Henry.
- Henry allowed Strongbow to keep Leinster as the lands he would manage on behalf of the crown.
- Strongbow was also allowed to keep the fortified towns of Dublin, Waterford, and Wexford.

Although having less power than he would have done under the deal he had struck with Mac Murrough, Strongbow had got off lightly. He hurried back to Ireland and probably breathed a huge sigh of relief.

To heck with it! Henry invades

Just as the situation with Strongbow looked to be going well, Henry received two messages. The first was from the Ostmen of Wexford who were fed up with the whole Strongbow situation, and the second from the Irish kings who were sick and tired of the way that the Normans (who were acting on behalf of the English Crown) were behaving in Ireland. Remember that the Irish had largely been running their own affairs, their way, for years. While they understood the power of the English crown, they weren't happy with all the upheavals that Strongbow caused.

Whether he liked it or not Henry had to go and sort out Ireland.

So he left the shores of home in October 1171, and landed near Waterford. His army was, by contemporary standards, huge. It comprised:

- 4,000 soldiers
- 500 knights
- 400 ships
- A selection of siege towers for attacking castles and fortifications.

This was warfare of the most modern order, and there was no one in Ireland who could hope to compete with such firepower. The Irish kings and all the Normans in Ireland, such as Strongbow, had two choices: submit or face annihilation. The Irish kings may well have been bloody-minded about invaders on their island, but they weren't stupid.

Norman or English . . . or, more to the point, when did the Norman rulers of England become English? William the Conqueror (who defeated King Harold in 1066) had been Norman. And people like Strongbow came from Norman stock, and therefore we talk about him as a Norman invader. Yet as the years went by, people like Henry started seeing themselves as English and slowly began forgetting the whole Norman part. As a result, the old Normans started emerging as definitely English. All the people that Henry brought to Ireland should be thought of as English – for that's where their loyalty lay – and no longer as Norman.

The kings submit

As Henry secured the towns of Waterford and Wexford, and moved towards Dublin the Kings began to fall in line and started to submit. It had been a largely bloodless invasion, and the sheer size of Henry's force had sent out the clear message that he was stronger and more powerful than anyone in Ireland.

The first King to submit to Henry was Donal Mac Carthy, King of Desmond. He acknowledged Henry as his boss, agreed to pay him a yearly *tribute* (he'd hand money over every year) and gave him *hostages* (a kind of deposit – if he misbehaved the hostages would be killed).

Everyone else, whether Irish or Norman, followed suit. Only two distant northern kings held out and refused to swear allegiance. Despite this refusal, this was a minor issue because the kings were in remote parts of Ulster and not in a military position to do anything to oppose Henry.

Quickly Henry had established himself in control of Ireland. He became lord of Ireland.

Henry hadn't had to lift a finger to beat the Irish into submission. When you think about the way all the different kings fought with each other for dominance before the Normans arrived (see Chapter 6), the peaceful capitulation in the face of Henry was quite something. The Irish kings realised they were dealing with someone who was not only militarily more powerful, but had connections in Europe and was closely allied with Vatican authority.

Stopping future rebellions

Before he left Ireland in April 1172, Henry was sure to put a system in place to prevent future acts of rebellion and disorder. He granted the whole of Meath to Hugh de Lacy. De Lacy was loyal to Henry, and would obviously keep Strongbow in check. De Lacy was also given the title of Chief Governor and all royal authority would flow through him. Strongbow had promised to behave and had been given enough land and power to keep him quiet. All the Irish kings had submitted, and while they were obviously not overjoyed about the whole thing, a sizeable English military presence in Ireland would keep them in order.

Doing Things the English Way

Henry had successfully completed the conquest of Ireland, but he hadn't managed to suppress it and control it. If he wanted to have Ireland under his rule, without the constant problems of rebellious kings, he needed to think about colonisation rather than occupation.

What Henry needed to do was make the Irish do things the English way. The Irish would have to accept not just the presence of Henry as their new lord, but also start conforming to English norms.

The following sections discuss the various ways that the English invaders and native Irish integrated the two cultures. In some areas, Henry's desire that English customs prevail were realised. In other areas, Irish customs and traditions won out.

The Irish Church

The Irish Church had, despite some attempts at reform (see Chapter 6), always been a bit independent in its ways and thinking. It had been loyal to Rome and the Vatican, but always liked to do things in a local way that suited Ireland.

Two Church-related issues had driven Henry II to Ireland. First of all there had been a papal licence for him to go to Ireland and reform the Church there so that it conformed to all the rules of the Vatican. Second, Henry had murdered Thomas à Beckett, the Archbishop of Canterbury (well, he hadn't done it himself, but he was blamed). Clearly the Pope didn't appreciate having his man in England attacked and murdered in Canterbury Cathedral. It also seems that part of Henry's desire to go to Ireland was to successfully implement the reforms of the Irish Church that the Pope wanted, in the hope that he'd forget the nasty business of murdering Beckett.

So, what did Henry do to reform the Church? He organised, in Cashel, County Tipperary, a church synod (a meeting of all the bishops and archbishops) in November 1171. What the synod produced was the standardisation of the Irish Church so that it was in line with practice elsewhere. This included:

- ✔ An end to abuses of the law of marriage (Irish clergy had kept getting married against the rules).
- ✔ Standard rules for the administration of the sacraments in Church and the form of the liturgy during services.
- ✔ Freedom of the Church from interference by the State, and the upholding of certain privileges for members of the clergy.

What all these very technical changes meant was that the Irish Church was now singing from the same hymn sheet as the Vatican. The synod also accepted that Henry was the lord of Ireland, and would effectively guarantee the existence of the Church, and its protection under law, in Ireland.

The proceeds of the meeting were reported on by the archdeacon of Llandaff, who told the Pope about everything that had gone on. He embellished the story so that the abuses of Church law prior to the synod looked even more dreadful than they were. As a result Henry came out of the whole thing smelling of roses. He looked like a real moderniser; the man who had brought the Irish Church kicking and screaming into the twelfth century.

The Pope was delighted and congratulated Henry for his good work in bringing the Irish back into line. The Pope also wrote to the clergy of Ireland and by proxy, the ordinary congregation, and told them they were lucky to have such a great chap as Henry in charge, and that they must remain loyal to him.

Henry had won the day. The Church had been modernised, the nasty business of murder in the Cathedral forgotten, and a religious dynamic had been brought to bear that supported Henry's rule in Ireland.

Intermarriage

The Irish had always been marrying off their daughters to attractive looking invaders who might also give them a bit of protection from their fellow kings. The specific process of the invaders from England marrying the Irish had really begun when Mac Murrough married off his daughter, Aoife, to Strongbow.

Initially this scheme had allowed the Irish to gain foreign friends. After Henry's whistle stop tour round Ireland, the marriage scheme seemed attractive to everyone. It allowed the Irish to make unions with the new English nobles, and gave the English a nice way into the Irish social scene.

Aoife, on her marriage, had become known by a new title: the Countess Eva. What this name change, and countless other acts, intended to do was to make the Irish accept the new English way of doing things. Hugh de Lacy – the King's new man in Ireland – also married an Irish woman. None other than the daughter of the old High King O Connor. These were clear political unions that tied the Irish and the new English together.

Language

The English didn't speak Irish. When English men married Irish women, their new wives learned their husband's language (French), but also stuck with their old tongue. So, despite the newcomers and their marriages, the Irish kept their own language too: invasion didn't destroy the native tongue. As a result Ireland became bi-lingual, which was great, but it also meant that some of the distinctions between the Irish and the English were unclear. Even for official court business, the participants had to use translators so that everyone understood exactly what business was being done.

Land charters

In the old days the Irish kings had ruled their lands by force. If they said they owned it and could force everyone to accept the decision, then it was theirs. This changed under Henry. Increasingly the Irish kings were no longer thought of as monarchs in their own right, but as lords of their land whose power was given to them by the English monarch. They'd have a charter to prove that the land was theirs, but in return would have to pay taxes to the Crown and provide men, when necessary, to fight in the King's army.

The middle nation

Henry had intended to Anglicise the Irish, in the same way his forefathers had brought Norman culture to England in 1066, but this strategy had two inherent problems. First off, the Irish could simply ignore the whole idea. Second, those English people who were sent over to colonise Ireland would have to remain true to the idea of the English monarchy and not start acting like the Irish themselves. A third problem exacerbated the challenges: England and royal authority was a boat ride away. Communications between England and Ireland were slow, and royal authority wasn't always easy to enforce.

Clearly when anyone moves to a new country they are going to be affected by what is going on around them. The English that Henry left behind him to run Ireland were no different. When they intermarried and had more dealings with the Irish leaders, they accepted, and sometimes adapted, Irish ways of doing things.

Also, the English were a minority population. All around them were the Irish who, for all their oaths of allegiance to Henry, kept on living as they always had. The Irish were still concerned with old struggles and control of their own land (whether those in control were called kings or knights and no matter where the authority came from).

As the English in Ireland adopted Irish ways, they steadily became more distant from their old home. They even started referring to themselves as the *middle nation*: effectively loyal to England, but thinking of themselves as Irish.

King John Takes Over

Henry faced the same problem that all fathers face – when can you trust your son to do something properly? This was a pressing issue for Henry, as the heir to the throne has to take on responsibility sooner or later.

For Henry's son and eventual heir, John, such responsibility came sooner rather than later. At the grand old age of ten, his father granted him the lordship of Ireland. For a country that had so recently been taken over by England – if that wasn't shock enough – they were now effectively ruled over by a schoolboy.

After years of training, young Prince John was finally ready to be dispatched to Ireland and, at the age of 18, in 1185, John went to Ireland for the first time.

Party time! Teen idol John in Dublin

Now, we've all read the celebrity life-style magazines, and we're only too well aware what young princes get up to: usually no good! For young John it was little different. He spent his time in Ireland with his mates, and was there for eight months.

The idea was that John's visit would herald in a new period of centralised English rule in Ireland, and that all the Irish leaders would come and pay homage and submit to him. In the event, John and his mates treated the whole thing like a teenage holiday and behaved appallingly. They were out of control, had a good time, and all the Irish refused to even visit him, let alone submit.

Despite the merrymaking, John's visit wasn't a complete waste. He didn't actually get out of Dublin and do anything himself, but he did set up a series of speculative grants, and thus extended the feudal area (*feudalism* was a system whereby land was granted in the name of the English Crown, and the owners ruled over it in the name of England). These speculative grants worked like this. John would give you a few hundred acres. You'd say thanks, that's great. John would tell you that the land, while yours, was actually occupied by a load of Irish people who thought the land was theirs. You could have it if you managed to throw them off the land. That was the speculative bit: could you throw them off?

King John takes on a changing Ireland

When John did come to the throne in 1199 in his own right he took control of an Ireland that was changing rapidly. The question was whether or not he had grown up enough to run the country properly and gain people's respect.

That Ireland had changed since the first Normans had arrived was unquestionable. The Church in Ireland was obeying the rules that were laid down by the Vatican and was becoming less of an identifiably Irish Church. With the work of Henry, and the additional numbers of English lords based in Ireland, the country was slowly conforming to an English way of life in respect of land ownership, law and order, and inheritance. Yet large swathes of the country were still under the control of the Irish, and they happily chose to ignore the rules for living as they were laid down by the English. The issue for King John and his successors was whether or not they could genuinely control the whole of Ireland, or merely those areas where the loyal English lived in greatest numbers. What was becoming clear, in a period of rapid change and external influences, was that the likelihood of another Irish High King emerging had been reduced to nil.

Lands of peace vs. lands of war

The real problem for King John was that Ireland had effectively become two separate places. They were referred to as:

- ✔ *Terra pacis* **or lands of peace.** These were where the English were in control, and were working in tandem with the Irish. In these areas the rule of law was respected, and all the necessary tributes and taxes were paid to the Crown. This was loyal Ireland.

- ✔ *Terra guerre* **or lands of war.** The *terra guerre* were effectively the border lands of English rule and the areas beyond. These were areas where the process of English colonisation of Ireland had stalled, and the Irish still controlled their own affairs.

For King John the difficulty was that the lands still controlled by the Irish always threatened those that were controlled by the Crown.

So how did King John try and control Ireland and ensure that the process of colonisation went smoothly?

- ✔ He had Dublin Castle built as the fortified home of English rule in Ireland.

- ✔ John developed a basic system of local government in Ireland that held everyone accountable and which was enforced by law. This system included the centralised collection of monies from Ireland thus bolstering the King's purse.

- ✔ A man was put in charge of Ireland on behalf of John. The justiciar would have all the authority of the King behind him and was his eyes and ears in Ireland (as well as his fist and his boot).

- ✔ Through the justiciar, the King regularly consulted local leaders and power brokers. Eventually such consultations evolved into Ireland's first parliament.

All John's reforms sound very impressive, as did the idea of centralised rule. However, all of this depended on everyone behaving themselves. Too many English people saw Ireland as a place where they could increase their wealth and free themselves from the tight confines of the royal court. Pursuing this path would lead to conflict. In 1209 two of King John's men in Ireland sought better deals by threatening rebellion and forming alliances with both the native Irish and the French. John returned to Ireland in 1210 and they were soon put in their place. Ireland would always be a place of potential rebellion. No matter what controls the Kings of England put in place, the country always seemed to be disloyal.

In a way John's new ways of ruling Ireland did just about enough. During the remainder of his rule there was no great sign of disquiet in Ireland, and for his immediate successors the same was true.

There were problems though:

- ✔ The process of the English becoming steadily more Irish continued. Increasingly they were referred to as the Anglo-Normans as their loyalties and customs were unclear.

- ✔ The Irish outside the colonised area became increasingly difficult. In 1258, Brian O Neill, King of Tyrone, even had the audacity to declare himself High King (he was killed in battle and his head displayed in Dublin as a reminder about the dangers of disloyalty).

✔ Arguments and battles between the English settlers and the Irish were not uncommon. These were often encouraged by opposing English lords in the hope that they would benefit financially from the chaos.

✔ In Ireland in the late thirteenth century there was an upsurge in crime that made the country, at times, an unstable and unsafe place to be.

Edward 1 and the First Irish Parliament

King John passed away in 1216, and was followed by Henry III (1216–72) and then Edward I (1272–1307). It was under Edward that the first Irish parliament was brought together in 1297 in Dublin.

The idea of bringing everyone together and talking about how a country should be run, and what rights everyone had, first emerged during the reign of King John. He had been forced to sign the Magna Carta, which was a basic rule book as to what everyone's role was in society. Effectively it introduced a basic written system of law that was to regulate the powers of the Irish kings and the new settlers from England. The principles had slowly filtered over the Irish Sea, and all the powerful people in Ireland came together. The parliament did some interesting things, including:

✔ **It placed the burden of sorting out the unruly Irish onto the local English community in Ireland.** The last thing that Edward wanted to do was to end up staying in Ireland for a long time. He didn't have the money or the resources to keep Ireland in order. What he wanted was for the settlers to defend themselves, and in doing so bring some kind of peace and stability to Ireland.

✔ **It passed laws against those settlers who had adopted Irish habits and customs.** There was a fear that these settlers had become so indistinguishable that they might be killed on sight because they would be mistaken as aggressive and dangerous Irish warriors. The Irish dressed differently from the English, wearing furs and cloaks, while the English preferred tailored clothes. Many settlers had adapted the Irish form of dress and were thus indistinguishable from the locals. The laws against the 'degenerate' settlers were supposed to pull these people back from their new Irish identity, and encourage them to regain their Englishness.

✔ **The parliament insisted that English common law be properly applied in Ireland.** All too often punishments were handed down locally without reference to the common law. This meant, in the eyes of London, that the Irish often went unpunished (or at least not punished harshly enough).

The Parliament of 1297 is important as it was the first such gathering, and a genuine attempt to make the English ways of doing things applicable to Ireland. Sadly, people in England didn't appreciate how difficult life was in Ireland for the settlers. They were surrounded by the hostile Irish and cut off from home.

While the Parliament put rules in place to stop the assimilation of the settlers and to encourage an English way of life, the reality was more complex. The English way of life couldn't be imposed on Ireland, and it would remain a place apart.

Part III

The Invading English Kings: The Fourteenth and Fifteenth Centuries

The 5th Wave   By Rich Tennant

14th Century Hospitality Committee

"Remember, whatever you do, don't tip the vats of boiling oil. We need to fry plenty of fish and chips to welcome our English guests."

In this part . . .

The history of Ireland is dominated by its relationship with Britain. In the fourteenth and fifteenth centuries the English kings kept getting frustrated with the Irish. The Irish were unruly, kept challenging the authority of the Crown, and just weren't behaving. To make matters worse they often rebelled. The Crown tried to control Ireland through the force of law and by using the military, but this wasn't always successful.

The English royal family wasn't exactly stable either. There was constant court intrigue, and eventually the question of succession broke out into what became the War of the Roses. People in Ireland were forced to take sides, and this set a trend for the future. Problems in England were often played out in Ireland, and the Irish too often got caught in the middle or simply backed the wrong horse.

Chapter 8

The Scottish-Irish Rebellion and Its Aftermath

*I*f Ireland caused lots of problems for the English, then Scotland was just as bad. Lots of men coming down from the Highlands, running round in kilts and looking for an Englishman to attack . . . well that's what Mel Gibson made it look like in *Braveheart*. Obviously it's far more complex than Mel made it appear in the film.

Right about now you may be wondering 'Why all this info about Scotland in a book of Irish history?' Well, the histories of the two nations got knotted up together occasionally. Which isn't surprising really when you consider how geographically close they are and how they shared the same historic animosity towards England. The Irish kings had been having a hard time under English rule (see Chapter 7) and looked to the Scottish to come and work with them against the English. They did, in the form of Edward the Bruce, and his more famous brother Robert (known for looking at spider's webs all day long).

In this chapter, you'll see how the possibilities of a combined Celtic uprising against England failed, and how the English, who were a bit miffed by the whole rebellion process, made Ireland pay through a series of laws, called the Statutes of Kilkenny.

The Scottish Rebellion

By the close of the thirteenth century the Irish were all a bit fed up with things. They hadn't had a really powerful and commonly agreed High King since the Normans had arrived, and they were finding the presence of the English in Ireland a bit bothersome. One of the leading Irish lords, Donal O Neill (who was King of Ulster, and died in 1325), decided he'd like to see the Irish get together, and actually try and take back control of Ireland. He knew they couldn't do it by themselves, and he looked around for a suitable ally.

The chiefs invite Robert the Bruce

In the early decades of the fourteenth century there was one King in Scotland and another in England. Robert I of Scotland (Robert the Bruce) didn't much care for Edward II of England, and they constantly squabbled.

The Irish saw in this long running Scottish and English row an opportunity. They were ruled over by Edward II in his capacity as Lord of Ireland, and wanted to see him gone. If they could form an alliance with the Scots, then there was a chance that they might be able to defeat the English.

The Scots had been busy bashing away at the English for years. What's known as the first War of Independence was fought between Scotland and England from 1296 until 1328. It featured some great Scottish leaders such as William Wallace (the character Mel Gibson played in *Braveheart*) and Robert the Bruce, who managed to invade northern England in 1328 and embarrass the English crown. The Scots would eventually be beaten, and the crowns of Scotland and England became united in 1603.

The Irish lords, led by Donal O'Neill, agreed that they should approach Robert of Scotland and see if he was interested in such an anti-English union. Robert loved the idea. He thought that if Ireland could become independent by expelling the English it would not only provide Scotland with an inspirational model of what might be but also give Scotland an ally.

Robert believed that Scotland and Ireland could produce a 'grand Gaelic alliance against England'.

Scotland and Ireland had a lot in common. Not only had they both resisted English rule, but they shared similar languages drawn from their ancient Gaelic ancestors and many aspects of culture. Also, their traditional systems of law, monarchy, and inheritance had much in common. The power of the English crown and, in Ireland, the presence of the settler population, were opposed by the Scots and the Irish. For the settlers, the prospect of such a grand Gaelic alliance was horrible because they'd be seen as the enemy and wouldn't be safe.

In 1315, Robert accepted the idea that had been put to him by the Irish lords, and signed up for a campaign against the English that would be fought in Ireland. As a measure of his serious intent, he sent his brother, Edward, to Ireland to do the job.

Defeating the English: Edward the Bruce

Edward the Bruce arrived in Ireland on 25 May 1315. He brought with him a large army, numbering into the thousands (it's said to have been as many as 6,000), and landed in Ulster. His army was made up of battle-hardened Scottish soldiers who were well used to fighting the English.

The Irish, who had invited Edward into Ireland in the first place, were encouraged by his arrival. They believed that the rebellion plan had substance, and rallied to the cause. All the major families across Ireland sent men and arms to fight alongside Edward.

The combined armies of Scotland and Ireland were hugely successful. They attacked English settlers in eastern Ulster, laid siege to and attacked the towns of Ardee and Dundalk in County Louth (and burnt them to the ground), and defeated the English army that was sent to fight them.

It was all going swimmingly, and the Irish were so pleased by the progress of Edward and his army that they crowned him King of Ireland at Dundalk in May 1316.

Despite the good news on the battle front, Ireland, still a largely underdeveloped country during this period, faced a looming problem. Playing politics and trying to get the Scottish to help free Ireland was all very well and good, but when it came to having thousands of troops in the country, mouths needed feeding. And that was the problem. As Edward's army and his Irish counterparts marched through Ireland, they had to gather supplies as they went along. That, in a nutshell, was the dilemma. The size of Edward's army, and the lack of thought that had gone into supplying them, caused real problems in Ireland.

While small towns could be raided or crops stolen to feed the army, what was plundered often didn't amount to very much, and certainly wouldn't feed a large army. Also, if you have to steal food from one mouth to feed another, what happens to the people you stole from? How, in other words were the Irish who had their food and crops stolen supposed to survive?

With lots of mouths to feed, Edward's army caused problems, but the whole situation was made far worse by a general famine. Bad weather in 1315 affected the sowing of crops, which was followed the next summer by a near total crop failure. It was an awful situation, and the presence of a large and hungry army in Ireland did nothing to help matters.

Joining the fun: Robert the Bruce arrives

Despite the success that Edward had won in Ireland, his brother, Robert the Bruce, felt that the whole war against the English would go a lot quicker if he joined in. In the winter of 1316, Robert the Bruce arrived in Ireland with a large army designed to help Edward in his campaign. Before his arrival, he wrote to the Irish explaining the point behind his campaign. The Irish leaders, he said, were fighting against the English 'so that with God's will our nation may be able to recover her ancient liberty'. And, things looked good – on paper at least. In addition to stamping his authority on Edward's campaign in Ireland, Robert's arrival brought a large, and fresh, force with him, a force that could help with the campaign in Ireland. With the size of the combined Scottish force behind them, the Irish, if they stayed united, had a real chance of a total victory over the English.

Unfortunately, events conspired against them:

- ✔ **The famine was rapidly developing and getting worse** (see the section 'Defeating the English: Edward the Bruce' for details). Edward's troops were already practically starving, and Robert's troops just added to the number of mouths that needed feeding and assisted the spread of disease that often accompanies famine. In 1317 the famine was so bad in Ireland that the fighting ground to a halt. Edward and Robert couldn't feed their men, the Irish couldn't feed themselves, and the English were in an equally perilous situation.

- ✔ **The Irish weren't united.** Petty squabbles had broken out between different Irish factions, and many of them had started acting alone. They were trying to seize land locally, rather than concentrating on the rebellion in its entirety.

With their forces struggling and the famine killing people off in the thousands, the Scots battled on. In 1317 they got as far as Dublin, but were eventually repelled by the citizens, who supported the crown, and who torched their own suburbs rather than submit. The Scottish army left Dublin and marched south, attacking Limerick. They hoped that the O Briens would come together and fight with them against the English forces in the area. But the Irish didn't get it together, and the starving Scots forces had no choice but to retreat.

Gotta go: Robert returns to Scotland

A year later Edward was on his own again. Robert had tired of the campaign in Ireland, and matters needed attending to in Scotland. There was still a chance that the rebellion could get somewhere if the Irish worked closely with their Scottish counterparts. But with the effects of the famine still being felt, it was going to be an uphill struggle.

Famine

A devastating famine, estimated to have killed many millions of people, hit Europe between 1315 and 1317.

In the absence of modern records it's difficult to say how many people were affected by the famine. Historians estimate that somewhere between 10 and 25 per cent of the Irish population succumbed. Disease was rampant and, as well as the basic starvation, many others would have died from pneumonia, bronchitis, and tuberculosis. The famine lingered for a number of years, and the effects were so devastating that stories of drawn-out deaths, cannibalism, and rampant crime (especially theft of crops, food, and animals) were common.

For all Robert the Bruce's pleas for an uprising in the name of a glorious Gaelic alliance between Scotland and Ireland, he was really only interested in number one. His aim for the Scottish incursion into Ireland seems to have been to destabilise the English position by opening another front in the Scottish and English war. While it would have been great if he could have taken Ireland, it seems that Robert was really driven by a desire to further unsettle the English.

The defeat of the rebels

The last stand of Edward the Bruce took place at Faughart, near Dundalk. The leader of the English army, John de Bermingham, had marched north to confront Edward. The battle was a bloody affair, and by the end of it Edward lay dead, and the Scottish army was finally defeated.

The ending of the Scottish rebellion was a major victory for the English. Although it would take years for them to finally suppress the Irish completely (if they ever did manage to do it), the rebellion led by Edward would be the last attempt to unite Ireland under a single King until the sixteenth century (see Chapter 12).

With the Scottish threat seen off, the English could sit back briefly and enjoy a sense of victory. They also had to be aware that Ireland was a mess, and that it had suffered terrible devastation from the combined effects of the rebellion and the accompanying famine.

Squashing the Irish: Edward III

While the arrival of the Normans, and then the full force of the English crown soon after, had changed Ireland forever (see Chapter 5), the country had never been fully taken over and suppressed. One reason why the Bruces had initially been so successful was because the Irish were very independent minded, didn't owe much of an allegiance to England and hadn't really adapted to English laws. So as much as the English might have wanted to control the Irish – squash them if you like – after their treasonous relationship with the Scottish invaders, it was not going to be an easy task.

Even after the Scottish rebellion had been put down, several problems remained for England:

✔ It simply didn't have the power to rule over the whole of Ireland. English rule was confidently asserted on the east coast, and around Dublin, but the rest of the country was pretty much separate.

✔ There were three different populations in Ireland:

- The native Irish who still worked within their own legal system and had their own customs.

- The Anglo-Irish who, although having originally come from England, had adopted Irish ways and saw themselves as lying somewhere between loyalty to the crown and adherence to the old Irish system.

- The English, or those who had arrived most recently and saw it as their role to occupy the country and defend the rights of the crown in Ireland.

✔ Because of the lack of conquest, and the complexities of the three populations, English common law (the bedrock of royal authority) had never been fully applied to Ireland.

As a result of all this confusion in Ireland, real power lay with the heads of the great families (the old Irish kings and chieftains). They accepted (grudgingly) that the King of England was in charge of them, and they owed him their allegiance. But in practice, they were the ones who ruled over the various regions and localities in Ireland – as their families had always done – and the English could not effectively challenge that authority without a major military intervention.

A sign of the acceptance of this situation came in successive Irish parliaments in the late thirteenth and early fourteenth centuries. The King accepted that the Irish and Anglo-Irish ruled their areas and, so long as they accepted that he had overriding authority, they were free to run their own affairs, collect taxes, and keep everything and everyone in order.

The lack of royal authority in Ireland meant that powerful men could make their own way. The absence of a central authority with teeth meant that Irish and Anglo-Irish both looked to enlarge their landholdings, and were creating ever more powerful local dynasties for themselves. These local power bases made Ireland unstable as people fought for control and challenged the authority of the crown in Ireland.

By 1330 there was a new King of England: Edward III. He was concerned about the way that people had been behaving in Ireland. One man caught his eye. Roger Mortimer had been using royal authority to gain more and more land and power in Ireland, and the King didn't like that. He had him arrested and executed. It was time to stamp his own authority on Ireland.

Edward's reforms

Edward was a man who wanted to ensure a quiet life for himself. He had Scotland as his pressing concern (they were still revolting in the glens), and didn't want Ireland distracting him. He was on the throne for half a century (1327–77) so had lots of time to influence life in Ireland. As a result of his need to keep some kind of order in Ireland, Edward tried to introduce a whole series of innovations to Ireland to try to keep a hold of the situation:

- ✔ He sent out a new justiciar (the King's agent in Ireland – think of him as an enforcer) called Anthony Lucy.
- ✔ He had Lucy attack some of the big Irish families, and even had some Anglo-Irish leaders executed for good measure.
- ✔ Archers were sent from Wales as part of a new force to control the Irish (watch those arrows fly).
- ✔ Edward insisted that only English people be allowed to hold the main jobs in Ireland, which sent a clear message that he didn't trust the Irish or Anglo-Irish.
- ✔ He closely examined all grants of lands and titles in Ireland and only gave them to those people who had shown themselves to be loyal.

It was the last of these steps that caused some real problems. Sir John Morris was appointed Justiciar in 1341. What he did was to take back all the lands and privileges that Edward III (and his father before him) had ever granted in Ireland. He also reclaimed all the debts that had been cancelled over the years, and demanded that the Anglo-Irish pay up. It was a radical step aimed at bringing some level of administrative order to Ireland.

Anglo-Irish response: Give us a break!

The response in Ireland was, in the short term at least, a peaceful one. They were perplexed by Edward's recent reforms and in 1341 came together in the Irish parliament (held this time in Kilkenny) to discuss matters.

During this meeting, the most important Anglo-Irish leaders in the country gathered. The prime movers behind the parliament were the Earls of Desmond and Kildare. (Apparently the King's ministers were so worried about the anger they might face from the Irish, that they refused to attend the parliament.) The participants stressed that they were loyal to the Crown. But, they said, they objected to the incompetence of the Ministers who were sent by the King to run Ireland. These men, they argued, simply didn't understand Ireland.

The parliament allowed the Anglo-Irish to vocalise their dislike and distrust of the English who they believed threatened local stability (the relationship between the Irish and the Anglo-Irish) because of the way they behaved. As demonstrated at the parliament, there was a clear division between the Anglo-Irish (who were loyal to the crown and a part of Ireland) and the English (who, although operating on behalf of the crown, alienated everyone in Ireland through their actions).

One of the Anglo-Irish, a man called Arnold Power, tried to explain what was happening in Ireland. He said that once the country had been the land of saints and scholars, but since the English were constantly arriving and interfering, the Irish were now made to feel that the were all heretics and savages. Basically, the Anglo-Irish resented being told that they weren't the equals of the men that arrived from England and feeling that they were somehow second class citizens.

The strength of feeling that came from the parliament in Kilkenny was so strong that Edward relented in his reforms and granted the requests of the Anglo-Irish. But the problems were far from over.

On-going problems in Ireland

In 1360 a great council of the Anglo-Irish came together to discuss the situation in Ireland. The country was a mess. The problems of how the English tried to run Ireland (or the bits they controlled) hadn't gone away. The borderlands between the Anglo-Irish and Irish areas were constant sources of friction, and the Irish themselves were in a near constant state of internal warfare or rebellion. The country was still suffering from the after effects of the Scottish invasion and the famine that had happened at the same time.

So what were the big problems afflicting Ireland?

- The Irish were attacking the Anglo-Irish and taking lands from them.
- The size of the army in Ireland wasn't big enough to protect the areas under control of the crown.

✔ People were leaving the border areas between the Irish and the Anglo-Irish and seeking safety in the towns. This left the borderlands even more prone to attack.

✔ Lands were being left depopulated and villages deserted. This just made the defensive areas even weaker.

✔ Because of the poor state of Ireland many people were choosing to emigrate to England rather than try and make a go of things in Ireland.

✔ A plague struck that was terrible in itself, but made all the other factors much worse.

The council sent a message to Edward warning him that unless something was done to remedy the whole situation, Ireland faced being lost. The King had to take decisive action if he wanted to retain control of Ireland.

Between 1349 and 1450 it's estimated that the population of Europe fell between 60 and 75 per cent, and that rural areas suffered the most. Exact figures for Ireland aren't really known, but if Europe is used as a guide, we can see how awful the loss of life must have been in Ireland. Given that the Anglo-Irish and the English were numerically the smallest groups in Ireland, the effect on them would have been devastating. They were struggling anyway, but with that kind of loss of population, their situation became even more precarious. No wonder they wrote to the King in such strong terms in 1360 – they literally were fighting for their very survival. If the English crown didn't come to their rescue, they faced being overrun by the Irish and Ireland could, as they predicted, be lost.

Plague!

The plague was a European-wide phenomenon. More commonly known as the Black Death, it killed millions across Europe, and was accompanied by famine in many areas.

The plague arrived in Ireland in the summer of 1348 in the eastern ports, and spread rapidly across the country. It was so bad that one friar in Kilkenny believed that everyone on earth would die. He himself did die of plague, but left behind a parchment recording what had happened 'if perchance any of the race of Adam may be able to escape this pestilence'.

The plague was terrible, and it came back to haunt Ireland and Europe in many forms over the years. The stories that are associated with the period are horrific, and clearly people did some terrible things just to stay alive. It wasn't just the risk of disease that was the problem — many people also struggled to feed themselves. It was recorded that the hunger got so bad that people started feeding off the corpses of dead criminals that had been hanged in the streets. It all sounds far-fetched and very gruesome, but as food costs rocketed during this period, the story might well have a grain of truth.

Sending his son to the rescue

Upon receiving the message from the Anglo-Irish council, Edward II acted quickly. In 1361 he sent his main men to help rescue Ireland. The man was Lionel, the Earl of Ulster (who was also his second son, and had been given the Ulster title in 1355). This was an important choice – the King wasn't simply sending some lackey to do his work, but his own son. This meant that Lionel arrived with a huge amount of authority and a lot of power invested in him.

Lionel had a lot of power – he also had 200 cavalry and 700 mounted archers at his disposal. By contemporary standards that was a sizeable and modern army, and was the biggest force to visit Ireland since 1210.

The plan was for England to heavily subsidise Lionel's mission, so that Ireland could get back on its feet and so that Lionel could recover any lands that had been lost to the Irish. Lionel was also charged with ensuring that the areas under the control of the crown were stable and well-protected. The ultimate aim was to make Ireland stable enough that the lands and estates would start making money for the royal coffers.

It was a great idea, and clearly had some success. Edward really hoped that it would all go so swimmingly that Ireland would become a nice peaceful place, and that he'd be able to start turning a profit on his investment of time and money.

Edward was particularly motivated to resolve the Irish issue. He was getting more and more involved in a long running struggle with France which he knew would lead, at some point, to a major war. He didn't need Ireland to be troublesome while he was off bashing the French. Also, major wars had a nasty habit of getting expensive. He needed to get a steady stream of income so that he could buy lots of nice weapons and support his army and he hoped that Ireland would be useful in contributing to the cause.

While Lionel was in Ireland things did go well. He called a parliament together in 1366, which began a process of transforming culture in Ireland so that it became, in theory, more English (go to the next section 'The Statutes of Kilkenny' for details on how that played out). But in 1366 he was also recalled to England because Dad wanted to marry him off. That was all well and good for Lionel, but the army went back with him. As soon as the English went home, the situation in Ireland worsened, and everything looked like it would simply slip back to being a mess again.

Lionel was eventually replaced three years later by William of Windsor. He was okay at his job but needed money to fund his mission. The parliament in England was getting all tetchy about funding the campaign in Ireland. William decided that he'd make the Anglo-Irish pay for his work instead but they hated the idea, and had him called back to England to find the money there.

Ireland needed securing, but the Anglo-Irish weren't in the position to pay for it – the bills would have to be met in England if the crown was serious about securing Ireland.

Edward III's involvement in Ireland was a costly affair. It is reckoned that between 1361 and 1376 the English spent some £91,000 (a huge amount by today's standards) on keeping the army in Ireland. Of that money, £71,000 came directly from the taxpayers of England. Considering that many people in England saw Ireland as an annoying burden, the expenditure of such a large amount of money was objected to. To put the spending into context one has to realise that the total income of Ireland at the time, in terms of taxes paid to Dublin, was only £2,000 per year. Staying in Ireland was a huge drain on English resources.

The Statues of Kilkenny

Clearly the English crown wanted Ireland to be a nice quiet place where everyone abided by the rules, was loyal to the King and, most importantly, behaved themselves. The English didn't want the population of Ireland to be constantly causing problems, rebelling and making a nuisance of themselves.

The Irish had different goals. They wanted to be left in peace to run their own affairs. They wanted to have control of their own lands, keep their own customs and traditions, and settle all their arguments the old way (either through battle, or by using the Irish system of law). And they had no great problem with the English King claiming to be the Lord of Ireland, so long as he didn't go sticking his nose in every five minutes.

Stuck in the middle between these two sides were the Anglo-Irish, a confused group of people in many ways. Although definitely loyal to England, they had been in Ireland long enough to know that it was a complex country to live in. They were the ones, after all, who had potentially violent Irish chieftains as neighbours, always wanting their land and their cattle. And because the Anglo-Irish often didn't have the military might to protect themselves, they had to make deals to placate the Irish, efforts that often involved friendly gestures such as of marriage, meeting the Irish halfway, and working within the Irish systems of law and tradition. As a result, they moved away from control by the crown and became part of Irish power structures. They began

- ✔ Speaking Irish.
- ✔ Dressing like the Irish.
- ✔ Wearing moustaches and beards.
- ✔ Riding their horses without saddles.

> ✔ Marrying Irish people.
>
> ✔ Employing Irish musicians and story tellers.
>
> ✔ Living according to Irish customs, and following Irish religious practices.
>
> ✔ Settling land disputes and other arguments according to Irish brehon law, rather than English common law.

While none of this sounds that serious, it all seemed completely alien to the English. The Anglo-Irish were supposed to be loyal people, who recognised the authority of the crown, yet here they were going around speaking Irish and being largely indistinguishable from the Irish themselves. It had to stop. If it didn't, then it wouldn't be long before the Anglo-Irish became completely Irish, and then the whole conquest of the country would be in real trouble.

So Lionel called together a parliament in Kilkenny, which met in 1367. The result produced a whole slab of legislation aimed at making Ireland an English-style country. Called the Statutes of Kilkenny, the legislation is some of the most far-reaching and restrictive ever forced on Ireland.

Outlawing Irish customs

The Statutes of Kilkenny were mainly aimed at the Anglo-Irish, but covered all aspects of society. The main problem, in the eyes of the crown, was that generations of English settlers in Ireland had become more Irish than the Irish themselves. They had gone native. While this situation continued, and the loyalties of the settlers remained unclear, the crown couldn't trust them. The Statutes of Kilkenny aimed to bring them back into line and make them identifiably English again.

Edward's son Lionel was the main author of the Statutes of Kilkenny. He had large landholdings of his own in Ulster, Connacht, and Munster, and so had a vested interest in making Ireland a stable and loyal country.

What specifically the Statutes were trying to do was to stop the Anglo-Irish from taking on Irish habits. So the statutes forbade the Anglo-Irish from:

> ✔ Speaking Irish.
>
> ✔ Dressing like the Irish.
>
> ✔ Riding like the Irish – they would have to use saddles in the future.
>
> ✔ Marrying anyone who was Irish.
>
> ✔ Using the Irish form of their name – it had to be an English one.

✔ Having Irish poets or musicians in their houses.

✔ Selling or giving the Irish any weapons or horses – that would be treason.

✔ Playing any Irish games, such as hurling, or taking part in Irish customs.

✔ Settling disputes using Irish brehon law – it had to be the English common law in the future.

Obviously this was the fourteenth century, and the rules weren't laid out in a nice straightforward list. They were set out as a long list of different statutes that covered each point individually. The statutes were quite clear in their rejection of the Irish ways, and enforced the English traditions in the strongest terms. For example, on marriage, the statute read, 'it is ordained and established that no alliance by marriage, gossipred, fostering of children, concubinage or by amour, nor in any other manner, be henceforth made between the English and Irish of one part, or of the other part'. Very flowery language, but the message was simple: Any marriages to the Irish, or children that came from alliances with the Irish, would have no legal status.

The Statutes of Kilkenny gave the Anglo-Irish a clearly defined template and set of rules by which they had to live. The Statutes aimed at completely killing off the process of Irish and Anglo-Irish interaction that had threatened the power of the English crown in Ireland. The question was whether such a large swathe of rules, that demanded that people instantly change the way in which they lived their life, could actually have any effect?

Defining the Irish

Clearly the main aim of the Statutes was to bring the Anglo-Irish community into line, and ensure their allegiance to England. Within the Statutes however, there was a mass of detail that would change the relationship that existed between the crown and the Irish, and which would potentially transform the localised relationships that existed between the Anglo-Irish and their Irish neighbours.

Effectively, the Statutes were making the Irish second-class citizens, whose job was to do what they were told, and not to interrupt the smooth running of daily life and crown authority.

The Statutes dealt with the Irish by:

✔ Making clear that there were two types of Irish: the Irish at peace and the Irish enemies. The Irish at peace would accept the Statutes and be bound by their rules. The Irish enemies would clearly ignore the Statutes and carry on behaving in an alien, Irish fashion.

✔ Seeing *all* the Irish as potential enemies (the reason for the Statutes that halted the selling of weapons to them) and spies (the reason for the Statute banning the employment of Irish poets or musicians in Anglo-Irish houses).

✔ Denying them their own cultural traditions and threatening them with loss of land and rights if they disobeyed: If the Irish ignored the Statutes as they applied to them (and intermarried, for example), they would lose their land and rights.

The impact of the Statutes

The Statutes of Kilkenny were potentially as tough on the Irish as they were on the Anglo-Irish. They demanded loyalty to the crown and the English way of doing things. For those Irish people who lived in English-controlled lands, the Statutes demanded total cultural loyalty, and those Irish who bordered the English had to keep their noses clean and not encroach on the areas that weren't theirs.

The penalties for anyone disobeying the Statutes of Kilkenny were severe, whether Irish or Anglo-Irish. For anyone breaking the rules, the penalties ranged from fines, a spell in prison, the loss of lands and privileges to, in the worst cases, execution.

The Statutes were introduced in the fourteenth century, which was a messy period in history. The Irish suffered, like everyone else in Europe, from famine and plague, and the English were involved in wars elsewhere (see the earlier sections in this chapter). The Statutes were clearly an attempt to bring about order in Ireland, and create, culturally at least, a clear sense of loyalty to England. But given the chaos of the fourteenth century, and the lack of a clear political and military strategy for Ireland, the Statutes were largely unenforceable.

Despite the huge expenditure that Edward sanctioned in Ireland, his aim of bringing the country to some kind of order failed. Ireland was a drain on the English purse, and despite the huge English army in the country, the country was probably in a worse state than when he had inherited it. When Edward died in 1377, the job of enforcing the Statues of Kilkenny and bringing some order and stability to Ireland fell to Edward's successor, Richard II. You can read about him in Chapter 9.

No more hurling

Hurling is one of the great games of Ireland, and is organised these days by the Gaelic Athletic Association (see Chapter 20). The game is said to be over 2,000 years old. It was certainly popular by the fourteenth century, and was a game played by both the Irish and the Anglo-Irish. The Statutes of Kilkenny banned the game. The Statutes stated that no one, 'henceforth, use the plays which men call horlings, with great sticks and a ball upon the ground, from which great evils and maims have arisen, to the weakening, of the defence of the said land'. The claim was that everyone was having such a great time playing hurling that they were neglecting proper defensive skills such as archery and sword fighting. If Ireland had a war, what good would a group of hurlers be? The country needed, or so it was argued, skilled fighters, and so hurling was banned.

Chapter 9

From Richard II to Henry IV: More Turmoil in Ireland

. . . .

In This Chapter

▶ Outlawing the Irish

▶ The English become Irish

▶ Trying to defend Ireland

▶ Making the pale

▶ English royalty begin arguing

. . . .

The fourteenth and fifteenth centuries were a complex period in Irish history. The country was a mess because of famine and plague, English dynasties were fighting each other over who should run the country, and the perennial enemy of France was always spoiling for a fight. Establishing any sense of continuity of rule was impossible, which made it very difficult for England to manage Ireland effectively.

The Statutes of Kilkenny had been a desperate attempt to culturally make everyone English, and undo a few centuries of social mixing and intermarriage (they stand out as one of the most famous exercises in the suppression of native Irish culture), but they failed. The Irish just carried on as they were. There were occasional rebellions locally – land and its ownership was always a big issue – and any form of stability was usually due to local agreements made between the Irish and the Anglo-Irish.

It was left to Edward's successor, Richard II, to try to impose English order on the wild Irish, bring the uncooperative Anglo-Irish back into line, and bolster support for the English settlers who found themselves in a foreign land among alien people.

This chapter examines Richard's efforts to save Ireland for the English and shows how the whole idea back-fired, leaving the English with less of Ireland than they started with, as the areas they controlled shrank back to covering just the four counties immediately surrounding Dublin. Known as the Pale, this area became the only part of Ireland that England could rule over with any confidence for decades to come. It also explains how the English Crown got locked into all kinds of silly arguments over who should sit on the throne, and why this had a dramatic impact on Ireland.

Richard II Arrives

With the death of Edward in 1377, Richard II took the throne. He was not however in the position to do much about Ireland: when he succeeded Edward he was only ten years old.

By 1385, with the situation in Ireland little improved from the time of Edward, the Irish parliament wrote to their monarch. In the same way that they had asked for help in 1360 (see Chapter 8), the Irish parliament again warned their King that without some kind of intervention, Ireland might be lost. Sadly for the Irish, Richard was fighting a war against the French at the time, and he wasn't able to turn his attention to Ireland until 1394.

When he finally did arrive, it wasn't all street parties, bunting, and red carpets. Richard came with a big army and wanted to play hardball.

34,000 armed tourists in Ireland

Richard was the first King to actually come to Ireland since King John had been there in 1210. For the first time in 184 years, the Irish were going to get to see what an English King looked like close up.

Richard wanted to restore the power of his lordship over the whole of Ireland. He also wanted to get all the different parts of Irish life – the Irish, Anglo-Irish and English – all working together under a unity that was loyal to the Crown. He was sick of all the infighting in Ireland. To accomplish his aims would take a big army and take some serious planning.

When he landed at Waterford, Richard had some 34,000 men under his command. Clearly this huge army hadn't come for a bit of sightseeing and to buy the odd souvenir: the Irish were suddenly confronted with a huge influx of tourists whose intentions weren't friendly.

Richard II

Interesting man Richard II. He was ten when he took over the throne from his grandfather. He married for the first time in 1382, but his wife died twelve years later. Politics impinged on his selection of a second wife, and to make peace with France, he had to take a French bride. All well and good, and duly the daughter of Charles VI was dispatched to London to marry him. But she was only seven years old! Richard's reign was hampered by the ongoing effects of famine and plague, and he even had to deal with a peasants' revolt in England in 1381. There was a struggle for the throne between Richard and Henry Bolingbroke (who would end up being Henry IV), and Richard lost out. He was deposed in 1399 and murdered in prison.

The locals don't like tourists

The reception for the incoming English tourists wasn't all good. Art Mac Murrough Kavanagh, a local Irish leader, was so incensed, that he burned down the town of New Ross in protest at the English invasion.

In the event though, despite the occasional resistance, and the dislike of the English forces, the Irish had no choice but to bow down before Richard.

Very quickly he was able to:

✔ March into Leinster, crush the leading Irish families and leaders, such as Mac Murrough, and demand their submission – all within ten days of his arrival in Leinster.

✔ Gain the submission of 75 Irish chiefs at meetings in Carlow and Drogheda in 1395.

✔ Get the majority of Irish leaders across the country to accept the authority of the Crown.

In February 1395 Richard accepted that many of the problems in Ireland had been caused by the mismanagement of the country over the years, and that some of the grievances of the Irish were justified. He made a distinction between different groups of the Irish. These were:

✔ **The wild Irish:** those Irish who refused to accept the authority of the Crown and would not submit.

✔ **The Irish rebels:** Irish and Anglo-Irish families who had largely tried to work within the law (and had eventually submitted), but who, he recognised, had justifiable grievances.

> ✔ **The obedient English:** those people who caused him no problems as they were carrying on the work of the Crown in Ireland and were completely loyal to England.

He also instituted these changes, meant to make Ireland a more peaceful place that was easily governable:

> ✔ Mandated that the Anglo-Irish respect local land rights and stop trying to claim their neighbours' lands as their own.
>
> ✔ The Irish chiefs accepted Richard's sovereignty as king and lord of Ireland.
>
> ✔ Richard accepted the Irish and Anglo-Irish alike as liege subjects of the crown. Through this equality of recognition he promised justice for all.

Richard left Ireland in the spring of 1395, and for the first time in a long time it looked as though an English monarch had actually managed to achieve some kind of stability in the country. The Irish had agreed to submit, and the Anglo-Irish nobility and English settlers were all supposed to support the system that Richard had put in place.

It all goes wrong

Rather than Ireland settling down and conforming to all the order that Richard had put into the country, it all started unravelling after Richard's departure.

Many of the Anglo-Irish aristocracy saw Ireland as their home, and also as the source of their livelihood. Richard's system of order had demanded that they respect local land rights and not go encroaching on the lands of their neighbours (be they Irish or Anglo-Irish). Within two years of Richard's departure, everyone had started trying to expand their holdings, and had started fighting with each other again. Local profit and security were more important to the Anglo-Irish than abiding by the rules that Richard had put in place.

By 1397 Leinster was in a state of war. Cork city had been burned by Irish chieftains and leading figures of royal authority in Ireland had been killed. Richard knew he had to go back to Ireland and try to restore order all over again. Sadly he had lots of problems in England and wasn't able to get away.

It took until 1399 when the situation in Ireland had deteriorated still further before Richard was able to head back to Ireland.

Whiskey

One of the great Irish drinks is whiskey. Its manufacture is one of the most important export industries in Ireland. There are distilleries across the country, and there are many famous brand names such as Paddy, Bushmills, and Jameson. But it was back in these distant times that whiskey first made its appearance. It's recorded, for the first time, as a drink that was produced in Ireland, in 1405. Shortly afterwards there is also the first record of an Irish lord dying of excessive consumption. He wasn't the last!

Richard comes back, goes home, and dies

Richard took a very impressive force to Ireland again, as he had done in 1394. This time, rather than rolling over and submitting, however, the Irish chiefs, supported by some opportunist Anglo-Irish leaders, decided to fight.

Richard's forces were constantly attacked through the Wicklow region. Poor weather didn't help his campaign. The Irish didn't engage with the English forces in open battle, but preferred to attack them on the move. Quickly, the English army, despite its size, was reduced to a state of disarray.

While it was all falling apart in Ireland, Richard's nemesis, Henry Bolingbroke (later to become Henry IV), invaded England to claim the throne. Richard had no choice but to abandon Ireland and head home.

Despite the growing importance of Ireland to the English Crown, holding the throne would always be more important. While there had always been arguments over the line of succession, the challenge by Henry to the throne of Richard would usher in a period of sustained instability (see Chapters 10 and 14). In the face of such disruption in England, Ireland would become a secondary concern, and quickly put to one side.

The return of Richard to England, followed by his imprisonment and murder (explained more fully in the next section), brought to an end his attempt to settle Ireland. What the fourteenth century had witnessed was a steady lessening of English authority in Ireland and the steady rise of the Irish again.

Henry IV's Impact

When Edward III had died, his throne had been inherited by Richard II. However, Richard's accession to the throne didn't go undisputed. Edward's third son was a man called John of Gaunt, and *his* son, Henry Bolingbroke, wanted the throne for himself. Realising the threat that Henry posed, Richard banished him from England for life when he took the throne, but, of course, Henry didn't listen. He turned up in England in 1399 and claimed the throne for himself. There was a brief struggle and Henry won out.

Ireland under Henry IV

With Henry IV on the throne, the Irish had to adapt to a new King. But Henry had real problems. Throwing someone else off the throne was bound to produce a response, and Henry had to watch everything at home very closely. He was less concerned therefore with Ireland than he might have been. For him Ireland was a potential threat: a place where contenders for his throne might emerge from. He was also hard up, skint, stony broke. He hadn't got his finances organised in England, let alone Ireland. Henry wouldn't be able to afford the kind of big venture to Ireland that his two predecessors had undertaken.

Clearly, running Ireland in these difficult situations was a big job for a big man. Henry IV decided to send his son, Henry (later to become Henry V), who was thirteen years old! Not only did Henry have the problem of his youth and inexperience to contend with, but his money, like that of his father, was tight. He had to quickly give away his jewels and other items to raise money to run Ireland, and by 1407, it's estimated that he was £20,000 in debt. Clearly such a deficit wouldn't allow him to go marching round Ireland demanding the submission of all the Irish nobles to him and the Crown. It was time to rethink the whole Irish strategy.

The Pale

Things were so bad in Ireland in the early fifteenth century that the English finally gave up the pretence that they ruled over the whole of Ireland in a secure and manageable fashion.

Income from Ireland had slipped to a measly £1,000 per year, and this wasn't enough to do anything more than defend what the Crown already had. At first the idea was to defend the four loyal shires, namely Counties Dublin, Meath, Louth, and Kildare. Even that became too much, and the decision was made to fortify and defend the area around Dublin. This became known as the Pale.

It was the area occupied by the English and Anglo-Irish who were loyal to the Crown. Outside of the Pale were the Irish, who were pretty much left to their own devices.

The phrase, 'beyond the pale' came to us from Ireland. Nowadays it's used to describe anyone who behaves in a way that is unacceptable to society. It comes from the belief that emerged in Ireland during the fifteenth century, that those Irish who lived beyond the Pale were wild savages and beyond the laws and force of civilised society. Anyone who lived outside the Pale was a savage, and anyone within it decent, loyal, and law-abiding. So, when you use the phrase now, you're not only rebuking the person you're talking about, but recalling the politics of fifteenth century Ireland.

Life in the Pale

To make the Pale secure, the area underwent a systematic process of fortification. Everyone understood that withdrawing into the area of the Pale was, in some ways, a defeat (although they never admitted it). What they had to ensure was that the Pale was completely secure from raiders and attackers.

The security concerns of the Pale were twofold. First, they had to stop aggressive attackers who wanted to attack the Pale and force their way in (fortunately these were few and far between). Second, they wanted to protect the economy of the Pale – they didn't want to see cattle and other livestock that they depended on for their living carried off into the night.

Castles and small forts were built along the length of the border of the Pale. Trenches were built along the border, and watchmen were employed to stand there all night and watch out for the invading Irish hordes. If they saw anything untoward, the watchmen were to light warning beacons that would alert everyone to what was happening.

Parliamentary grants were given to build impressive castles in the various parts of the Pale. These were supplemented by a £10 royal castle building subsidy, and the remains of some of these Pale castles can be found in places like Luttrelstown, Kilgobbin, and Dundrum.

More worryingly for the security of the Pale, it became obvious in the early decades of the fourteenth century, that all the rules put in place by the Statutes of Kilkenny were being completely ignored.

The Statutes of Kilkenny were supposed to make the Anglo-Irish behave like the English, and therefore make the whole English settlement of Ireland more secure. There were ongoing problems though. Many English people kept emigrating back home, and Ireland was suffering a lack of population that would stay in Ireland and be loyal and useful. As a result Ireland was suffering a lack of skilled people to make the Pale secure.

Life outside the Pale

So what was life like beyond the Pale? Royal authority was left in the hands of the various local families so long as they didn't directly challenge the Crown.

There were a wealth of local power struggles though:

- ✔ In the north, Niall Garbh O Donnell took the kingship of Tír Conaill after a series of struggles with the O Neills.
- ✔ Callhach O Connor began his successful rise to power over the borderlands of Leinster in the 1420s.
- ✔ The Ulster Irish lords attacked counties Meath and Louth in the 1420s, looted the area, and forced the locals to pay them rent money.

These are only a few examples of the kinds of disorder that Ireland beyond the Pale suffered. They were examples of the long-standing desire of local chieftains to gain the upper hand over their neighbours, claim valuable lands, and make themselves powerful.

The Anglo-Irish beyond the Pale

The Anglo-Irish, who were in an even more precarious position now that the English settlers had secured themselves in the Pale, were less likely to abide by the Statutes. With no one to either enforce the Statutes of Kilkenny or support their application, the Anglo-Irish did what they could locally to make their situation more secure.

In 1440, the people in the Pale were so alarmed by the Anglo-Irish that they passed a law that reclassified them. Rather than seeing them as settlers and agents of the Crown, the Anglo-Irish were seen as closer to the Irish and not changed at all by the Statutes of Kilkenny. The decision was made to label all the Anglo-Irish people as alien. They too were now beyond the Pale: not just geographically, but also culturally and politically. All this did was to convince them that they were perhaps Irish and owed little allegiance to the Crown.

Making matters worse: Snow and plague

If all the problems caused in Ireland by the decision of the so called rulers to hole up in the Pale weren't enough, the country suffered two calamities: both were caused by natural forces and so there was little that could be done about them.

The first problem was a terrible period of weather which began in the winter of 1435 and froze everything. It affected the crops, and the harvests in the following years were poor. With everyone weakened by the poor harvests, the second problem was the return of plague to Ireland in 1439 which was a disaster. The plague severely affected Dublin (the one thing that fortifying the Pale couldn't keep out), and would revisit the area on a regular basis until 1492.

Henry VI, Richard Plantagenet, and Irish Chutzpah

Henry died in 1413, and his crown went to his son, Henry V. Henry V was very successful, and won some great victories against the French. In 1422 he died at the age of 35, though, and was succeeded by his infant son, Henry VI.

Even after he grew up, Henry VI wasn't that good at being King. He lost all the French territory that his father had secured. He also suffered from mental illness, and this affected his ability to run the country. When he was sick, during 1453, Richard Plantagenet, Duke of York, took control. Although Henry got better in 1454 and ruled the country again, Richard wanted the throne for himself.

Even before all this, as far as King Henry VI was concerned Richard was clearly a mischief maker. Henry believed that Richard had his eyes on the throne and wanted him out of the way. Where better to send him than to Ireland?

Richard was duly dispatched to Ireland in 1449 as lieutenant. He had an interest in the island as he was the proud owner of the earldom of Ulster, and he owned lands in Connacht and Trim.

The Henrys were all from the House of Lancaster, but were opposed by the House of York. Richard Plantagenet was from the House of York. The Wars of the Roses (named after the two emblems of the two fighting Houses: a red rose for Lancaster, a white one for York) began, and they would continue, in one form or another, from 1455 to 1487. Ireland would get sucked into the whole struggle (see Chapter 10), and different Irish factions would take opposing sides.

Richard Plantagenet arrives in Ireland

Once he arrived in Ireland, Richard marched his army out of the Pale (refer to the earlier section 'The Pale' for info about this region), and demanded that the Ulster chieftains submit to him. They did, and were soon followed in submission by the chiefs of Leinster. It all looked great, but there were complexities:

- Securing the submission of Irish chieftains was great news for Richard, but a problem for Henry. If Richard got all the chieftains behind him, he might well use his strength in Ireland to mount a campaign against his opponent on the throne.

- By securing the support of O Neill in Ulster (including 500 cavalry), Richard was building himself a military powerbase in Ireland.

- Many of the chieftains who submitted to Richard weren't actually those recognised by the authorities, but were rivals to the existing chieftains.

- Richard's arguments with Henry were well known in Ireland. It seems that many Irish chieftains submitted to him in the hope that they might benefit from any instability caused by a struggle for the throne.

While in Ireland Richard's troops caused problems. In the late summer of 1449 the soldiers and their families swarmed over the Irish countryside stealing food and drink. They felt that they had a right to help themselves, but this only annoyed the locals. The thefts became more and more common, and in many cases peasants who were defending their produce were killed by soldiers. The actions of Richard's troops were seen as so outrageous that an Act of Parliament had to be passed to stop them.

Marauding troops damaged Richard's reputation, and in 1450 he went back to England. In his place, Richard appointed the Earl of Ormond as his deputy to run Ireland. Ormond was a loyal Yorkist and supported Richard's claim to the throne.

Take your places please: Yorkists versus Lancastrians in Ireland

Richard seems to have done well in Ireland (apart from the hungry troops) in winning the main chieftains over to the idea of supporting the Yorkist cause. With Ormond as deputy, his interests should have been looked after, but, unfortunately for Richard, Ormond died.

Ormond's son, James Butler, succeeded him as Earl of Ormond which you'd think would be good news for Richard, except that James Butler, unlike his father, was a Lancastrian. All the Butlers followed suit and, like James, declared for the Lancastrians. The Butlers' opponents in Ireland, the Geraldines in Kildare, took the opposing view and declared for the Yorkists.

Ireland split into two camps: those, like the Geraldines in Kildare, who supported the claims of the Yorkist Richard to the throne, and those, like the Butlers, who backed the sitting monarch, the Lancastrian Henry. But despite the splits, Richard had the majority of chieftains behind him.

Successive English monarchs had feared that Ireland could become a seat of rebellion. They had always presumed that such rebellion would either come from the Irish themselves, or from one of England's European opponents such as France or Spain. They had never really anticipated that the challenge would be led by an English pretender to the throne using Ireland as a launching pad.

Ireland: Dick's our man!

While the various Anglo-Irish families and Irish chieftains were deciding which side they'd take in the struggle between Richard and Henry, decisive action had been taken in England.

In 1459 Richard had been forced to run for it – the English parliament had declared him a traitor and Henry was after him. Richard made the decision to head for Ireland and look for support there.

An Irish parliament met in 1460 and backed Richard. They also declared that any action against Richard that might harm him was a treasonable offence. Even an unfortunate messenger arriving from England, with orders from King Henry that Richard should be arrested, was executed under the treason rule.

By supporting Richard, the Irish parliament openly challenged the authority of King Henry and the English parliament. In practical terms, this meant that any decisions made in the Irish parliament were now more binding, and had primacy, over any decisions that were made in England.

With these actions, the Irish parliament had effectively proclaimed the independence of Ireland. All decisions would be made in Ireland, and neither the authority of the English parliament nor King Henry had any power in Ireland.

By rejecting the authority of the parliament in England, the Irish parliament had reinstated what it called the 'ancient laws and customs of Ireland'. While this was all specifically driven by the battle between Richard and Henry, it also had the effect of ripping up all the work of the Statutes of Kilkenny and the attempts to settle Ireland.

With the backing of the Irish behind him Richard was in a strong position. He decided the time was right to strike against Henry. He would do this, not in Ireland, but back on the home turf of England.

The Irish parliament agreed to back Richard's plan, and passed a law that allowed anyone who wanted to sail with Richard a leave of absence. The force would be made of up Richard's son, the Earl of Warwick (later Richard III), Yorkist supporters in England, and the Irish.

The battle begins and goes on and on and . . .

On 10 July 1460 the first major battle was fought between the forces of King Henry, and those of Richard's son, Warwick. The battle took place at Northampton, and Warwick won. The Yorkists were on the march, and seemingly in control.

Realising that the writing was on the wall, Henry agreed that when he died, Richard and his descendants could have the throne. It looked like the Irish had backed the winning horse in the royal stakes (probably for the first time ever).

But with such bitterness in the air, such a deal wasn't likely to last. Instead of sticking to the agreement, both sides started sniping at each other, and the battles started again. The battles of 1460 and 1461 had serious repercussions:

✔ **Battle of Wakefield, 30 December 1460:** Leading his own forces, Richard attacked a Lancastrian army twice the size of his own. It didn't work. He lost the battle and he was killed.

✔ **Battle of Towton, 29 March 1461:** Led by the son of Richard, Edward, the Yorkists defeated the Lancastrians. Henry VI fled to Scotland.

After his victory, Edward marched to York where, on 28 June, he was crowned King of England. Irish luck was holding and they were still supporting the winning side.

The problem for the future was that Edward IV's victory wasn't complete. Henry had got away, and would rally his troops and continue to campaign to reclaim his throne. The struggles between the Yorkists and Lancastrians – the Wars of the Roses – would dominate affairs in Ireland for the future decades (see Chapter 10) and lead to further rebellions and splits that would harm the country.

Chapter 10

Family Feuds I: The Wars of the Roses

*T*he war between the Lancastrians and the Yorkists over who should sit on the English throne affected Ireland deeply. Rather than sitting on the fence and letting the English sort out their own squabbles, the Irish were forced to take sides.

By and large the Irish decided that they'd support the Yorkists – a decision they'd made when Richard Plantagenet was in the country (see Chapter 9). The Wars of the Roses went on from 1455 to 1487, and the Irish were involved from start to finish.

In the end the Irish ended up on the losing side, and it was the Lancastrians who won the day. As the Irish had been disloyal (as far as the Lancastrians were concerned), they were made to suffer by the eventual victor, Henry VII. Despite this, the Irish, led by the Geraldines, managed to chart a careful course, and actually brought a good degree of stability to the country.

This chapter shows how the Irish got involved, why they chose to support the sides that they did, and how the Wars affected Ireland. The chapter also shows how important these events were in England and Ireland. The two countries were intertwined whether they liked it or not, and the Wars of the Roses were the most ambitious attempt by the Irish to shape the future of the English Crown.

A Rose by Any Other Name? An Enemy

There were two sides battling it out for the English Crown (see Chapter 9 for more details).

- ✔ **The Lancastrians**, led by the former King, Henry VI, who was in exile in Scotland.
- ✔ **The Yorkists**, who from 1461, were in charge and led by Edward IV.

As with all power struggles that affected Ireland, everyone had their favourites and could change their mind quickly depending on who was winning.

Picking sides: The Butlers and the Geraldines

During the Wars of the Roses, two of the main families in Ireland came out clearly in support of the opposing English factions. The support offered for either side in Ireland was as follows:

- ✔ The Butler family, led by the Earl of Ormond, supported the Lancastrians. Their powerbase was in the area surrounding Kilkenny.
- ✔ The Geraldines, headed by the Earl of Desmond, supported the Yorkist cause. The family's powerbase was in Munster, and another branch of the family controlled Kildare.

The Geraldines and the Butlers had long been in competition with each other, and there was little love lost between them. Although the Wars of the Roses added an extra spice to their struggles, and raised the stakes, the fact that they were in competition with each other was nothing new.

The Battle of Pilltown

Although the Wars of the Roses had a profound effect on Ireland (discussed in the later section 'Rejecting the Hunchback'), only one battle was actually fought in Ireland, and it came early on.

After having left Ireland to go and claim their throne in 1461, the Yorkists were happy to leave their supporters, the Geraldines, in control of the country.

The Lancastrians had other ideas. Henry VI wrote to his followers in Ireland encouraging them to rise up against the Yorkists. In 1462, Sir John Butler, who had been in England, led a force to Ireland to try to take over.

Butler's army, although containing many Irish who supported the Lancastrians, was mainly made up of English soldiers. The hope was that once they were in Ireland, other people would rally to their cause and they could carry the day.

Sir John landed his force in the south of the country, and quickly took New Ross and Wexford. The Butlers in Kilkenny and Tipperary went into open rebellion in support of the cause, and others joined them in Meath.

Sir John and his cousin Edmund mac Richard Butler led a force into battle at Pilltown, near Carrick on Suir against the Earl of Desmond. Whichever side won would take control of Ireland, and the result would have ramifications for the royal struggle in England.

In the end it was Desmond and his Geraldine forces that won the day. He managed to put 20,000 men onto the field of battle at Pilltown, and ensured that the Yorkist cause was victorious.

For having had the gall to challenge the authority of the Geraldines, the Butlers were severely punished. The family was disgraced, and had all its lands taken away. Those families that had fought with the Geraldines were rewarded, and a whole new period began in Irish life.

The Geraldines in Charge

Having fought so loyally and secured Ireland for the Yorkist Crown, the Geraldines were in line for some big rewards. The Geraldines had supported the Yorkists throughout the various stages of the royal intrigue. This support was rewarded when they were given the full backing of the crown. This enabled the Geraldines to take all the top jobs in Ireland, make themselves more wealthy, and enjoy the fruits of having backed the winning horse in the royal struggle.

Thomas fitz James fitz Gerald, Earl of Desmond

Edward IV made the seventh earl of Desmond, Thomas fitz James fitz Gerald, the head of the Irish government. It would be his job to run Ireland on behalf of the monarch, and to make sure that the country was secure.

Desmond came from one of the great Anglo-Irish families that were so important in Ireland, but he had no direct experience of being in government or holding high office. His family was very involved in the Irish way of life, and Desmond, despite his loyalty to Edward IV on the battlefield, was in fact more Irish than English.

Desmond wasn't that popular among the English people of the Pale. They felt that he allowed too many abuses to go unchecked, and that aspects of English law were ignored in favour of the old Irish way of doing things. Desmond was quite happy, so long as the Pale was secure, for the Irish beyond it to embrace the indigenous way of doing things. To security-minded English people this seemed a dangerous way of going about relationships with the Irish. That said, Desmond did do many things that made the King like him:

- ✔ He ruled Ireland on a genuinely national basis, and tried to take care of the distant regions as much as he looked after the interests of Dublin.

- ✔ He regularly brought the parliament together, and oversaw the passage of a great deal of legislation.

- ✔ He stopped the collection of *black rents* (protection money that was paid by many Anglo-Irish families to their Irish neighbours to ensure their safety). Instead this money was to be paid to the authorities who would look after everyone's interests.

- ✔ He kept the Pale secure.

Desmond was especially keen on making the Pale a place where English forms of behaviour were the norm. He wanted to make the place very secure and ensure that any Irish who were in the Pale were kept in line. He passed laws that demanded that everyone in the Pale had to have an English name and had to dress in the English fashion. He also passed legislation that made it legal to decapitate any thief who wasn't English or accompanied by an Englishman. This may seem an extreme version of community policing, but it really did happen.

Drogheda: The New University

When one thinks of the great Universities of the world, Trinity College in Dublin might come to mind. One that doesn't instantly shoot to the top of the list is the University of Drogheda. Drogheda is a small town, some thirty miles or so north of Dublin. Given its royal charter in 1194, it's also one of the oldest Irish towns. Nowadays it has a population of about 40,000, and is well known for its annual Samba festival. It doesn't have a university – but it could have!

One of Desmond's great ideas was that Ireland needed a new university. He wanted to develop a seat of learning that would benefit intellectual life in Ireland, and chose Drogheda as the site for his marvellous new institution. In 1465 the necessary laws were passed in parliament, and on paper at least, the university was ready to go. Sadly, Desmond never got the money together for the new institution, and the university was never built.

Desmond seemed to be able, unlike many of his predecessors, to keep most people happy. The English praised him for trying to enforce the spirit of the Statutes of Kilkenny (see Chapter 9), which stopped the spread of Irish customs and practices amongst the Anglo-Irish. And the Irish praised him for his encouragement of traditional Irish culture, and the way in which he allowed the Irish to pursue their own traditions.

Sadly for Desmond, it all went wrong in 1466 – a group of people in Offaly, the O Connors, captured Desmond, and complained to the King that they didn't like him very much. The King listened to the Offaly people, and poor old Desmond, despite his successes, was out of a job. The O Connors received a hearing from the king for two reasons. First, they had Desmond as a hostage, and second, unless the O Connors' demands for the removal of Desmond were met, they could potentially threaten the security of the Pale.

John Tiptoft, 'The Butcher'

Sir John Tiptoft was officially titled the Earl of Worcester. Everyone actually knew him as 'The Butcher'. The title came from his reputation as someone who had excelled in executing Lancastrians. Here was someone who took his job, and his political loyalties, very seriously. Edward IV thought he'd be the right man to run Ireland.

As well as being good at hanging people, Tiptoft was also a very experienced administrator. His first year in Ireland was a success. He was a respected scholar, passed no outrageous legislation, and managed to keep all the old feuds in Ireland quiet. Perhaps The Butcher had given up the old ways.

But then again, perhaps not.

Hitting him when he's down: Charges against Desmond

In 1468 the Irish parliament came together. They were a difficult lot, and had never been over enamoured of Desmond. It was time, they decided, to exact their revenge. The parliament accused Desmond of:

- ✔ Being treasonous as he had given (allegedly) arms and horses to the Irish.
- ✔ Endangering the safety of the English and the Anglo-Irish because of his close links with the Irish.
- ✔ Using his position at the head of the Irish government to plot to become King of Ireland.

Clearly most of these charges were utterly ridiculous. The record shows that Desmond had actually been quite good at his job. This was a case of his enemies attacking him when he was weak. But what would The Butcher, as the representative of Edward IV, do? Would he throw out these charges, or allow them to proceed?

Well, once a butcher, always a butcher. Desmond was found guilty, taken off, and executed. But why? The most logical explanation seems to be that Edward IV was getting rid of Desmond so that he could not build up a local powerbase. He did the same thing in England too: if the King didn't like you, watch out!

Avenging Desmond

Clearly the Anglo-Irish and the Irish weren't overjoyed with The Butcher executing one of their own. They fell back on the age-old Irish way of doing things – they rebelled.

Desmond's brother, Garret, marched north, destroying everything and everybody that got in his way. He was joined by Thomas fitz Maurice, Earl of Kildare, and a number of local Irish chieftains. Although Tiptoft, The Butcher, met them in battle and was successful in defeating Garret, the rebellion continued to spread: Louth and Tipperary were raided, and the Irish in Ulster and Leinster also rebelled.

Tiptoft had to try to get hold of the situation. He couldn't really call on forces from England, so he had to sort out the mess himself. He made a deal with Thomas fitz Maurice, Earl of Kildare (one of the leading rebels, and a Geraldine from the Kildare branch of the family). If Kildare brought about peace, he would be pardoned for his treasonous activity and looked after.

While it might seem strange to make a deal with your enemy, this was quite normal in fifteenth century Ireland. Tiptoft knew that he couldn't militarily defeat the whole of Ireland when it was in such a state of rebellion. He had to get one of the leading rebels on board, and use them to calm the situation. This kind of deal making was how politics worked back then.

Bye-bye, Tiptoft

For Tiptoft, this was the end of the line. He had won over Kildare, and with his help had put an end to the rebellion. He left Ireland in the late summer of 1470 and went back to London. Sadly for Tiptoft he arrived in the middle of another crisis in the Wars of the Roses. Edward IV had been forced to abandon England, and the Lancastrian Henry VI had been returned to the throne. In the middle of a major riot, Tiptoft, who was well known as the butcher of so many Lancastrians, was captured. In front of an admiring crowd the butcher was publicly executed. He probably didn't appreciate the irony of his situation.

Thomas fitz Maurice, Earl of Kildare

With Tiptoft gone, Kildare was elected justiciar by the ruling Council in Dublin. A man named Sir Edward Dudley had been left behind by Tiptoft as the King's Lord Deputy in Ireland, but it was Kildare who was the man with all the power.

Kildare was a supporter of the Yorkist cause. Edward IV had just run away to France (see the section 'Bye-bye, Tiptoft'), and left Henry VI, the Lancastrian, on the throne. Kildare, and most of Ireland, was therefore supporting the deposed King. They were all disloyal and treasonous.

Ignoring Henry VI

In November 1470 an Irish parliament was brought together. Kildare was fully aware of what had happened in London, and knew that the King whom he supported was no longer on the throne – a fact that Kildare chose to ignore. To make clear his allegiances Kildare:

- ✔ Declared that the parliament was being held in 'the tenth year of the reign of King Edward IV', which pretty much denied the change of power that had happened in England.

- ✔ Began minting new coins that carried the line, 'Edward by grace of God King of England and Lord of Ireland'.

Kildare was therefore refusing to accept Henry VI as his King. He remained absolutely loyal to Edward IV, and waited to see what, if anything, happened in the ongoing struggles that were the Wars of the Roses.

England was in a real state of disorder. It had taken Henry VI eleven years to get his throne back, and Edward IV wasn't going to sit idly by and let him remain on it. With all this chaos, and continual fighting, Ireland was really the least of anyone's problems. Once back on the throne, Henry VI had to concentrate on securing England and not worry about Ireland.

Henry VI, although probably knowing full well that Kildare's real loyalties lay with the Yorkist cause, had no choice but to accept Kildare as his Lord Deputy in Ireland. It was simply easier to leave Kildare in charge, than challenge him and face a battle in Ireland.

But then Edward IV reclaimed the throne in April 1471. Rather than have an opponent hanging around (a lesson had been learnt from the last time), Edward did the honourable thing and had Henry murdered. The Yorkists were back in charge, and Kildare sat rather smugly in Ireland having stayed in charge of Ireland during the whole mess that was English royal affairs in 1470 and 1471.

Building a brand new army

With Edward back on the throne, and Kildare in charge, everything should have been rosy. But Kildare had the perennial problem of how best to secure the Pale and the counties immediately around Dublin. A long running series of attacks were taking place on the borders of the Pale and the outlying counties which lay between the Irish and the Anglo-Irish populations. Kildare wanted to protect the Pale, and the counties around it, more effectively so he asked parliament for a permanent force of 80 archers.

These men, with their bows and arrows, would, Kildare argued, be able to better defend Dublin, Meath, Louth, and Kildare. This would be Ireland's first permanent army.

The army had two purposes – one publicly acknowledged, the other not.

- ✔ The army would be able to defend the area of the Pale effectively, and this would help the residents feel more secure. This was the public argument in favour of the army.

- ✔ The same army would be under the control of Kildare in his role of deputy, and therefore loyal to him. The part of the argument in favour of a standing army, that wasn't publicly stated, was that it would make Kildare and the Geraldines more secure and more powerful.

The Fraternity of St George

In 1474 the Irish parliament legislated for the establishment of the Fraternity of St George. This elite group would be headed by the twelve most important men in Ireland (and surprise, surprise, Kildare got to be in charge), and under their control would be a standing army of 40 cavalry, 40 pages, and 120 archers.

This force allowed Kildare to bring a degree of stability to Ireland, and to the Pale specifically. He'd done a good job, but in 1478, after eight years in charge, Kildare died.

Gerald: The new Kildare

Kildare was succeeded by his son, Gerald, who took the title of the eighth Earl of Kildare. He is an important figure in the history of Ireland, as he managed to live a long life, governing Ireland under four successive monarchs.

England sent over Lord Grey as Lord Deputy to Ireland in July 1478, and he replaced Gerald who had been voted into the post by the Irish Council. Despite the fact that he was accompanied by 300 archers, Grey was met with stern resistance. Gerald had been put into the top job by the Irish Council, and they objected to the interference from England. The arrival of Grey was also a direct challenge to the power of the Geraldines in Ireland.

A measure of how far the powerful people in Ireland were willing to go to keep Gerald in charge, rather than Lord Grey, was illustrated when Grey arrived in Dublin. As Lord Deputy, he was the agent of the King, and everybody should have acted very reverentially towards him and done exactly as he asked – not the case!

✔ When Grey arrived at Dublin Castle, the seat of English rule in Ireland, the constable in charge destroyed the drawbridge and refused to allow Grey to enter.

✔ The chancellor of Ireland, Roland fitz Eustace, refused to give Grey the great seal. Without the seal, Grey could have no legal authority.

With his authority undermined, and no one playing ball with him Grey was in a difficult position. He decided the best way to proceed was to call together an Irish parliament and get their support. Gerald decided to do the same thing. Ireland had two parliaments! Each of them declared the other null and void, and each told the King that they were the real thing.

Edward IV despaired (and who could blame him). In 1479 Gerald went to see him, and explained everything. Edward was so impressed that he agreed to recall Grey and let Gerald act as Lord Deputy.

Gerald was clearly a very powerful man in Ireland. There was no sense that he was trying to take the role of the High King of old, but he did dominate politics in Ireland. It's easy to see Gerald as someone who was challenging royal authority. The Geraldines had an extensive power network, and brought together the powerful families from both the Irish and Anglo-Irish areas of the country. Yet Gerald, it is argued, was the best option the King had. He needed someone who could manage the King's affairs in the Pale, as well as communicate effectively with the distant parts of Ireland. The only alternative that Edward IV had to Gerald was an extensive and costly military campaign which he could ill afford.

The Fifteenth Century Success Story

Under Gerald Ireland actually started, by fifteenth century standards, to flourish. Sure, there were still lots of problems, such as localised wars and land struggles, and development was uneven. But there were good points, including:

✔ The steady development of towns and fortifications meant that the settler populations were steadily becoming more secure and less open to attack.

✔ Relationships between the Irish and Anglo-Irish were, in many cases, very peaceful, and the Irish population benefited as tenants on the land and as artisans employed to work.

✔ The management of agricultural land improved. With a more settled population (and the absence of famine or plague) land was tilled properly.

✔ Towns such as Dublin saw an increase in the level of commercial activity.

✔ The number of trades that flourished in Irish towns was evident in the number of prosperous tradesmen's guilds that were established.

✔ Many churches and religious institutions, that had fallen into disrepair, were restored and rebuilt on a grander scale.

✔ The amount of money flowing into the Irish exchequer became more constant and steadily increased.

This isn't to argue for one minute that this was some fifteenth century equivalent of the Celtic Tiger (see Chapter 23), but things were definitely looking up. Despite the chaos of the Wars of the Roses, Ireland had achieved a degree of continuity of rule under the Geraldines. The English Crown had little choice but to let them get on with it, and in return the Geraldines were responsible in the way they ran Ireland.

Rejecting the Hunchback

Richard III is always portrayed as a horrible man, with a hunchback. We can probably blame Shakespeare for that as he wasn't a fan of the King. But clearly Richard did do some nasty things so that he could climb the greasy pole to the throne.

So what did Richard do that was so wrong? Well, he was very powerful, and was in a strong position after the death of Edward IV in 1483. He believed that Edward's son, Edward V, was too young to take the throne and that his youth would lead to more instability. He got Edward V's succession declared illegal (arguing that he was illegitimate), and had him and his brother, Clarence, locked in the Tower of London. They were soon, mysteriously, dead. With no young Prince left around to claim the throne, Richard was crowned Richard III on 6 July 1483.

Richard was opposed by the Lancastrians again, in the form of Henry Tudor. In 1485, at the Battle of Bosworth, Richard's army was defeated and Richard III killed. He became the last English King to die on the battlefield.

In Ireland the reign of Richard, who had wanted to challenge the authority of Gerald and the Geraldines, was a worrying time. Richard was threatening to work with Irish leaders other than Gerald. Fortunately for Gerald, Henry Tudor arrived just in time, and Richard's plan for Ireland was never implemented.

While Richard potentially threatened Gerald's power in Ireland, at least Richard was a member of the Yorkist lineage. With the defeat of Richard at Bosworth, the Yorkists went out of business, never to re-emerge. Gerald and the Irish were now faced with Henry Tudor (who had been crowned Henry VII – the first Tudor King of England) who was allied to the Lancastrian cause. Although the Lancastrian dimension had weakened over the years, and Henry was descended directly from, and represented, the House of Tudor, his Lancastrian sympathies potentially caused problems for the Irish. They had been loyal to the Yorkists since the start of the whole Wars of the Roses.

Plotting Against Henry VII: Part 1

In March 1486, less than a year after having defeated Richard at Bosworth, Henry VII accepted that Gerald should continue as the King's Lord Deputy in Ireland. This was a great result for Gerald. He might have expected that he'd be got rid of because of his Yorkist sympathies. It seems that Henry simply accepted that he had no other options in Ireland. If he tried to remove Gerald, it would only lead to problems. It seemed as if Gerald would be all right if he accepted Henry as his King, and was content to let the whole Yorkist loyalty that he had fade away.

It wasn't to be.

Hail the King: Lambert Simnel

In the new year of 1487, a priest arrived in Dublin with a ten year old boy in tow. The priest claimed that the boy was in fact Edward, Earl of Warwick, and therefore a living and legitimate Yorkist heir to the throne.

The boy, whose real name was Lambert Simnel, provoked a real dilemma for Gerald. Ignore him, and hope that he would go away, or champion him as the Yorkist heir to the throne. Never one to miss out on a bit of drama and king making, Gerald decided on the latter course.

Yorkist sympathisers arrived in Ireland to herald their new King, and brought some 2,000 troops with them to fight the cause. Gerald and the Irish were now on a collision course with Henry VII. If they continued to support the claim that Lambert Simnel was indeed the heir to the throne, then Henry would have to act against them.

Now, these things can either be done quietly and with diplomacy, or you can make the big, loud statement that no one can ignore and provoke a crisis.

On 24 May 1487, and for the first and only time ever on Irish soil, the coronation of a King of England was staged. With full honours, and under the guidance of the Bishop of Meath, Lambert Simnel was crowned Edward VI at Christ Church, Dublin.

What to do next? Gerald decided, along with the other Yorkist sympathisers, that they had to force home Lambert Simnel's claim to the throne. How to do that? Simple . . . invade England, kill Henry VII, and put Lambert on the throne!

Bang, bang: You're dead

Battles in Ireland were nothing new, but people had always been killed with sharp implements such as swords. Towards the end of the fifteenth century all this changed, when the new military technology of the gun arrived on Irish shores. In 1487, the forces of Ardh Ruadh O Donnell started using imported firearms. It's not recorded who was the first to die from gunshot wounds, but the arrival of the firearm changed the way that battles were fought in Ireland forever.

The invasion didn't go as planned:

- The army – mainly Irish and Flemish – landed in Lancashire on 5 June 1487.
- Many supposed local sympathisers refused to join them.
- Henry's army met them at the Battle of Stoke Field on 16 June 1487.
- Henry won.
- Gerald was captured.

Clearly by supporting the false claims that were made about Lambert Simnel, the Irish had caused Henry lots of problems. But Henry was a nice man. He accepted that Lambert Simnel wasn't to blame, as he was only a young boy, and found him a job in the kitchens (he eventually rose to the position of royal falconer). Gerald was slapped on the wrists and sent home to Ireland. In May 1488 he was given a full pardon and continued in his job as the King's Lord Deputy in Ireland.

Yes, Gerald was a Yorkist, and would clearly have preferred to have seen a Yorkist on the throne. Most historians have argued that Gerald knew early on that Lambert Simnel was a fake, and not the Earl of Warwick. It seems that Gerald's motivations were personal. He probably didn't care one way or the other whether there was a Yorkist or Henry Tudor on the throne, as Henry was being perfectly nice to him. What Gerald was doing was gambling. If they could get Lambert Simnel on to the throne, then Gerald would benefit massively and get even richer and more powerful. The gamble failed, but Gerald was no worse off.

Plotting Against Henry VII: Part 2

Richard III had the sons of Edward IV killed in the Tower of London . . . or did he? Well, a man called Perkin Warbeck thought not. Why not? Because he was one of those princes! Warbeck was actually a Fleming, who had been born in 1474. He went around the place pretending to be Richard, Duke of York (one of the murdered princes), and telling anyone that would listen that the throne was rightfully his. Henry had dumped him in the Tower of London, after he had been heard at the court of Burgundy telling everyone who he was (or thought he was). Perkin Warbeck escaped though, and made for Ireland.

Hail the King: Perkin Warbeck

Warbeck landed in Cork in 1491, and started telling everyone who he was, and that they should rally to his cause. Locally, the Earl of Desmond took him at his word, and declared that he supported Warbeck as the rightful heir to the throne.

Henry VII was worried that Warbeck would spark off the same kind of silliness that had accompanied Lambert Simnel's claims that he was the King. The last thing that Henry needed were the Geraldines to start supporting Warbeck and kick-starting the whole rebellion against the Crown thing again.

Henry sent James Ormond and Thomas Garth to Ireland with an army. They were told to defend Tipperary and Kilkenny so that any Warbeck-inspired rebellion was confined to Cork. In the event everyone backed down and Warbeck left Ireland.

The Perkin Warbeck saga was absolutely nothing to do with Gerald. Warbeck claimed later that Gerald had helped him, but Gerald was firm in his denial. He said that he had never supported Warbeck or housed him or even met him. But mud sticks, and for Henry the mere fact that two Yorkist pretenders to the throne had emerged in Ireland was enough evidence to doubt the loyalty of Gerald.

In June 1492 Gerald was sacked. Royal authority was divided between the Archbishop of Dublin, Walter fitz Simons, and James Ormond (who had come to Ireland to head off the Warbeck threat).

Trouble in Ireland

With Gerald off the payroll, all his enemies came out of the woodwork. The Butlers, who way back at the beginning of the Wars of the Roses had supported the Lancastrians against the Geraldines, pledged their support for Henry, and attacked Gerald and his supporters. Violence was rife, and gangs even fought in the streets of Dublin. The Irish chieftains joined in, and the whole place looked like it was going downhill fast.

Henry sent in the army in March 1493 and tried to calm the situation. It didn't work, and in the summer of 1493 regular fights were still occurring between the Geraldines and the Butlers. Henry spent some £4,000 in 1493 trying to calm the situation, but really to no avail. He decided that it was time for a radical plan.

The New Broom: Edward Poynings

Henry argued that the problems in Ireland had been caused by faction fighting and the presence of the 'savage' Irish in the country. He decided that he would send a huge army to Ireland, and that he would militarily bring the country to order. Once he had won the peace, he could then establish the kind of administration that was necessary for the smooth running of the country.

The man for the job was Sir Edward Poynings, who was appointed deputy to Ireland in September 1494. It was agreed that he would work with the one man who knew Ireland best: Good old Gerald, the Earl of Kildare (he was back again!).

Warbeck's back, and so is Gerald

In July 1495 Warbeck (yes, the confused gentleman who thought he was a prince) landed in Waterford, and Poynings had to march down there and sort him out. Warbeck fled to Scotland. He continued to cause trouble for a while until he was finally captured in England in 1498 and hanged a year later.

To get rid of Warbeck, and bring Ireland into some kind of order, Poynings had spent £23,000, making his intervention in Ireland one of the most expensive to date. The Crown could not stand that sort of expenditure in the long term, and so it had to revert to the old system of ruling Ireland. What they needed was a local magnate who could boss everyone about, was strong enough to keep everybody in order, but wouldn't be a drain on the English exchequer. Who was there that could do such a job? Re-enter Gerald, Earl of Kildare please!

In 1496 Gerald was appointed Lord Deputy, again, and was given the job for ten years. He was given full power over land grants and the Irish exchequer. It seemed that the only way that the English were going to be able to rule Ireland on a day-to-day basis was through Gerald.

Poynings and his Reforms

On his arrival in Ireland Poynings had been accompanied by a crack force of civil servants. Their job, while Poynings was sorting out the country militarily, was to introduce reforms into the way Ireland was administered.

These men were good at their job. Everything was accounted for, and started running more smoothly (in the short term at least). A series of parliaments brought together by Poynings introduced a number of laws that would shape Ireland into the future. Although it would be Gerald who would see to things on the ground, Poynings' laws gave the English administration shape and direction.

His reforms were:

- ✔ No Irish parliament could be called without the King's prior consent.
- ✔ No bill could be introduced to the Irish parliament unless it had first been approved by the King and his Council in England.
- ✔ All laws in Ireland were to be based directly on laws that had been passed in Ireland: there would be no local distinctiveness in Irish law.
- ✔ The authority of the great seal of England, the privy seal, and signet of England were absolute in Ireland.

What did all this mean in practical terms? Effectively the Irish were being punished for their behaviour in recent decades. During the Wars of the Roses the Irish had been passing laws by themselves, and using the Irish parliament to challenge the authority of England. The parliament had even been used to declare pretenders such as Lambert Simnel as King.

But no more. In the future government in Ireland would be totally controlled from England. Anything which differed from the English system would effectively be treasonous. Whereas the Irish had acted with a degree of independence by calling together their parliament nearly annually, from 1495 to 1536, it was only called together by the King eight times. England was setting up a system that would allow direct rule.

Part IV

Religious Wars and Family Feuds: The Sixteenth and Seventeenth Centuries

The 5th Wave   By Rich Tennant

THE REFORMATION IN IRELAND BEGINS

His majesty thought this might help win some hearts and minds.

Kiss Me, I'm Protestant

s Me, tant

In this part . . .

Religion – one of the great problems for Ireland. The country was very devout (after all, St Patrick had done his best work in Ireland) but was caught out-of-step when Henry VIII decided he didn't like Catholicism anymore. The Reformation (swapping the Roman Catholic Church for a Protestant one) had a deep and lasting effect on Ireland. Henry VIII and his successors sought to control, and eventually suppress, the Catholic Church. However, the Irish weren't prepared to give up their Church without a fight.

While the English had learnt to control the Irish through force, the sixteenth and seventeenth centuries witnessed a new tactic: the plantations. Rather than try to make the Irish see the virtues of the new Protestant Church, the Crown decided to send Protestants to Ireland to settle the country. The hope was that they would establish themselves so dominantly that Ireland would fall into line. All the plantations actually did was to increase the tension between the Irish (Catholics) and the newcomers (Protestants). At the end of this period, the issue of royal succession once more affected Ireland. The battle between Catholic King James and Protestant King William was fought out in Ireland and killed off Catholic hopes for a long time.

Chapter 11

Popes Versus Archbishops: The Reformation and Ireland

*H*enry VIII is best known for getting married lots of times, falling out of love with his wives, and then either divorcing them or chopping off their heads (actually he got someone else to do the messy bit). While all this marital strife makes for a good royal story, Henry's actions had a far-reaching impact on Ireland.

While it was all right for Henry to have the lives of two of his wives brought to early ends (he was the king after all), divorcing them was strictly against the rules. Henry was, like everyone at the time, a Catholic, and Catholics didn't believe in divorce. While the ordinary man in the street may have had to abide by the Church's rules against divorce, Henry sidestepped the issue by setting up his own Church.

This chapter explains how Henry's divorces changed the dynamics of religion in Ireland forever, and what impact the invention of a new religious denomination had on the country. It also helps you understand why the Irish resisted the Reformation so strongly and what Henry had to do to get them behind his new view of the world.

Henry VIII: Large and in Charge

Henry VIII sat on the throne from 1509 to 1547 and is seen in most British history books as one of the great monarchs. He was certainly controversial, but it's doubtful that the Irish loved him as much as their English counterparts.

Henry came to the throne when he was still a young man. He hadn't been first in line to the throne, but when his elder brother, Arthur, died in 1502, the eleven-year-old Henry was suddenly the heir-apparent. He would assume the throne when his father, Henry VII, died, which he obligingly did in 1509. A few weeks after his accession, Henry VIII married for the first time. The wedding bells were the start of all of Henry's problems.

Royal marriages at the time weren't stories of true love. More often than not they were business arrangements between different European countries to cement alliances and ensure a degree of stability.

The wife that Henry took, Catherine of Aragon, had previously been married to none other than Henry's brother Arthur. Henry's father, Henry VII, had been keen that Catherine, a Spaniard, stay in the family as it ensured good relations between Spain and England. Poor old Henry didn't have a choice in the matter and was saddled with his second-hand bride. Despite being King, Henry still had to do the right thing: diplomatic relations were all important.

There was only one key issue in any royal marriage at the time: children. Catherine produced five children for Henry. Four of them died shortly after birth, and only a daughter, Mary, survived. Female heirs were no good to a Tudor king, and Catherine's inability to have a healthy boy was a problem. By the 1530s Henry had seen enough of Catherine to know that she would never give him the son he needed.

The wives and woes of Henry VIII

It's clear that Henry liked women. While married to Catherine he had two long-term mistresses: Mary Boleyn and Elizabeth Blount. In 1526 he also started a relationship with Mary's sister, Anne Boleyn. From all accounts, it seems that Henry was truly infatuated with Anne, and this spelled the end of Catherine.

Working with his advisor, Cardinal Wolsey, Henry set out to rid himself of Catherine. Doing so would leave him free to marry Anne and then he could set about trying to create a male heir. But Henry's plan had two big problems:

✔ **The Catholic Church didn't recognise the concept of divorce.** Unless Henry could prove that the marriage was never valid, he had no other acceptable way of separating from Catherine. He argued that the Papal dispensation that had allowed Catherine to marry him was flawed, and that Anglo-Spanish diplomatic relations had been the driving force behind the marriage.

✔ **His marriage to Catherine had been part of a diplomatic pact with Spain.** Throw Catherine out of the door, and the Spanish would be mightily upset. By the time Henry was looking to get rid of Catherine, the Anglo-Spanish relationship had changed. Henry was closer to France, and didn't need to worry about Spain so much.

The whole attempt to prove that the marriage was invalid failed. The Spanish wouldn't stand for it, and the Papal authorities just got tied up in knots over the issue.

Henry was livid. He sacked Wolsey and stripped him of his power and money. (Luckily for Wolsey he died before he got to trial on the charge of undermining the king's authority.) And then Henry took matters into his own hands.

When he couldn't get the Pope to support his claim, Henry dismissed the Pope – as the head of England's church, at least – and appointed a new team to run his affairs: Sir Thomas More (Lord Chancellor), Thomas Cranmer (Archbishop of Canterbury), and Thomas Cromwell (Chancellor of the Exchequer). Things moved swiftly from there.

In January 1533 Cranmer married Henry and Anne Boleyn, and in May of that year, he declared Henry's marriage to Catherine null and void (the first divorce!). Then the dominoes began to fall. Because the marriage was invalid, Henry and Catherine's daughter, Mary, was declared illegitimate. As a result, Mary lost her position as natural heir to the throne.

Henry also had to face some unexpected opposition from his own Lord Chancellor. Thomas More argued that, while Henry and his parliament could make any decisions they wanted, they had no religious authority. The Pope, More argued, was still head of the Church. Henry charged More with high treason and had him beheaded in 1535.

Clearly Henry's actions weren't going to win him friends in either the Vatican or in Spain (who were increasingly thinking of England as an enemy anyway). The Pope was really miffed, and in July 1533 excommunicated Henry. The king was out of the Church.

Love's labours lost on Henry

Even though Henry got his way and was able to divorce Catherine and marry Anne, his personal life didn't get any better. Although Anne gave birth to Elizabeth, she never produced the much needed son (although she was given only three years to try). She was charged with witchcraft and adultery, and beheaded. After that Henry married again (and again):

✔ Jane Seymour, married 1536. She managed a son, Edward, but died shortly after his birth

in 1537. Edward, a sickly child, actually lived to inherit the throne from Henry in 1547.

✔ Anne of Cleves, married 1540, annulled 1540. She never had children and died in 1557.

✔ Catherine Howard, married 1540, annulled 1541. No children and she was executed in 1542 for adultery.

✔ Catherine Parr, married 1543. No children, but Henry died before her and she kept her head.

No more Pope: The Reformation

Parliament supported Henry and passed a series of laws to undermine the place of the Catholic Church in England. The Pope was denied revenue from England, all clerical appointments would in future be approved by Henry, and the Church could make no decisions that would apply in England without Henry's say so. In 1534 Henry topped it all by declaring himself the Supreme Head on Earth of the Church of England. Anyone who denied Henry this position and supported the divine right of the Pope was to be charged with high treason and beheaded.

Catholics were in a perilous position. Under the Act of Supremacy of 1534, which declared Henry as the head of the Church, any act of allegiance to the Pope was considered to be an act of treason. Catholics could not deny the power of the Pope, who they viewed as God's divinely appointed representative on Earth, so effectively they all became treasonous in the eyes of the Crown. Members of religious orders were executed and Henry began seizing the possessions of monasteries and closing them down. Unless you signed up to Henry's new view of the world you were in big trouble. To really clamp down on the Catholics he:

✔ Ordered the destruction of all Catholic shrines in 1538.

✔ Dissolved all the monasteries and took all their land in 1539.

✔ Removed all members of the Catholic hierarchy from the House of Lords.

Although it would take years before the break was complete and the country firmly Protestant, Henry essentially created a religious authority separate from the Catholic Church in Rome – the Church of England – with himself (or the king) as its head. Meanwhile, the Irish, still Catholic and still wary of England, were watching these events very closely.

Irish Eyes Aren't Smiling

The decision by Henry to separate from his first wife Catherine would have profound effects in Ireland. Given the changes that Henry wanted to instigate, namely a split with Rome and the Catholic Church, Ireland had two choices: go along with the whole scheme, or rebel. Perhaps unsurprisingly, the Irish chose the latter course.

Under Poynings' laws (see Chapter 10) the Irish were ruled aggressively by England and her agents in Ireland. The various factions in Ireland were interested in local power, and had no strong allegiance to the Crown. While they were loyal to Rome and the Catholic faith, controlling their local affairs, and the ending of English rule in Ireland, was equally important.

Clearly the changes that Henry was making in religious terms were cataclysmic. As much as the Irish loved their Church, they also saw the chaos in England as an opportunity. By swearing allegiance to Rome, they had a reason to reject English rule. The support of Catholicism by the Irish, although a genuine act, was also a vehicle that would allow them to confront English authority in Ireland.

The Catholic question wasn't the first issue to spring up between Henry VIII and the people of Ireland. They had a bit of history before he booted Catholicism from English shores.

The most important man in Ireland during the first two decades of Henry's rule was the ninth earl of Kildare, Gerald. Kildare wasn't particularly well loved by many of his countrymen, but as the Irish Lord Deputy, he was the one through which royal authority flowed. And, because Henry wasn't that interested in Ireland (European court politics were far more interesting, after all), Kildare got away with a lot.

By 1519, ten years into Henry's reign, the situation in Ireland had deteriorated as many of the powerful Irish families had started ignoring English laws and were not remaining loyal to the Crown. So Henry sent the Earl of Surrey to Ireland with a small army to kick the Irish into some kind of order. He also sent a message. While he would respect the Irish and their ways, his power as monarch was absolute. Cross the king, and you would be in trouble! But then Henry lost interest again and pretty much forgot about Ireland.

Ireland's rebellion

With the news of Henry's effective divorce, the Irish saw their opportunity. News arrived in London that Gerald, ninth earl of Kildare, was plotting treason. It was evident that he had plundered the royal arsenal at Dublin Castle and removed all the weapons to his own castle in Maynooth.

Rebellious men in Ireland were nothing new for the English authorities to deal with. The constant fear was that any rebellion would reach out to England's potential enemies, such as Spain or France, and that Ireland would be used as a launching pad for attacks on England. With the split from Catherine, Henry had also caused divisions between England and Spain. The fear was that the Irish would form an alliance with Spain and that England would be threatened. Henry couldn't allow that and should have been keeping his eye on them.

Worried by Kildare's light-fingered activities in Dublin Castle, Henry summoned Kildare to London to explain himself. Kildare stalled for a while, but reluctantly agreed to travel to London in February 1534. In his absence, he put his son, Thomas, Lord Offaly (Silken Thomas as he was known) in charge.

Poor old Thomas was left alone in Ireland without his father, and worried about the intentions of the English. Things got worse when Thomas was informed that the English planned to arrest him, and other members of his family, transport them to England, and have them executed.

Rather than face the executioner's block, Thomas decided to go before the Irish Council and encourage a rebellion (something that Dad had written from London and told him to do anyway). So on 11 June, Thomas spoke to the Irish Council of his fellow countrymen. In his speech he resigned his Sword of State (the thing that gave him the backing of English authority), and defied the king. He denounced Henry as a heretic and swore allegiance to the Pope and the King of Spain and warned all Englishmen to leave Ireland or face death.

Clearly this was a fairly overt statement of intent (especially the bit about Henry being a heretic). Although a dangerous path to go down, Thomas was supported by the most important Irish chieftains. The rebellion spread quickly and to many observers it seemed as though the English were on the verge of losing Ireland. The anger felt in Ireland was also enhanced by news that Kildare had been arrested and died shortly afterwards in the Tower of London.

Henry's response

Henry was made of stern stuff. If he could see off the Pope, a few rowdy Irishmen shouldn't pose too much of a problem. The response was full on.

Henry dispatched Sir William Skeffington to Ireland with 2,300 troops armed with the most modern weapons of the time. The fights in the war that ensued were brutal, but English technology was far better than that of Irish. By the winter of 1534–5, most of Thomas' allies saw the writing on the wall and deserted him and his cause. In March 1535, Skeffington attacked Thomas' castle in Maynooth and the fortress was taken. Thomas wasn't in the castle at the time and evaded capture. The rebellion continued until August 1535, but without sufficient forces and facing a superior enemy Thomas surrendered.

So, the Irish rebellion against England, and by default against the idea of the Reformation, had failed. Clearly Ireland remained a potential problem. How would Henry deal with it?

Hanging the Irish in London

Usually troublesome Irish lords who had rebelled were, after a short term of imprisonment, pardoned and given their lands and title back. The hope was that they'd fall into line and not misbehave again. Thus, when Thomas surrendered, he did so on the understanding that too he would be spared life and limb.

The situation during the Reformation was different, however. The Irish may have seen their rebellion as a bid for freedom from England, but Henry recognised it as a threat to his own sovereignty. Because of his actions against Rome, Henry had cast himself as the adversary of all Catholic nations which, at that time, meant all the nations of western Europe. Given these circumstances, Henry couldn't be seen to be weak. He had to enforce his rule in Ireland.

Henry had three options regarding Thomas:

- ✔ **Execute him immediately.** Although this option may have appealed to him personally, Henry feared that it would start a new rebellion in protest.

- ✔ **Give Thomas the traditional pardon.** Although precedent made this option viable, Henry didn't think such leniency would send the message to the Irish that Henry meant business.

- ✔ **Imprison Thomas and execute him later when things had calmed down.** It might cost him a little something in food and lodging, but . . .

Obviously, Henry went for the third option. Thomas and his key followers were imprisoned in London for nearly a year and a half. Once Ireland was a bit quieter and everyone had forgotten about Thomas, he was, to put it mildly, *dispatched*.

On 3 February 1537, at the famous public execution spot of Tyburn, in London, Thomas was hanged and then beheaded. That was nasty, but his five uncles who accompanied him to the gallows were hanged, beheaded, and quartered.

Hanging a few more Irish back home

To drive the message home that rebellion would not be tolerated, Henry had another 100 of the main rebellion leaders and supporters of Thomas executed in Ireland.

Considering the size and seriousness of the rebellion, Ireland had got off lightly. For now.

Enforcing the Reformation in Ireland

Although the Reformation had been shocking to people in England, there had already been some questioning of the absolute rule of the Church. Ideas such as Lutheranism, anti-papalism (opposition to the idea that the Pope was God's representative on earth), and anti-clericalism (mistrust of the power and religious beliefs of the clergy) had been circulating in England and Europe for a while. In Ireland, these ideas had simply never arrived, and no one seriously questioned Church authority.

Having split with Rome and put down the rebellion of Thomas, Henry now had to find some way of enforcing his rule, and the idea of the Reformation, on Ireland. He made these changes:

- **Declared himself Head of the Church of Ireland.** In England, Henry had been declared Head of the Church in November 1535. This meant that he took the place of the Pope at the head of all things religious and was therefore the chief authority in the new Church of England. In May 1536, the Irish echoed this move and made Henry the 'supreme head in earth of the whole Church of Ireland'. This church was under Henry's sole rule and was legally established in Ireland without much fuss.

- **Applied much of the legislation to Ireland that had been used in England to suppress the most obvious symbols of the Vatican's authority.** In the years from his first marriage split, to the time of his death, half the monasteries and one third of the friaries had been suppressed. Inside the Pale this suppression was almost total. Outside it was more patchy.

- **Removed symbols of devotion and sites of pilgrimage, such as the shrine of Our Lady at Trim.** At the time the Irish weren't as attached to such sites as their English counterparts, and these acts of destruction met with little opposition.

- **Enforced a series of liturgical reforms.** English prayers were enforced, for example, and acts such as confession were condemned.

The changes Henry brought to Ireland to enforce his separation from the Roman Catholic Church went rather smoothly. But given that the Irish had never seriously considered questioning the Pope's authority or the authority of the Roman Catholic Church, it may come as a surprise that they didn't raise a stink over Henry's actions. There are a few reasons why they took the changes in their stride:

- ✔ The English rule of Ireland was not complete. It only really had total control of the Pale (the area around Dublin) and some other English districts. Because Henry didn't have the military strength on the ground to enforce the Reformation across the whole of Ireland, outside the Pale life went on pretty much as normal.

- ✔ The Irish had just witnessed what Henry would do if he was crossed. They saw how he put down a rebellion (refer to the section 'Henry's response'), and decided it was easier to go along with his wishes than to try to oppose him.

- ✔ Many of the Anglo-Irish felt that there was a need to try to get to grips with the Church and welcomed the reforms. This was long overdue. The Irish Church, although Catholic, had always retained a degree of separation from Rome, and mixed Catholic theology and practices with traditional beliefs. The Anglo-Irish felt that the Irish Church needed a greater sense of direction and discipline.

- ✔ Most Irish people outside the Pale saw Henry's change in title as another political episode in Anglo-Irish life. They were accustomed to political intrigues – the shifting and re-shifting of power – and saw these latest changes as not fundamentally changing the real order of things. In other words, it didn't matter what Henry called himself; they continued to see those in Rome as the natural Church leaders.

Aiming for Supremacy in Ireland

In the years from the start of the Reformation until the time of his death Henry had a dilemma. Ireland was clearly a concern, a powder keg that could explode at any time. However, Henry had enough on his plate at home and in Europe without devoting too much time and energy into sorting out Ireland.

What happened was a partial attempt to sort out Ireland. The policy was not to completely take over Ireland or suppress it, but to try and win people over and, when necessary, give them a good kicking to remind them who was boss.

A smallish rebellion

In the late 1530s, Henry put a new man in charge of Ireland: Lord Grey (Leonard Grey, 1490–1541). He didn't much like the Irish, and thought the best way of managing Ireland would be to suppress all forms of resistance.

Grey launched military campaigns into the west of Ireland towards Galway, and as far north as Armagh. He was basically trying to kick the Irish beyond the Pale into some form of submission where they would acknowledge English authority in Ireland. After his army had threatened or defeated any Irish forces they came across, they were forced to submit to English rule.

But not everyone liked the idea. The lord of Donegal, Manus O Donnell, led a small rebellion under the name of the Geraldine league. The league was opposed to the Church reforms of Henry and the strong arm tactics of Lord Grey. O Donnell brought together a coalition of Irish lords to stop the English.

Coalitions of Irish lords, despite their regular infighting, were nothing unusual. The Geraldine league came together because of a need for self-preservation. Lord Grey's tactics were successful in suppressing those Irish he came into contact with, and the others feared what he would do next.

The league took the audacious step of invading the Pale in August 1539. Rebellion was one thing, but breaking and entering into the preserve of English rule was a real innovation. Problem was that the Irish got a bit greedy and stole so much from the Pale that their booty slowed them down. Grey didn't have much trouble finding them, and the league was defeated.

Making a deal with the Irish

After the Geraldine league had been defeated, the Irish lords complained to Henry. They argued that Grey was a bully, and that peace would never happen until he was removed. While Grey remained in Ireland, they said, the Irish would just simply be forced into further acts of rebellion.

The last thing that Henry needed was the Irish lords in a state of rebellion. He needed them to be supportive of the Crown and not kicking up a fuss. Henry did the usual trick to get rid of troublesome people: He sacked Grey, charged him with treason, and had him beheaded.

Under the new boss for Ireland, Sir Anthony St Ledger, things changed, and Henry set about trying to win the Irish over so they'd learn to love him a bit more. To do this Henry set out to make the Irish feel more secure in their position. So he introduced a 'surrender and re-grant' scheme, in which the

Irish would surrender all their land to the Crown, and in return they would be given a legal title to the land underwritten by the authority of the king. To sweeten the whole deal, the Irish were also given a nice new English title, such as earl or baron, that would make them feel loyalty towards Henry.

It sounds like a great deal, and in some ways it was. It didn't come without a price however. The new Irish lords had to contribute to the army, renounce the Papacy, accept the English legal system, and adopt English habits and manners.

Basically England was offering the Irish outside the Pale a choice. Be like us, and we'll recognise your authority and your wealth. . .or else.

Here's an example showing how the surrender and re-grant process worked. A lesser Irish chief, MacGillapatrick, agreed to enter the scheme. He renounced his Irish title, surrendered his land, and had them re-granted. He swore to use English habits and manners, and agreed to introduce English forms of agriculture and architecture to his lands. In return he was renamed the Baron of Upper Ossory and was given a seat in the upper house of the Irish parliament. A good deal, and one that secured his place in society, but it meant that he stopped using Irish ways in favour of English ways.

Henry, from Lord to King of Ireland

Henry had always had the title of lord of Ireland. Clearly as monarch he had plenty of authority. But he wasn't king. Given the removal of the Pope from the scene, and Henry's increase in position, the time was ripe for his promotion from the status of lord.

It was actually the Irish who suggested that Henry's title be changed from that of lord to King of Ireland. Henry blushed at the suggestion and told everyone that such an honour was quite unnecessary, but jumped at the chance.

The official business was done in the Dublin parliament in June 1541. Once passed, Henry and his heirs were given the title of king of the realm of Ireland. Two thousand people gathered in St Patrick's Cathedral in Dublin to take part in a celebratory mass. Three cheers for King Henry of Ireland!

But what did this new title actually mean? In effect it finished the whole surrender and re-grant process. With Henry as king, all the people in Ireland were now his subjects. They had a clear legal status and were part of an alliance between two kingdoms that were joined together by the crown.

The first parliament after the new title had come into force was well attended by the lords from across Ireland. All these local leaders, despite their continued reservations about changes in the Church, seemed content to accept the new situation and all seemed well.

It couldn't last, though. Wars in France and Scotland meant that the size of the army in Ireland was reduced. A new administration in Ireland was accused of provoking the Irish lords and another small rebellion broke out. Although it was easily put down, the rebellion of O Connor and O More in 1547 coincided with the death of Henry VIII.

He'd married lots of times, had set up his own Church, and become King of Ireland. Without him in charge how would Ireland fare? And there was still the ongoing Reformation to worry about. Ireland was in for some interesting times ahead.

Chapter 12

Religious Roundabouts and Irish Rebellion

*W*hen Henry VIII died women around the world must have breathed a sigh of relief. At least with him dead there was no chance he might marry them and chop their heads off. More seriously, the question of the Reformation remained. With Henry dead and the process of making England and Ireland Protestant incomplete, what would happen to the Reformation? Would his successors fall back in line and accept the authority of the Catholic Church, or would they forge ahead with their own version of religion?

These questions were really important in Ireland. In this chapter, you see how Henry's successors – son Edward and daughters Mary and Elizabeth – all had different ideas as to what do with the Reformation and, as a result, what they should do with Ireland.

Edward VI: Young, Sick, and Protestant

After Henry died he was initially succeeded by his son, Edward VI, who had two problems. First off he was very young, and so had to take advice off a varied group of powerful men who all said they had his best interests at heart (but they probably didn't). Second, he was a sickly boy and always had been. It was unlikely that Edward would last long, and he didn't. He only sat on the throne for six years, dying in 1553.

During his reign, however, Edward was a believer in what his Father had tried to do with his various Church reforms and carried on implementing the transformation to Protestantism. That was a problem for the Irish, as they simply didn't want to be pushed in that direction.

First gift to Ireland: A closed fist

Just as Henry was dying, the decision was made that trying to be nice to the Irish was pointless and so the powers-that-be implemented a policy of suppression and coercion. Edmund Bellingham, a military man, was given the post of Lord Deputy in Ireland, and he ran the place like an occupied country. He fought his way through the various counties east of the River Shannon and squashed any sign of rebellion against the Crown.

While Bellingham's policy of military intervention was successful (at least for the Crown), it was costly. By the time of Edward's death in 1553, England had spent around £250,000 in Ireland – the majority of it for the military excursion in Ireland. The significance of this? By 1551, there were some 2,600 troops more or less permanently based in Ireland. In addition, this kind of expenditure and commitment showed the real problem that faced the Crown: if the suppression of Ireland was your only policy option, you had to remember that it took serious amounts of money.

Second gift: The Book of Common Prayer

As well as stomping the army around Ireland and making sure everyone understood who was in charge, Bellingham also tried to enforce the religious aspects of the Reformation on Ireland in a much clearer fashion. To do this he introduced the *New Book of Common Prayer*. This was an entirely Protestant prayer book, and was designed to replace the Catholic one.

The new prayer book was written in English. Many people in Ireland still spoke Irish and could not, whether they wanted to or not, use the new prayer book. This led to a stark division between those who could adapt to the new ways (the Anglo-Irish and the English in Ireland) and those who could not (the Irish).

When Edward died there was a real problem for those who believed in the Reformation, and real hope for many of the Irish. The next in line was Henry's eldest daughter, Mary, who was a devout and practising Catholic.

Mary, Mary Quite Contrary – and Catholic

Mary had never seen eye-to-eye with her dad's reforms, and had, throughout her life, stayed true to her Catholic faith. As a result, her succession to the throne led to an exciting, although rather bloody period, called the counter-Reformation.

The counter-Reformation in Ireland

As soon as she was Queen, Mary took all the big jobs on offer. One of these was as supreme head of the Church of Ireland. Her view was quite straightforward: The Reformation that had been undertaken by her father and brother had been an aberration. She would simply cancel the whole thing and realign her kingdom with the Catholic Church and the Vatican.

In England and Scotland, the counter-Reformation was a bloody process. Mary and her agents rooted out the die-hard Protestants, and those who refused to convert back to Catholicism were killed. This led to a whole string of Protestant martyrs who would be venerated by the oppressed. In Ireland, however, there were no such martyrs. Everyone was quite happy to go back to the old ways of Catholicism. The ease of the transformation shows how ineffective the Reformation had been in Ireland anyway. Two key facts facilitated the smooth return to Catholicism in Ireland:

✓ **Ireland was still Catholic.** For all the chaos of the Reformation in Ireland and the violent ways in which it had been enforced (discussed in Chapter 11), it had been a largely unsuccessful project. The bulk of the Irish population supported the Catholic Church. Although the Catholic Church may have, to a degree, gone underground, it had never disappeared and had never been replaced by Protestantism. The only sections of the population who followed Protestantism were the English who arrived during Henry and Edward's time, or the Anglo-Irish who simply did what they were told to do. Ireland didn't have to learn how to become a Catholic country again under Mary, as it had never ceased to be one.

✓ **Protestantism never fully took control of the infrastructure that was supposed to make everyone loyal to the new religion.** One of the key ways that Henry had tried to enforce the Reformation was to mandate Protestant education at school and University level, but there weren't enough Protestant school teachers, and many of the men who actually educated the Irish were Catholic. In addition, Catholic universities and Jesuit colleges flourished across Europe. The sons of well-to-do Catholics were sent there. Such an education provided Catholicism in Ireland with future leaders and made this group immune to the charms of the Reformation.

The counter-Reformation was not simply a project that lasted the six years of Mary's reign. The Irish were convinced that they were on the right track in terms of religion, and would try to continue the process of counter-Reformation (or preserving Catholicism and resisting Protestantism) whoever was on the throne and whatever their beliefs.

A delicate balancing act: Divided loyalties

With the counter-Reformation, the situation in Ireland became more convoluted. Although the Irish were pretty pleased with the return of Catholicism, the Anglo-Irish and the English, who had gone along with Protestantism as faithful subjects of Henry VIII and Edward VI, now found themselves at cross-purposes with their new, Catholic monarch.

These three populations had to decide where their loyalties lay – with the Catholic Queen of England or elsewhere.

The Irish

During this period, the Irish had complex ideas about who they owed their loyalty to. Obviously, their first allegiance was to the Pope, as he was head of the Church, God's representative on earth, and a fully impressive kind of bloke. But what of their allegiance to England? English monarchs still wielded legal and civic authority over Ireland. As a Catholic, Mary was certainly more palatable to the Irish than Edward VI had been, but someday (in the not too distant future, in fact; see the section 'Elizabeth, the Virgin – and Protestant – Queen') she would be gone and someone else would be in charge. So what was a good Irish Catholic to do if the day came when, once again, a Protestant English monarch sat on the throne?

Why, be politically pragmatic, of course. Many Irish saw themselves as primarily Catholic, but they also accepted that the English Crown was the legal and civic authority that they owed allegiance to. This position was bolstered by the Pope, who, until 1570 (when he excommunicated Elizabeth), argued that the Irish should not get involved in rebellion, even if the monarch in question was heretical (code for Protestant).Until the later decades of Elizabeth's reign, the Irish wanted recognition and respect for their religious rites, and did not necessarily want the overthrow of the (Protestant) Crown.

The Anglo-Irish

The Anglo-Irish were in a difficult position, as they always seemed to be. They were certainly loyal to the idea of having a monarch, and believed in the value of a close relationship between England and Ireland. But many of them had remained true to the Catholic faith and had rejected the changes brought about by the reformation. They liked what happened under Mary, but wouldn't be so sure of themselves once Elizabeth was on the throne.

The English settlers

The English settlers, as the most recent arrivals in Ireland, usually reflected whatever was in vogue in England. They hadn't been in Ireland long enough to have their way of doing things transformed by the Irish. As such most of the English in Ireland believed in the reformation as it had been carried out under Henry, they were lukewarm on the changes that Mary brought in, and didn't like the idea of a return to Catholicism. They were delighted when she died and Elizabeth took over.

The death of Mary

Mary died in 1559. Elizabeth was now heir to the throne. Although they may have been sisters, Mary and Elizabeth didn't like each other very much. They had different mothers (Mary's mother was Catherine of Aragon; Elizabeth's mum was Anne Boleyn, the woman Henry threw Catherine over for), widely opposing views on their father (Mary thought Henry a heretic, while Elizabeth saw him as a hero), and totally incompatible religious beliefs (Mary was Catholic, Elizabeth was Protestant).

So when Mary died and Elizabeth took over, the Catholics in England and Ireland rightly feared what the new Queen might do to them. Although they may have wanted to stop her accession, they simply weren't powerful enough to do so.

Mary was buried and with her, despite some sterling resistance during Elizabeth's reign, was buried the last real hopes that England could ever again be a Catholic country. Resistance to the onward march of Protestantism as the state religion would happen in Ireland where Catholicism was strongest. During Elizabeth's reign there was a steady realisation that a belief in the Catholic Church was not compatible with support for the English Crown in Ireland.

Elizabeth, the Virgin – and Protestant – Queen

Elizabeth was a tough cookie. This was the Queen who would see through the Reformation in England, send men around the world to find new territories for her country (she got potatoes and tobacco from a small place called America), and, in her finest hour, saw off the Spanish who wanted to throw her off the throne. In the same way that her father is still seen as one of the great Kings, Elizabeth was, without doubt, the greatest English Queen. Not that she'd be that popular in Ireland though!

When Elizabeth came to the throne, she had to deal with the same problems that English monarchs before her had to deal with. The Irish were resentful of the way that Ireland was ruled by force, and becoming increasingly so, and no one felt secure. And the Anglo-Irish didn't like the newly-arrived English who were all very aggressive and didn't understand the complexities of Ireland. In addition to these seemingly never-ending problems, Elizabeth also faced the problems relating to the religious upheaval of the past years. Ireland had resisted the first Reformation, loved the period under Catholic Queen Mary, and would undoubtedly resist any attempts to return to Protestantism.

Ireland was a complex enough place for England to run and manage without any interference from outside, but Elizabeth and her advisors had to be wary of the threat that Ireland posed as a potential ally for enemies such as Catholic France and Spain. These countries didn't like the power that England had anyway, but the fact that the English had rejected the authority of the Pope just heightened the animosity.

Elizabeth would stay on the throne from 1559 until her death in 1603. The fact that she was in control for nearly half a century gave the Crown a period of stability and continuity that it had not known for a long time. Unlike the quick switches between Edward and Mary, and then Mary and Elizabeth, all in the space of just over a decade, the Elizabethan era was long, and the control that the Crown brought to bear impressive. With such longevity and stability, Elizabeth was able to work through her ideas, see off her opponents, and bring her will to bear in a way that neither Edward nor Mary had been able to do. The length of her reign also meant that the Irish – especially those who wished to resist the renewed Reformation – were facing a more powerful and wily opponent.

What to do in Ireland? Carry on

So, when Elizabeth came to power, in addition to her many other problems, the big question facing her was what to do about Ireland. Three options were open to her:

- ✔ **Just give up.** Accept that the Irish were difficult and didn't much care for the Crown or Protestantism, so leave, and just let them get on with whatever it was they wanted to do.

- ✔ **Take over completely.** The problem for Elizabeth, indeed all English monarchs of the period, was that no one had ever fully taken over and suppressed Ireland. Rather than having it as a festering boil next door, the answer could be to attack the irritating parts of Ireland that refused to be loyal, and put enough troops and civil servants in there to run the place properly.

> ✔ **Carry on as before.** The English had been suppressing Ireland for years. It only worked at the margins, and only meant that you only really controlled the Pale (the area round Dublin). Outside that area, anything could happen as the Irish were always busy causing trouble!

The first and second options, as logical as they may have been, were off the agenda for Elizabeth. The first potentially left Ireland open to occupation by either the French or the Spanish, and they might then use Ireland as a launching pad for an invasion of England. The second was just too expensive. To take over and suppress the whole of Ireland was a complex and costly business that no one had the stomach for, or could really afford. So Elizabeth decided that the last option was best: carry on as before, keeping the Irish in place and defending what the Crown had.

The first challenge to Elizabeth's resolve came from a man called Shane O Neill who wanted to inherit the title of Earl of Tyrone that had become vacant. O Neill challenged royal authority and made clear to Elizabeth just how difficult Ireland could be.

Trouble in Tyrone: Shane O Neill

Conn O Neill had ruled over Tyrone and accepted the inevitability of royal rule. When he died in 1559, he had no clear direct successor. Shane O Neill, a legitimate relative of Conn's, stepped forward to claim what he saw as his birthright.

While Shane's claim was good, it presented a problem for England. Shane didn't want to sign up to a cosy relationship with the authority of the Crown. He wanted to step backwards and rule Tyrone as a traditional Irish king or chieftain.

Although the decades before Elizabethan rule had seen the steady development of royal authority, and an acceptance by the Irish of English titles and land charters, the old ways had not been completely killed off. The Irish were still keen on the old ways. Although they had new titles such as earl or baron, they often ruled over land that had been held by their families for centuries. There was always a chance that the Irish would try to turn the clock back and seek authority on their own terms rather than have it underwritten by the Crown.

When it became clear that Shane wouldn't accept the norms of English law, and would pursue a specifically Irish direction, the authorities decided that he could not inherit the title. Instead in May 1560, it was given to his nephew, who was recognised with the official, English-styled title of the Earl of Dungannon. Shane was incensed. But what do you do in the face of royal authority?

Dearest Elizabeth . . .

Shane wrote a nice letter (actually a whole series of them) to Elizabeth asking if he could visit and discuss things. Flattering though his approaches were, the Earl of Sussex, the Lord Deputy in Ireland, had seen enough and moved against Shane.

Sussex invaded Ulster and defeated Shane in a series of battles. But Shane rallied and then beat Sussex and his army a few times. Fed up, Sussex tried to have Shane assassinated but this failed too. And so, with the two opposing sides at an effective stalemate, Shane was given an invite to meet the Queen in London.

This story is important as it shows, no matter what the Crown wished to do in Ireland, its authority was far from complete. Shane was initially rejected, and then launched a counter-attack. Despite this clear attempt to enforce the English will on Ireland, Shane successfully resisted, and the English had to start talking to him. This was not supposed to be the way that royal authority functioned in Ireland.

Dearest Philip of France . . .

Once in London Shane met the Queen, and had his authority recognised, though not fully, and neither was he given the title of earl. Shane returned to Ireland believing that he had shown the English a thing or two, and the Crown just had to cross their fingers and hope that he wouldn't misbehave when he returned home. Not a chance!

Once back home Shane marched on his only rivals in Ulster, the O Donnells, and attacked them. Then, in a boldly reckless move, he asked the King of France for 6,000 troops to expel the English from Ireland and offered to become a French subject.

The English had long feared that the Irish were disloyal and would allow the island to be used as a launching pad for a foreign invasion. France was one of England's great enemies, and Shane's request for French help to expel the English from Ireland was clearly an act of treachery. While the English might allow Ireland to be a chaotic place internally, they would not stand for any potential foreign involvement.

Shane's head on a pike

By this time there was a new Lord Deputy in Ireland, Sir Henry Sidney. He had a radical plan for Ireland that might finally bring the place under control. Sidney argued that Ulster had always been the real problem in Ireland, and that Shane was just the latest in a long line of annoying Ulstermen. To deal with this problem Sidney suggested defeating Shane and removing the Irish from their positions in Ulster. English colonists, who would be completely loyal to the Crown, would replace the displaced Irish. Sidney knew that his plan would be a messy and difficult business, and he wanted the full support of the government, a whole heap of cash, and a big army. Which he got.

In 1565 Sidney took a large army to Ulster and won a series of battles. He didn't get the pleasure of defeating Shane himself, however, because Shane had been killed by someone else while he sat eating his dinner at a banquet. As the symbol of disloyalty in Ireland Shane's head was taken to Dublin where it was put on display on the Castle walls. It's claimed it was still there four years later!

After Shane

Sidney had been successful in crushing and killing Shane O Neill. He even had the Dublin parliament declare, in 1569, that the O Neill family ceased to exist and held no power or authority. But could he make his plan for conquest actually work? Theoretically it could have. In actuality, it didn't.

Shane's successor in Tyrone was a relative called Turloch Luineach. He accepted the Queen as boss, but married a Scottish woman who arrived with 1,200 galloglas (angry looking Scottish soldiers) in tow. As Turloch also gathered a force of 3,000 together, a large part of Ulster was quickly under the control of an armed Irish chief again, and Sidney's big idea had stalled before he had started.

New goal: Conquering Ireland

Although Sidney had failed to instantly enforce some new kind of order on Ulster, he had big plans for Ireland. They involved:

- The creation of new Presidency Councils that would govern Munster and Connacht.
- Colonising Ireland with loyal English people, funded by private enterprise rather than by the Crown.
- The full enforcement of English common law and the prohibition of the traditional laws that the Irish had always used (called the *brehon* laws).

Sidney's plan was a bold one. The aim was (as had been tried many times before) to make the Irish fully respect the power and authority of the Crown and of English law. It differed from other plans in an important way: This plan wasn't simply an attack on the Irish, but also the Anglo-Irish. There were to be no halfway houses in the future. Everyone would have to adapt to the new way of doing things, or else face the full force of English military power and the law.

Sidney's idea of conquest was an important one. Ireland had never been fully conquered and controlled, even though the English had been there since the twelfth century. The reforms he would institute in the implementation of his plan formed the bedrock of the Elizabethan reorganisation of Ireland. But Sidney's changes weren't simply about getting Ireland organised and less troublesome. They were also about proving the supremacy of Protestantism, and the men who came from England to administer or run military campaigns in Ireland were Protestants. They believed fully in the process of the Reformation, and saw the Irish adherence to Catholicism as completely wrong. The religious practices that Catholics followed were seen as acts of superstition; idolatrous and barbarous. The Irish were viewed, because of their religion, as a savage people. Normal civil law wouldn't work on them because of their beliefs. The only thing they would understand would be the use of force as they were thought of as being more like animals than civilised people. And they treated them accordingly.

If the English wanted to control Ireland, it would have to invest a lot of money and commit a big army to the problem. Without such a commitment Ireland would remain a constant source of concern and potential military uprising. The big question was whether the Elizabethans were up to the job. Most historians accept that militarily the Elizabethans could have taken Ireland if they had wished, but argue that other concerns, such as the war against Spain, always stopped them from fully committing the necessary resources to Ireland until it was absolutely necessary.

Reforms and reprisal in Connacht

The Presidency was established in Connacht in 1569. All Irish laws were banned, and the land reorganised so that it was arranged into shires. All the landholders were forced to go along with the new way of doing things and to promise their future good behaviour.

Although changing a culture by legislation and might is never going to be a smooth process, matters were made worse in Ireland by Sir Francis Fitton, the man charged with carrying through the reforms.

Fitton travelled across Connacht destroying all things Catholic that he could lay his hands on. He destroyed Catholic shrines, attacked the images that he found distasteful in Churches, and closed the monasteries at Athenry and Kilconnell. The changes that were being introduced to Ireland were never going to be popular, but the attacks on Catholicism made the whole thing seem worse for the Irish.

Elsewhere

In other places across the country, the changes were enforced. Irish law was banned, chieftains were made to submit, and all the Irish lords had their power restricted. Troops were swiftly employed against anyone who dared oppose the new world order. Previously, Irish lords had paid a tribute to the English in the form of goods. By this time a system of coinage was well-established, and the payment was transformed into a money rent. It still meant that the Irish were paying the English, but it showed how the economy had moved on.

Big problems in Munster

It was obvious that all these changes weren't going to go unchallenged. The Irish were having a new system of land ownership, law, and government forced on them, and the whole process was accompanied by the use or threat of violence. To make matters worse, the process was underpinned by the religious fervour of the Protestant English who believed totally in the Reformation and objected wholeheartedly to the Irish belief in Catholicism.

During the 1560s small rebellions started in Munster, but were put down relatively easily. The most important rebellion was led by James Fitzmaurice Fitzgerald (from Munster, and the cousin of the Earl of Desmond). He wasn't only fed up with the English changes to the old way of doing things, and their constant need to throw their weight about, he was really fed up with the religious dynamic of the changes. He even called the Queen a heretic, for trying to make the Irish follow a Church that God himself didn't agree with.

If you believe this strongly but have no real hope of defeating the English military, you're probably going to ask for outside help. That's what James Fitzgerald did.

From Munster to Spain: You are cordially invited . . .

As the religious figurehead of Fitzgerald's potential rebellion, the Archbishop of Cashel travelled to Spain and asked for the help of the King of Spain, Philip II. The Archbishop asked him to come to Ireland to defend the Catholic faith and condemn the Reformation and the heresy of Henry VII, Edward VI, and Elizabeth. In exchange, allegiance would be given to any Catholic prince whom Philip nominated.

Nothing happened immediately, but this was a huge step. The Irish were actively inviting the Spanish to come into Ireland and fight a religious war against Protestant England.

The Queen's man Humphrey in Munster

Before any response came from Spain, the localised rebellion in Munster was tackled by Humphrey Gilbert (1537–83). He suppressed the rebellion by force and ruled Munster through intimidation and violence. He declared that anyone who refused to acknowledge the new laws would be killed and that any rebel building would be attacked and burnt to the ground.

Gilbert clearly didn't like the Irish, and was keen on making them understand who was boss. He killed lots of people because they disobeyed him, and the story is told that he cut all their heads off and collected them together. Once he had a good pile of heads, he would lay them out on either side of the pathway that led to his tent. Anyone visiting him would have to walk down an avenue of dead and slowly rotting heads. He claimed that this would bring 'great terror to the people when they saw the heads of their dead fathers, brothers, children, kinsfolk, and friends'. Clearly Gilbert was a horrid man, but whether or not he left heads by his doorstep is another matter. First of all they would have smelt terribly, but it's also likely that the story emerged as a way of discrediting the English presence in Ireland.

Invasion Number 1: A bust

In July 1579, James Fitzmaurice Fitzgerald returned to Munster to lead a big rebellion against the English. Sadly for him the Spanish had never really taken up the idea of invading Ireland, and he only managed to gather together one ship, seventy men, and a Spanish friar. He called for an Irish rebellion against Elizabeth in the name of the Pope. Everyone ignored him, and he was killed soon afterwards in a skirmish with his local rivals.

Invasion Number 2: Another bust

In September, 1580 the Spanish finally arrived. Along with some Italians, the combined force was going to fight for the Pope in Ireland. They landed in Smerwick harbour, but the force of 600 men was soon cornered by the English. They did the noble thing and surrendered. The newly arrived English Lord Deputy, Lord Grey, accepted the surrender and then had all the Spaniards and Italians killed. Grey was ruthless.

Rebellion in Ulster

Ulster had always been a problem. The English had never quite got hold of the place, had never successfully settled it, and simply failed to control the various families who ruled over it. In 1573 the Earl of Essex led an expedition to colonise Ulster. You can imagine how the folks in Ulster felt about his plans, but Essex was ruthless. He had one of the leaders of Ulster, Sir Brian O Neill executed, and killed 200 of Brian's followers. He also developed a reputation for killing women and children. Not a nice man and everyone was very happy when he died in 1575.

Given that Essex had taught everyone in Ulster to quite dislike the English, how could the power of the Crown be brought to bear on the area? Who would ensure that Ulster was a manageable place, and not a chaotic seat of the next rebellion?

The man that the English turned to was Hugh O Neill. He was a descendant of the great O Neill clan, but had been educated in England and was, in terms of dress and custom, English rather than Irish. He appeared loyal to the Queen, had worked in Munster for the English, and had even assisted Essex during his colonisation of Ulster. What could be better for the English than an Ulsterman who seemed more loyal to the Crown than he did to his ancient family heritage? They signed him up, and gave him, in 1587, the title of the Earl of Tyrone. Perhaps Hugh O Neill would be the man to make Ulster loyal (and if not loyal to England, at least quiet).

How wrong they were . . . how very, very wrong!

The worm turns

When loyal subject and Irishman Hugh O Neill, newly minted as the Earl of Tyrone, took over control of Ulster at the behest of the English, he did exactly what they were hoping him to do. He was all very loyal: He married well to a nice girl from another family loyal to the Crown, was nice to the Queen, and helped out the English army in Ireland. But then, O Neill turned on the English:

- ✔ He fought the English army (which was actually headed by his brother-in-law) and defeated them at Clontibret.

- ✔ He built an alliance of Ulster chieftains, of which he was the head, to fight against the English.

- ✔ He started writing to the King of Spain asking him for support in his struggle to defend Catholicism and defeat England.

Throughout the years of Elizabeth's rule, the Irish had begun looking to Spain for support. The thinking was simple. Ireland was a Catholic country and so was Spain. The Spanish hated the English and so did the Irish. If the two countries could be brought together in a single force, they could take on the English in Ireland. If they were successful they would save Ireland from Protestantism, and pose a serious threat to English authority.

The rebellion spread across Ireland, and O Neill, who had once been seen as the ideal man to bring the Irish round to the English way of things, was declared a traitor by the Crown. What happened?

At this time, it was common for powerful people and families in Ireland to take on English habits and customs. This wasn't necessarily because they wanted to be English, but because they understood how to get ahead in society. If they wandered round in animal furs, looking all dangerous and Irish, then the English would give them a hard time. If they had at least the appearance of the English and some of their manners, they'd have a quiet life and their local power base would be secure.

The rebellion spreads

The rebellious forces were caught up in the excitement of the possibilities that O Neill's leadership promised them. First all the Ulster chiefs joined with O Neill. Then the Irish leadership in Munster and Leinster joined them after O Neill had appealed to them directly to defend Catholicism.

By 1595, England was facing its most serious and complete rebellion in Ireland since the time of the Norman invasion. By 1598 O Neill had defeated another major English force at the battle of the Yellow Ford in County Armagh, and Connacht joined in the rebellion. Outside of the Pale, there was no part of Ireland that wasn't rebelling. O Neill had emerged as the great Irish leader who could potentially drive England out of Ireland.

This was not just a rebellion of the Irish. It was the most sustained and powerful military act of counter-Reformation of the whole era.

The unsuccessful English response

Clearly the English weren't going to take the rebellion lying down. They were somewhat annoyed about O Neill's uprising, and the threat that it posed, given England's ongoing problems with Spain and the wars they were fighting.

England decided that the only response was a military one. During the winter of 1598–9 the English sent an extra 10,000 troops to Ireland. Elizabeth appointed a new chief governor, Robert Devereux, the Earl of Essex. When he sailed to Ireland an additional 17,000 men went with him. This was the largest ever force to enter Ireland.

There was a problem though. Essex was as about as much use in a military campaign as an umbrella is in a tornado. His forces were regularly defeated by the Irish, and within a few months he had to agree to a truce with O Neill. He was charged with treason when he returned to England, and Ireland was still in open rebellion and had the upper hand.

Madeira for everyone! The Spanish arrive

O Neill had been constantly negotiating with the Spanish. In 1596 Spain had sent arms and ammunition to the Irish and had landed briefly in Donegal to make the delivery. In October that year a fleet had sailed to take part in the rebellion but bad weather forced them back.

Although the English, under Sir Francis Drake, had seen off the Spanish Armada in 1588, Spain was far from a spent force. Arms were sent to Ireland again in 1599 and 1600.

In 1601 the decision was made to send a force to Ireland to assist the rebellion.

Spanish interest in Ireland wasn't particularly driven by a love of Ireland. It was more to do with the balance of global politics between the two biggest powers of the time – Spain and England. And the Spanish badly wanted to defeat the English. Any defeat they could inflict would be welcomed. They felt that by assisting the Irish they would not only defeat England on Irish soil, but also badly weaken the country. The Spanish felt that a victory in Ireland would badly dent the English fighting spirit and make Spanish holdings elsewhere in the world, for example in the Caribbean, more secure.

In September 1601 Spanish forces, amounting to approximately 2,500 men, landed at Kinsale (they'd lost a lot of ships and men on the way because of bad weather). The Spanish were poorly equipped, badly served in terms of supplies, and suffering from disease. Despite the threat that a Spanish army in Ireland should have posed, this one was far from scary.

Their presence managed to spark a rebellion in west Cork, but by then the English had got wind that the Spanish were in town and were determined to do something about it.

England versus the Spanish and Irish combined team

The English decided that the threat from the Spanish and Irish team was serious and chose to put their best squad onto the field. Lord Mountjoy and Sir George Carew became the captains of the English team, and had 4,000 men on their side. Carew didn't have much luck against O Neill's forces, but everywhere he went he destroyed things. The idea was simple – burn the houses and the crops, and the population would go hungry. Once starving, they'd fall into line. It was harsh, but effective, sapping the will of the Irish population.

Quickly the Irish started submitting, and the English started reclaiming control of the country. Mountjoy figured out that the Spanish would land in Munster, and left the rest of Ireland open while he diverted his forces there. He believed that if the English could defeat the Spanish, the Irish ability to effectively rebel would be severely dented.

Faced with the large English army under Mountjoy, the Spanish decided that fighting was pointless. They apologised profusely for any inconvenience caused and were allowed to go home quietly.

England won the match. The Spanish never really entered the field of play, and without one half of their team, the Irish were in a hopeless position. In October 1603 O Neill surrendered and the rebellion was over.

Just as the Battle of Kinsale – that never really was – came to a close and the Spanish went home, Queen Elizabeth died.

The flight of the earls

Whereas the Spanish had been able to say a simple, 'So sorry for the trouble' and been allowed to go home, the Irish weren't so lucky. At the end of their failed rebellion, the English forced through many of the reforms that they had long desired. The Irish who had rebelled were stripped of their titles and land, which were then granted to loyal Irishmen or given to incoming Englishmen.

In addition, in March 1604 a law was passed that declared that all the Irish were subjects of the King of England and not any local lords or chiefs. The days of the Irish kings and lords had, in law at least, come to an end.

By the end of the summer of 1607, many of the old Irish leaders, and those who had led the rebellion, knew there was no place for them in Ireland. They gathered together at Lough Swilly and sailed away from Ireland forever and headed for Rome. Known as the flight of the earls, this departure left Ireland, and especially Ulster, without a local and traditional leadership. England, it seemed, had finally gained the upper hand.

Chapter 13

James I and the Plantations; Charles I and Chaos

*A*fter trying and subsequently failing to upset the English apple-cart with the help of the Spanish (see Chapter 12), the death of Queen Elizabeth meant that the Irish had to face life under a new monarch – James I. James offered a lot to the Irish, but failed to deliver. What he did carry on was a system that Queen Elizabeth had started – swamping Ireland with loyal subjects from England and Scotland so as to finally gain control of the unruly island (they had finally figured out that beating the Irish into submission wasn't working).

The idea was that these new settlers, known as the *planters*, would buy land, make it profitable, and become the loyal heart of Ireland. At least that was the idea, anyway. As you can imagine, the Irish didn't much care for the Plantation system.

This chapter also looks at how the dashing King Charles I took the throne in England, and the effect that this had in Ireland. Despite his good looks, Charles was a difficult character, and many people didn't like him. In opposition emerged warty Oliver Cromwell, about whom you can read more in Chapter 14, one of the most despised figures in the whole history of Ireland.

James I and Ireland

James I started life in Scotland. He was born in 1566 and was the heir to the Scottish throne. In 1567 he became James VI, the King of Scotland. James was also Elizabeth I's cousin. When she made it clear that she wasn't going to have a man in her life (and therefore no children), James was first in line to inherit the throne of England as well as Scotland.

James' succession was a potential difficulty. He was Scottish and, although brought up Protestant himself, had connections with the Catholic Church because of his mother's (Mary Queen of Scots) fervent Catholic beliefs. For the English who had spent much of the last century fighting against Scotland and the previous decades battling through the Reformation, the whole idea of James as King of England was, quite frankly, a little bit scary.

That said, when Elizabeth died in 1603, James became James I, King of England. In one move, the kingdoms of England and Scotland were united under a common monarch.

The fractious Irish populations

When James came to the throne, he was the first monarch in history to reign over England, Scotland, and Ireland simultaneously.

James really encouraged the plantation scheme – the settling of English families on Irish land (see the later section 'The Plantation System' for details on this scheme) – and as such introduced a new population to Ireland. These three groups made a potentially explosive mix:

✔ **The Planters:** The newest population, arriving in Ireland to take advantage of the plantation scheme, was mainly from Scotland and England. They were a combination of Protestants and Presbyterians and very loyal to the Crown and their religion. Certainly the Crown saw the planters as its most avid supporters in Ireland.

✔ **The Old English:** These people (who used to be called the Anglo-Irish) had been around for ages, and were the descendants of all the families who had settled in Ireland over the centuries. They were loyal to the Crown, and many had converted to Protestantism – others remained Catholic. But they were also a source of suspicion for the English as they had often seemed to adopt Irish ways and customs. They had land holdings, but had often lost land to the plantation scheme and as a result were often ambivalent to the new population.

✔ **The Irish:** The biggest group in the population. Nearly all Catholic, many of the Irish accepted the authority of the Crown, but just hated many of the English changes such as the plantation scheme and the laws outlawing Irish culture (refer to Chapter 8) that they saw as unfair. They had little effective political power, and were at the bottom of the ladder.

These three populations were divided in many ways. Sources of contention included their religious differences, how much the Crown trusted them, their access to land and wealth, and their access to political power.

Saving Catholics from their addiction

The religious difficulty for James in Ireland was that, although the majority of the population was Catholic, the minority Protestant population, which happened to hold the political power, made very clear that, in their opinion, Protestantism was superior.

The Reformation hadn't been fought for nothing. As head of state and leader of the Church, James's job was to promote the Protestant religion by continuing the work of Henry VIII and Elizabeth I to ensure that the whole kingdom, including Ireland, was Protestant.

In 1605, the Protestant Church of Ireland demanded that the attack on Catholics continue. They claimed that many people in the country were 'addicted to Popery', and wanted that changing. The government acted and:

✔ Banished Catholic priests.

✔ Made attendance at Protestant Church services compulsory.

✔ Fined anyone not attending Protestant services twelve pence.

For a while this compulsory Church attendance seems to have worked, but then after a while, the fuss died down and, across Ireland, the Catholic Church continued to function.

To get round all the legal restrictions on Catholic worship, the Catholic Church:

✔ Organised Mass in private houses and chapels (the Protestants had taken over the church buildings).

✔ Quietly re-established the parish system and allocated priests to each parish.

✔ Employed priests as 'singing men' at celebrations and funerals. Clearly they were there in a religious capacity, but the renaming of their function kept them free of the authorities.

Despite all this religious fervour and debate, the people who lived in Ireland at the time weren't teetotal. In 1611 Ireland's first ever public house licence was granted and the great tradition of the pub started. 'Cheers!', they all said (or in Irish, 'Sláinte!')

Power plays in Parliament

The only Irish parliament of James's reign sat in 1613. In the run up to the parliament it looked as if the Old English would cause problems. They were unhappy about the restrictions being placed on Catholics and all the religious fervour of the new settler population and wanted to see more liberal laws brought in.

To stop a move towards liberal laws for Catholics (which would potentially bring Ireland into conflict with the resolutely Protestant English parliament), James stacked the numbers in his favour by creating 40 new parliamentary seats. These were the so called 'rotten boroughs' which had small electorates and voted always in favour of the government (democracy was a rare thing in the seventeenth century). With all these new members of parliament duly elected, all of whom were Protestant, the Catholics were left in a minority in parliament.

At the start of the 1613 parliament there was a dispute over who should act as the Speaker (the person in charge of proceedings). John Everard, a member of the Old English, decided that the job was his so he took the chair. His rival for the post, Sir John Davies, didn't quite know what to do, so he decided that he would sit on the chair too. The Irish parliament was faced with the sight of Davies sitting in the lap of Everard, with both of them claiming that the Speaker's role was theirs. Eventually Everard was removed, and Davies was able to get on with the job.

After the dispute over who should be Speaker in the parliament, and the ejection of Everard, all the Catholic members of parliament walked out fearing that the whole parliamentary session would attack Catholics.

James agreed with them, and had all the anti-Catholic legislation for the parliament withdrawn. James had shown that, despite his responsibility to the Protestant Church, he was fully aware of the situation on the ground in Ireland. Great swathes of anti-Catholic legislation would only lead to trouble, and that's something that James wanted to avoid.

Remember, Remember the 5th of November

Much beloved by children in Britain, November 5th is Bonfire Night. It actually celebrates the gunpowder plot, and the attempt of Guy Fawkes to blow up the English parliament on the day James was due to make an appearance. The goal of the gunpowder plot was to kill the King, and take large numbers of parliamentarians with him, in the name of Catholicism. The assassinations failed (the plot was discovered before the gunpowder could be lit), and Fawkes and his fellow conspirators were hunted down, captured, and executed. The whole episode made James very wary of Catholic plots against him and quite paranoid. Although the 5th November is now a harmless night of loud bangs and colourful explosions in the sky, it actually celebrates the successful foiling of the plot and the execution of Guy Fawkes. The Guy on top of bonfires is the embodiment of Guy Fawkes. The whole 5th November celebration has its roots in the failure of Guy Fawkes and his Catholic plot. No wonder that they don't celebrate bonfire night in Ireland.

James is dead

In 1625 James I died. He hadn't had a bad innings, and compared with some of the kings that the Irish had dealt with, he hadn't done too badly by them. The process of plantation was ongoing, and would be his lasting legacy in Ireland. Although he'd given the Irish thousands of planters (for which they were no doubt ungrateful), he'd also tried to be, within the context of Reformation politics, fair-minded in his approach to Catholics.

James was succeeded by his son, Charles I, who went down in history as the King who was executed in Britain's only serious anti-monarchy revolution. But it would take more than twenty years before he met his grisly end, and in the intervening time he had a profound effect on Ireland.

The Plantation System

For all the English armies that had been sent to Ireland since the time of the Norman invasion, the conquest of the country had never been successfully achieved. All too often, England sent in the troops, sorted out whatever rebellion or difficult Irish king was causing them problems, and went home again. Many of the English settlers who did stay found themselves isolated and facing aggressive Irishmen on the borders of their land. For all the riches and opportunity that Ireland might offer, it wasn't actually a very attractive place to live – far too unstable. Many settlers retreated to the safer lands around Dublin, merged with their Irish neighbours, or simply packed up and went home.

The result was that the only parts of Ireland that England could rightly claim it controlled were those areas in the Pale. Beyond that, Ireland still belonged to the Irish, regardless of what the English monarchs might have tried to claim. After having suffered one too many rebellions, the last one involving the Spanish, the English, or more specifically Queen Elizabeth, had had enough. She wanted some stability, and if she couldn't get it militarily, which she obviously couldn't, she'd get it another way. Hence the plantation system was born.

The plantation idea was quite simple:

- The Crown divided land up into blocks of 12,000, 8,000, 6,000 or 4,000 acres. Where did it get the land you may ask? England owned some of it; what it didn't own, it simply took from the Irish.

- Undertakers, who were in charge of the scheme, were to run the land. Their job was to find tenants, but – and this is a big but – they had to promise that they wouldn't lease land to the Irish.

- Families would be found in England who were willing to take their chances in Ireland, and they would be shipped over to their new homes.

If the scheme worked, then Ireland would be full of happy, industrious English families. If they lived off the land successfully, they would bring stability to the country, enhance the strength of the Crown in Ireland, and most of all they would be loyal to the Crown and Protestantism. And best of all, in English eyes, the Irish would be kept off the land.

Alas, the Elizabethan plantations were a disaster. For Elizabeth the problems were:

- This was social engineering on a grand scale. To make it work, all the instruments of government had to be fully behind it and aware of their responsibilities. Elizabethan central government wasn't up to the task.

- The Irish who had lost land that was to be provided for plantation were able to petition to have it returned. Despite the aim of the scheme being the wholesale importation of English people to Ireland, the Irish kept winning their petitions and getting their land back.

- The undertakers struggled to get English families who wanted to take the risk of moving. As a result, they carried on renting land to the Irish, which defeated the whole idea of the scheme.

- Under Elizabeth, Ireland wasn't stable enough to attract people, nor allow such a grand scheme as this to be put in place.

Although a disaster for Elizabeth, her experience gave King James a blueprint to work from and showed him what pitfalls to watch out for. In addition, by the time James came to the throne, the rebellious earls had fled (see Chapter 12), and the situation in Ireland was, in theory, much brighter. James decided to go ahead with a wholesale plantation scheme.

The first plantations in Ulster

With the rebellious earls that had challenged Elizabeth gone, the Crown claimed all their land in Ulster. This was a big coup for the Crown. It had long struggled to maintain any kind of order in Ulster. Now the very men who had caused them so many problems had simply gone away and left all their lovely land behind. It was Sir Arthur Chichester who had the big idea for the Ulster plantations. He argued that plantation was a great idea because:

✔ It would bring about better cultivation of the land. New settlers would know more about modern farming than the Irish.

✔ If the settlers were drawn from the loyal people of Scotland and England, then Ireland would be civilised and it would also have lots of people who weren't Catholic.

✔ If land was given to men who had loyally served in the English army – he called them *servitors* – they'd be useful for defending the whole scheme.

✔ There was so much land available in Ulster that the Crown could give the native Irish as much land as they wanted (so long as they paid their rents). That would mean that the Irish wouldn't be so upset about the new arrivals.

In 1608, parliament declared officially that all the land previously held by the earls was now the property of the Crown. It was all surveyed, divided up into plots, and by 1610 was ready for distribution for plantation.

Ireland's first survey

Before you can go and start giving land away, you have to know exactly what it is you actually have to give. While there had been maps of Ireland before, these weren't very precise.

For the process of plantation, exact maps had to be drawn up. The Crown needed to know exactly where the boundaries were between different plots that they were giving away, where those plots were, and what kind of lands they consisted of. It was a big job.

The land that was going to be planted was in six counties: Tyrone, Donegal, Armagh, Fermanagh, Cavan, and Derry.

The first survey was done in 1608, but was such a bad job (they got all the maps wrong so that they couldn't be worked from), that the whole thing had to be redone in 1609. This time they got it right. All the six counties were visited by cartographers (map drawers) between August and September 1609, and the work finally finished with the drawing of Cavan. The maps were very detailed, and covered in comments that explained all the drawn detail and local conditions. By March 1610 the maps were in their final form and in London, ready to be worked from.

The man in charge of the whole survey was so pleased with his work that he recorded that 'the most obscure and unknown part of the King's dominions is now as well-known and particularly described as any part of England'.

So with the maps in place, all that had to be done now was divide it up, move the people over, sit back, and watch the whole thing work.

The Beginners' Guide to Plantation

Okay, the land is owned by the Crown, maps have been drawn up to show exact boundaries and terrain, and everybody agrees that the whole plantation thing is a really, really good idea. So how does it work?

Who Can Have Land?

There were three classes of people that it was agreed could have land:

- ✔ **English and Scottish undertakers** who would be responsible for the plantation of the land given to them. Undertakers were often investors who saw the chance of making a quick buck. To make it work they had to ensure that they got people out of England and Scotland and on to the land.

- ✔ **Servitors,** mainly ex-soldiers who had served the Crown in Ireland. This land was a reward for them – think of it as their pension.

- ✔ **Native Irish.** The Irish, like everyone else involved, had to recognise the English Crown and promise to be loyal to it always.

Sir Arthur Chichester had suggested that the Irish should have as much land as they wanted as this would make them think better of the whole scheme. In actuality, the Irish were severely restricted in the lands that they could access and began to feel that the whole scheme was more of an invasion that made them lose land, rather than a plantation from which they benefited.

Plantation system rule-book

To ensure that the whole scheme ran properly, and that people actually made a go of it, the rules for the planters were very strict. They had lots of obligations to ensure that they stayed on the land and made it profitable.

- ✔ Each undertaker had to, within three years, build a stone house, a fortified yard, and get 24 able bodied men from England and Scotland planted onto each 1,000 acres that he owned.

- ✔ Everyone had to pay rent. These were deferred for the first few years to allow everyone to get on their feet, but after five years the undertaker had to pay £5 and six shillings for every 1,000 acres, servitors £8, and the Irish £10 and 13 shillings. You'll notice how the Irish had to pay more than anyone else – not very fair was it?

- ✔ The undertakers, once they had been granted their lands, had to ensure that all the Irish population was moved off it. This was effectively enforcing a segregation between the settler and Irish populations. The goal was to try and ensure the purity of the settlers and to prevent them feeling endangered by the Irish, or slowly integrating with them.

Attracting settlers

Once the scheme had begun, and the lands allotted, the undertakers had to try to find people to fill the lands. This was difficult. Many people believed that Ireland was a dangerous and unsettled place. Why would they want to move somewhere so hostile? The authorities worked hard to promote the scheme – books were even published trying to sell the idea to people. So, who came to Ireland to try and start a new life for themselves?

There were two main groups that got involved in being undertakers. The first were a series of London Livery companies who saw the whole thing as a potential investment. The second was mainly made up of Scottish nobles who had been encouraged by King James to get involved.

With the Scottish settlers there was a direct link between the barons who acted as undertakers, and the lands that were settled. For example:

- ✔ **Armagh:** The undertaker was the Fews barony, so all the settlers came from his lands in East Lothian and Midlothian.

- ✔ **Cavan:** The undertaker was the Clankee barony, so the settlers came from Ayrshire, Renfrewshire, and Stirlingshire.

- ✔ **Fermanagh:** The undertakers were from the Knockninny and the Magheraboy baronies. As a result, the lands were settled by people from Fifeshire, Kincardinshire, and Kinrosshire, and East Lothian, Lanarkshire, and Midlothian respectively.

The Scottish planters were the most successful and came in the largest numbers. These settlers were radical in their religious beliefs, and the purest believers in the process of the Reformation. The majority were Presbyterians and as such became an active and radical voice in Ireland.

The plantations, although they took place across Ireland, were most successful in Ulster. Here the land was of good quality and people could make a living, and also, because of the high numbers of planters in the area, the people were fairly secure and surrounded by religious fellow travellers. Because the majority of settlers were Scottish Presbyterians, this changed the religious and political dynamics of Ulster. If it wasn't for the plantations, Ireland probably wouldn't have had a large non-Catholic population. Because of this, the roots of religious conflict, so important in the nineteenth and twentieth centuries (see Chapters 19 and 23), lie with the plantations of the early seventeenth century.

The results: A mixed bag

Many of the undertakers and settlers looked for short-term profits rather than trying to make a long-term go of their new homes in Ireland.

In the original plans, just over half a million acres were allotted for plantation. Fifty per cent of the land was to go to the settlers, 25 per cent to the Protestant Church, and the remainder (the last 25 per cent) divided between the servitors and the Irish. To chart the plan's progress, successive surveys of the plantation scheme were made in 1611, 1615, 1618, and 1622. The Plantation scheme wasn't as successful as had been hoped. The 1618 survey, for example, showed that the six planted counties of Ulster contained only 1,974 new families. As it happened, many undertakers had no choice but to rent lots of the land out to the Irish because there weren't enough settlers or servitors to claim the land that had been earmarked for them.

Still, there were some successes. The London Livery companies' settlement of Derry was a particular success story, and Londonderry was incorporated as a town in 1613. By 1616 the town had 215 stone-built houses within its walls. Elsewhere the scheme was less successful. By 1630 Enniskillen only had 60 adult males who had settled, and Virginia, County Cavan, only 19.

With other plantations happening in Munster and Connacht, by 1641 the total number of settlers had reached about 100,000. Their experiences differed widely. Those in Munster became the most affluent, those in Ulster the most numerous.

Considering that the population of Ireland was probably as small as 750,000 in 1600, the arrival of settlers boosted the country's population, and made them a significant proportion of the total. Although the economic success of the scheme, or its ability to achieve the original goals, can be doubted the plantations of the early seventeenth century changed the make-up of Ireland forever.

Charles 1 and His European Unions

As always, England was busy looking out over the English Channel and seeing what the continentals were up to when Charles came to the throne. In the early 1620s the English had been quite keen on making friends with Spain, and they had tried to marry Charles off to a Spanish royal. The whole thing failed, and Charles, who was a bit miffed at having been turned down (never good for a man's ego), called for a war against Spain. Just after his succession he married a nice French girl (the sister of the King of France no less). By September 1625 he acted on his rejection by Spain, and went to war with them. Oh, and by 1627 he also went to war with France as well.

Clearly all this warring was keeping Charles busy, and his Irish subjects saw their chance to win some concessions.

Appeasing the Old English: Round 1

The Old English had got fed up with being treated as second-class citizens in comparison with the oh-so-glamorous and loyal settlers. They made it clear to Charles that they were fed up with the way that they were treated and felt that they were being discriminated against. Fearing that any discontent might look for an alliance with one of the Crown's foreign enemies, the English government changed their approach and started treating the Old English much better. It stated that the Old English should be treated favourably, and provided them with soldiers that they could use for the defence of Ireland.

But then the Protestants in Ireland objected saying that the loyalty of the Old English wasn't clear and that they shouldn't be trusted with soldiers and the Crown took the army away from the Old English.

To try and win the Old English over for the loss of their soldiers, Charles promised:

- An increase in the size of the standing army to defend Ireland.
- The abolition of the bar on Catholics practising law.
- Reforms to inheritance law that would mean that the descendants of Catholics weren't penalised when their parents died.

The Old English took a look at these reforms, and said no.

Appeasing the Old English, Round 2: The Graces

Charles was in a tough position. The longer it took to convince the Old English that he loved them really, the more he feared that they might either rebel or ally themselves with his opponents.

In June 1627, Charles met with an Irish delegation to discuss what he could do to try and make everyone happy.

The Protestant and Presbyterian settlers in Ireland had very strong views and were very anti-Catholic. If they thought Charles was making too many concessions to the Catholics they'd let him know. Charles was stuck in a tricky position. He had to do something to keep the Old English on side, but he couldn't risk alienating the settlers by doing too much.

After meeting the Irish delegation who promptly agreed to give Charles a £40,000 subsidy over three years (he spent a lot did Charles), he sent what was called 'His Majesty's instructions and graces' to the Irish parliament.

The graces, and there were 51 of them, were aimed at making the Catholic Old English position in Ireland better. Overall the graces were a way of making, or at least acknowledging, that the Old English were loyal. They didn't fundamentally change the Protestant domination of Ireland, but gave just enough to keep the Old English quiet. The graces included improvements to the Catholic position in Irish society including their guaranteed rights to land, access to certain professions that had previously been barred to them and the agreement that they could take command positions in the army.

Things were looking up for the Old English, but then Charles made peace with both France and Spain, and the whole issue of Catholic loyalty in Ireland became less important. The Irish parliament, which was dominated by Protestants anyway, wasn't recalled to make the graces law, and the whole idea was quietly dropped until 1634.

The Old English were outraged. They felt that Charles had let them down and the situation was made worse by renewed attacks on Catholics. The Irish government reintroduced fines for those not attending Protestant Church services, and all Catholic religious houses were closed down.

Wentworth: No friend of ours

In 1632 Thomas, Viscount Wentworth, was appointed to the job of Lord Deputy of Ireland – he was the man in charge. Over the coming years he would make Ireland his own, and get very, very rich in the process.

Wentworth's policies, which served both himself and the Crown, were as follows:

- ✔ Make Ireland, whether Old English, Irish, or Protestant, completely loyal to the interests of the Crown.
- ✔ Use Ireland to pay for the 'King's wants' or, in other words, subsidise Charles's extravagant lifestyle.
- ✔ Take advantage of the opportunities in Ireland to make himself wealthier.

Wentworth made sure that the Irish whom he charged with disloyalty, were removed from their land, and that their properties were transferred to the Crown. Half the rent would then go to the Crown, and half for himself. It's reckoned that Wentworth was eventually earning about £19,000 a year from his schemes (most government officials would have been lucky if their earnings made it into three figures), which made him one of the richest men in England.

Wentworth's wealth allowed him to build himself a new house. This was built at Jigginstown, County Kildare. It was one of the first brick houses in Ireland, and at a size of 390 feet by 120 feet, it was one of the biggest.

Wentworth called a parliament in 1634 to further his plans for Ireland. This parliament:

- ✔ Made the graces law – good for the Old English
- ✔ Got six big subsidies (cash gifts if you like) for the Crown over four years – good for Charles
- ✔ Allowed Wentworth to investigate what he called defective land titles. This meant he could claim, by legal sleight of hand, whatever land he wanted for the Crown – good for Wentworth and Charles' purse

Wentworth moved quickly, and claimed lands for the Crown in Mayo, Sligo Galway, and Roscommon (the areas that hadn't been fully planted). Rather than introducing a systematic scheme of plantation, Wentworth gave this land to his mates.

While Wentworth achieved his original aims, everyone in Ireland (apart from his friends that benefited) hated what he had done. He'd alienated all three main groups in Ireland, and steadily the Old English, Irish, and settler populations began to see that they had much in common: they all loathed Wentworth.

Bad times for Good Time Charlie

While Wentworth was annoying everyone in Ireland (see the preceding section), his king, for whom he'd done all this work, was in big trouble.

The Presbyterian Scots had rebelled against Charles, and all hell was breaking loose in England. By 1640 a Scottish army had defeated royal forces in the north of England, and Charles was on the ropes. His Parliament was refusing to grant him money to fight with Scots, they didn't like the way he was running the country, and they hated his flamboyance. While Charles had loyal supporters (called the Royalists), he had many enemies across England and they began turning against him.

Wentworth, and Ireland, became very important to Charles's sense of security. Wentworth brought an Irish parliament together, and convinced them, despite their misgivings, to call up an army of 9,000 men which the residents of Ireland would pay for. Wentworth manipulated parliament by using his friends as allies to vote the legislation through, and an Irish army, for the defence of England and King Charles, was brought together.

Things moved very quickly from here:

- The army (mostly Catholic) was brought together at Carrickfergus in July 1640.
- The English parliament, which was now opposed to Charles, feared what the Irish army would do if sent to England.
- Wentworth was seen as the villain in the piece and the English parliament sought to impeach him.
- The Irish cheered, and sent lots of evidence to England to show what an objectionable man Wentworth was.
- Wentworth was impeached, imprisoned, and executed.

While this was a good result for everyone in Ireland – as they all hated Wentworth – it would pave the way for a disaster (see Chapter 14). Charles was in a weak position, and Civil War would soon break out in England. His opponent there was Oliver Cromwell, who would become the scourge of Ireland.

Wentworth's death also heralded splits in Ireland. The Old English thought their best chance of concessions lay with supporting a king who needed friends – and that would be Charles. The settlers, whose natural sympathies lay with Charles's opponents, such as Cromwell, looked to oppose him.

What was going to be fought out was not just the future of the English Crown, but also the choice between a Protestant supremacy in Ireland (championed by the settlers) or an Ireland that accepted and acknowledged its Catholic population (led by the Old English and supported by the Irish).

Foras feasa ar Éirinn: A History of Ireland

By the seventeenth century, Ireland had been around for a long time. Through its oral history and the books that Irish monks wrote centuries earlier, Irish history had been passed down from generation to generation, sharing the stories of Ireland's great past. While there had been many history books written, it took until the early seventeenth century until one of the most famous emerged.

In Europe at the time the fashion was for histories that told the story of what was called the *patria* or the fatherland. Effectively these were national histories that explained what had happened in the past and how the nation had emerged.

The work, when it was finished, was called *Foras feasa ar Éirinn* (basically 'A History of Ireland'). It tells the story of Ireland from the earliest times to the end of the twelfth century when the Normans arrived and spoilt everything.

Introducing Geoffrey Keating

Geoffrey was born sometime around 1580, and lived until 1644. He was born in County Tipperary. His family were of Anglo-Norman heritage and seem to have been quite well-off with significant landholdings.

Evidence of the wealth of his parents is obvious when we consider young Geoffrey's education. He was able to afford to travel to Europe and attend university in France at Rheims and Bordeaux, where he got a doctorate in theology – clever lad our Geoffrey.

Once back in Ireland Geoffrey put away his academic cloaks, and swapped them for the clothes of a priest. He was ordained as Catholic priest, and returned to his local area and was attached to the diocese of Lismore.

Keating was theologically very strict. He was well known for his powers as a preacher, and produced a whole series of theological writing on complex themes such as death and repentance. Given his firm beliefs it appears that Geoffrey would have hated the whole idea of sin, and it's reputed that he publicly denounced people in his congregation for sins such as adultery.

The author, Geoffrey Keating, finished the manuscript in 1634, and it proved very popular (see the nearby sidebar 'Introducing Geoffrey Keating' for more on Geoffrey). In the early years the history was read in the language it had been written: Irish. Steadily, and because of its popularity, the history was translated into Latin and English. Eventually it was published in book form, and the revised translation into English in 1723, proved really popular. It's constantly been reprinted ever since. Shame Geoffrey's not around to collect the royalties.

The idea of a national history was a contemporary fashion in the seventeenth century. This is one reason it appealed to people. But it was important during the seventeenth century for another reason: It gave the Irish, especially during the period of plantation when all these outsiders were arriving, a sense of who they were and how great their history had been. Still, it wasn't until the second half of the nineteenth century that Keating's history really came into its own. When the Cultural Revival was at its peak (see Chapter 20), Irish people needed to know where they came from and what their country had been like before the English arrived. Keating gave them all this, and the book sold heavily again during the Cultural Revival period.

Chapter 14

Family Feuds II and III: The English Civil War, then William and James

The middle of the seventeenth century was a tense time. The authority of Charles I was shaky, and he was being challenged by a parliament in England which was rapidly losing faith in their high-spending and rather arrogant King. In Ireland there was widespread fear about what the anti-King lobby was about. The Irish feared that the plantation population (also known as the New English) were not only anti-monarchy but also bitterly anti-Catholic and anti-Irish.

Not only did the Irish have to worry about the New English, but they also had the bloody rebellion of 1641 – and how this got caught up with the Civil War in England – to consider. Oliver Cromwell, once he had beheaded Charles, came to Ireland, and the Irish suffered, according to many people, their worst suppression ever.

England couldn't cope with the idea of not having a monarchy, and eventually the son of Charles, Charles II, was restored to the throne. This led to another struggle for the throne, when Charles II's chosen successor, James II, was challenged by William of Orange.

Ireland didn't just get caught up in the James versus William struggle, the whole war was fought out in Ireland. In this chapter we'll see how the royal struggle became one that completely divided Ireland along religious and nationalistic lines.

The Civil War

The English Civil War ran from 1642, in various guises, until 1651. The three stages of the Civil War were:

- ✔ 1642–45: King Charles I (the Cavaliers) against the supporters of the Long Parliament (the Roundheads).

- ✔ 1648–49: The second Civil War was a rematch of the first, and the sides were the same.

- ✔ 1649–51: The third Civil War involved the forces of the heir to throne, Charles II (Charles I had been executed in 1649) and the supporters of the Rump parliament.

Ireland got involved in all this, and was seen as a key battleground in the Civil War. Many people blamed the Irish for starting the whole Civil War because of events in Ireland in 1641.

The Rebellion of 1641

The Irish Rebellion of 1641 is one of the most significant events of Irish history, and is one that has gone down in the folklore of the country.

There were four main reasons that lay behind the rebellion:

- ✔ **The failure of assimilation:** The three sections of the Irish population, the planters (now often called the New English, but who were mostly Scottish and English Protestants and Presbyterians), the Old English (assimilated settlers of old who were often Catholic) and the native Irish, had all failed to get along and were divided along religious lines in their attitudes towards the monarch versus parliament struggle.

- ✔ **The Plantations:** The settlement of Ireland under King James (see Chapter 13) had changed the landscape of Ireland. The settlers were very different from the people living in Ireland and tensions were inevitable. The taking of land, by the planters, from the resident Irish was a cause for dispute and resentment.

- ✔ **The Conspiracy against the Crown:** There had been a Scottish rebellion in 1640, which was effectively supported by the English Long Parliament (so called because it sat for many years; the Parliament is important for its opposition to King Charles). The rebellion had been started by the Scots (who were very driven by their Protestant and Presbyterian beliefs) in opposition to what they thought were Charles's liberal attitudes towards Catholicism (see Chapter 13). Charles asked the parliament for money, but they kind of agreed with the Scots and said no. Charles turned to Ireland for support, and there he found a sympathetic hearing. They put together an army to help him, which grew on the news that the Scots were talking about invading Ireland to suppress Catholicism once and for all.

- ✔ **Economics:** In 1641 the Irish economy suffered from a recession and the harvest was pretty awful. Many of the Anglo-Irish leaders were heavily in debt, and had no way of repaying their loans. Neither the leaders (debt-ridden) nor the Irish people (hungry and poor) had anything to lose by agitating in favour of Charles I – who knows, they might even benefit.

It was clear during the summer of 1641 that there was a crisis. The Old English and the Irish feared an invasion of Scots who wanted to destroy their way of life. Only support for Charles I, who was opposed to the Scots support for the Parliamentarians anyway, offered any real hope. The New English, who were fully supportive of the Scots' religious fervour, supportive of the Long Parliament, and opposed to the King, were worried. They feared that if the Old English and the Irish rebelled in defence of Catholicism, it would be they that suffered.

Planning the rebellion

The rebellion was planned at a meeting on 5 October 1641. The main leaders were mainly from the Catholic gentry of the Old English in Ulster, who were supported by locally powerful Irish leaders. The strategy for the rebellion was first an attack on Dublin Castle – the headquarters of English rule in Ireland – and then the capture, by force, of all the most important fortified towns in Ireland.

Drink played an important part in foiling the plan. It's said that a man called Owen O'Connolly, who knew what the plans of the rebels were, got drunk. Once intoxicated, he told the authorities what the plans were, and how they were about to lose Dublin Castle. Forewarned, the authorities were able to mount extra defences and hold the castle.

The rebels didn't think of themselves as rebels. They firmly believed that they were fighting to defend themselves and for the rights of the Crown. One of the leaders, Phelim O'Neill wrote that, 'we do really fight for our prince, in defence of his crown and royal prerogatives, which we shall continue and die to the last man'. This was a powerful statement. Not for the first time, the Irish were coming out in favour of the King (as he was seen as pro-Catholic). The problem was that Phelim said that he had the authority of Charles to attack the English in Ireland (his documentation was actually fraudulent). This claim gave the parliament in England all the ammunition that it needed against Charles, and it would be used against him as evidence of his intrigue against seventeenth-century democracy.

Massacres in Ulster

When the rebellion began, in late October 1641, it quickly descended into a violent and bloody series of massacres that were fuelled by local sectarian tensions. Any plan that there had been for the rebellion, or sense of clear political objectives, was quickly lost.

- ✔ In Ulster the Irish peasantry began attacking English and Scottish settlers whom they hated for their religious beliefs and for taking the land.

- ✔ The leaders of the rebellion tried to stop such brutal sectarian attacks, but couldn't control the peasantry.

- ✔ The authorities believed that this was going to be a total rebellion of the Irish population, and over-reacted. They sent Sir Charles Coote and William St Leger (both Protestant settlers in Ireland) to sort the mess out.

- ✔ Irish attacks on settler populations led to counter attacks on Irish civilians by the English forces, and this became the cycle of action during the rebellion.

The rebellion of 1641 was later used in propaganda showing how evil and degenerate the Irish were. It was seen as a moment in history when the Protestant population had been ruthlessly attacked, and if the Protestants wanted to prosper in Ireland they would always have to be wary of such attacks in the future. To instil fear in Protestant populations of the future, 1641 was always remembered as a time when more than 100,000 settlers had been brutally murdered by their Catholic neighbours. This total is still quoted in many histories, but completely overstates the actual numbers killed. Most historians now recognise that the real figure is nearer to 4,000 Protestants being killed during the 1641 rebellion.

1641 is a key date in the history of Ireland's Protestant population. It is used as a constant reminder of the state of siege under which they live. Until the end of the nineteenth century Ulster Protestants used to parade every year to commemorate the loss of life during the rebellion. While they no longer parade to commemorate the event, pictures of the 1641 rebellion, and the massacre of Protestants, are still used on Protestant banners when they parade on 12 July, and the date regularly features on loyalist murals.

1641 Propaganda

The massacres of 1641 soon became the stuff of legend, and dominated the gossip in England that autumn and winter. The evidence, whether or not it was real, of what had happened to the settlers was all the evidence that the English (and Scottish) needed to prove that the Catholic Irish were a bunch of Godless savages. Refugees fled the massacres of Ulster and began arriving in Dublin – many would eventually return to England where they told stories about the awful things that had happened to them. Pamphlets and books were quickly produced that told of the horrors in Ireland with subtle and understated titles such as *Bloody news from Ireland or the barbarous cruelties by the papists used in that kingdom*. To a hungry readership these publications recorded the horrible murders, the rape of women, and the killing of babies. By August 1642 the English parliament was recording that there had been 154,000 deaths in the rebellion, and by 1646 a book recorded the number at 200,000. The facts didn't matter: this was all anti-Irish propaganda aimed at instilling and reflecting anti-Catholic hatred in the minds of the English.

The fighting in the rebellion was made worse by the poor state of the economy and a harsh winter. In addition to those who were killed, thousands more settlers were driven from their lands by the Irish, and lost their livelihood. Without anywhere to live and farm, they often died of exposure. In Armagh, one of the centres of the rebellion, it's estimated that somewhere between 17 and 43 per cent of the settler population died in the 1641 rebellion.

England responds

The English response to the rebellion was swift and dramatic. Force of arms was used against the rebellion as well as the passing of laws that were designed to suppress Popery in Ireland. It moved the rebellion into a new and bloody phase, and also made things even more complex for Charles.

- In December 1641 the English parliament decided that Popery in Ireland wouldn't be tolerated.

- In March 1642 the parliament confiscated some 1 million hectares of land from the Irish and Old English because of their treachery.

- The land was made available to adventurers who could buy it and make landholding in Ireland a thoroughly Protestant affair.

- Sir Charles Coote led an army in Ireland that hanged disloyal Irishmen (whether or not they had done anything wrong) and engaged in a bitter rearguard action against the Irish forces that were winning.

The whole situation was a mess. The English Civil War had started by 1642, and most of Ireland was in the hands of the rebels. The Irish and Old English forces swore their allegiance to the Crown (much preferable to the Protestant fervour of the parliamentarians) but had successfully acted alone to take control of most of the country.

By 1642 there were three different forces in Ireland:

- ✔ One under the control of the English parliament fighting against the rebels.

- ✔ One under the control of Charles, which was supposed to be fighting against the rebels, but was increasingly working with them against the parliamentarians.

- ✔ One that was made up of Irish and Old English who were in open rebellion against the English parliament.

The fighting escalates

By 1642, and especially with the start of the English Civil War, Ireland was in near total rebellion. Many of the different groups – especially the Old English – that had first been ambivalent to the idea, joined in.

With the outbreak of Civil War in England, and the success of the parliamentary forces, it was clear that the Irish were facing a powerful, and very committed enemy. The parliamentarians were driven by the hatred of Charles, and their strongly held religious beliefs. They feared Charles as a tyrannical king and opposed what they saw as a tyrannical church. The parliamentarians considered themselves, by the standards of the time, as democratic: a principle underscored by their fervent Protestantism. They detested Catholicism in all its forms, and events such as the 1641 massacre just proved to them, if proof were needed, how dangerous Catholicism was. The Irish were not simply fighting for the control of their own country, but for the survival of their religious beliefs.

The near-total rebellion in Ireland was driven by a number of factors. These included:

- ✔ The English parliament's stated intention to punish all Catholics in Ireland for the massacre of 1641 and the rebellion. It didn't matter whether or not some groups such as the Old English had initially stayed out of the rebellion; just being Catholic would make you guilty. It was better then for everyone in Ireland to join the rebellion and take their chances.

✔ Many of the Old English who initially stayed out of the rebellion were fearful of their Irish neighbours who had enthusiastically supported the rebellion. The Old English worried that if they didn't join the rebellion, they too would be attacked by the Irish in the same way the settlers had been. Again, it was easier to fight alongside local neighbours, than risk attack.

✔ By early 1642 with victory over English forces at Julianstown, it looked as if the rebellion might actually be successful – always better to try to be on the winning side.

The Confederation

In March 1642 the Irish forces, although doing brilliantly well in the battlefield, were only too aware of their one weakness: they had no central leadership.

The Earl of Clonricarde, one of the leading men in Ireland, suggested that there should be a system of councils that would rule over the whole of Ireland beginning at county level, through to provincial and then at national level. In May 1642 this body met for the first time at Kilkenny, and was a meeting of 'the lords and gentry of the confederate Catholics'. The Irish confederation had been formed, and would become an important force in Irish politics.

The Catholics were loyal to the king, but this was not a slavish devotion. What the Old English leadership of the confederation wanted was the reinstatement of the graces (see Chapter 13) that had offered so many benefits to the Catholic population of Ireland.

Despite the presence of the confederation, and their expressed loyalty to the king, Charles himself was ambivalent. He believed he had a divine right to rule, and was no more going to take his orders from the Irish confederation than he was from the English parliament. The Irish thought that, now that Charles was facing Civil War in England, the king would be glad of their support and would sign up to anything.

The confederates wanted:

✔ A parliament for Ireland that would have the same rights as the one in England.

✔ Secure tenure and recognition of all land rights.

✔ No reprisals against the Irish for their supposed disloyalty against the Crown by starting their rebellion in 1641.

While such a deal was not unreasonable, it was fraught with difficulties. It gave the Irish, and Catholicism, a series of rights that would be unique in history, and would, if agreed to, give Charles's enemies in Ireland further ammunition. Also, Charles was in England (based in Oxford), busy with the Civil War. Direct and speedy negotiation with the confederation was difficult. His man on the ground in Ireland, the Earl of Ormond, fully believed in Charles's divine right, and wouldn't make any decisions without communicating with the king.

Into the gulf emerged a new player: The papal envoy Rinuccini.

The Pope interferes

Given the problems that Charles was having, his wife, Queen Henrietta Maria, left for France in 1644. Once there she tried to negotiate between the royal forces in Ireland, the confederation representing the Irish rebels, and the Vatican to create some kind of settlement.

The Pope sent his envoy, Rinuccini to Ireland, and he would become a pivotal player. He arrived in November 1645.

Rinuccini was very critical of the confederation. He argued that they were more interested in securing the ownership of the land than they were in securing the position of the Catholic Church. Rinuccini threatened to excommunicate people who didn't take a strong line with the king, and had members of the confederation put in prison if he thought they were being weak on the issue of religion.

Clearly the arrival in Ireland of Rinuccini, and his rapid accumulation of power, changed the nature of Irish politics again. The rebellion changed complexion, and became a more overtly religious struggle. The ever more vociferous promotion of the Catholic cause in Ireland, under the command of a Papal envoy, put the Irish completely off-side with the Protestant parliamentarians.

Death to Charles – and the Confederation

In January 1647 King Charles was captured by the Scots and handed over to the parliamentary forces. He was executed in London on 30 January 1649. Before his execution, and during his time of imprisonment, it was clear that the attempts of the confederation to win concessions from the king had come to a dead end.

Rinuccini left Ireland in February 1649, and the confederation was on its own. Ireland was in the control of the confederation forces, but they were, with the death of Charles, ever more isolated. Charles's man, Ormond, controlled the areas outside Dublin, but he too, lacked a leader. The city of Dublin was the home to the only parliamentarian force in Ireland.

The forces of the English parliament had won the English Civil War. The army, under the control of Oliver Cromwell, was called the New Model Army. These were professionally trained soldiers, who were paid for their services. This was the first modern army in history. Armed, as it was, with all the most up-to-date military technology, the New Model Army was highly effective. Not only were they professional, they were also committed Protestants, and ideologically driven. They were the antithesis of the outdated way in which the Irish rebels were organised.

Cromwell in Ireland

Oliver Cromwell is one of the most despised figures in Irish history – and famous for wanting to be painted 'warts and all' (not very vain our Oliver). He is charged with some of the worst atrocities ever seen in Ireland and responsible for the destruction of long-standing patterns of religious observance, landownership, and government. The Catholic Irish didn't care much for warty old Cromwell.

As the leader of the parliamentarian forces, Cromwell's first target was to assist the remaining parliamentary stronghold in Ireland based in Dublin. But before Cromwell could even arrive, a combined force of Irish confederates and royalists attacked Dublin.

The leader of the parliamentary force in Dublin struck out of the city to surprise his opponents, and routed them. Some 3,000 Irish and royalist soldiers were estimated to have been killed. Cromwell's campaign was going well before he had even arrived.

Defeating the Irish

Cromwell arrived in Ireland on 15 August 1649. He moved quickly to suppress his opponents:

- ✔ Cromwell attacked the 3,000 royalist troops occupying Drogheda. He took the town and the entire royalist force was killed, as well as many local residents. The leader of the royalists, Arthur Aston, was even reputed to have been beaten to death with his own wooden leg.

- ✔ 5,000 men were sent north to Ulster to secure the province. Upon completing that mission, the army then headed south to take Wexford and Waterford. Wexford was taken and 2,000 of the townspeople killed.

By the end of 1649 Cromwell controlled most of the eastern side of Ireland, and had the major fortified ports in his hands. It was all very controversial though, and the cruelty of Cromwell's forces struck fear into the hearts of the Irish. Events at Wexford were a particular issue. It was argued that Wexford was actually in the process of surrendering, and that Cromwell's forces used this as an excuse to attack and massacre the people of the town. For the remaining Irish towns this provoked a dilemma. If they said they'd surrender, what guarantee did they have that they would survive? Better to resist until the last man.

Cromwell's campaign in Ireland has been dismissed as one of intolerable cruelty. Some historians have said that this is not the case. While accepting that Cromwell was never going to be a loved figure in the country, his actions were fairly standard in the context of seventeenth century warfare. Wars at that time, and especially when they involved laying siege to towns, were a nasty business. Cromwell just did what was accepted as the normal practice of the time. Others reject this view and say that Cromwell was deliberately cruel. They argue he was trying to suppress Ireland as quickly as possible and that he was driven by a hatred of Catholics.

Cromwell would eventually leave Ireland in May 1650, and leave the job to other people. Before he left, his campaign continued to crush the Irish.

- ✔ In the spring of 1650 Cromwell's forces took Kilkenny (which was allowed to surrender).
- ✔ The important strategic town of Clonmel was taken.
- ✔ Troops who were fighting for the royalists in Munster rebelled against their leadership in Cork, and handed the Province to Cromwell.

By the time of Cromwell's departure, the parliamentarians had control of Leinster, Munster, and Ulster. The remaining confederate and royalist forces in Ireland had retreated to Connacht, and awaited their fate.

In 1651 Limerick fell, and in 1652 Galway followed it. The parliamentarians had won a complete victory and the Irish rebellion and the period of confederation were at an end.

No more Catholicism

With Ireland under the control of the parliamentary forces, it was time for the Irish to really suffer. The Cromwellian campaign in Ireland had been terrible. During the period of Cromwell's campaigns in Ireland it's estimated that 616,000 people were killed or else died of disease. This reduced the population of 1,466,000 to a remaining 850,000. Of these 160,000 were Protestant. The Irish population had been massively reduced, and the majority of those who had died were Catholic. Those who remained alive would now feel the full weight of the Cromwellian settlement.

For Cromwell his campaign in Ireland had been as much about the eradication of Catholicism as it had been with the restoration of order. Cromwell was vehemently opposed to Catholicism, and during his campaign in Ireland Catholic buildings and clergy had been amongst his prime targets.

When Cromwell took the town of New Ross, the citizens of the town had asked him that they be granted 'liberty of conscience' – in plain terms, the right to follow their own choice of religion. Cromwell replied in no uncertain terms: 'I meddle not with any man's conscience. But if by liberty of conscience you mean liberty to attend mass, I judge it best to use plain dealing and to let you know, where the parliament of England has power, that will not be allowed of'. Cromwell was making it clear that there would be, if he had anything to do with it, no Catholicism. To try to kill off the religion he:

- ✔ Destroyed Churches and other religious buildings during his campaign.

- ✔ Killed or executed many clergy. The remaining clergy were transported to the Caribbean to work as slaves, or else allowed to travel to Europe.

- ✔ Put a price on the head of any priests that were found in the country.

- ✔ Banned Catholicism and the celebration of it.

- ✔ Forbade anyone openly confessing the Catholic faith to live in an Irish town.

These draconian measures didn't kill off Catholicism, but severely restricted it and drove it firmly underground.

No more land for Catholics

Along with religion, the other big issue was land. In the same way that Cromwell hated Catholicism as a religion, he thought that anyone who saw themselves as Catholic was completely unfit to own land. He used the involvement of the Catholics in Ireland with the 1641 rebellion, the ensuing confederation and their support for the monarchy as the marks of their disloyalty. This activity against England and Protestantism would be the mechanism by which he could remove them from the land.

The nature of landownership in Ireland changed completely after Cromwell.

- ✔ In 1642 parliament had given more than 1 million hectares to adventurers prepared to settle in Ireland. After Cromwell's time in Ireland this scheme was acted on.

- ✔ The troops that had fought under Cromwell, on behalf of the parliament, were owed wages. Parliament was strapped for cash, and decided to pay the 35,000 troops who had fought in Ireland in land. As a result Ireland was flooded with New Model Army veterans.

✔ Anyone who had been involved in the rebellion or the confederation was sent away from Ireland and their lands confiscated. By 1656 an estimated 60,000 Catholic Irish had been transported to Barbados and elsewhere in the Caribbean as slaves.

✔ Many pre-Cromwellian settlers in Ireland, who had suffered during the 1641 rebellion, took the opportunity to claim more land from their Catholic neighbours.

By 1660, Protestants owned 80 per cent of the land in Ireland, and Catholics the remaining 20 per cent. Prior to the 1641 rebellion these figures had been 40 per cent and 60 per cent respectively.

Cromwell achieved what all the previous English rulers who had encouraged plantation (see Chapter 13) had tried, but failed, to do. He had managed to completely destroy the Catholic landholding system in Ireland, and introduce into the country a huge number of Protestant Englishmen who would remain loyal to their homeland. The Cromwellian settlements destroyed the native Irish and Catholic landowning class, and made Ireland, almost overnight, a place owned and farmed by the Protestant English. It took until the end of the nineteenth century before the Catholic Irish would again own the majority of the land (see Chapter 19). No wonder the Irish never cared much for Cromwell.

The Wart Is Dead, Long Live the King (Charles II, That Is)

Cromwell died in 1658 and many Catholics in Ireland were heartily relieved. But for Cromwell's supporters in Ireland, his former soldiers and the Protestant settlers, there was a sense of unease: What would happen next?

Old warty had always refused to take the title of king. He inspired great loyalty, but with his death the coalition of his supporters in parliament fell apart, and didn't really know what to do.

After all the chaos and bloodshed of the English Civil War, the parliament decided, twenty months after Cromwell's death, that they'd go back to the old ways, and have a monarch again. But who to have? They had chopped off the head of King Charles, so he was no use. Luckily his son was still knocking about (and still had his head attached). He was brought back to London and proclaimed King Charles II.

The reinvention of the monarchy posed all kinds of problems in Ireland. The Catholics they had to wonder what his attitude to religion would be. For many of the settlers, who believed firmly in the ideological and religious significance of their life in Ireland, the return to monarchy looked like a backward step.

To get everyone behind his monarchy, Charles announced, in April 1660, that anyone who had opposed the royalist cause during the Civil War would be pardoned. At first this big announcement wasn't extended to include Ireland. But the Catholic Irish were a wily group, and kept petitioning the king. In November 1660 he made a further announcement that said that all settlers and soldiers could keep their land (loud cheer from them), except those lands that belonged to 'innocent' Catholics (loud boos from the settlers and soldiers).

What this meant was that any Catholics who could prove that they never had anything to do with the rebellion and the confederation could have their land back. A court was put in place in Dublin to settle the claims of the innocent Catholics and, by the end of 1663, some 350,000 hectares had been returned to Catholics.

This wasn't a great deal of land in the grand scheme of things, but it did mean that the total percentage of land owned by Catholics was nudged upwards by two or three per cent.

While Charles II's attitude towards Catholics who were innocent was all very well as a means of trying to make him popular with everyone, it flew in the face of the power structures on the ground. After the Cromwellian settlements there were no Catholics holding office in Ireland and only one in parliament. The Protestants that ran Ireland lobbied Charles hard, and by 1663 got the court that was giving land to 'the innocents' closed down.

Charles II died in 1685, and the throne passed to his brother, James II. This caused a real stink. Whereas the Protestants in Ireland had been a bit ambivalent towards Charles because of his promotion of the claims of innocent Catholics, they hated James. He openly believed in Catholicism and wanted to make all his kingdom Catholic again.

The Rollicking Rule of James II

Once in charge James believed that it was his job to give Catholics a fair go in society. He wanted to end all the laws that discriminated against Catholics. People in England, who had fought for Protestantism during the Civil War, and those in Ireland who had settled the country in the name of their religion, hated the whole scheme.

Although the Reformation had happened a long time ago (see Chapter 11), the lineage of the monarchy had changed since the days of the Tudors. Men like James had been brought up with a belief in the supreme right of monarchs to rule. During his time spent in exile in Europe during the English Civil War, James had become fervent in his belief in Catholicism. By championing Catholicism James wanted to turn the clock back to the days before Henry VIII, and make England and Ireland Catholic again. It wasn't going to be easy.

It all came to a head when James's wife gave birth to a son. This meant that James had a direct heir, and everyone had to face the potential continuation of a Catholic monarchy. It was time to act!

The opponents of James looked for a champion, and they found one close at hand: James's sister Mary and her husband William of Orange.

The Williamite Wars

James's sister, Mary, had remained true to Protestantism. Her husband, William of Orange (a Dutch aristocrat) was also a committed Protestant. These two were invited to come to England, knock James off the throne, and take it for themselves. If they were successful it would ensure that the Crown reverted to Protestantism and all the talk of Catholicism ended.

✔ In an attempt to protect himself, James brought four regiments of Irish Catholic soldiers to England. The presence of the soldiers proved to James's opponents that the world had gone mad.

✔ In November 1688 William of Orange landed at Newton Abbott, in Devon, and the Williamite Wars began. England quickly united behind William and proclaimed him as king.

✔ James knew his goose was cooked, and had no choice but to make a run for it. He headed initially for France, but knew that his one remaining powerbase was in Ireland. In March 1689 he landed at Kinsale in County Cork and resolved to fight for his crown in Ireland.

Getting another go at rebellion

It's easy to see the Williamite wars as a straight fight between James, representing the Catholics, and William, fighting for the Protestants. By the end of the war this was indeed the case. However, when James was first deposed it wasn't that clear-cut.

James had wanted equal rights for Catholics and dissenters. This second group mainly comprised Presbyterians who, although Protestants, were discriminated against because of their refusal to accept all the rules and theology of the established Protestant Church. When William landed in

England, many Protestants and Presbyterians in Ireland initially were supportive of James – he was their king for better or worse.

The chaos caused by the upheavals in England encouraged the Catholics of Ireland to begin attacking Protestants and Presbyterians – seeking revenge and taking land – and it was the fear of attacks by Catholics that drove most Protestants and Presbyterians to supporting William. If James had been better able to keep the Catholics of Ireland in line, and prevented them from settling local scores, he would have been far stronger.

The real killer for James was the decision by a parliament dominated by Irish rather than settler interests, in May 1689, to turn back the clock on the Cromwellian settlement. The parliament annulled all the Cromwellian land laws and the grants of lands to settlers and soldiers. Effectively, in legal terms at least, the Protestants were off the land, and the Catholics back on it. The Protestants had no choice: if they wanted to keep their land, they would have to fight against James (who supported the Catholic parliament) and side with William.

Initially the campaign of James went well in Ireland. He amassed a large army, and marched on Dublin largely unopposed. Ulster was the sticking point. No matter how enthusiastically the Catholic population supported James, it was Ulster that was the strongpoint of Protestantism in Ireland: it was there that the war would be decided. With Ireland in open rebellion against William, Protestantism, and the English parliament, the battle lines were drawn once more.

It goes wrong . . . again

Back in November 1688, just as William was preparing to land in England, an army supporting James marched on the most important Protestant fortified city in Ireland: Londonderry. When they arrived in December 1688, the walls of the city were famously shut on them, and the siege of Derry began.

The siege lasted until July 1689. In April that year James had arrived in Londonderry hoping to take the city: he failed. By July a Williamite fleet had landed off Londonderry, and they relieved the city. James and the Irish were on the run and in trouble.

Painting the Boyne orange

The major battle of the Williamite war took place in Ireland on the banks of the river Boyne. William had landed in Ireland (near Belfast) in June 1690. He was concerned that although his forces were achieving steady successes in Ireland, the war was dragging on.

The Battle of the Boyne took place on 1 July 1690. The two armies were vast: William had 36,000 troops, James, 25,000. William's forces were victorious, and some 2,000 died in the battle.

James's soldiers deserted him in huge numbers, and William was able to take Dublin a few days later without a fight. James knew that he was finished and left Ireland for France. In Ireland he was christened Séamus an Chaca (or James the Shit) for his desertion of his army, his cause, and the Catholic people of Ireland.

Although leaderless, the Catholics of Ireland decided to fight on. It took until October 1691, and the fall of Limerick, before the Williamite forces were in complete control of Ireland.

William, Orange Not Green

With the final defeat of James's forces William was in complete control. The Catholics had been defeated, and they had to wait to see what would happen to them – as they had done after defeat at the hands of Cromwell.

The effects of the Williamite victory were profound:

✔ The end of organised Catholic resistance in Ireland.

✔ The enforced departure of the Irish forces and their leaders from Ireland. This was known as the 'Flight of the Wild Geese', and meant that some 24,000 Irish people had to leave their homes for France.

✔ The re-establishment of the Cromwellian land settlement and the domination of Protestants in positions of power and on the land.

✔ The reintroduction of laws that barred Catholics from public life, and prevented the observance of the Catholic religion.

The Glorious Twelfth

The victory of William is celebrated annually across Northern Ireland. Protestants, and members of the Orange Order, parade through towns and villages to remember the victory of Protestantism over Catholicism. The parades feature marching bands, banners commemorating the battle and have, in the past, included displays by Loyalist paramilitaries. The parades are hugely contentious. The Orange Order, who organise the parades, argue that they have the right to march the routes they always have done and to celebrate their heritage. The Catholic population argues that the parades are aggressive displays of Protestant supremacy and have no place in contemporary Northern Ireland.

Part V
Catholic and Protestant: The Eighteenth and Nineteenth Centuries

The 5th Wave   By Rich Tennant

"Does anyone know how to work one of these Wolfe Tone dolls?"

In this part . . .

The eighteenth and nineteenth centuries saw the rise of nationalism within Ireland as well as one of the greatest natural disasters the world has ever seen, and a campaign for the rights of Catholics.

New ideas of liberty, inspired by the revolutions in France and America, influenced Irish thinkers and activists and led to the first great modern rebellion against the British in Ireland. Led by Wolfe Tone, the rebellion was crushed but left an important legacy of freedom. To try and calm Ireland the British would eventually concede equal rights for Catholics, but this simply led to further demands for reform.

The Irish became increasingly bitter about British rule in the middle of the nineteenth century when the Great Famine struck. The population was decimated, and a million people chose to emigrate rather than face starvation. This led to the start of the great Irish diaspora that would influence the histories of many nations around the world. For many Irish people the only solution they could find to the perennial problems of British rule and the decision of whether to emigrate was a demand that Ireland become an independent nation.

Chapter 15

Going Irish? Grattan's Parliament and Wolfe Tone's Rebellion

In This Chapter

▶ Innovation in eighteenth century Ireland and the arrival of Guinness

▶ Changes to religious laws

▶ Establishing a parliament in Ireland

▶ Revolutions in France and America

▶ Wolfe Tone's Rebellion

In some ways the eighteenth century was good to Ireland. There was a degree of economic innovation, and some wealth flowed from that. Two of the great Irish institutions flourished – both of which have to be experienced if you're in Dublin – Trinity College and Guinness.

This chapter explains why these two institutions were so important to Ireland, and has a look at the harsh treatment of the Catholics by the government.

The end of the eighteenth century provides some great stories, and a whole period of change. At first it looked as if Ireland might get some degree of freedom from Britain when a more self-assertive parliament was convened in Dublin. That was all very exciting, but it all went horribly wrong. Not for the first time, one group in Ireland decided that things weren't as they wished, and started a rebellion.

Led by Wolfe Tone, and supported by the French, the 1798 rebellion is one of the key events in Irish history. As well as telling that story, the chapter also explains why the French got involved in the first place, and why events in Paris and America had such an impact on life in Ireland.

The More Things Change: Irish Innovations and Institutions

Across Europe (and in America) lots of interesting things happened in the eighteenth century. The industrial revolution got going, and all kinds of clever things were being done with cotton and iron. Factories started appearing, and the people's way of life changed. Although agriculture remained important, many were attracted by a new way of life working in factories.

It was a great time for inventors. People started understanding things like steam-power, industrial machinery, and even developed new forms of transport by building canals. Universities became very important as they functioned as centres of invention and innovation.

The importance of philosophy and politics in the contemporary world began to be discussed and in France that led to all kinds of thinking about the state of the monarchy and whether it was fair that someone was born to be a ruler. People started asking what rights the ordinary citizen had. In America the thinking was much the same, but their target was the right of Britain to rule a territory 4,000 or so miles away.

Travel was still relatively difficult in the eighteenth century and people didn't have instant access to the world through things like the internet and rolling news programmes, but ideas began to move about. Certain sections of society were highly literate; they read newspapers and books that reported on ideas and events that were happening away from Ireland. Also, despite the problems of poor roads and long sea crossings, many people travelled to different countries and witnessed events elsewhere in the world. Ireland wasn't isolated from the world, and events, ideas, and inventions all had an impact.

Inventions from Ireland

A real sign of how advanced a society is can be measured by their scientific advances. By the eighteenth century Ireland, and especially Dublin, was a place of real innovation. Some of the best scientists of the age were working there, and places such as Trinity College were absolutely central in creating an environment for scientific advancement. All this was a mark of Ireland's sophistication and learning. Clearly this scientific knowledge and innovation wasn't shared by everyone: it was limited to a rich, Protestant elite.

Some inventors and innovators that emerged from Ireland around this time were:

✔ Aeneas Coffey invented the world's first heat exchange device that was a mainstay (and still is) in the process of whiskey production.

✔ John Kyan developed wood preservatives.

✔ Alexander Mitchell invented a device for constructing lighthouse and ship moorings in deep water.

Trinity College

At the heart of Irish scientific and intellectual life in the eighteenth century was Trinity College in Dublin. Trinity College was founded in 1592 and was set up specifically to educate Protestants at the University level, partly as a reaction to events during the Reformation (see Chapters 11 and 12). In 1685 its work had been boosted by the founding of the Dublin Philosophical Society, which was modelled on the Royal Society of London. This Dublin Society, which was closely linked with Trinity, was a home for the brainy ones in society, and led to a flourishing intellectual climate in Ireland.

In 1775, the brainy set grew even bigger. The Royal Irish Academy was founded to explore and understand Ireland's history. Again, this august body had close links with Trinity. One of the founders of the Academy, Henry Flood, liked Trinity so much that he left the College his estate when he died. He specifically wanted the money to be used to set up a professorship of Irish and to allow the library to buy important Irish manuscripts.

Trinity's great buildings were erected during this period, and make it the beautiful place it is today. The buildings of the eighteenth century (basically what you see when you first enter Trinity College) include:

✔ The Long Room Library designed by Thomas Burgh.

✔ The Printing House, on the famous entry quad, created by Richard Cassels.

✔ The Dining House, used to feed all the hungry students and dons of the period, designed by Hugh Darley.

✔ The Examination Halls, sadly for the students, was built by Sir William Chambers.

Trinity College has, because of its beauty and grandeur, been filmed many times. It was the backdrop for the Julie Walters and Michael Caine film, *Educating Rita,* but more intriguingly many people argue that the Long Room Library was the inspiration for the look of the Jedi Archives in *Star Wars Episode II: Attack of the Clones.* Not sure whether any Jedi Knights have ever made it to Trinity, but it's a great story.

As well as the great buildings, eighteenth century Trinity also produced some great people, including:

- ✔ Edmund Burke (1729–97), statesman, philosopher, and libertarian.
- ✔ Oliver Goldsmith (1730–74), writer and physician, most famous for his book, *The Vicar of Wakefield.*
- ✔ Jonathan Swift (1667–1745), writer best known for *Gulliver's Travels.*

The Black Stuff: Guinness Arrives

In addition to the emergence of Trinity College as the scientific and intellectual centre of Irish life in the eighteenth century, during this period another important institution arrived (some say the great Irish invention of all time) – Guinness.

A very clever man named Arthur Guinness opened the now famous Guinness brewery in 1756. Three years later Arthur pulled off the property deal of several lifetimes when he agreed to lease a plot of land for nine thousand (yes, that's thousand) years for a mere £45 per year. This meant that Guinness has been permanently located on one site (and will stay there a good deal longer) at St James's Gate on the banks of the River Liffey.

Arthur's great contribution to the modern world was his 'invention' of a dark stout drink, also known as porter. It's made from Irish barley and water from the Wicklow mountains (and not from the Liffey as popular legend has it).

It's a great pint, and an essential part of Irish life. But remember that Guinness grew rapidly from its foundation in the eighteenth century and became a cornerstone of the Dublin economy. By the early nineteenth century roughly a quarter of the city's workforce was employed in jobs connected in some way or other to the brewery. It was also a great place to work as the brewery workers had access to free pints during the day (just to keep their mind on the job!).

Despite the importance of Guinness to Dublin, it's anything but a local drink. Guinness is sold across the world, and the company have breweries on all five continents. There probably isn't a decent-sized city anywhere in the world that doesn't have a pub or bar that sells the black stuff. The manufacture and selling of Guinness is now a multi-million pound business that employs thousands across the globe. But wherever you happen to drink it, think of old Arthur Guinness and his desire to give the workers of Dublin a decent pint.

Guinness for Tourists

The Guinness brewery at St James' Gate is one of the most popular tourist attractions in Ireland today. It's well worth a visit so you can see the history of how the drink came to be made, tour the old brewery, see how Guinness has been advertised over the years and, best of all, get to taste a pint while looking over the Dublin skyline. The arguments over which place in Dublin serves the best pint of Guinness are legendary. Everyone has their favourites (I still think it's the Palace Bar on Fleet Street), but many people argue that the best pint is served where the stuff is made, so that gives you another reason to visit.

The More They Stay the Same: Troubles for Irish Catholics

Despite the progress that Ireland had made in some areas, it had not advanced in others. The wealth and success of Ireland, or at least parts of it, in the eighteenth century, was largely produced by, and reserved for the Protestant population. There was no real place for the Catholic population in Ireland at the time, and they certainly weren't invited to take part in running the country.

After all the violence at the end of the seventeenth century between Catholics and Protestants, and the battles between kings James and William, hostility and suspicion remained. After William III's victory at the Battle of the Boyne Protestants remained deeply suspicious of Catholicism and its advocates and Catholics found themselves relegated to a firm second place in society. Like the power-holders before them, the Protestants in eighteenth century Ireland aimed to keep the Catholic population powerless and marginalised.

One priest per parish only

In the first few decades of the eighteenth century, Catholics outnumbered Protestants by three to one. Despite their numerical supremacy, they had no real access to power. To try to keep the Catholic population in its place the following laws were passed:

- ✔ Catholics were forbidden from owning weapons.
- ✔ Catholics weren't allowed to own a horse that was worth more than £5.
- ✔ Catholic schools and teaching were banned.

Clearly many of these laws were difficult to enforce. Shortly after the victory of King William, a law had been passed that banished the Catholic hierarchy from Ireland. This was particularly hard to enforce as the religion simply went underground.

To try and regulate Catholics, a new law was introduced in 1704 that ordered all Catholic priests to register with the authorities, and provide assurances of their good behaviour. What it meant in practical terms was that each parish in Ireland would be allowed one priest, and no more.

Did the regulation of the Catholic clergy actually have any effect? In 1704 when the law first came into force, some 1,100 priests registered with the authorities. By 1731 that number had risen to around 1,600. That might not sound like many, but actually equates to one priest for every thousand Catholics. So, despite the laws, Catholics were well served.

No votes

In addition to the general attempts to suppress Catholics and their Church, there was a specific political dimension to the laws which kept Catholics away from the machinery of power.

The eighteenth century wasn't an age of enlightened liberalism. Only men could vote, and then only if they were rich and owned property. (There was a property qualification that afforded people the right to vote.) Most Catholics were so poor they didn't have a hope of ever qualifying for the vote, but there were some Catholics who owned enough land, and they had previously had voting, as well as other, rights.

That all changed though when various laws were introduced to ensure that the political power of Catholics in Ireland was even more severely limited. From the 1720s the following laws were put in place:

- ✔ It was reiterated that Catholics could never hold public office.

- ✔ All Catholics were disenfranchised (lost the right to vote). So now, even those Catholics who qualified to vote because of their wealth were disqualified from voting because of their religion.

- ✔ Catholics were barred from entering officer ranks in the army or the legal profession (the fear being that if they got these jobs, they would have influence).

Catholics did have a get-out clause. By publicly declaring that the celebration of Mass was superstitious and idolatrous, and denouncing the worship of the Virgin Mary, they could have their rights back. Clearly few people would turn their back on their religion in this way. But some did: by 1731 the so-called 'convert rolls' listed some 704 families who had turned their back on Catholicism.

As all these laws were so effective, any remaining hopes of a Catholic power base in Ireland diminished. It would take until the nineteenth century before rights were restored to the Catholic population as voters and office holders (see Chapter 17).

Famine

Although the eighteenth century saw lots of agricultural innovations in Britain, such as the use of crop rotation and the move to enclose agricultural land to make it more efficient, the impact was slight in Ireland. Rather than modernising, Irish agriculture was largely unchanged from previous centuries. Also, because of a growth in population, there were more people trying to make a living on the land. Then, between 1739 and 1741, a famine struck Ireland.

At the start of the eighteenth century more and more Irish families had become dependant on the potato as their main source of food. A high yield crop, it was ideally suited to the poor quality of most land, and could feed lots of mouths year round.

In 1739, and for the next two years, the potato crop failed. The main problem was that the winter of 1739–40 was very cold, which didn't help the potato. This was followed by a short, wet summer (not very unusual most people would say).

Potatoes were in such short supply that their price jumped six times. If people couldn't grow their own, they could scarcely afford to buy them on the open market.

Eventually it is reckoned that:

- One in three of the rural poor died.
- The problems of starvation were made worse by outbreaks of typhus and dysentery.
- Overall 400,000 people, out of a total population of 2 million, died – that's nearly a quarter of the population died in the three years of famine.

Trouble Brewing

The last twenty years of the century saw a series of challenges to the existing power structures. There were three main forces that impacted on Ireland:

- The revolutions in France and America.
- Resentment from all those sectors of society that had no power.
- Increasing tension between the parliaments of Dublin and London over who really ruled Ireland.

An Irish Parliament for some people

The Irish Parliament had met regularly during the eighteenth century. Entry to it was completely restricted to Protestants, and their freedom of legislating was restricted by the greater power of the British parliament in London.

In the second half of the eighteenth century there were increasing calls that the Irish parliament should have a greater freedom of action and full legislative independence.

The demands for legislative independence for the Irish parliament in the eighteenth century were radically different from those of the nineteenth and twentieth century. Later demands for Irish independence were driven by nationalists who wanted separation from Britain. The eighteenth century Irish parliament was fully loyal to Britain, and shared a common Protestant heritage. The legislative independence they wanted was so that they could better administer and legislate their own country: they were not trying to undermine the relationship with Britain.

In the 1770s there were increasing demands for the Irish parliament to have its own voice. In 1782 the British parliament accepted these demands and gave the Irish full legislative independence. This would last until 1800 and meant in practice that the Irish parliament could make laws that could not be amended or changed by the British legal or parliamentary system.

Despite this promise of freedom, the reality was somewhat different. The problems that the parliament had in using its newfound powers were as follows:

- ✔ Corruption still continued. This corruption allowed the British government to have people elected to parliament in Dublin that would resist change. Known as the 'undertakers', these men worked against Irish reforms from within parliament.

- ✔ Despite its legislative freedom, Ireland retained an executive in the form of a lord lieutenant and chief secretary who were directly appointed by London. These men ensured that the power of the parliament was muted.

- ✔ There were some people in the parliament who favoured liberalising attitudes towards Catholics. Any such moves were deeply resisted and made London suspicious of the parliament's motivations.

- ✔ Moves were made in the Irish parliament to pass legislation that would ensure free trade between Ireland and Britain. This idea was fiercely resisted by the merchants of Britain and was not implemented. Such thinking again demonstrated to many that parliamentary freedom for Ireland was a bad idea.

The Irish Parliament Buildings

The Building that housed the Irish parliament was the first purpose built parliamentary building anywhere in the world. Designed by Edward Pearce and completed by James Gandon, the parliament was constructed between 1729 and 1797. It housed the parliament during its most exciting phase, and was the scene of many of the great speeches by Henry Grattan. After the Act of Union, the building was sold to the Bank of Ireland on the condition that no political meetings be held there. It is still a working bank, and is open to the public who can visit the old debating chamber.

Clearly the Irish parliament, whatever great hopes there were for its potential freedom, was effectively a lame duck. Despite Britain's seeming generosity in allowing the parliament to have its freedom, power was never really transferred to Dublin. In the end bigger problems killed off the parliament, and ended any hope of legislative power in Dublin until the twentieth century.

French and American ideas

Ireland couldn't escape the forces of change that were happening elsewhere in the world in the later decades of the eighteenth century. Two big events happened over the oceans that had profound effects on Ireland.

In America there was a revolution against the British, and in France there was revolution against the monarchy. The American Revolutionary Wars lasted from 1775–83, and ended with American independence and the British withdrawing. The Irish parliament initially sent 4,000 troops to fight on the side of the British but they were doomed to be on the losing side.

In France the revolution started in 1789. From the storming of the Bastille to the execution of Louis XVI in 1793, the whole thing was a bloody mess. In Britain the whole episode was abhorrent. The popular mass had taken charge, dangerous ideas such as liberty were circulating, and worst of all, the revolutionaries had sent the royal family to the guillotine.

Henry Grattan

The years of legislative independence can't be separated from the life of Henry Grattan. Indeed, most historians refer to the parliament during the period 1782–1800 as 'Grattan's Parliament'. Grattan was born in 1746 and was a lawyer by trade. He had entered the Irish parliament in 1775 and was well known for his power of oratory. He was the champion of the cause of legislative independence, and as a result the Irish collected £50,000 for him as a thank you. His support for a more liberal attitude towards Catholics alienated him from many of his Protestant supporters. Despite opposing the Act of Union (see Chapter 16), the cause of legislative independence was lost. He served in the British parliament from 1805 until his death in 1820. He was rewarded for the efforts of his public life with a key burial spot in Westminster Abbey and a statue in the lobby of the Houses of Parliament at Westminster.

But what did these two events mean for Ireland?

✔ The British defeat in America gave hope and inspiration for any countries under colonial rule who wanted their freedom.

✔ The behaviour of French revolutionaries was terrifying to observe, and press reports constantly returned to the feeling of terror on the streets of Paris.

✔ Intellectually the French and American revolutions were both underpinned by radical ideas of democracy, personal freedom, and religious equality.

✔ The British, and many people with an investment in the status quo in Ireland, wanted to avoid the spread of revolutionary fervour. They didn't want to see radical liberal ideas taking hold, they didn't want to suffer any more military defeats, and they certainly didn't want the Royal Family to get the chop.

The 1798 Rebellion

For the Protestant population in Ireland, the bulk of the eighteenth century passed quite happily. They were in charge, mostly affluent, and there were some real educational, social, and economic advances taking place in their society. The Catholics meanwhile were in a sorry state. Despite being in a majority, they had no political power, little recourse to the law, and were economically downtrodden.

It couldn't go on forever.

A shot across the bow: The United Irishmen and Wolfe Tone

As it became clear that the Irish parliament was in fact a toothless body, the stirrings of protest began. In 1791 the Society of the United Irishmen was founded. Led by Theobald Wolfe Tone, the Society was headed by a Protestant political elite. Their main aim was to bring democratic reform and a greater level of political independence to Ireland. Additionally, many in the Society, including Tone, wanted to see Catholic emancipation; for others in the Society this was not a desirable outcome and this was a cause of some division.

The French connection

The United Irishmen looked to the French revolution for inspiration, and argued that genuine reform in Ireland could only be achieved by breaking the connection with Britain. Wolfe Tone also sought the help of the French revolutionary government in support of his planned rebellion.

Taking the French revolutionaries as an inspiration and forming alliances with them was an act of treason. The British would never stand idly by while such an unholy alliance was formed. Protest in Ireland was one thing, making friends with Britain's enemies something completely different.

The French liked Tone's idea of a rebellion against the British. After all, the British were as much the enemies of the French as they were the cause of Irish independence. In 1796, French General Hoche led a force of 15,000 French troops to the Irish coast to assist Tone. The weather was awful (it was December) and the landing cancelled.

An inspired alliance: Catholic and Protestant together

The real importance of Tone, the United Irishmen, and 1798 was the alliance that they brought together. This wasn't simply an Irish Catholic or nationalist rebellion against British rule. It was a union of Catholics and Presbyterians (adherents of a radical form of Protestantism that was especially strong in Ulster), an alliance against Britain that stretched across sectarian divisions. Because of this union, Tone remained a hero to future generations of Irish Republicans. He understood that the real goal was the expulsion of Britain from Ireland, not the supremacy of the Catholic people.

Out-and-out war

The sight of 15,000 French troops off the coast of Ireland understandably caused a few alarm bells to ring in the minds of the government. A campaign of repression began against anyone connected with the United Irishmen, and murder, torture, and house burnings became the order of the day.

With the movement under threat, and many leaders arrested, the United Irishmen decided to go for open rebellion with or without French help. The rebellion started in 1798, and by the end of it some 30,000 people were dead.

The main events in the rebellion were:

- ✔ May 1798: Rebellion starts in Dublin, and spreads quickly to Wicklow, Meath, and Kildare.

- ✔ The British response is quick and brutal. Where rebellions have started, the United Irishmen are attacked, and where there is no sign of activity, known United Irishmen are attacked anyway (just to be on the safe side).

- ✔ The rebellion spreads to Antrim by 7 June, where a force under the Presbyterian Henry Joy McCracken occupies the town. They hold out for a week.

- ✔ In Wexford the rebellion is strongest. The rebels take the towns of Wexford and Enniscorthy.

- ✔ Suppressing the Wexford rebellion takes some 20,000 troops. British forces win a decisive battle at Vinegar Hill. The suppression of the rebels is swift, brutal, and barbaric.

- ✔ A bit late in the day – 22 August to be exact – the French finally arrive. One thousand soldiers land in County Mayo. They win one victory, but within two weeks are defeated and sent home by the British.

The last act of the rebellion came in October 1798 when another French force, accompanied by Tone, tried to land in County Donegal. They were met by the British navy and surrendered. Tone was recognised, tried, and sentenced to hang. Rather than face the noose, he cut his own throat.

To the victor . . .: Britain takes over

Clearly the British response to the United Irishmen rebellion was swift and effective. A combination of good luck and military supremacy helped them see off the French factor in the rebellion and order was restored.

Irish disloyalty, and especially the adoption of French revolutionary ideas, was a real threat to Britain.

The answer in the minds of the British was quite simple. The only way to secure the future peace of Ireland, and prevent all this quarrelsome behaviour was to run the place directly from London, especially because the Irish elite had shown themselves unable to cope with the threat of the United Irishmen.

A union of Ireland and Britain was the answer. It would end any façade of Irish independence and was legislated for in 1800. Sadly for the United Irishmen, their rebellion had produced the one thing they didn't want: even stronger British rule. You can read about the Act of Union in Chapter 16.

Chapter 16

Going British: The Act of Union

After all the problems that Wolfe Tone had caused (see Chapter 15), the British were in no mood to placate the Irish. They decided that rather than let the Irish have control of their own affairs, they'd rule Ireland directly from London, and that the country would be legally united with Britain. It was a bold step, and Ireland would remain as part of the Union until Irish independence in 1922 (see Chapter 21). Although the Union did bring a level of stability and wealth to certain sections of the population in Ireland, the spirit of rebellion that Wolfe Tone had inspired wasn't dead, and the Irish (well, a small number of them), led by Robert Emmet, had another go at rebellion.

Politics wasn't the only problem the Irish faced in the first half of the nineteenth century. Bad weather, outdated agricultural systems, and poor harvests led to a series of famines that made everyone suffer – and foreshadowed the Great Irish Famine (which you can read about in Chapter 18). Equally problematic was the strengthening of religious feeling that only served to separate the two communities in Ireland. In addition, the series of famines and the increasing population resulted in real difficulties that led to death, disease, and emigration.

Explaining the Act of Union

After the chaos of the 1798 rebellion, politicians in Britain and Ireland came to the opinion that the only way that Ireland could be secure and stable in the long term was to merge the two countries together formally. This would give the Protestants security, and make all the laws and systems of rule the same in Ireland and Britain. It was also supposed to give Britain more security by making Ireland a stable place, and also act as a defence against attack from France.

Understanding the Act

By the turn of the century, Catholics outnumbered Protestants in Ireland by five to one. This made the Protestant situation one that was, numerically at least, very weak. If Ireland and Britain came together as a Union, the tables would be turned: Protestants would then outnumber the Catholics by nearly six to one. Rather than having to worry about the problems of Catholics in parliament, and being a numerical minority, the Protestants in Ireland would be in the majority and would be ruled directly from the Westminster parliament that was very definitely Protestant.

The United Kingdom of Great Britain and Ireland was formally ratified by the Irish and British parliaments, and created by law on 1 January 1801. The practicalities of the Union were:

- ✔ Ireland would be run from, and legislated for, by the parliament at Westminster.
- ✔ 32 Irish peers would have seats in the House of Lords (they were chosen by virtue of their titles and not elected).
- ✔ 100 Irish Members of Parliament would enter the Westminster House of Commons (they would have to win an election in their local constituency).
- ✔ Free trade between Ireland and the rest of Great Britain would be introduced.
- ✔ The Church of Ireland and the Church of England would be united.

A new flag for everyone

Before Union, the British flag was a combination of the flags of England (the Cross of St George) and Scotland (the white saltire with a blue background). When the Union happened, a new flag was created for the United Kingdom. It wasn't likely that the British would try to merge anything that was too Irish into the flag (such as a harp or a Celtic Cross), so they decided to use the saltire of St Patrick, which was red. When combined with the existing flag for Britain, the Irish dimension helped create what we now know as the Union Jack.

The really negative part of all the deals that went into the making of the Act of Union was the failure of Ireland's Catholic population to gain any concessions. The British knew that they had to try to offer the Catholics something so that they wouldn't get too angry about the whole Union idea. The government supported the idea that a central part of the Act of Union would be the emancipation of Catholics (at this point they were still barred from many public jobs, and couldn't vote, because of their religion).

The talk of emancipation was well received, and when the British cabinet agreed to it, in principle, in January 1801, it looked like the Act of Union might benefit both sections of Ireland's population. The problem was that George III hated the idea (and didn't really like Catholics much) and had the idea taken out of the legislation. Catholics would have to wait nearly three more decades before they got their emancipation (see Chapter 17).

What Union meant: The good bits

So long as you weren't a poor tenant farmer, things under the Act of Union weren't so bad. The Act of Union had improved a number of things. In some ways, the political situation, although far from peaceful, stabilised a bit and the Irish – well, the Protestant Irish, at least – experienced an economic boom.

Politically speaking

With the Act of Union, Ireland was now part of the British state – it wasn't just some apparently independent difficult and troublesome backwater. As part of Britain Ireland gained a bit more status in the world and had a few more opportunities than it had had before:

- ✔ Irish MPs went to Westminster. They still often acted in self-interest (which parliamentarian doesn't?), but at least they were able to bring Irish issues to the attention of the powerful in London.

- ✔ As part of the Union, Ireland was also placed at the centre of the ever more powerful British Empire. Ireland would benefit economically from Empire, as well as sending its people across the globe to work.

- ✔ Under the Act of Union Ireland and Britain started a free trade relationship. Before that Ireland had to pay duties on any goods it exported or imported. Although the relationship with Britain was never going to be an equal one economically, at least this meant that Ireland could compete better in the British market, and was able to buy things more cheaply.

Leinster House

What was originally built as Kildare House changed its name to Leinster House when the Earl was made Duke of Leinster. The floor plan of Leinster House, and its external appearance, were supposed to have inspired James Hoban, who was the architect who designed the White House. Apart from the colour, they actually look quite similar in some ways. The Duke finally sold the House, in the late nineteenth century, to the Royal Dublin Society. In turn they were persuaded to sell it on in 1924. Why? So that it could be used as the home of Ireland's first independent parliament. Ever since then Leinster House has been the home of both houses of the Irish Parliament – the Dáil and the Seanad. So, what started out life as the home of an elite Anglo-Irish noble, ended up as the home of the independent Irish.

In addition, the decades either side of the Act of Union – broadly speaking the reign of George III (1738–1820) – saw a boom in Ireland. The two main cities, Belfast and Dublin, benefited massively and the cities that we know today were created. In Ulster, industries such as shipbuilding and textiles followed the British path of industrialisation and these developments would, by the end of the nineteenth century, make Belfast one of the richest cities in the Union.

Architecturally speaking: Building up Dublin

In the eighteenth century there had been a property boom in Georgian Dublin. At first this was dominated by the building of fine wide streets on the north side of the River Liffey. Big squares were built, such as Ruthland Square (now Parnell Square) and Mountjoy Square. In the grand houses of these squares the most prominent residents of Dublin lived, such as Archbishops, Lords, and Commercial leaders.

In the mid-eighteenth century one of Dublin's most important people, the Earl of Kildare, decided that he wanted a new house for himself. Rather than squeeze in with everyone else, the Earl decided to build his new place on the very unfashionable south side of the Liffey. Kildare House was the biggest residence in Dublin, and one of the grandest ever constructed. It is a perfect example of Georgian building.

The move to the south of the river by Kildare, inspired everyone to follow. In the latter years of the eighteenth century, and into the nineteenth, a massive building programme started in the south of the city.

The years before and during the period of Union saw some of the great spaces and places in Dublin built. These included:

✔ The three great squares of the south of the city: Merrion, Fitzwilliam, and St Stephen's Green.

✔ The Royal College of Surgeons' Building, designed by Edward Parke and William Murray.

✔ University Church, designed by John Hungerford Pollen.

✔ The Harcourt Street Railway Station (the trains stopped running in 1959).

✔ The Grand Masonic Lodge on Molesworth Street. Designed by Edward Holmes, and built as late as 1866, it's a Georgian classic.

Basically there wouldn't be all the amazing buildings there are now in Dublin, if it hadn't been for Georgian styles of architecture, and the wealth that flowed into the city during the years before and after Union.

What Union meant: The bad bits

All in all then, the Act of Union wasn't a disaster for Ireland. True, a sense of national identity and self importance had been lost, but the country, and especially Dublin, benefited in other ways, as the preceding sections outlined.

Yet while the development of cities and industries was great for some people, the wealth wasn't evenly distributed (either by religion or geographically). There were pockets of Georgian wealth and splendour in Ireland that benefited from the Act of Union, and whole areas that stayed massively underdeveloped and poverty-stricken.

The advances made by Union were also overshadowed by the many complex structural issues (such as the land and food supply) and the social issues (namely religion) that bubbled away. These simmering issues, soon to come to a boil, would make the remainder of the nineteenth century calamitous for Ireland.

Great houses but lousy social scene

The passage of the Act of Union did have some negative effects. While Grattan's parliament sat (see Chapter 15), there were regular meetings of the parliament in Dublin. This meant that all the officials, and their servants would descend on Dublin. It's also why many decided to build houses: they needed to be in Dublin for work.

(continued)

(continued)

Accompanying the parliament was a great social scene. Dublin in the second half of the eighteenth century became famous as a place where the great parties were held – it was the place to be seen.

Once the Act of Union was passed, and parliament moved to London, there wasn't the same social season in Dublin. The Duke of Leinster and Viscount Powerscourt were so aware that life would change with the parliament in London, that they sold their Dublin houses immediately. The social scene suffered because of Union. That said, there were still some great parties. The Lord Lieutenant hosted the annual St Patrick's Day Ball (a must for anyone of social standing), as well as debutant balls, state balls, and dances.

Robert Emmet's Small Rebellion

After the Act of Union, Ireland plodded on much as before. For the bulk of the population, the fact that Ireland was now ruled from London had little direct impact. The Protestants were still in charge, and the Catholics were still downtrodden, leaving one group holding the reins and the other group chafing at the bit. Enter Robert Emmet.

Robert Emmet, a Protestant, was born in Clonakilty (famous for its black pudding) in West Cork in 1780. He made his way to Trinity College in Dublin, and there became involved in the United Irishmen – the organisation that had been responsible for the 1798 rebellion. He even became the secretary of one of the United Irishmen branches in the College.

After the failure of the 1798 rebellion, Emmet had no choice but to get out of Ireland. He went away to France, and there met lots of other men who had supported the United Irishmen's cause.

Emmet's grand plan

Hanging around in Paris, Emmet's mind constantly returned to the whole question of Ireland, and how he could continue Wolfe Tone's work. In 1802 he even went to see Napoleon to see if he'd help with a rebellion in Ireland. Napoleon had, at that point, just made a peace deal with Britain, and didn't want to upset anyone, so turned down Emmet's request for help.

In October 1802, Emmet travelled back to Ireland, and started plotting again. The grand plan was as follows:

✔ Emmet would lead a rebellion in Ireland.

✔ Supporters of the United Irishmen's cause in England would rebel there.

✔ The French, who had fallen out with Britain again, would join in.

✔ The whole thing would go well, and Ireland would be free.

It was a great plan, but one that was absolutely riddled with flaws. No matter how well Emmet organised things in Dublin, he couldn't rely on anyone else further afield. All these revolutionary movements were riddled with spies, and the authorities were aware that something was up. Also, the French were notoriously fickle when it came to supporting Irish rebellions, and they were no help to Emmet at all.

The best laid plans

In Dublin Emmet planned his end of the rebellion meticulously. Even the prosecutor at his trial would acknowledge that Emmet had done a good job. To try to make his part of the rebellion successful, Emmet:

✔ Had a large quantity of arms either imported or made locally. Included in these arms were special pikes made to be used in close quarter street fighting, explosive devices to be thrown in Dublin's streets at any attacking cavalry, and a rocket that could be launched from a distance against oncoming troops.

✔ Regularly drilled willing rebels to make them better able to fight when the rebellion happened.

Often go awry: A riotous rebellion

The big event happened on 23 July 1803. Rather than creating a revolutionary spirit across Ireland, and bringing British rule in Ireland crashing to its knees, Emmet's rebellion was a bit of a farce.

He led his troops in an attack on Dublin Castle. The thinking was good – this was the seat of British authority in Ireland – but with his men behind him, and dressed as he was in full General's outfit and carrying a sword, Emmet was a bit obvious.

The forces of the state stood firm, and Emmet's rebellion stalled. Rather than creating a well organised assault on British rule, the whole thing descended into a general riot of the population in Dublin. Emmet realised it was all going wrong, and tried to disperse his forces rather than fight on. Everyone ignored him, and the rioting continued – Lord Kilwarden, the Chief Justice of Ireland, was even dragged from his coach and murdered by the mob.

Riots in Dublin weren't that unusual, and the forces of law and order, after some street fighting, always managed to restore order. The way that Emmet's rebellion played out meant that his forces posed little more of a threat to the authorities than any other urban riot. Where it differed was the political meaning – freedom for Ireland – that Emmet was putting on the event. It seems though that the people of Dublin had little enthusiasm for his message, and were content to riot as normal.

By the end of the day, the authorities were back in control, and Emmet had fled. He was now public enemy number one, and they started searching for him. Eventually Emmet was arrested on 25 August 1803, and thrown in prison to await trial.

Emmet's trial

Emmet's trial was always, legally at least, going to be a straightforward affair. He would be found guilty and executed – and that's how it turned out.

Many historians see Emmet simply as another in the long line of Irish revolutionaries who tried to free Ireland, but failed. They argue that he acted in good faith, but couldn't win enough of the general population over to his cause. Others argue that Emmet became a tool for the authorities. The government had always believed, or so it is argued, that the forces of Wolfe Tone had not been fully defeated in 1798. Historians have claimed that the authorities had deliberately sought to flush out all the remaining supporters of the spirit of 1798 by encouraging Emmet's rebellion. Spies encouraged Emmet to rebel, they claim, and once he was in custody, he was taken into the confidence of the prison surgeon and his lawyer, both of whom actually worked for the government. Poor old Emmet, if it's all true, was just a pawn in the game.

Emmet was sentenced to be hanged. But he was also allowed to make a long speech from the dock. Although his rebellion turned out to be less than effective, the sentiment he expressed in his speech became a cornerstone of Irish nationalist thinking. He argued that no one should mourn him, inscribe his tomb, write his epitaph, or celebrate his life until Ireland had won its freedom '. . . when my country takes her place among the nations of the earth, and not till then, let my epitaph be written'. It was powerful stuff, and would have much more of an effect than the actual rebellion that he had led.

A traitor's death

The day after his trial had closed (which had only lasted a single day anyway), the twenty-five-year-old Emmet was taken to Kilmainham Gaol and hanged. When his body was taken down from the rope, his head was cut off and displayed to the crowd. For dramatic effect – and always a crowd pleaser – the hangman, Thomas Galvin, announced that 'this is the head of a traitor, Robert Emmet'.

Robert Emmet's missing body

Once he'd been dispatched by the hangman and the crowd gone home, Emmet's body was put to one side. His relatives were either in prison, or else too scared to come and get it, so Emmet was buried in a common grave in a place called Bully's acre. Later no one was really sure exactly where he was buried, and his grave was unmarked. What his supporters thought was that his body was later dug up, and taken to St Michan's Church. But then others claimed that the body had been taken to St Anne's Church in Dawson Street or the Glasnevin Churchyard. Others said it had gone to his family's vault at St Peter's Church in Aungier Street. In 1903, the centenary of Emmet's death, it was this last option that was investigated, but nothing conclusive was found. It was later argued that a headless corpse found at St Paul's Church in King Street was that of Emmet, and that it had been hidden there by the authorities who didn't want any Emmet grave to become a shrine. St Peter's has now been demolished and is a YMCA, while St Paul's has been converted into an enterprise centre. No one really knows where Emmet's remains are, but the story never goes away. In 2003, DNA tests were carried out on a skull found in Tralee which people believed was Emmet's head. It wasn't. So basically we still don't know where poor old Robert Emmet lies.

After Emmet: The disloyal Catholics?

The Act of Union had been brought about in response to the failed 1798 rebellion. It was an attempt to stop such rebellions occurring and make Ireland a more secure and peaceful place. By 1803, Emmet's rebellion had caused everyone to reassess the question about where the loyalties of Irish Catholics really lay.

In the early years of the nineteenth century:

✔ The authorities remained suspicious of the Catholics.

✔ Books such as Richard Musgrave's *Memoirs of the Different Rebellions of Ireland,* published in 1801, warned the Protestants of Ireland that the Catholics were just waiting to massacre them all. Musgrave was a notorious anti-Catholic propagandist. This kind of propaganda instilled a sense of fear.

✔ After Emmet's rebellion, the lord lieutenant of Ireland accused the Catholic bishops of having prior knowledge of what Emmet was intending to do (and in effect of having supported it).

✔ Attitudes against the idea of Catholic emancipation – first suggested as part of the Act of Union – hardened. No one in parliament or the Lords wanted to pass such legislation.

✔ In the 1807 election, the popular slogan of the winning party in Britain was 'No Popery!'

It's pretty clear that the first few decades of the nineteenth century were pretty bleak for the Catholics in Ireland. No one in power really trusted them, incidents such as the Emmet rebellion just made matters worse, and the Protestant Church actively campaigned against Catholicism.

The Battle for Converts

With the atmosphere building against Catholics, the bad feelings between Irish Catholics and Irish Protestants became increasingly entrenched.

Across Ireland the numbers of sectarian attacks and clashes rose dramatically. Secret Catholic Societies sprang up across rural Ireland, wanting better conditions for the non-Protestant population of Ireland. With no effective public platform, these societies were reduced to making attacks on local Protestants.

The wholly Protestant yeomanry, which was responsible for law and order in the years before a police force was organised, combated the activities of the secret societies, and, for good measure, staged indiscriminate attacks on the Catholic population. Such sectarian violence did little to convince either side to trust the other, and made rural Ireland a deeply unpleasant and, at times, dangerous place to live.

Many Protestant Church leaders believed that if the Catholic Irish could be made to see the errors of their ways, and convert, then they wouldn't be such a threat.

The early nineteenth century was a period during which religion changed. Across Britain and Ireland, Protestants moved out of their Churches and into the communities. They were evangelical and wanted to convert people to the Protestant faith. The evangelical missions were very important in England, especially in the urban areas that were industrialising, and convinced many people that they had to be closer to God. The evangelicals saw the conversion of non-believers or people from other faiths, rather than the blanket dismissal of the beliefs of others, as their role.

In Ireland Bible societies assisted the work of the Evangelical missions. The societies (a bit like the Gideon people that leave Bibles in hotel rooms across the world) believed that Bibles and religious tracts should be made available to everyone free-of-charge. If they had access to these works they were more likely to read them and change their ways.

In a single decade at the start of the nineteenth century, the Bible societies distributed 4.5 million Bibles and religious tracts across Ireland. The evangelical missions worked very hard, and with their religious fervour, began converting people from Catholicism to Protestantism.

The evangelical movement worked so well, that the Catholic Church in Ireland was forced to act. The Catholic Church invested in its educational programmes across the country, and spent more time teaching people about the importance of their religion. The Church was put on a better organisational footing across the country, and public events staged to encourage devotion.

This battle for converts was important. It made people – Catholic or Protestant – far more aware of, and committed to, their particular denomination. It made them understand that their religion was not something that they were simply born into, or engaged with on a Sunday, but was a central part of their identity. It linked together personal identity with religious and national identities. The Protestants therefore saw themselves as ever more stridently British and superior, while the Catholics saw themselves as Irish and discriminated against. The close links between religion and identity are important in the battle over Catholic emancipation (see Chapter 17) and the struggle between nationalism and unionism (see Chapters 19 and 21).

Land and Famine

One of the biggest structural problems facing Ireland in the nineteenth century was the ownership and tillage of the land. The problems would be most fully demonstrated during the Great Famine of the mid-nineteenth century (see Chapter 18), but even in the first half of the nineteenth century the problems were evident.

These included:

- ✔ Poor agricultural techniques – many of the Irish farmers weren't using modern ways of farming because they couldn't afford to. Also, many Irish farmers distrusted the new technologies and feared that their application would result in them losing their jobs.

- ✔ Inefficiency on the land and poor farming methods reduced the yields from crops and made them more prone to disease and weather problems.

- ✔ The subdivision of lands among Catholic families led to ever smaller plots of land being farmed.

- ✔ Family size, and the size of the general population, was increasing: There were more mouths to feed, but no improvement in farming yields.

- ✔ The systems of rent and land tenancy were unfair. Catholics suffered from a lack of legal protection in terms of their rented land, and rents were often unfairly high.

✔ Although many landlords did live in Ireland, and worked hard to improve their lands, many other English landowners chose not to live in Ireland and left their lands in the hands of middlemen. These men had no interest in the long-term future of the land, and exploited the tenants to make their own wallets fatter. Their actions only increased the number of abuses, and made the yields from the land even more unstable.

With all these problems the situation was becoming precarious. Whilst the winters were mild, and the summers good, then all would be okay, and everyone would get by. But what if anything went wrong (plant disease, heavy frosts, and so on)? Would the system be able to cope? The short answer: No.

Going hungry

In Ireland, the crops failed in 1800, between 1816 and 1819, and again in 1822. The effects were devastating. Crop failure was bad enough, but each time the shortage of food was accompanied by disease.

The problem of crop failure, starvation, and famine was nothing new to Ireland. In 1741 an estimated 250,000 people died from famine, and in the years 1816–42 there were 14 partial or complete famines in Ireland. The agricultural infrastructure of Ireland was a mess, and people were dying very regularly. Without the political will to sort out the landholding system – which didn't exist – such crop failures sadly became the norm.

The year of no summer

1816 was known as the year of no summer or, in many of the records, 'a year without summer'. This wasn't just an Irish phenomenon, but affected much of Europe. It was caused by volcanic dust that was covering the sky after a major volcanic eruption in 1815 in Indonesia.

The effects of all the heavy cloud and dust cover blocked out the sun, changed the weather, and killed the summer. Heavy rains during spring months were followed by snow in June and July, causing widespread harvest failures. In England and Ireland the wheat harvest was at least 75 per cent lower than normal. England was better able to deal with the loss

of crops than Ireland because England had a more diverse agricultural system and could more readily import extra food. Too many Irish farmers were reliant on a subsistence system, and if their crop failed, they had no food.

In Ireland writers noted that the number of beggars on the street had reached 'unmanageable proportions'. The poor state of everyone's health before the crop failures didn't help. One Irish doctor wrote how everything was made worse by 'the low conditions of bodily health arising from the deficiency and bad quality of the food'.

Stay or go? Irish emigration begins

The nineteenth century is known as the century during which the Irish started leaving their homeland in great numbers (people had been leaving since the seventeenth century, but these were mostly Protestants). Most of the emigration is linked to the mid-nineteenth century Great Famine but the movement of Irish Catholics had already started in the wake of these early nineteenth century famines and the year of no summer.

The Irish didn't really have much of a choice. Stay, and you'd probably die (or at least have a pretty miserable existence) or go, and try to make a new home and life somewhere else.

Heading to America and Canada

Prior to 1827, there had been limits on the number of people that the American government would allow to land in its country. These rules were changed and the government repealed all restrictions on immigration. Immediately the unrestricted opening of America changed things. Between 1828 and 1837 almost 400,000 Irish men, women, and children departed for a new life in America (including what was then called British North America, or Canada as we know it today). For more details of what life was like for the Irish in America, see Chapter 18.

The opening up of North America, and the effects of the famine, changed the nature of emigration. Prior to 1832, about half of the emigrants came from Ulster and were largely Protestant and Presbyterian. These people weren't necessarily the richest in society, but at least they could afford to go, and would be allowed into America. After the rule changes in 1827, Catholics from the three southern provinces dominated the numbers landing in America.

Across the water to Britain

Despite all the political differences between Ireland and Britain, it was close by. It was also one of the most powerful countries in the world, and full of towns, factories, and opportunities.

For the poorest Irish, who would never get enough money together for a ship fare to America, Britain became the final destination.

From 1830 to 1835 some 200,000 Irish men and women went across the Irish Sea and found new homes in the towns and cities of England and Scotland. By 1841 over 400,000 lived permanently in Britain. These congregated in the largest cities such Glasgow, London, Manchester, and Liverpool.

All the problems that the Irish had in Ireland, were replicated when they got to Britain. They were treated suspiciously because of their religion, given the worst jobs, and often fell into lives that were dominated by drink, crime, and violence. They were also regularly attacked by Protestant mobs who hated them for their religion. Sectarianism became as much a feature of life, particularly in Liverpool and Glasgow, as it had ever been in Ireland.

Travelling conditions

As ship technology improved, and trading links between the countries of the Empire increased, there were more and more boats crossing the world. The hungry Irish just became a new potential cargo for the ship-owners, and the Irish were willing passengers.

Compared to a crossing to America (which was becoming ever cheaper) the trip across the Irish Sea was a bargain. It cost just a few pence to buy a deck passage across to Britain. That meant that you got to stand outside the whole way – whatever the weather.

But conditions on open deck crossings were terrible. Deck passengers had a lower priority than baggage or livestock. On many crossings an estimated 2,000 people would be crowded on to an open deck. For the ship-owners it meant good business (the more people they packed on board, the higher the profits). Any safety regulations were never enforced, and the poor Irish were hardly in a position to complain. Records of people being washed overboard were common, as were injuries sustained in the crush.

The Population Explosion

One of the root causes of the problems with land ownership, and the inability of Irish farmers to produce enough food was the rapid increase of population in the first half of the nineteenth century.

The growth of population was dramatic (as it was in Britain, but there they had industrialisation to sustain and employ huge numbers of people). In Ireland there was no great industrialisation, and a rapidly growing population was reliant on a poor agricultural infrastructure. Table 16-1 shows the dramatic growth between the beginning of the eighteenth century and 1841.

Table 16-1	Population from 1700–1841
Year	*Population*
1700	Approximately 2 million
1754	2.3 million
1800	Between 4.5 and 5 million
1821	6.8 million
1841	8.1 million

The big wind

The fragile nature of the Irish agricultural system, and its openness to devastating attack from the elements, was proven on the night of 6 January 1839. A storm which ripped across Ireland was seen by many people as the precursor to the Day of Judgement. It showed them just how angry God could be. Others blamed it on the Freemasons, and some, with an eye on the old fashioned legends, on the fairies (it was rumoured that English fairies had invaded Ireland, and that the Irish fairies blew the wind to blow away the invaders). Whatever the cause, the Big Wind was devastating.

Damage to shipping around the Irish coast was put at half a million pounds, the Liffey flooded, and many of the trees in Dublin's Phoenix Park were blown down. What crops that were in the ground were ruined, and stored cattle feed simply blown away. One hundred people died, and buildings across Ireland, whether simple dwellings or big houses, were damaged and destroyed.

There was a massive relief effort in Ireland to rebuild everything, but critics were very vocal about how little assistance came from England (a mirror of what would happen during the famine). The impact of the Big Wind changed the way in which buildings were constructed in Ireland, and increased the pace of poor law reform. The replacement buildings were either constructed of new materials (thatched roofs were replaced by slate) or else in sheltered areas rather than on open land. The chaos that was caused by the wind, and the dislocation of people, encouraged the government to make sure that the provisions of the 1837 Poor Law were fully applied to Ireland.

One surprising legacy of the Big Wind happened in 1909. In that year the Old Age Pension was introduced. In an age before birth certificates and driving licences, how do you prove that you're over seventy and entitled to the money? The answer was simple: if you could remember the Big Wind, you were old enough.

As Table 16-1 shows, the real spurt in population happened in the decades between 1780 and 1830. Unlike Britain and other parts of Europe, this wasn't an urban phenomenon helped along by industrialisation, but a mainly rural growth. It was the poorest labouring classes, those who couldn't really afford the extra mouths, that saw the biggest increases in Ireland.

The reasons why Ireland's population grew so rapidly are still argued over. The fascination with the growth is driven by the lack of development in Ireland: usually the reason why numbers start increasing. Most historians agree on at least some of the reasons why Ireland's population grew. They argue that the marriage age was relatively low during this period, which led to people starting their families earlier, and this in turn led to very large families. Also, because there was a tradition of subdivision of Catholic landholdings between all male members of the family, everyone got some land to live off. While these pockets of land were increasingly reducing in size, the inheritance of even a small plot of land allowed people to stay where they were. They didn't have to look for alternative ways of finding a living, and could marry and stay on the land. So although their standards of living increasingly decreased, people fed their ever larger families, subsistence-style, off the land they occupied.

The growth in population, and the causes of it, was a time bomb. As more people tried to survive on ever smaller plots of land, so the room for manoeuvre, in the event of a poor harvest, reduced. Ireland was heading for some real problems (see Chapter 18).

Chapter 17

Three Strikes for Irish Independence: O'Connell, Davis, and Mitchel

The first half of the nineteenth century saw lots of changes in Ireland. The Irish started getting organised politically, and in Daniel O'Connell found a great leader. This chapter explores why the issues of Catholic emancipation and the repeal of the Act of Union dominated Irish (and British) political life until the 1840s.

But these years weren't all peaceful protest and politics. There were also violent attempts at driving the British out of Ireland; and the land, and the ways it was managed, also began dominating Irish thoughts.

Agitating on the Land

The administration of land in Ireland had always been a contentious issue. The bulk of the land was owned by Protestants (the descendants of settlers), and by the start of the nineteenth century many Protestants were absentee landlords who preferred to live in England rather than in Ireland. The majority of the Irish themselves owned little land, and many of them were forced to try and make a living off small, uneconomic plots. The poor state of Irish agriculture and the unequal distribution of the land were structural problems that would lead, in part, to the disastrous Irish famine in the mid-nineteenth century (see Chapter 18).

Ireland was plagued by a series of issues relating specifically to the land and its management. These issues, like poverty, violence, and tithing systems put in place years earlier by a Protestant parliament, exacerbated the political problems the country faced (which you can read about in the later sections of this chapter). During the nineteenth century, some efforts were made to eliminate or, if not eliminate, at least lessen the instability and dissatisfaction that the majority of the Irish felt. These efforts had varying degrees of success.

The mass of problems in Ireland were all interconnected. Irish Catholics felt detached from the system of government, and this feeling of alienation filtered down to their relationships with local authorities, their landlords, and the economic system that they had to work in.

Rural violence

In the 1830s, rural Ireland was a violent land. As one historian noted, 'violence, murder, injury, and destruction of property were endemic'. Crime was a common feature of daily life. The forces of law and order barely functioned, and secret societies (read more about them in the section 'Secret societies') fighting against all kinds of grievances were common across the country.

To deal with the violence, a new police force, the Royal Irish Constabulary was established in the 1830s. Although mistrusted by many people, at least its presence led to a semblance of order and fairness.

Tithing

One of the most immediate gripes in the 1830s was the tithe system. Anyone owning or renting land had to pay an annual tithe (think of it as a tax) in the form of produce to the Church. The problem for most people in Ireland was that this meant the established Protestant Church, not the Catholic Church that they followed. This was a payment that most Irish could ill afford to make, and the fact they were paying it to their religious opposite made it worse.

Also, some important British figures in Ireland, such as the Under-Secretary in Ireland (a very important civil servant), Thomas Drummond, began vocalising their concerns about the way that land was managed pointing out that many aspects – particularly the tithes – were unfair.

In 1831 a Catholic Bishop, James Doyle of Kildare and Leighlin, denounced the tithe system and told his parishioners that they should oppose them 'with all the means the law allows'. What he was trying to encourage people to do was to protest peacefully. He was opposed, as all of the Catholic Church was, to secret societies that were violent. The Catholic Association, which had been started by Daniel O'Connell in 1823 (see the section 'The Catholic Association' later in this chapter) supported the movement to change the tithe system as they felt it was yet another piece of legislation that made it difficult for Irish people to have a stable lifestyle.

Given the weight of unease that everyone felt about tithes, and the religious connotations of such a tax, the British government acted. In 1838 they changed the system. It didn't offer as much reform as people in Ireland wanted – but when did reform ever go far enough?

The new system annulled all unpaid tithes and exempted many of the poorest tenant farmers in Ireland from having to pay. In future, rather than having to hand over produce that could have fed their own families or made them money at market, Irish farmers would have to pay a money charge to their landlords which would replace the tithe. Although not perfect, the changes did just enough and ended the arguments over the tithe system.

Poverty

Poverty was a big issue. There was no welfare state system in the nineteenth century, and if you were poor you had to rely on charity or else turn to crime. More likely than not, poverty would lead to illness and death.

In 1838, the British government introduced the Poor Law Act to Ireland. This law set up 130 workhouses across the country that would take in the poorest citizens. In return for hard, and often brutal work, the residents of the workhouse would be given food and a bed.

Workhouses were a last resort. They were horrible and unpleasant places run with a strict regime. People would go to any lengths to avoid going to the workhouse, but eventually they often had no choice. Think of Charles Dickens' Oliver Twist asking for more gruel, and you get an idea of the kind of place I'm talking about. The Victorians believed that they were doing the right and charitable thing in providing workhouses, but the people who supported them didn't have to live there.

Railways

One of the biggest changes in Irish society in the first half of the nineteenth century, in fact across the whole of Europe, was the arrival of the railways.

Ever since George Stephenson had perfected his train, the Rocket, in England, railway lines had spread across Britain. They had an incredible impact on the economy, on the way people travelled and helped moved goods quickly and cheaply. Many entrepreneurs had made their millions from railway building in Britain, and it was only natural that they extended their endeavour to Ireland. The railways had been built by thousands of Irish navvies who had emigrated to Britain to take advantage of the employment opportunities. These men didn't get rich from their work, and many of them died doing what was hard and dangerous work.

The first railway opened in Ireland in 1834, and ran from Dublin to Kingstown. It was followed two years later by the 36 mile line between Belfast and Armagh. Railway fever had begun.

The Drummond Commission was established by the British government to ascertain whether railways would be economically viable in Ireland. The Commission felt that because of the scattered Irish population, and lack of industrial development, railways would struggle. How wrong they were! By 1848 Ireland had 360 miles of railway, and by 1920 this had grown to 3,750 miles.

Most of the railways joined together the large towns and cities of Ireland. They ran to the major ports and helped their passengers to emigrate. Railways also ran to major sporting arenas such as race courses, and assisted the flow of goods being imported into, and exported out of, Ireland via the main ports.

While the railways made certain investors rich, they didn't bring about the kind of wealth that was made in Britain. That said, they played a key role in making Ireland a smaller place and bringing about a good deal of economic modernisation.

Secret societies

Ireland had always had lots of secret societies. In the second half of the eighteenth century, the inhabitants of rural Ireland had been terrified by the activities of a host of such organisations. Usually these societies were very localised and driven to action by abuses and unfairness in the areas of rural employment and access to the land.

In the first half of the nineteenth century these organisations continued to pop up across Ireland. The organisations often have colourful names such as the Whiteboys, the Oakboys, and the Hearts of Steel, and were led by mythical leaders such as Captain Fearnought and General Right.

The nineteenth century secret societies were not as powerful as their eighteenth century equivalents, but were still a concern to the authorities. Both the civil and religious authorities condemned such societies.

One of the most common tactics of such societies was to attack the property of absentee landlords. It was argued that these people who owned the land, yet lived elsewhere, weren't being fair. Why should they have land if they couldn't be bothered to live on it?

The tactics of the protesters were varied and included:

- ✔ Sending threatening letters and signs to the landlords and their agents.
- ✔ Gatherings of large numbers of people at the landlord's house or property to intimidate them or their family.
- ✔ Physical attacks on landlords and their agents.
- ✔ Attacks on and intimidation of people renting land from such landlords.

The attacks were viciously opposed by the state authorities, and many people were arrested and imprisoned for their part in such protests. The net effect was to make rural Ireland a dangerous place to live.

Although popular, and active for nearly a century in various forms, the secret societies began to diminish in importance by the time of the Great Famine. Rather than joining localised protests, most people realised they could more powerfully make their point by joining broader political campaigns such as the Land League and the later crusade for Home Rule.

Daniel O'Connell and Catholic Emancipation

Because the Act of Union meant that all major political decisions were made in London, and usually in favour of the Protestant population (refer to Chapter 16), Catholics had only the barest political, economic, and social rights, despite outnumbering Protestants on the island by five to one. Clearly, the Irish needed an inspirational leader, but they had lacked one since the deaths of Wolfe Tone and Henry Gratton (see Chapter 15). And then along came Danny.

Daniel O'Connell was from a Kerry family. His family, although Catholic, were landowners, and his upbringing was relatively well-off. Because of family money, young Daniel was educated in the law, a profession he was able to enter at the end of the eighteenth century after studying in London, Dublin, and Paris. Daniel was very good at his job. By 1805 he was earning an amazing £1,000 per year, which rose to £3,500 soon afterwards. This man was becoming seriously rich.

Castle clergy

Equal rights for Catholics, although opposed by the majority of Protestants in Ireland, wasn't a particularly radical idea. Unsurprisingly the Catholic Church in Ireland thought it was a good idea.

But the Catholic Church had a problem. Many of the leading clerics in the country didn't particularly like the Irish peasantry. They preferred preaching to the well-off in Irish Catholic society. O'Connell dismissed this mentality as belonging to the 'castle clergy' – priests who were more interested in good living and the approval of Dublin Castle, the seat of British rule in Ireland, than in the real needs of the mass of their parishioners.

Class was still a difficult issue in the early nineteenth century. The French Revolution had been driven by the support of the poorest classes who held the Church in as much disdain as they did the French monarchy and upper classes. There was a constant fear that if the Irish peasantry got organised, they would reject the Church as easily as they would attack the representatives of their British rulers.

But rather than simply being interested in wealth, which would have been easy to do, O'Connell was socially minded and felt he should do something to improve the lot of his fellow Irish. The root of all evil in Ireland, or so O'Connell thought, was the lack of rights that Catholics had. He wanted them to be equal with Protestants, and so his thinking led him to the idea of Catholic emancipation – and not armed rebellion.

So where did these big ideas come from?

- ✔ He had witnessed the French Revolution during his time in Paris and rejected the use of such violence and terror in the pursuit of social justice.

- ✔ He had also opposed the 1798 rebellion. He distrusted what the French were trying to do in Ireland in 1798, and believed that while Britain was far from perfect, Ireland had more in common with them than outsiders.

- ✔ He read lots of European literature about freedom. As a result he believed in humanitarianism and equality. For example, while it was still deeply unfashionable O'Connell supported the emancipation of Jewish people and the abolition of slavery.

The campaign for emancipation

What O'Connell wanted, put simply, was for Catholics to have the ability to vote for Catholic Members of Parliament. If they had that, he argued, they would have a stake in the society they lived in, and Ireland would be a better place for all.

Some Catholics could vote. Those who had freeholds valued at 40 shillings or above could vote (some 230,000 people out of a population of seven million). What O'Connell was campaigning for was not votes for all – that wasn't even on the cards in Britain – but for the rights of Catholics to enter parliament.

O'Connell argued that any movement that supported Catholic emancipation had to be a mass movement. It was no good having the support of an elite if the bulk of the Irish people weren't involved and didn't benefit. O'Connell wanted to make his movement for change a genuinely national one. In line with his humanitarian thinking, he wanted his movement to give a voice to everyone.

The Catholic Association

In April 1823 O'Connell established the Catholic Association that would campaign for emancipation. All such political campaigns need two things: money and mass support. O'Connell figured out a way that he could have both. By the time he was done, O'Connell had half a million members – middle-class Catholics, the peasantry, and their spiritual leaders – at his disposal.

The middle-class

While many Catholics were poor and lived a subsistence, peasant-based lifestyle, many others, like O'Connell himself, were affluent. They were professionals and landowners, and many had made money in the booming world of commerce of the early nineteenth century. Like their peasant brethren, however, they were equally disenfranchised. They had grievances.

So O'Connell set the membership fee for the Catholic Association at one guinea. The money collected from these wealthy members funded O'Connell's campaign.

The peasantry

To get the people behind him, O'Connell offered cut-price membership of the Catholic Association. In 1824 he decided that anyone could join as an associate member for one penny a month. Even the poorest peasant could afford this, and associate members flooded into the Catholic Association making a mass movement.

The priests

To complete his sweep of members, O'Connell also made all priests ex officio members of the Association. The Priests were essential to the whole movement. Not only did they support O'Connell, but they collected the penny associate membership subscription at the Church gates before Mass. This was not simply a political movement, but one that was linked with popular devotion to the Catholic faith.

Meanwhile, at a place called Waterloo

While O'Connell was busying thinking about what to do for Irish Catholics, there were far bigger things happening in Europe. The period of the French Revolution had led to all kinds of chaos, and eventually Napoleon Bonaparte had taken charge in France. He fought a long and bitter war against the British that finally ended, as the ABBA song went, at Waterloo. The Napoleonic Wars overshadowed everything else. Thousands of Irishmen (159,000 by the end of the war) went to war, fighting for the British, and until the final battles of 1815, the struggles against Napoleon overshadowed everything.

The campaign begins

After the uprisings led by Wolfe Tone (1798) and Robert Emmett (1803), the Protestants in Ireland and the British establishment were deeply suspicious of Catholic desires. Simply put, the Catholic population of Ireland was seen as the enemy. They had made an alliance with the French in 1798, and followed the religious doctrines of Rome. The idea that they should have equality in Ireland seemed absurd to most Protestants. Instead it was easier to mistrust them, and when necessary, squash them.

In this climate, O'Connell had to transform his popular support into meaningful political action that the British would respond to. To that end, O'Connell combined popular protest with electioneering and this strategy struck at the heart of British attitudes towards Ireland and the Catholic population:

- ✔ The Catholic Association began convincing sympathetic Protestants to stand in the general election of 1826. Supported by the machinery of the Catholic Association, these candidates were able to unseat members of the Protestant ascendancy who opposed emancipation.
- ✔ In January 1828 three quarters of parishes across the land held rallies clamouring for Catholic emancipation.

O'Connell stands for election

In June 1828, O'Connell announced that he, a Catholic, would fight the by-election in Clare. He was the first Catholic since the seventeenth century to stand for election. O'Connell was going to test for himself whether his campaign was working.

The priests in the area campaigned for O'Connell, and the full apparatus of the Catholic Association was brought to bear on the electorate of Clare.

Nice Mr Wellington and a compromise

O'Connell won the Clare by-election. The politicians in Britain had two choices: accept the demands of O'Connell and the Catholic Association, or crush them.

The Prime Minster, the Duke of Wellington (an Irishman), decided that compromise was the best bet. If he refused to yield to the demands for Catholic emancipation what would the next step in the campaign be? Rather than face some form of violent insurgency, Wellington understood that it was best to try and meet the demands of O'Connell and his followers.

In 1829 the necessary laws were passed that allowed for the emancipation of Catholics. But, this victory for emancipation came at a cost. The Catholic Association was banned by law, and the threshold for voting was raised from the previous 40 shillings to £10, effectively cutting the Catholic electorate in Ireland from 230,000 to a mere 14,000. Nevertheless, O'Connell had won: Catholics were now allowed to enter parliament, and as a result, the voice of Catholic Ireland could be heard in the debating chambers of Westminster.

Repealing the Act of Union

Catholic emancipation was great news, but O'Connell wanted more than that. He argued that the biggest stumbling block for any real sense of Irish freedom was the Act of Union. O'Connell believed that while Ireland was ruled directly from London, it could never have any real control of its affairs. He began a campaign for the repeal of the Act of Union. The bottom line, which many British politicians understood only too well, was that while the Catholic question had been settled, this did not mean that arguments about the future of Ireland were finished.

The Duke of Wellington

Famous as a war-time general, his victories over Napoleon and the invention of a boot, the future Duke of Wellington was born as Arthur Wellesley in Ireland. Very much of the upper class, and from a land-owning family, Wellington did little in his political career to advance the cause of Irish Catholics. But when it mattered, as it did in 1829, he knew enough about the dynamics of Ireland to make concessions. Wellington was permanently remembered by his countrymen shortly after his death. In Dublin's Phoenix Park an obelisk was built – the second tallest in the world – that celebrated his military victories.

Taking the idea to Parliament

After emancipation the representation of Catholic Ireland increased. In the 1835 general election 65 of the 105 Irish seats were won by anti-Tory candidates. O'Connell could count on the loyalty of 60 of them. What the Irish members of parliament were doing was forming themselves into a block around O'Connell and supporting the liberal-minded Whig party rather than the conservative Tory party. The Whigs understood that they were expected to act sympathetically on Irish issues in return for the support of the Irish in parliament. They were not supportive of the ideal of repeal, however.

Whether Whig or Tory, the main political parties in Britain were Protestant minded and committed to supporting the Union and protecting the stability of the British Empire. While the Whigs understood the need for a sympathetic policy towards Ireland to keep it peaceful, this did not equate to supporting the break-up of the Union.

In 1834 O'Connell forced a vote asking that the Union be discussed: he lost, 523 votes to 38. If O'Connell wanted repeal, he'd have to find a way to do it that didn't rely on parliament.

O'Connell's plan

In the early 1840s O'Connell turned all his attentions to trying to win repeal of the Union. He built on the model he had used to gain Catholic emancipation: a mass movement demanding change.

O'Connell worked the parishes across Ireland and encouraged everyone to join his Repeal Association. He managed to recruit three million members into the Association. The support of the Catholic Church was once more critical, and he was successful in convincing the majority of Irish bishops to join the Association and become vocal supporters. In 1843 O'Connell was so confident that his movement was becoming unstoppable that he declared that the year 'is and shall be the great repeal year'.

O'Connell understood that the British parliament would not simply grant repeal. Instead he proposed his own approach that would force the British to act. He set out a timetable for 1843:

- ✔ A series of mass public meetings to show the popular support for repeal.

- ✔ Elections to be held in Ireland to establish a Council in Ireland.

- ✔ This Council would then (i) Repeal the Act of Union, and (ii) establish a new Irish House of Commons.

- ✔ The existence of the Council would force the British to act. O'Connell believed that the British would either have to crush the Council or accept the ideal of repeal.

O'Connell was playing a high-stakes game. He knew that the British wouldn't take a mass movement demanding repeal lying down. If O'Connell pushed too hard, he risked a vicious repression of Ireland by British forces. This in turn could lead to violence (which O'Connell deplored) and the loss of the moral high ground. O'Connell had to try and convince the British that repeal was the right thing to do, but he also had to make sure he stayed within the law and did not give the British any reason to suppress his movement.

Monster meetings

One of O'Connell's key strategies was to bring ordinary Irish people together at mass meetings to support the call for repeal. O'Connell wanted these meetings to be well-ordered and carefully controlled. He did not want to give the British any ammunition that would allow them to dismiss the meetings as those of a dangerous Irish rabble.

Throughout 1843, O'Connell staged a series of these rallies, termed 'monster meetings' by the London *Times.* Over forty of them were held across the country, and the average crowd seems to have been somewhere in the region of 300,000. Considering that these were the days before electronic amplification, it says much for O'Connell's skills as a speaker and the popular belief in the cause that so many people attended.

In August 1843 O'Connell held his biggest meeting to-date. An estimated one million people came together to hear him speak at Tara. That crowd, like all the ones before it, had been well behaved. The careful control of the crowds meant that the British had no reason to crush O'Connell's popular movement or stop the calls for repeal.

Another monster meeting was planned for October 1843. The leaflets announcing the meeting were deemed by the British to be seditious, and they banned the meeting and the military were put on to the streets to stop the meeting from going ahead. O'Connell had two choices:

- ✔ Go ahead with the meeting and risk a major confrontation between his followers and the forces of the Crown that would undoubtedly lead to loss of life and the banning of his movement.
- ✔ Stand down the meeting, obey the letter of the law, and try to maintain the momentum behind the repeal movement.

O'Connell decided to obey the British order. He circulated notices cancelling the meeting, and members of the association turned back people who had travelled to Dublin for the event.

The end of the Repeal efforts

Acquiescing to the British demands that the October 1843 meeting be cancelled, and thereby avoiding a potential crisis, gave the British grounds to claim seditious activity on behalf of O'Connell and his Repeal movement. O'Connell and eight other leaders of the Repeal Association were arrested. O'Connell was sentenced to a year in prison. Although released after six months, O'Connell was seventy years old when he was finally freed. He didn't have the energy to re-energise his movement.

Not only had O'Connell's movement lost momentum, his time in prison meant that other more radical forces moved into the void and began stirring up trouble. Also, although no one knew it at the time, the famine lay just around the corner (see Chapter 18) and this would completely dislocate everything in Ireland. The movement for repeal died, for the time being, in October 1843.

Rebelling Against the Union

Into the void left by O'Connell stepped a new organisation – The Young Irelanders. This group, led by Thomas Davis, wanted pretty much the same thing that the Repeal Association wanted – some form of Irish independence from Britain – but their methods were radically different.

The fluid politics of the 1840s were important for exposing Irish people to various ways of thinking. On the one hand they had the mass popular, and legally-minded, movement of O'Connell, and on the other they had Davis and the Young Irelanders.

Thomas Davis and the Young Irelanders

Davis is one of the most important thinkers in the history of Irish nationalism. He was a member of the Repeal Association, and highly thought of by O'Connell despite their regular differences of opinion. Whereas O'Connell closely allied his campaigns with Catholicism, Davis argued that the Irish nation embraced all shades of religious belief and tradition across the island. Davis also argued that the Irish language had to be at the heart of any Irish nation as it made the people see themselves as genuinely and distinctively Irish.

Davis established a newspaper, the *Nation*, in 1842 to spread his message. It was hugely successful and had a readership of some 250,000 people across the land. The paper was full of essays and poems that linked the struggle for

Ireland in the 1840s with the ancient struggles of history, and embraced the 1798 rebellion as a great moment for the Irish.

Whereas O'Connell had simply wanted an end to the Union and the establishment of an Irish parliament that would reflect the Catholicism of Ireland, Davis considered that vision too short sighted. Through the *Nation,* Davis and his fellow writers introduced their readers to Irish songs and history of a patriotic flavour. But while Davis painted a picture of an Irish nation that, while free of Britain, included all religions, O'Connell's view was of a limited independence that was almost entirely Catholic.

Davis was dead in 1845 (he was 30 years old) and in his short life he had vocalised many important ideas, and offered Ireland an alternative to the Repeal Association. O'Connell followed him to the grave in 1847. With the two main leaders in the grave, which view would persevere?

John Mitchel and the Irish Confederation

In 1846 there was a major split between the Young Irelanders and the Repeal Association over the Association's decision to completely reject the use of violence in pursuit of its aims. The Young Irelanders didn't agree and set up their own organisation: the Irish Confederation.

With the death of Davis, the leader of this new organisation was now in the hands of the radical Ulster Presbyterian, John Mitchel. He thought that the direction of the movement and the *Nation* was too moderate, and set up his own newspaper, *United Irishman*, in early 1848.

1848 was a year of political upheaval across Europe. There were major revolutions and political struggles in France and other countries on the continent. The intellectual spirit of the time was one of revolution, of challenging old orders. In Ireland, men like Mitchel found the atmosphere of revolution intoxicating. The British were fearful that the spirit of revolution could spread to Britain or Ireland and kept a close eye on the rabble rousers.

In April 1848 Mitchel set out his stall. He wrote that the Irish people should 'strike for a republic… and raise the Irish tricolour, orange, white and green, over a forest of Irish pikes'. His call was a revolutionary one. He talked openly of a republic that would take in all of Ireland, and his reference to the forest of Irish pikes brought to mind the failed rebellion of 1798.

The British weren't stupid though, and recognised a revolutionary when they saw one. Mitchel, along with other Young Irelanders, was arrested shortly after the outbreak of revolution in France and sent to Australia for a prolonged holiday at his Majesty's pleasure.

In addition to arresting the main leaders, the British made the Irish Confederation illegal. The remnants of the leadership, who weren't on their way to Australia, decided to act.

The cabbage patch revolution

Revolutions usually rely on some level of organisation and, most critically, on popular support. The Young Irelanders of 1848 had neither. Although men and arms had been promised from sympathisers in Scotland these never arrived. Many people, although they may have been sympathetic, never joined the revolution.

In the end the whole thing became a farce. The main body of rebels, numbering just a few hundred, found themselves pinned down in a house in Balingarry, County Tipperary. The house belonged to Widow McCormack and the rebels understood that if they held their ground the British forces would destroy them and the widow's property. Rather than deprive an old woman of her home and livelihood, the rebels surrendered. The main fighting before surrender had taken place in the garden of the widow's house, and the whole event has been dismissed as the 'cabbage patch' revolution.

The revolution of 1848 was a farce. But its long-term effects were very important. The British sent its leaders off to Australia to join Mitchel, whereas others evaded capture and fled to North America and France. The Irish revolutionary organisations that would appear in the second half of the nineteenth century (see Chapters 18 and 19) were founded by these men. In America they raised money to bring an end to what they considered to be the British oppression of Ireland, and in France, one of the 1848 rebels, James Stephens, was responsible for founding the Fenian movement that would underpin all moves towards expelling the British after the famine.

Young Irelanders in Australia

The leaders who took part or were implicated in the Young Irelanders uprising were exiled to Australia. This was a lucky escape as the initial sentence in court was that they should be hanged. Rather than wasting away in Australia, these men flourished. Some escaped from Australia and settled in America, while others remained after the end of their sentence in their new home. Eventually these men rose to the following positions: John Mitchel (prominent New York politician), Thomas Francis Meagher (Governor of Montana), Gavan Duffy (Premier of Victoria), Michael Ireland (Attorney General of Australia), Richard O'Gorman (Governor General of Newfoundland), and Morris Lyne (Attorney General of Australia). So, rather than suffering for the insurrectionary acts against the British, the Young Irelanders all seem to have done rather well.

Pinning your colours to the mast: The first Tricolour

One of the great innovations of 1848 was the first appearance of the flag that would eventually become the Irish national flag. Prior to 1848 most Irish nationalists had used a simple green flag, or else one decorated with a harp.

The Young Irelanders thought differently. Taking their inspiration from the French flag, they used a tricolour flag of green, white, and orange. In its modern form the flag has the green stripe nearest the flag pole, but in 1848 it was the other way round.

Whichever way the flag was flown though, the Young Irelanders gave each stripe a meaning:

✔ Green: Representing the Gaelic Catholic community in Ireland

✔ Orange: Representing the Protestant community in Ireland

✔ White: Symbolic of the two communities living in peace.

The flag made periodic appearances after 1848, but was given renewed significance when it was used by the insurgents of 1916 (see Chapter 21). It was finally adopted as the Irish national flag in the 1920s after independence, and enshrined in the constitution of 1937.

So, despite failing in its political aims, the Young Irelanders rebellion did have a lasting legacy.

Chapter 18

The Great Hunger and the Land War

· ·

In This Chapter

▶ Enduring the Famine

▶ Emigrating from Ireland

▶ Making it in America and elsewhere

▶ Fighting for Ireland

· ·

*I*n 1826, Dominic Corrigan, a Dublin doctor, warned the government that 'a pestilence and disease of unprecedented magnitude will befall us' unless the Irish people were provided with new sources of food. Sadly for Ireland Corrigan was spot on in his prediction. A famine struck Ireland in the years 1846–51, and nearly a million people perished.

This chapter takes a look at what triggered the Great Hunger in Ireland, and what it meant for the people living there at the time. It will also explore what happened to those Irish people who decided to leave Ireland because of the famine, and the impact that they had on their new homes. Finally the chapter introduces one of the stickiest issues in Irish history: the ownership of the land, and the attempts that were made to rectify the situation.

The Famine

In September 1845 the first signs of a fungal disease in Irish potatoes appeared. The humble tuber, which had fed generations of Irish people, was rotting in the fields and people started to go hungry. In 1845 only one third of the crop was lost, but in 1846 the fungus reappeared and the failure of the potato harvest was near total. The crops failed again in 1848 and 1849, and the knock on effects of poor harvests and lack of food began taking their toll on the population.

Family loss

Families across the affected areas were decimated by the famine, and in many cases entire generations perished. On the Blasket islands, off the west coast of Ireland, a woman lost her entire family to the famine: her husband and eight children. She had to bury each and every one of them herself, digging a hole in the ground for each of them in Ballynahown. Having buried each of them she began her blessing, 'Rest in peace, dear children and gentle husband . . . I leave you at rest in God's grace till the Angel sounds the trumpet on the last day.'

During the course of the famine Ireland suffered terribly. Compared to the population peak of eight million in 1841, the post-famine figure of 1851 had fallen to six and a half million. More than half of this figure had died from hunger or associated disease. The remainder had fled the famine and emigrated. The wave of the Irish leaving their home would continue unabated until the end of the nineteenth century. By 1860 there were 1.6 million Irish people living in America, and a further 800,000 in Britain. These figures represented a 6–700,000 increase, in both countries, on the numbers for a decade earlier.

The numbers who lost their lives in the famine, or who chose to emigrate, represents a disaster of epic proportions. It changed Ireland forever, and had a profound effect on those countries where the Irish chose to settle. But underneath the figures lie a host of personal and family tragedies, stories of charity and, in some cases, weak and misguided government decisions that exacerbated an awful situation.

Black '47: The worst year of the famine

In 1847 the fungus that had struck the potato did not return. Despite this good news, 1847 was one of the worst years of the famine, and has earned the name Black '47.

Although the fungus did not return to blight the potato crop in 1847, the loss of life and dislocation that had been caused in 1846 meant that few potatoes had actually been planted. As a result the crop in 1847 was small and inadequate to feed the population. In the winter of 1847, 400,000 people died in Ireland as a result of the famine.

While the potato crop either failed or was small during these years, much Irish land was actually farmed commercially and was designed to produce crops for export out of Ireland. In 1847, while people were dying in great numbers, exports of food crops from Ireland were high. The British government believed in free trade, and for them the market was king. Ideologically they did not believe in government intervention. Rather than the food being kept in Ireland to feed people, it left the ports for its intended export market. In 1847 alone, it is estimated that 4,000 ships left Irish ports laden with food grown in Irish soil, but destined for sale in foreign markets.

With only a small yield of food from the potato crop, people were dependant on charity. Otherwise they would die.

The government had three main approaches to feeding people:

- Employing them on large-scale public work schemes. In return for their wages these workers could then buy food. Some 715,000 men were employed in this way in 1847.
- Feeding them directly through soup kitchens. These were established across Ireland and managed to supply basic rations to three million people.
- Providing food and shelter for them in workhouses. In 1849, a million people were catered for in this way.

Believing the worst was over at the end of 1847, the government scaled down the public work programme and closed the soup kitchens. The following year the potato fungus returned with renewed ferocity and people starved once more.

Soup kitchens

The soup kitchens that were established across Ireland in 1847 were invaluable in keeping countless people alive who would have otherwise starved. The effort, which was undertaken by government, local authorities, charities, and private individuals, was an amazing achievement in the context of the enormity of the crisis. There were, however, negative aspects to the endeavour. Stories circulated that Protestant organisations established soup kitchens, but would only feed those families who converted from Catholicism to Protestantism. The level of desperation meant that many undertook the change and were derided with the label 'soupers'. In Dublin, the famous London chef, Alexis Soyer, set up a soup kitchen to feed the city's hungry. While he was able to deliver 100 gallons of soup for a mere pound in cost, he supplemented his efforts by charging Dublin's elite five shillings to watch. A newspaper at the time was outraged, and compared the choice of watching paupers eat unfavourably with the small extra charge, only six shillings, it cost to see the animals in nearby Dublin Zoo.

Succumbing to disease

One of the biggest killers during the famine wasn't the actual starvation, it was the diseases that the weakened bodies succumbed to. Contagious diseases were a common feature of mid-nineteenth century life, and epidemics of diseases such as cholera weren't unusual. In addition, during the famine years, the conditions in Ireland were unsanitary – even by nineteenth-century standards. People were in weakened states, and less resistant to the various diseases that affected the country.

The most common diseases in Ireland during the famine years were typhus, cholera, dysentery, and scurvy. As with modern famines, it was simple illnesses such as diarrhoea which were devastating to the starving population.

Disposing of bodies was a huge problem. Given the faith of the Irish, the act of burial was an important one. But in an environment of numerous deaths, such procedures could not always be followed. Bodies were found in cabins, in the fields, and by the roadsides. Until they could be buried, rats and stray dogs were devouring the corpses. Such conditions only hastened the spread of disease and forced the authorities to act. At various times during the famine bodies had to be buried, without coffins, in large trenches.

The cycle of starvation and disease was a difficult one to break. In the context of the famine, 1849 was one of the better years in terms of the potato crop, and saw a slight decline in the number of dead. However, that year a cholera epidemic hit Ireland and many of those who had survived the famine succumbed to the disease.

The absence of food in a society will always lead to hunger and starvation. The most virulent killer in such situations will always be those diseases associated with unsanitary conditions, problems with the water supply, and the difficulties of disposing of dead bodies. The Famine Museum in Strokestown, county Roscommon, memorialises the loss of life in Ireland, and explains how it happened. It also links the events in Ireland in the period 1846–51 with other famines that have since struck elsewhere in the world. Despite the passage of time, the lessons learnt from the Irish famine, and what responses should be employed in such a situation, are still sadly relevant.

Half-hearted attempts to solve the problem

When the potato crop failed, and people started dying in Ireland, British Prime Minister Robert Peel was forced to act. To be fair, he did buy £100,000 of American Indian meal to feed people in Ireland, and set up a scientific commission to investigate what had caused the fungus to strike the potato.

Memorials

For such a terrible event, with such tragic consequences, it is perhaps inevitable that the famine has been memorialised in Ireland and elsewhere. Over the years, and particularly on the 150th anniversary of the famine, people have come together to raise money to erect permanent memorials to those who died or chose to emigrate. Such memorials exist across Ireland and in the US. There are two in Dublin – one in St Stephen's Green that depicts a dying family, the other by the side of the River Liffey and the Docks which commemorates the enforced emigration of the Irish from that site. In New York, there is a memorial in the form of a reconstructed Irish famine village, and in Boston there are statues of two family groups, one dressed in rags and dying from hunger, the other, an affluent American group, stretching their hands to assist. While such memorials have often been controversial, they ensure that the famine is remembered.

He also repealed the controversial Corn Laws, which had protected the British markets against cheap imports, and Britain became a free trading nation. The industrial workers of Britain let out a huge cheer as Peel's change in direction meant that food became cheaper for them. In Ireland no one cheered. They were too busy trying to survive.

Who lives, who leaves

The effects of the famine didn't have the same impact on Ireland's individual regions. While all areas were affected by a lack of food and the spread of disease, the resulting number of deaths was not uniform.

It was the poorest areas, those whose agricultural development was lowest, that were worst affected. In parts of the country where peasant farmers had large families, but small plots of land, the death toll was highest. Two groups suffered most: Families that depended on their income from *smallholdings* (subsistence farming on a small acreage that produced food for the family), and landless labourers (those who relied on employment working on the farms of others).

If you were lucky enough to live in Ulster, where there was industrial employment, the effects of the famine were negligible. If you lived in the poor rural areas of the west and south-west, and were trying to survive on a small plot of potatoes, then your chances of dying were highest.

Put simply, three broad outcomes can be understood;

✔ The smallest and poorest farmers, who lived year-on-year through subsistence farming, were most likely to die.

✔ Families who were affected by the shortages of the famine, but had access to some form of savings or belongings to sell, were most likely to emigrate.

✔ If you lived in an unaffected area, worked in a region of industrialisation, or were from the middle and upper classes, you survived and stayed.

Clearly some people did survive the famine in the most terrible circumstances, and some who would have been expected to make it through those terrible years succumbed.

In addition to the high numbers who died or emigrated, many families were evicted from their land. These families lived as tenants on land that was valued as being worth less than £4. Their landlords were supposed to pay the rates for this land to the government. As the landlords would receive no rent from their tenants because of the famine, they evicted them instead.

Evictions exacerbated an already dreadful situation. In 1849 17,000 families were evicted from their land, which was their only source of income. In 1850 this number rose to 20,000. Many of these people joined the ranks of those emigrating, others became part of the horrendous statistics of famine dead.

Apparitions: Something stirs at Knock

On the evening of 21 August 1879, two women from the small village of Knock, in County Mayo, Mary McLoughlin and Mary Beirne, were walking near the local church when they noticed luminous figures at the gable end. They identified one of them as the Blessed Virgin, and the others as St Joseph and St John the Evangelist. Soon other neighbours joined them who said they could also see an altar, with a young lamb on it, in front of a cross, while one boy saw angels over the altar.

A commission of enquiry was set up in 1879, and another in 1936, that both considered the witnesses reliable and trustworthy. Knock quickly became a place of pilgrimage, and many cures were attributed to visiting the shrine.

In 1979 Pope John Paul visited Knock. Half a million people came to hear him, and while there he honoured the shrine and celebrated its centenary. Knock remains the largest site of pilgrimage in Ireland and one of the holiest places in the world.

While the apparition at Knock was good for local business because of the large number of pilgrims, its context is important. The visitation of the Blessed Virgin, while of huge religious significance, also had a political and social impact. The whole event happened at the height of a period of evictions from the land, and shortly before the intense period of the land war (see the section 'The Land War: Davitt and Gladstone' for details about that).

Many observers linked the apparitions at Knock with events in Ireland. They argued that the appearance of the Blessed Virgin was God's message to his oppressed children in Ireland. The apparition linked the popular piety of Ireland's Catholics with the struggle against the landlords and the British.

The process of eviction was brutal, and made a bad situation worse. Evictions were seen as cruel in such terrible circumstances, and bred even greater resentment against the British. This resentment was carried by many emigrating Irish to their new lands.

Assigning Blame

At the time of the famine, there were two competing versions of the reasons behind the famine:

✔ One opinion, which was commonly held in Britain, argued that the famine was the fault of the Irish. They claimed that there were too many of them, their agriculture was inefficient, and that the loss of population would force them to modernise in due course. This view was also extended to view the whole famine as an unchallengeable act of God.

✔ The opposing view, advanced in Ireland as well as by Irish emigrants, was that the disaster had been caused by British mismanagement of Ireland, and that Britain was to blame.

The truth – or at least modern conjecture – indicates that the causes of the famine and the situations that worsened the tragedy were more complex than simple acts of God or government mismanagement.

The question of who was to blame for the famine, indeed whether blame could even be apportioned, has become a hot potato in recent years. While many historians have argued that the tragedy was caused by a combination of a multitude of circumstances, others, especially in America, have sought to have the famine redefined as an act of genocide. They argue that the loss of life was deliberately caused by British mismanagement of the affair, and that the history of the famine should be taught, alongside the Holocaust of World War Two, as part of genocide studies.

The life of the poor

Historians have argued that the causes of the famine were multifaceted. These include:

✔ Most Irish people had become entirely dependant on the potato for their source of food.

✔ Too many people were trying to survive on plots of land that were too small. A government commission in 1843 showed that 326,000 people were occupying plots of land that were insufficient to support families of more than five – but the average Irish family at the time was larger than this.

> ✔ Ireland had undergone rapid population increase. In 1821 the population had been seven million. By 1841 this had risen to just over eight million.

> ✔ Apart from small pockets of development, Ireland had not witnessed an industrial revolution, and was still dependant on small-scale agriculture.

In this environment, with an increasing population, a lack of alternative sources of income, and ever-decreasing plots of land, the only option for the Irish was to survive on the highest-yielding crop available – the potato. Then, when the fungus hit, the whole house of cards collapsed.

Nasty Mr Peel and government policy

Robert Peel is seen in Britain as one of the great Prime Ministers. Statues of him adorn many British cities, and when he died after falling from his horse, the nation, especially the working classes, mourned him.

In Ireland, Peel was not remembered with such affection. Not only had he opposed O'Connell's campaign to repeal the Union (see Chapter 16), he also believed, as a Tory, in protecting the British market from cheap imports by charging tariffs. Throughout the 1830s and 1840s Peel had faced opposition on this stance from the Liberals and the Anti-Corn Law League who believed in free trade. But why was this debate relevant to Ireland?

Peel's stance of protecting the British market meant that cheap imports of food from overseas weren't available. Prices were kept artificially high on items such as bread, as Peel's policy favoured those large farmers who grew wheat. However, poor farmers in Ireland (and in Britain too) were not only uncompetitive, but couldn't avail themselves of cheap food in the shops. Many argued that Peel's policy of protection had led to the structural problems in Irish farming that caused the famine. However, once free trade became a reality many Irish farmers found that they were unable to compete in an open market, and began arguing in favour of protection.

Sailing Away: The Irish Diaspora

Leaving Ireland was nothing new. The Irish had been emigrating since the eighteenth century in steady numbers. What the famine did was turn the steady stream of emigrants into a tidal wave of people.

The famine and its effects were clearly a factor that pushed people to leave. They were aided by the ready availability of ships that plied a trade between Ireland and countries such as America, Australia, and Britain. These weren't cruise ships though. The conditions on these ships were often basic, and better equipped for the transportation of animals than of people.

Grosse Isle

Grosse Isle is a small island in the Saint Lawrence River, some thirty miles east of Quebec. The authorities in North America had always been concerned about the health of incoming immigrants and had designated the island a quarantine stop for new arrivals. In 1847, given the rush to get away from Ireland and the famine, Grosse Isle was swamped. In that year over 100,000 Irish immigrants landed on Canada's eastern seaboard, with 398 ships arriving at Grosse Isle. Of these, 77 ships had carried passenger numbers in excess of 400 on their 60-day crossing of the Atlantic. Conditions on board ship were dreadful, and 5,000 people are known to have died at sea. The Irish had carried disease with them, and the conditions on ship had only made a bad situation worse. While in quarantine a further 5,242 people died and were buried on the island. Grosse Isle is now a Canadian National Park and has been dedicated as a memorial to all the Irish who died there.

One group departing Ireland said: 'All we want is to get out of Ireland . . . we must be better anywhere else than here.' For many Irish people that sentiment just about summed it up.

Despite the many stories of successful Irish emigrants finding their way in a new land, many more had a terrible time. If they survived the ship journey, Irish emigrants found themselves at the bottom of the social hierarchy in their new homes. If they could find work, it was often menial and low-paid. They lived in poor conditions, suffered racial abuse, and were viewed by the authorities as an irritant – dirty, lazy, violent, and drunken. Rather than being welcomed, the Irish were often viewed with suspicion.

The Irish in America

The most favoured destination for Irish emigrants – if they could afford the fare – was America. By 1990, 44 million Americans claimed Irish as their ethnicity or background in the national census.

Emigration to America began long before the famine. The large-scale movement of the Irish had begun as early as the 1720s. In the eighteenth century 200,000 Irish people went to America, three-quarters of them Ulster Presbyterians. Mass Catholic emigration was very much a feature of the famine years and the subsequent decades.

Between 1815 and 1921, six million Irish emigrants settled in America, more than the entire current population of Ireland. Of those six million, 90 per cent were Catholic. Once in America the Irish had an amazing impact. They were important simply because of the sheer number of them, but also because they were very socially mobile. There was not an aspect of American life that the Irish failed to influence. Also, they were organised through institutions such as the Church and in the labour movement, and made sure that they wouldn't suffer the same discrimination that had been a feature of their lives in Ireland.

Many emigrants left for America direct from Irish ports. Others first went to Britain, which was a cheaper destination, where they tried to raise the money for the more expensive Atlantic crossing. The emigrant trade was so profitable for shipping lines that most small towns in Ireland had an agent's office selling tickets to America.

Most Irish emigrants arrived at the big east coast ports in America such as New York and Boston, and these cities developed large Irish communities. But not all of the emigrants could or wanted to stay in the big cities. The Irish played a key role in opening up America. They were central in the building of the railway system across the continent, and also shifted west in large numbers chasing opportunities such as the Gold Rush.

Although many of the stories of the Irish in America concentrate on the male experience as unskilled workers and navvies, men were only about half of the total number of emigrants. As women did not inherit land in Ireland, and had limited opportunities for social advancement or marriage, they formed half of the total number of those leaving Ireland. They found work in the industrial mills of the north-east of America, and dominated the service sector catering for middle-class Americans who employed them as servants and domestics in their homes.

Micks on the make

When they first arrived in America the Irish were not much loved. In the period through to the 1880s, the Irish were the most socially disadvantaged immigrant group (only Native and African Americans were more disadvantaged). Given their circumstances of having left Ireland, and struggling to make it in a new home, the Irish unsurprisingly had their problems. Drink, violence, unemployment, and vagrancy were common features for the Irish in America. They also suffered from attacks by Americans who were fearful of the effect of the Irish presence in their country. Such attacks were often displayed in religious terms. America was a predominantly Protestant country and it was feared that all these immigrant Irish Catholics would swamp the settled population, and so there were regular incidents of sectarian violence.

Fortuitous timing and support from the Church

But it wasn't all bad news. By the beginning of the twentieth century the Irish had climbed the social ladder and were the most successful immigrant group. Their wages and social standing rapidly became equal to that of the settled population. Although never free of discrimination and anti-Irish jibes, the Irish in America assimilated themselves into the mainstream of society remarkably quickly.

The American Wake

When people left for America in the nineteenth century they knew, as did their families, that they were unlikely to ever return home. The decision to emigrate was a difficult one, as it meant leaving home and family forever. Effectively the emigrant, once they boarded their ship for America, would never be seen again. For those left in Ireland, it was as if that person had died. Throughout the nineteenth century a tradition existed called the American wake. It was a gathering of friends and family to bid the emigrant farewell. Although supposedly a party to wish them well, such gatherings were always mournful affairs. Rather than a party, it became known as the American wake to mourn the passing of the emigrant who would never be seen again.

Why were the Irish so successful? In the last half of the nineteenth century America was expanding rapidly. The Irish arrived at a time when there were great opportunities. Initially the Irish had been discriminated against and excluded by native-born labour leaders and trade unions from the best paid trades and jobs. The Irish organised themselves in their own labour organisations and began campaigning effectively for better pay and conditions. At the end of the century, they had been so successful that they dominated the American Trade Union movement. In 1900 the Irish occupied the Presidency of 50 out of 110 unions in the American Federation of Labour. Rather than being the outsiders and the low-skilled who could be discriminated against, the Irish were in a position of power and couldn't be pushed around anymore.

One of the major forces behind the Irish influence in American life was the Catholic Church. The Irish brought their religion with them, and the Church was very important in supporting them. Not only did the Church provide religious support, it also gave newly arrived immigrants a support network through which they could find work and lodgings. The Church also became very important politically, with Archbishops such as New York's John Hughes becoming powerful advocates for the Irish. With the influx of other Catholic immigrants from places such as Italy, and more recently the Hispanic countries, the Catholic Church became, and remains, the single largest Christian denomination in America. Even as late as 1970, more than half the Bishops in America were of Irish descent. Although recent debates surrounding abortion, divorce, and child abuse have alienated some from the Church, it still remains a powerful advocate of Irish Americans and provides that community with support.

The Irish in American politics

While the Irish did well in social and economic terms in the decades after the famine, it was in politics that they really made their mark. From the 1830s the Democratic Party had seen the Irish influx as an important reservoir of support and actively courted them. In the second half of the nineteenth and into the twentieth century, the Irish came to dominate municipal politics.

John F Kennedy

Kennedy was from a powerful and successful Irish-American family, and he played up to his Irish background. He famously visited Ireland in 1963, and charmed the country. He claimed that his time in Ireland was the most enjoyable and relaxing visit that he had been on during his Presidency. He told the crowd at Shannon airport when he departed that he'd 'be back in the springtime'. Sadly Kennedy was assassinated months later and never made the return journey. The Kennedy family have, however, remained staunch supporters of Ireland, and played a key role in the 1990s peace process in Northern Ireland.

From 1871 to 1924 the Irish dominated New York politics and ran City Hall with only minor interruptions. Patronage became an important tool in securing support, and the Irish came to dominate those areas of employment that the city provided, such as the police force and the fire service. While city bosses such as Richard 'Boss' Croker and Charles Francis Murphy became legends, the Irish control of City Hall was also marked by corruption. Favours, such as jobs, were freely given in return for votes. Despite such corruption, the Irish presence in City Hall secured the advancement of the Irish society and transformed them from the 'dirty immigrant Irish' into respectable Americans.

It wasn't just in New York that Irish politics prospered. They also dominated cities with large Irish populations such as Brooklyn, Boston, Chicago, San Francisco, Buffalo, and Kansas City. James Curley in Boston and Richard Daly in Chicago controlled their cities with almost total authority over a number of decades.

Although the Irish did well in controlling those cities where there was a sizeable Irish and Catholic population, they struggled to translate this dominance in the area of national politics. Alfred E. Smith, who had been Governor of New York, ran for President on the Democratic ticket in 1924 and 1928, but was easily defeated both times. While there were cities that were Irish-dominated, much of the country still remained suspicious of having a Catholic President. It was the election of Kennedy, in 1960, that would finally allow a Catholic of Irish descent to take the Presidency.

Painting the town green

For all its impact on American society, the one great lasting legacy of the Irish has been the annual celebration of Ireland's patron saint on 17 March. St Patrick's Day had been celebrated as a religious festival in Ireland, but it was Irish-Americans who made it the big public event that it is today.

The first St Patrick's Day parades took place in the 1730s. These were military parades and were organised by Irishmen serving in the British army in America. With the growing number of immigrants in the nineteenth century St Patrick's Day became an important marker of Irish identity. Not only did it allow the Irish to come together and celebrate their identity, but it also became an important way for the Irish to announce their presence, and their numerical size, to their nativist opponents.

St Patrick's Day in America is now a day celebrated by everyone, whether they are Irish or not. Parades and celebrations take place across the country, much green beer is drunk, hundreds of thousands of greetings cards are sent, and shamrock is everywhere. The first St Patrick's Day greetings cards were produced in the 1890s, and live shamrock was imported from Ireland by air from the 1930s. Many of the American traditions have now been re-exported back to Ireland, and Irish celebrations appear ever more American. Corned-Beef-and-Cabbage lunches have remained an American speciality though.

St Patrick's Day celebrations now take place across the world. In Dublin there is a four day Festival to celebrate 17 March, and events and parades take place in such far flung corners of the world as Tokyo, Lagos, Monserrat, Buenos Aires, Sydney, and Beijing. One reason for the global spread of St Patrick's Day has been the power of Guinness. They have successfully marketed the day as an event where 'everyone can be Irish'. With the spread of Irish theme bars across the world, the popularity of Irish dance and music, and the sheer number of Irish people about the globe, partying on 17 March has become a pastime that everyone wants to embrace.

The Irish down under

The British first started using Australia as a penal colony in 1788, and the Irish were amongst the first convicts to be sent there, arriving in 1791. Since those first prisoners, so many Irish have made the long trip down under that it's the most Irish country in the world after Ireland itself: a third of Australia's 19 million population claim Irish ancestry.

Picking a place to party

Choose your place of celebration carefully. The biggest parade is in New York, but more people watch events in Dublin. The smallest parade, in County Cork, is only seventy five yards long (from one pub to the one next door) and the fastest growing in recent years is in Savannah, Georgia. In New Orleans they throw vegetables at the floats, and in Chicago they dye the river green. Wherever you go, enjoy it.

By the time the British had got fed up with transporting its criminals half way around the world in 1868, an estimated 40,000 Irish had made the trip. The Irish were such a central part of the criminal world – or so the British thought – that they made up a quarter of all people transported down under. Most were ordinary criminals, and many had been sentenced to a trip to Australia for fairly minor crimes. An act such as stealing a pig often resulted in a seven-year sentence in Australia.

Rather than face the long journey home at the end of their sentence, many Irish chose to settle in Australia as free men and women. Many of them were successful on the land, and were vital in opening up the vast continent.

During the nineteenth century a new type of Irish flooded into Australia. These people were no longer criminals, but people fleeing the hardships of life in Ireland. Many were given assisted passage by the Australian government that was desperate to populate its country. Most of them were Catholic, but roughly one in ten Irish landing in Australia were Protestant.

The Catholicism of the Irish caused problems in Australia as it did elsewhere. There were claims – remember Australia was a loyal country of the British Empire – that the Irish were attempting to undermine Crown rule by adhering to their religion. It became a huge issue in the First World War when it was Catholic votes that ensured the Australian government's conscription referendum failed. To many Australians that supported Britain, the rejection of conscription was treachery.

The Irish-born now make up only 0.5 per cent of the Australian population, but the diaspora remains strong. Also, Australia has become the place for young Irish to spend a year working after college. Every barman in Sydney or Melbourne now seems to have an Irish accent!

Ned Kelly

One of the most famous Irish Australians was the outlaw Ned Kelly. He was born into an Irish family in Victoria, and grew up in poverty in the bush. He was regularly in trouble with the law, and at sixteen was sent to prison. On his release he began cattle rustling with members of his family, the infamous Kelly gang. On the run from the law, Ned Kelly raged against the treatment of Irish Catholics in Australia, and was so aware of potential attack from the police, that he bought himself an iron suit for protection. In 1880 Kelly and his gang were finally surrounded by the police, and in the subsequent shoot out he was shot twenty-eight times. Once captured he was tried and executed. Kelly became an Australian folklore hero – a symbol for the working class Australian struggling against the forces of colonial rule. Many books and films have explored his life, and during the opening ceremony of the 2000 Sydney Olympic Games actors dressed as Ned in his iron suit represented the Australian spirit of independent action.

Across the water to Britain

As it's only next door, Britain was an obvious place for the emigrant Irish to settle. The history of the Irish in Britain goes right back to the Middle Ages. They were disliked then, and the history of anti-Irish attitudes and actions in Britain is a long one.

It was the Industrial Revolution and the success of the cotton industry that first brought the Irish to Britain in large numbers. There had always been a tradition of people going over to Britain for seasonal agricultural work, but these people rarely settled permanently. Before the famine, the Irish became a significant proportion of the population in cities such as Manchester, Liverpool, London, and Glasgow.

The famine really caused the numbers to swell. The numbers of Irish born in Britain in 1841 was 289,404; twenty years later and shortly after the end of the famine, the numbers had leapt to 601,634.

The Irish weren't much loved by the British. They were seen as dirty, drunken, and violent, and the root cause of many of the problems associated with nineteenth century towns and cities. The biggest problem of all was that the Irish insisted on retaining their belief in Catholicism which in Britain was an alien and potentially subversive religion. Violence between Irish Catholics and the native population was frequent, and many leaders of the Church of England and anti-Popery lecturers helped to stoke up the feelings of hatred.

The Irish did make an important contribution to British life. They were central to various liberal and socialist movements during the nineteenth century, such as the Chartists (a working class movement that campaigned for better conditions and greater democracy), and were a key element in the establishment of trade unions. Also, without Irish workers Britain would have never been able to build its canals and railways.

The Irish kept coming over to Britain right through the twentieth century. The depression in Ireland in the 1920s, 1950s, and 1980s encouraged countless young Irish men and women to try to make a new life for themselves in Britain. Even as late as 1971, 957,830 people in Britain were of Irish birth – the largest single immigrant group.

Despite various pieces of British legislation since the Second World War that have tried to control the number of immigrants entering Britain, such laws have never applied to people coming from the Irish Republic. They have always had the ability to move to Britain, and there has never been any quota on the number of Irish who could enter. In the light of restrictions that have been placed on the numbers of Irish who could enter America or Australia, this has meant that Britain has always remained a popular destination.

Irish everywhere?

It seems that wherever you go in the world you'll always find an Irish community or, at the very least, an Irish bar. The Irish have been the most successful people in the world at spreading themselves across the globe. Not bad for such a small population.

Why have the Irish been so successful at conquering the globe?

- ✔ Much emigration, especially as a result of the famine, was effectively forced. The Irish had no choice but to seek a new life overseas.

- ✔ The Irish economy was stagnant for so long that the tide of emigration didn't cease until the 1990s.

- ✔ Economic depressions, such as those in the 1920s, 1950s, and 1980s, forced high numbers to emigrate and therefore topped up the numbers of Irish around the world.

- ✔ Much emigration was assisted. Family members who had made it in their new home would send money back to Ireland so that their parents or siblings could come and join them.

- ✔ The Irish network around the world was extensive. The pain of emigration was eased as the Irish got looked after by institutions such as the Church, county associations, or the Gaelic Athletic Association when they arrived on foreign shores.

- ✔ The Irish Catholic Church was very busy in sending priests and nuns across the world to do missionary work. These religious initiatives attracted other Irish people such as teachers and nurses to go to work in developing countries.

- ✔ While the Irish have been good at assimilating into their new societies, they have also been aware of their heritage. This has meant that the Irish, even later generations who weren't born there, have remained highly visible.

- ✔ For all the problems that the Irish had with Britain, they played a key role in staffing the British Empire. Wherever the British claimed a colony, the Irish were there as well.

- ✔ Although emigration is no longer a product of a weak Irish economy, the boom of the 1990s has meant that the Irish are an important part of the global job market in areas such as finance and information technology. Go to a major corporation in Hong Kong, Dubai, London, or New York, and you'll find the new Irish emigrants.

The Land War: Davitt and Gladstone

The issue of land ownership was central to political life in Ireland in the later decades of the nineteenth century. It was clearly understood that the ways in which Irish land was owned, rented out, and inherited had contributed to the appalling effects of the famine. The question was how the situation could be rectified.

In the late 1870s and early 1880s, before a solution could be found, another series of bad harvests occurred, and the threat of famine again hung over Ireland. The landlords, who believed that their tenants would not be able to pay their rents in a time of poor harvest, began evicting them from the land.

In response, a new movement, the Irish National Land League, emerged to fight for the rights of small tenant farmers. The goal of this movement was to bring about a more equitable system of land ownership. The League wanted three main things:

- ✔ Fair rent in line with the market price for land, rather than an inflated charge set by the landlord.

- ✔ Fixity of tenure. The League wanted rent agreements to state how long tenants could stay on the land rather than leave them with no security.

- ✔ Freedom of sale. The tenants had no rights over the land when it was sold – they wanted to have a say.

More broadly it wanted to get Irish land into the hands of Irish small farmers and away from the ownership of absentee landlords who didn't care for their tenants' welfare.

The founder of the Irish National Land League was Michael Davitt. His family had been evicted from their land in the 1840s and forced to emigrate to England. Davitt was sent to work at the local cotton mill in Lancashire. Like many other young boys he was working in dangerous conditions. At eleven he lost his arm in an accident, and was unemployable. He educated himself, and began seeing the British as being responsible for all Ireland's problems. He was sentenced to 15 years in prison in 1870 for Fenian activity, but released in 1877. On his release he turned his attention to the landlords whom he saw as the root of all evil in his native land.

The struggle over the future of Ireland was often presented in religious terms. Britain, as a Protestant country, was struggling to control Ireland, which was predominantly Catholic. The Catholic Church supported its parishioners, and backed the campaigns for land reforms and the principle of Irish self-determination. In the twentieth century (see Chapter 20) this would be very important.

Boycotting unscrupulous landlords

To achieve its aims the Land League attacked the landlords who treated their tenants badly, who charged unfair rents, and who evicted their tenants. Many of these attacks took a physical form, and landlords and their families were beaten. Some, such as Lord Leitrim (a landlord who was notorious for his poor treatment of tenants), were even murdered.

The greatest tool of the Land League, and the one that has found a place in the English language and in protests everywhere, was the boycott. The basic idea was that people would stop doing business or socialising with landlords whom they opposed because of their unfair practices. Farmers would refuse to work for them and the rest of the community was encouraged to ostracise the guilty party. One of the first targets was Captain Charles Boycott, of Lough Mask House, County Mayo, after whom this strategy was named.

The Land League didn't boycott only the landlords, however. They also boycotted those Irish people who chose to take on the land from which others had been evicted. In one speech, the President of the Land League told the crowd that anyone who had taken on the land of the evicted should be:

- ✔ Ignored on the roadside when they were seen.
- ✔ Ignored when met at the shop counter.
- ✔ Ignored at the fair and market place.
- ✔ Ignored even in the house of worship.

Because of these tactics the Land League became very effective and feared. It didn't make rural Ireland a great place to live, but the Land League's pursuit of its goals would ultimately be successful.

Land and country: The link to nationalism

This was a period when demands for some kind of Irish self-determination were becoming very popular. Politicians, the press, and the people began to link the land issue with the question of Ireland's relationship with Britain. Was it possible to solve the land question without also addressing the issue of self-determination? Because of this link between the two questions, the agitation over the land issue became one that was heavily influenced by ideas of Irish nationalism.

Everyone understood that the land ownership question was a key cause of complaint by the Irish. The British general election of 1880 had been fought over the issue, and many commentators also picked up the question. One nationalist even said: 'Damn Home Rule! What we're out for is the land. The land matters. All the rest is talk.'

Opinions differed greatly in Britain about what to do with Ireland. The Liberals argued that Irish demands should be met, whereas the Conservatives thought that the Irish should not be allowed to be so lawless in the pursuit of their goals. Some historians have argued that land reform was the best option as it calmed the situation and prevented a revolutionary movement that violently linked the land issue with national freedom. Others have argued that the British, by enacting land reform, deliberately sought to divert Irish attention away from their aspiration for political freedom.

Nice Mr Gladstone and the Land Act

The Land League was so effective that the British Prime Minister, William Gladstone, decided to do something about the situation. Rather than try to squash the protests, he made the decision to actually address the issues.

Gladstone's Land Act (which was agreed by parliament in 1870) began a process by which the old landlords were steadily replaced by Irish owners of the land. The process has been called 'a social revolution which transformed Ireland'.

To stop the disruption caused by the Land League's tactics, Gladstone first restored some kind of order to Ireland by clamping down on the League's activities by passing a series of coercion acts that tried to prevent political activism.

The Land Act finally gave Irish tenants what they had wanted: fair rent, fixity of tenure, and free sale of tenant's interest.

While the Act was quite revolutionary, it did have shortcomings. Tenants who already owed rent were not covered by the new law, nor were leaseholders. As a result Land League activity continued, and the Land League initially boycotted the act and told their followers not to pay their rent. It all got sorted out a while later, and the details are in Chapter 19.

Chapter 19

The Fight Over Home Rule

*A*fter the horrors of the Famine (head to Chapter 18), Ireland, according to Gavan Duffy, 'lay dying on the dissection table.' The country's population had been decimated by death and emigration, and many laid the blame on the British. By the late nineteenth century many believed that the only future for Ireland was to have an independent parliament, free of Britain. That wasn't a consensus view, however: The British establishment – many of whom owned land in Ireland – wanted the country to remain as part of the Union and in the Empire, and the unionist population in Ireland also wanted to stay British.

As a result, this period saw the rise of the Home Rule movement and organised unionism.

The Irish, although wanting their own parliament, still understood the value – economic and political – of staying in the British Empire. Home Rulers wanted a parliament in Dublin for which the Irish people would elect the MPs and that would have power over all aspects of running Ireland – well, almost all; imperial and foreign matters would still be decided at the British parliament in Westminster. Home Rulers wanted Ireland to remain a part of the British Empire but the Irish would have the final say in how Ireland was run. Demands for complete separation only became popular in the period after the First World War (see Chapter 21).

The Great National Leader: Charles Stewart Parnell

There's a statue of Parnell at the top of end of Dublin's O'Connell Street – he was so important to the people of Ireland that they celebrated his life on the capital's main street. Parnell was important to Ireland because he made the Home Rule movement a reality rather than an aspiration. Without Parnell's inspirational leadership it's doubtful that the Irish would have been able to voice its demands so effectively. He was, like O'Connell before him, one of the great leaders of constitutional Irish nationalism.

His rise to prominence

Parnell was born a Protestant to a large landowning family in Wicklow. His family was wealthy, and many of his male relatives, including his father, had served as MPs in the Westminster parliament. Parnell followed their footsteps when, in 1875, he was elected MP for Meath as a supporter of Home Rule.

In the 1870s entry into a political career was still restricted on the basis of class and wealth. Not just anyone could stand to be an MP or vote, and certainly no women. Parnell was the perfect model of a Victorian MP: rich, of the right class, and with no clear career path. If he didn't enter politics he would have to join the army!

At the time of his election the Irish Home Rule party was led by Isaac Butt. While committed to the cause of Irish independence, Butt was also a believer in the political traditions of Westminster and played by the rules. Not so Parnell. He believed that the Home Rulers were unlikely to get what they wanted because the Liberal and Conservative parties were uninterested in Ireland (see Chapter 16 to know which party is which). Also, no matter how many seats the Home Rulers won in Ireland, it was unlikely that they would ever be in a position of power.

In an attempt to draw attention to the Irish cause, Parnell decided to make life difficult for everybody else. Rather than working with the parliamentary system, he decided to disrupt it. The policy of obstructing parliamentary business by making long speeches and adding countless amendments and procedural questions to laws that were going through the House of Commons did have a history, but Parnell took it to a new level. He droned on for hours in debates, making one last for twenty-six hours, and managed to bring everything to a grinding halt. Obstruction intensely irritated the government but made Parnell popular in his party and brought him wide acclaim in Ireland.

Butthead Parnell

Parnell didn't have a stable upbringing though. When he was six his parents separated, and he was so disruptive that his sisters christened him Butthead. Like many of his class he was sent away from home to be schooled in England. He eventually made it to Magdalene College, Cambridge, but never finished his degree. He was rusticated (booted out to you and me) from the University for brawling. With no degree and no obvious career path, Parnell travelled to America before settling in Dublin. One historian said of the young Parnell that he had 'a marked upper-class English accent, an interest in horses, hunting, and cricket, and the manners of a gentleman.' No sign of the great political leader there!

In 1879 Butt died, and a year later Parnell replaced him as the leader of the Home Rule party. A year later there was a general election, and Parnell, perhaps being a bit greedy, stood for election in three seats. As a sign of his popularity in Ireland, he managed to win all three, but decided to sit for Cork. Within five years of first being elected as an MP Parnell had risen to national prominence, was well-known in Irish-American circles, and impressed everyone who supported the cause of Irish independence.

His allies: Radicals and politicians

The home rulers weren't the only force in Ireland. Although Parnell concentrated on bringing about political change in Westminster, he also made alliances with more radical movements such as the Land League. The Land League was an important popular movement that wanted to reform the system of land ownership in Ireland and ensure that the Irish were able to own or rent land fairly. (For more info about the Land War, head to Chapter 18.) Parnell also made an alliance with the Fenians, a more shadowy but equally important group. They were a revolutionary nationalist organisation, funded and organised by Irish-Americans (find more about them in Chapter 21).

But what did they all want?

- ✔ Parnell and the Home Rulers wanted a separate parliament for Ireland, which would be based in Dublin, as well as continued parliamentary representation at Westminster where foreign and imperial matters would be decided.

- ✔ The people involved in the Land War wanted to end the abusive relationship between British-based absentee landlords and their Irish tenants. Rather than suffering from evictions and increased rents, those involved in the Land War wanted to see Irish people owning the land.

> ✔ The Fenians were driven by the spirit of previous rebellions against the British – Wolfe Tone, Robert Emmet, and the Young Irelanders (see Chapters 14, 15, and 16) – and wanted to create an Irish Republic: a country totally free of British rule and one that left the Empire as well. To do this they believed that the use of violence, rather than strictly constitutional means, was acceptable.

If the Land League and the Fenians joined with the Home Rulers the combination would make a powerful and potentially troublesome mix. Parnell's success in parliament had come to the attention of both the Land League and the Fenians, and the Home Ruler was only too aware of the power and potential of land agitation and violent republicanism. An alliance was brought together that would both challenge and terrify the British as they sought to control the Irish situation.

His balancing act

In 1879 Parnell was elected the President of the Irish National Land League and although, as befitted a constitutional politician of the Victorian era, he was opposed to the use of violence in the pursuit of political goals, he understood that the land question was one that motivated Irish public opinion. Parnell actively joined public demonstrations by the Land League in 1880 and 1881, and was vociferous in his protests against evictions. In 1879 and into 1880 Parnell toured America in search of support for Home Rule. In doing so he engaged with Irish-American republicans, and won them over to supporting his campaign. While the alliance was never official, the Fenians were active in the more violent aspects of Land League activity, and brought a level of disorder to the Irish countryside.

By 1882 Parnell headed a three-way coalition: the Home Rulers in parliament were backed throughout the countryside by the populist activities of the Land League and this was underpinned by the threat of violence by the secretive, yet shadowy Fenians.

The forces of Irish nationalism have rarely been centred solely around constitutional politics. In the same way in which Parnell's parliamentary campaign for Home Rule was supported by radical and violent forces, so modern nationalism in Northern Ireland has been a complex mix of different groups. Throughout the 1980s and 1990s, the constitutional party, the Social Democratic and Labour Party, had a working relationship (though not always public) with Sinn Fein. They both wanted similar things for the North of Ireland, but believed in different methods of attaining their goals. The same has been true since the mid-1990s. While Sinn Fein has embraced the constitutional political process, their force (and threat) has been underpinned by their relationship with the Irish Republican Army (IRA).

His prison time: the Kilmainham Treaty

As always in Irish politics, the big question (other than what will the Irish do next?) was how will the English react? If you suspect, not particularly well, you're right.

In April 1881, the Liberal government sought to undermine agitation in Ireland by creating a new tribunal, the Land Court, to fix fair rents and recognise tenants' rights. While it was a step in the right direction, Parnell knew that it wasn't enough for his more radical Irish-American and Land League supporters. It was decided to test the new legislation, and demonstrations were held across Ireland opposing the idea – basically breaking the law by attending proscribed meetings. In the thick of the protests was Parnell, and the British, not understanding his need to be seen fighting for land rights alongside his supporters, were very upset. As far as they were concerned, he had been to a banned meeting and broken the law. So they arrested him.

By all accounts, Parnell behaved like a gentleman when arrested. He was taken to Kilmainham Gaol on the outskirts of Dublin where generations of political rebels had been held by the British. Given his status Parnell was well treated. He kept his own clothes, was given two cells to himself, and was even allowed to bring his own furniture into the prison. The British may have been the long-standing oppressors of Ireland in the popular mind, but with Parnell they knew that special allowances had to be made.

Throughout his six month imprisonment, Parnell continued a dialogue with Prime Minister Gladstone (see Chapter 18 for details on him). The aim was simple: to ensure that the land reforms were enacted but with everyone's honour intact. Parnell demanded one last concession – that the government settled all outstanding rental arrears – and in return he would ensure that the level of land agitation and associated outrages would decline. A deal was done between the two men – called the Kilmainham Treaty – and Parnell released. While it didn't solve all Ireland's problems, the Treaty offered a significant step forward on the land debate and brought the two leaders to a closer understanding.

Gladstone tries to help

In the 1885 general election, the Home Rulers swept the board in Ireland. With the exception of unionist seats in Ulster and the University seats in Dublin, Parnell's men won everywhere. In all there were 86 Home Rule MPs. Best of all for Home Rulers, the Liberal party had not won a big enough majority throughout the United Kingdom and were dependant on Parnell's votes at Westminster to get any legislation passed.

After some messy political activity during which Liberals and Conservatives took power – both refused to make a deal with Parnell – Gladstone knew he had no choice. If he wanted to form the government he would have to make a deal with Parnell's party. In February 1886 he went to see Queen Victoria, and told her that he wanted to introduce a Home Rule bill for Ireland.

Had Ireland's day finally come? Well, no. While the Irish were delighted, many members in Gladstone's party opposed the idea. In two successive votes, the House of Commons voted the proposed bill down, and that was that. The Liberal government collapsed, and the Conservatives took over. They hated the whole Home Rule idea, and looked at other ways to win over the Irish without talking about independence. Parnell was left in a vacuum politically, but then his personal life, as with all good political stories, intervened to finish him off.

As well-organised and vociferous as the Irish were in their quest for Home Rule, and no matter how much support they got from Gladstone, it wasn't there for the taking. Many British politicians hated the idea of letting Ireland leave the Union (and the effect this would have on the Empire) and the unionists were totally opposed. In the event Ireland wouldn't get its independence until 1921, and even then they didn't get all of it.

Parnell's Fall and His Party's Decline

Parnell would eventually fall from grace because of his involvement in one of the great scandals of the Victorian age. His relationship with a married woman, and his appearance in the divorce courts caused the Home Rule movement to fracture. It would take until 1900 before the Home Rule movement reunited under a single, commonly agreed leader again.

The scandal

Despite his political success and popularity, Parnell's personal life was far from straightforward. He became involved with an Essex girl, Katharine Wood. She had been born a year earlier than Parnell and came from a wealthy family with an upbringing that was typical for a woman of her time. When she was 22 she met a dashing young hussar, William Henry O'Shea, and married him. In 1880 O'Shea entered politics. He won the Clare seat on behalf of the Home Rulers and went to work in parliament. For the sake of appearances, as their marriage was far from happy, Katharine supported her husband in his new career and attended many political functions. At one such gathering she met Parnell, and an affair began. Parnell and Katharine went on to have three children who, upsetting for O'Shea, looked just like their father!

One of the best stories about the Parnell-O'Shea love triangle, and there are many, was that the two men challenged each other to a duel to settle the issue of which one should have the affections of Katharine. It's hard to imagine a modern politician being caught up in such a situation (the newspapers would have a field day), and common sense also prevailed in 1881 – the duel was never fought. It would have been an interesting contest though. O'Shea had been in the armed forces and would have been well-used to a gun, whereas Parnell, who preferred to unwind according to his housemate, Auguste Moore by 'spending the evening playing with a boy's train set', might not have been the best competitor in such a duel!

In Victorian society such an open affair was, given Parnell's position, problematic. Although it seems that he had always been aware of the affair between Parnell and his wife, O'Shea decided in 1889 to give the couple a present in poor taste, and on Christmas Eve, started divorce proceedings. Given the celebrity status of those involved, the press and the public pored over every detail of the court case. Stories included the regular escape of Parnell from his trysts with Katharine down fire escapes, and a counter claim that O'Shea had committed adultery with Katharine's sister. The divorce was granted but it spelt the end of Parnell.

The political fallout: No party for the Irish

Victorian society valued moral righteousness, and divorce, although legal, was seen as scandalous. Even today – as Bill Clinton and others have found out – we expect high standards of our politicians. For Parnell it was far worse. Not only did the media focus in on his affair with Mrs O'Shea, but such immoral behaviour from a leading politician could not be condoned by Victorian Britain nor Catholic Ireland. Gladstone, a devoutly religious man, withdrew his support from Parnell on moral grounds, and the Irish party split. Neither did Parnell's behaviour win him many friends in Catholic Ireland. Although he married Katharine in 1891, and remained popular with many – especially in Dublin – Parnell's career as leader of a united Home Rule party was over. He remained an MP until October 1891, when he died in Hove, in Sussex. Katharine survived until 1921, but never again in her life did she visit Ireland, which is probably a good thing given the reception she would have received.

With Parnell gone, in body and in spirit, and a huge row left behind, the Home Rulers were in a mess. They continued to be split along the lines of the Parnell divorce case for the best part of a decade. It seems that they just couldn't move on. Accusation and counter accusation dominated party debates, and rather than worrying about the big questions of Home Rule, or monitoring what the Conservatives were doing, the Home Rulers seemed content to just keep on fighting with each other. During this period the pro-Parnell wing of the party was led by John Redmond and the anti-Parnellites, in the form of the People's Rights Association, was led by T.M. Healy. The

Parnell split had been bitter, and this remained the main point of contention between the two groups. They didn't actually disagree too much about the general direction of the Home Rule movement.

Like any family feud, the period of the split was bitter, and many of the arguments advanced at the time now seem petty. In the midst of the feud the Home Rulers, although maintaining a degree of efficiency within parliament, lost coherence and the party organisation on the ground suffered. Even Gladstone's introduction of a second Home Rule Bill in 1893 didn't bring the party back together and, once again, the very thing that Ireland dreamt of was lost.

Although they were eventually brought back together in 1900, the wounds of the split would hamper the party into the twentieth century. The different sides remained suspicious of each other. When faced by the threats of a nationalist alternative in the form of Sinn Fein, and the belligerence of the unionists, the Home Rulers inward looking self obsession was revealed. Parnell it seemed, still dominated the party even from the grave.

What kept nationalism going, at least in part, during the years of the split was the broader cultural movement that spread across Ireland during the 1880s and 1890s (see Chapter 20) that made people feel Irish in a way that Home Rule politics had failed to do.

The Land Purchase Act of 1903: Killing Home Rule with Kindness

Parnell was gone. And for many of the Conservatives who were now in government their response would have been, good riddance! But while they had got rid of the leader of the Irish nationalism, and the Home Rulers were in disarray, Ireland was still there, and causing endless problems. Land reform was still a big issue, crop failures and economic downturn were regular occurrences, and there were still violent movements operating in the countryside.

But what were their options?

- ✔ Try and introduce their own Home Rule bill – but this was impossible given the opposition to such a course within the Conservative party and their close links with unionism.

- ✔ Stamp down on all the political agitation in Ireland and make the Irish do what they were told. Well, in part this is what the Conservatives did do. They introduced and used several coercion acts to control the country, but in the long term they had to actually try and address the issues if they wanted a quiet life.

✔ Meet the Irish halfway. One of the arguments that had been made by Gladstone was that Irish violence was the result of Irish grievances. The Conservatives understood this, and felt that if they could make conditions better for Irish people, then their demands for political change would evaporate.

In the end, rather than giving the Irish what they wanted, the Conservatives decided that the way forward was to kill Home Rule with kindness. The Conservatives believed that if they could solve the whole land question the Irish would settle down to peaceful and productive lives, would forget about Home Rule, and would be content with effectively being British. They argued that most small farmers weren't actually concerned with the national question, but had been convinced by unscrupulous nationalist politicians that the constitutional status of the country was somehow linked to their economic well-being. Solve the national question and land reform would follow, the Home Rulers had argued. The Conservatives turned this on its head, and argued that small farmers, left to their own devices and farming their own land, wouldn't care who ruled Ireland.

Whatever the rights and wrongs of Conservative policy in Ireland, it is clear that in the last decade of the nineteenth and first years of the twentieth, the party introduced the most far-reaching land reforms in Ireland ever undertaken.

Under Arthur Balfour in the 1890s, the Conservative government began buying huge tracts of land from large landowners, and redistributed it to the Irish under the terms of a long-running, but affordable loan. Okay, so while the Irish were in debt to the British government for decades to come, at least they did, for the first time ever, own their individual plot of land. The Land Purchase Act of 1903 meant that 317,000 smallholdings were transferred into the hands of the Irish farmers.

While the Conservatives didn't move the Home Rule issue forward one inch – if anything they forgot about it – they reformed Ireland. In doing so they didn't actually kill demands for Irish independence, but they did remove some of the angst and aggravation that had accompanied the issue of land ownership that had dominated the post-famine decades.

Unionist Response: Just Say No

While the campaigns of the Land League, the Fenians, and Parnell were all well and good if you were a small Catholic farmer – after all, they were battling for you – many in Ireland didn't share this enthusiasm. A large proportion of people in Ireland, especially in Ulster, didn't want any form of Home Rule; they wanted Ireland to stay part of the British state.

Such people, the unionists, were backed by powerful interests in business, land ownership, the Protestant Church, and the Orange Order. They wouldn't take Home Rule lying down. During the last decades of the nineteenth century they began organising and campaigning to ensure that Ireland, or at least some part of it, would always remain British.

Unionist ideas

The unionists believed that

- ✔ Ireland was theirs (and for many, it had been since the plantations) and an integral part of Britain and the Empire.

- ✔ They didn't want Home Rule, and they certainly didn't want to be included in a state where the majority of people were Catholics.

- ✔ They were often well-off or, if they were workers, believed that industrial stability came from the link with Britain. Unionists were contented precisely *because of* Britain and its Empire, so why change? If Ireland left the union, what would happen to their wealth, influence, and power?

Deciding that there was little in the idea of Home Rule that appealed to them, the unionists took matters into their own hands and set out to oppose Home Rule by whatever means possible. At an anti-Home Rule meeting in Belfast one opponent of Home Rule stated that 'Ulster will fight, and Ulster will be right.' That pretty much summed up what the unionists felt about the whole situation.

Signing the Solemn League and Covenant

In the decades leading to the turn of the century the unionists started getting organised. In 1867 the Ulster Defence Association and the Central Protestant Defence Association were formed by elite unionists to fight any moves towards Home Rule. These were followed by the Ulster Loyalist Anti-Repeal Association, the Ulster Defence Union, and a host of local-based Unionist Clubs.

By 1912, when the Liberal government were again backing Home Rule, over 400,000 unionists came together in Belfast to sign the Solemn League and Covenant, which pledged them to 'use all means necessary to defeat the present conspiracy to set up a Home Rule Parliament in Ireland.' In 1913, things really came to a head, when the Ulster Volunteer Force, with 100,000 men and 20,000 rifles to hand, prepared to fight, if necessary, against Home Rule. The message was simple: while the majority of Ireland might want its freedom, and the Liberals, for their own domestic purposes might be happy to give it to them, unionists would fight. The black clouds were gathering.

The Ulster Volunteer Force continued to demonstrate its loyalty to Britain during the First World War when a substantial proportion of the organisation enlisted to form the predominantly unionist and almost wholly Protestant 36th (Ulster) Division. The Division was decimated on the first day of the Battle of the Somme in 1916 and became a potent symbol of the sacrifices made by unionists in defence of the Union. In 1966 the name, the Ulster Volunteer Force re-emerged to defend Ulster, and became one of the most notorious Loyalist paramilitary organisations, responsible for scores of murders.

Protecting the Protestant way of life: The Orange Order

The most important motivation for the unionists, and their most powerful tool, was religion. They feared enough from Home Rule in terms of economics and politics to motivate them, but what really got them upset was the link between Irish nationalism and Catholicism. Unionists were not only loyal to Britain, but absolutely wedded to their own religion: Protestantism.

The trouble really began before the first Home Rule Act had been introduced in 1886. In an attempt to make everyone happy in Ireland and head off more serious demands for reform, Gladstone had passed an Irish Church Act in 1869. For the Catholics the act looked like an equalisation of the rights of worship in Ireland. To unionists, the act resembled only one thing: the disestablishment of the (Protestant) Church of Ireland. To unionists the Irish Church Act proved to them that their way of life was under threat. All the first Home Rule Act did was underpin their belief.

To combat the attack on their way of life and the threat from home rule, the unionists turned to the Orange Order. The Order, as one historian summed up, 'provided the only credible basis for loyalist opposition to both the Land League and the National League.' The Orange Order brought together politically minded unionists with members of the Church of Ireland and Presbyterians, all of whom felt threatened by an aggressive Catholicism with political goals.

What the Orange Order did, with great effectiveness, was link together all strands of unionist life. It was an organisation that was run by the social elites, but included and welcomed members from all social levels. The Order offered a potent mix of politics, religion, and ritual which translated the unionist campaign against Home Rule and the Land League from one that was merely political, into one that was underpinned by a religious sense of righteousness. It would be an organisation that would dominate the agenda of unionism and be a central force in the mobilisation of Protestant opinion from the late nineteenth century to modern times. Crucially it linked the survival of unionism with the power of a non-Catholic God. If Irish politics weren't complicated enough, the Order brought religion fully and publicly into the equation.

The Irish in Antarctica

Despite the demand for Irish independence and a desire to reject British rule, the Irish played an important part in supporting and staffing the British Empire. Irish people, both Catholic and Protestant, were to be found working wherever the British flag flew. The last great unknown part of the globe, the Antarctic, became a British obsession before and during the First World War. Britain wanted to get to the South Pole before anyone else. Problem was that the Norwegians had the same idea (and got there first). The Irish played an important role in Antarctic exploration during this period. Tom Crean, from Anascaul, County Kerry, travelled with Captain Scott to the Antarctic in 1901 and 1910, and also went along when Ernest Shackleton (born in Kilkea, County Kildare) tried to cross the icy continent. It all went horribly wrong when they got stuck 800 miles away from where they should have been. To get back to their ship they rowed an open boat across the cold waters. The fact they all survived is amazing, and their journey has been called 'one of the greatest boat journeys ever accomplished'. Crean retired back home after all his adventures and opened a pub called the South Pole Inn. His fame was such that his story featured in a 1990s advertising campaign for Guinness. Not that there was much competition – the number of pub-owning Antarctic explorers never got past one.

The Orange Order was popular in the late nineteenth century and has lost none of its vigour. The movement is still important in unionist politics in Northern Ireland, and publicly declares its allegiance to Britain and the Crown on the 12th July every year by marching to celebrate the victory of Protestant King William over Catholic King James at the Battle of the Boyne. In recent years the rights of the Orange Order to parade have been challenged. At Drumcree, there were a series of violent demonstrations by the Orange Order in the late 1990s when the British Army blocked the path of the Order's traditional parade route. It was blocked because the government felt that such a parade would offend Catholic residents who lived on the route.

Protecting the Protestant economy: Belfast the powerhouse

The Orange Order and the unionists weren't just concerned about their political and religious freedoms; they also believed that Home Rule would make them poorer.

Belfast was at the heart of the British industrial success in the second half of the nineteenth century. During the American Civil War, and the resultant downturn in cotton exports to the UK, linen came into its own. And where was the linen industry? Belfast. By 1894, the amount of linen thread produced in Belfast would have circled the earth a staggering 25,000 times, a rate of production making many people rich along the way. At the same time the railways delivered raw materials and finished goods from Ulster's towns and cities, to the docks that would allow their rapid and cheap transport to the British market. Ulster was booming.

Shipbuilding was one of the core industries in Belfast. In the 1890s, the Belfast yards made more ships than anyone else. Engineering industries grew up that supported the shipyards and all these added to the wealth and skill base in Ulster. They also turned themselves to more self-indulgent products – Belfast became the largest producer of aerated water (that's fizzy), made 60 per cent of Ireland's whiskey and at Gallagaher's made cigarettes for the whole of Ireland and Britain. It might have been a dirty and noisy city, but it was one of the great Victorian industrial success stories. The high levels of income and work that were available in Ulster made unionists even more wary of the Home Rulers – if Ireland left the Union, would their profits be threatened?

Protecting the Empire

The unionists were enthusiastic supporters of the Empire, and their political beliefs were as vociferous in their support of the imperial idea as they were in their belief in State and Crown. Here's why. They, like the British, were opposed to Home Rule in Ireland because of the impact separation would have on the rest of the Empire. The British felt that if Ireland, a landmass that was so close to Britain, could challenge British rule, this might encourage other colonial nations to also try and leave the club. The British were especially worried about the behaviour of separatists in South Africa (the British were fighting a war against the nationalist Boers at the time) and India. If the Irish got what they wanted, who knows what might happen? Also worrying the British was the widespread and vocal support for the Boer cause across Ireland, fearing that it could indicate an emerging union between the oppressed people of Empire.

Home Rule at Last!

In 1898 huge celebrations were held across Ireland to mark the centenary of Wolfe Tone's rebellion (although the unionists were certainly not joining in the fun!). These events brought together various strands of nationalism in Irish life, and allowed for a very public display of the enthusiasm for an independent Ireland.

At the turn of the century there was a renewed interest in the idea of Irish nationalism. The nationalist spirit had never gone away, but because of the split following the fall of Parnell, its voice and focus had been lost. The 1898 celebrations encouraged people to begin voicing their demands for independence.

Reuniting the Home Rule party

In this atmosphere, the Home Rulers finally managed to put aside their arguments, and pulled themselves together. In the mid-1890s, William O'Brien had formed the United Irish Land League in Mayo. The League was brought together to fight for the rights of smallholders in the West of Ireland (and proved that no matter how far reaching the government land reforms, more was always needed). O'Brien also had another agenda. He understood that the land issue had always been central to Irish politics and a point of consensus and he aimed to use the League to bring the Home Rulers together around an old point of agreement.

In 1900 the League was formally integrated into the Home Rule party, and a popular dimension restored. No longer was Home Rule politics to be dominated by political infighting amongst its leaders – it had real work to do.

Later the same year, John Redmond was elected to the Chair of a reunited party. By virtue of the League's popularity, and its ability to refocus everyone on the real issues, rather than the legacy of Parnell, the Home Rule movement came back together. The real question was whether the damage of the split would hamper it as a political force.

Party leader Redmond's juggling act

Although the Home Rulers had got back together, there was still a lot of bad blood. Not only did the party fail to forget all the animosity that surrounded the Parnell split, but during the period of division a host of strong and opinionated men had risen to the fore. Redmond's leadership of the party has been called by one historian, 'at best, a balancing act'. In many ways he was more like a juggler, trying to keep all the different demands and pressures in the air without dropping anything. One half of his party expected him to be aggressive, and to challenge the British government at every turn, while the other encouraged him to accept reforms such as the Land Purchase Act without criticism, and to consider them as positive actions. While the Conservatives were in office, and maintaining their hostility to any talk of Home Rule, there was little he could do anyway.

Redmond had a series of problems in trying to stamp his authority on the Home Rule movement:

- ✔ He believed in doing things the 'right' way, or as a contemporary said of him, he had a 'prejudice in favour of the truth that was almost English'. As a result Redmond was committed to strictly parliamentary means for most of his career, and did not build the broader nationalist coalition that Parnell managed to bring together.

- ✔ Other main figures in the party, who had been active during the period of the Parnell split and perhaps imagined themselves as the leaders of the Home Rule Movement, such as James Dillon and William O'Brien, while accepting him as leader, spent a lot of time publicly criticising him and offering alternative suggestions – not good for party cohesion.

- ✔ Although small in scale, a nationalist alternative, in the shape of Sinn Fein emerged in 1907 to challenge the Home Rule agenda. By 1918 they overtook the Home Rulers in terms of popular appeal.

- ✔ While the Conservatives were in power, and trying to kill Home Rule with kindness, Redmond could only have a limited impact on politics at Westminster.

Attacking the House of Lords

Redmond had to keep this difficult juggling act up for some time as he had no real power in Parliament until the election of 1910 when, despite their confidence, the Liberals only managed a two-seat majority. Suddenly Redmond was the king maker. He promised the Liberal leader, Asquith, his support in whatever he wanted, so long as an Irish Home Rule bill was brought before parliament.

The problem Asquith faced, as had reformists in British history before him, was that the House of Lords didn't really appreciate reform, and had an annoying habit of blocking anything that they didn't like as they could hold bills back and sometimes veto them. Asquith decided to act. He went to the country in a second election in 1910 with this simple agenda: If elected, Asquith and the Liberals would curtail the powers of the House of Lords to veto bills from the Commons; instead, the Lords would only be able to delay a bill for two years. The electorate supported the Liberals and Asquith was able to convince the Lords that their day had passed.

Asquith and the Liberals were more interested in their own agenda than that of Home Rule. The House of Lords had rejected the Liberal Party's reforming budget in 1909, so the 1910 election had been fought on the issue of the powers of the Lords. Having won the popular vote (just), Asquith announced a plan to limit the powers of the House of Lords, threatening to create enough new pro-reform peers to swamp any opposition. The resulting Parliament Act, passed in August 1911, ended the Lords' veto over financial legislation passed by the House of Commons. This in turn paved the way for the passage of the Home Rule Bill through the Lords in 1912.

In 1912, and true to his word, Asquith placed a Home Rule bill before parliament. Redmond and the Home Rulers would get their reward. After much acrimony, vicious debate, and aggressive campaigning against the bill by unionists, the bill was passed in the Commons. The bill was unsuccessful in the Lords, but as they no longer had a veto, the bill would only be delayed for two years. Home Rule would become a reality on 18 September 1914. The Irish rejoiced.

Many people thought that Redmond had delivered to Ireland what it had always wanted: Home Rule. But in the months before the outbreak of the First World War, the government watered down the proposals. Redmond was convinced that he should allow the six counties of Ulster with majority Protestant populations to be excluded from the Home Rule Act for six years. So while Redmond had won Ireland its independence, he quickly allowed parts of it to opt out because of the power of the unionists within British politics. Had Redmond achieved freedom for Ireland, or had he been outmanoeuvred by a combination of unionist and British politicians? Some historians feel that Redmond had put too much trust in the British political system and was duped by more powerful forces, while others think that he got the best deal he could.

But then a million Germans marched into view on the Western front, and the world changed all over again.

Part VI
Divided in Two: Life from the 1880s

The 5th Wave   By Rich Tennant

In this part . . .

In the 1880s Ireland embraced its traditional culture, and tried to distinguish itself from Britain. This was an important process and made people in Ireland feel more Irish. The more Irish they felt, the more they argued that Ireland's future would be improved by separation from Britain. The demands for separation found a political voice in the early years of the twentieth century. After the chaos of the First World War, the Irish took matters into their own hands and rebelled against the British. They won freedom from Britain by fighting a war, but the freedom was only partial.

In 1922 Ireland was divided in two. The partition of Ireland would play an important part in Western history in the twentieth century, and would lead, to some extent, to the Troubles in Northern Ireland from the late 1960s. The violence in Northern Ireland over the last three and a half decades has been bitter and divisive, although the signs for peace have been promising of late. Since the 1990s, Ireland has changed once more, switching from a period of boom, to a new one of bust.

Chapter 20

Balls and Books in Irish: The Cultural Revival

. . . .

In This Chapter
▶ Understanding Irish culture
▶ Why the Irish needed a Cultural Revival
▶ Sporting ways of the Irish
▶ Ireland in literature and at the theatre

. . . .

A fter the Famine many thinkers, artists, and political activists began realising that traditional Irish culture was in danger of being lost. Ireland was undergoing a process of Anglicisation. Most aspects of Irish life were being replaced by British forms. The Irish were increasingly exposed to British authors, playwrights, newspapers, sports, music, business practices, and laws.

There was a fear that unless the process of Anglicisation was arrested, Ireland would cease to be distinctive. There was also a realisation that without an indigenous Irish culture the demands for a separate Irish nation would be meaningless. Ireland had to remain distinctive in terms of its culture to truly be free. If Anglicisation continued unchecked, any future freedom would result in an independent nation that was culturally indistinct from the rest of Britain. To confront the challenge of Anglicisation, a series of movements in art, literature, drama, and sport emerged that would champion traditional Irish culture.

Preserving Everything Gaelic

During the nineteenth century traditional Irish sports, such as hurling, Gaelic football, and handball, went into steep decline. The reasons for this were:

⤷ The loss of population and stability caused by the Famine.

⤷ Legislation that prevented the holding of fairs and other gatherings on holidays and Saint's Days. Traditional sports had been a feature of such days, but the British authorities and the Catholic Church considered them too rowdy.

✔ The spread of British sports through the schools and colleges of Ireland. It was felt that games such as cricket taught young men how to become gentlemen whilst Irish games were for the savages and not to be encouraged.

Similarly, people felt that the Irish language was being supplanted by English. Although not a dead language, over the centuries it had been replaced by English. The same problem existed with Irish art and culture. People feared that it was either imported straight from Britain or that Irish artists and writers simply copied the styles from across the Irish Sea.

The numbers of Irish speakers fell in the decades after the Irish Famine of the mid-nineteenth century, but was preserved by the work of organisations such as the Gaelic League (discussed in the next section) and the policies of Irish governments after 1922. There is now a daily Irish language newspaper, and a national radio and television station. All school children learn Irish, and specific areas, known as the Gaeltacht, are preserved as places where Irish is the everyday language. Irish is more vibrant than the *Mead Cile Failte* (a thousand welcomes) of the tourist brochures!

The Cultural Revival was a wide ranging movement that operated in many different areas of Irish society. The work of the cultural revivalists were felt in many disparate areas of life and would play an important role in arresting the spread of English forms of culture. In doing so, the Cultural Revival would play an important role in making people feel more Irish and develop a sense of nationalism.

Keypoints of the Irish Revival

The Irish Cultural Revival had many different features and motivations. These included:

✔ A promotion of the language and traditional culture in the arts, literature, theatre, and sport.

✔ Support for indigenous agriculture and industry.

✔ A rejection of British forms of culture which were viewed as destroying the fabric of the Irish nation.

✔ A realisation that the preservation of Irish culture was linked to demands for national independence.

✔ An overall vision of the Cultural Revival as one that was primarily Gaelic and Catholic.

Why the Irish wanted to be different

The Irish weren't being difficult in their demands that they play their own sports, speak their native language, and embrace indigenous culture, they simply wanted to preserve their sense of identity in the face of one of the most powerful empires in the world. Also, the desire to preserve their heritage didn't mean, as many observers in Britain argued, that the Irish were backward or savages. Many sectors of Irish society, such as the middle and upper classes, had embraced British culture. The Cultural Revival aimed at removing the appeal of British Culture and demonstrating how vibrant and important Irish Culture could be.

In fact what they wanted to embrace were traditions of culture that emerged during the pre-British era. These traditions, symbolised by work such as the Book of Kells, were based on high levels of learning. Traditional Irish games, such as hurling, relied on physical and technical skill. By attempting to preserve an Irish culture, the Gaelic League, Gaelic Athletic Association, and others were building on traditions of innovation and excellence. Just because it was different to British culture didn't mean that it was a bad thing.

The Irish weren't alone in trying to retain and define an indigenous culture that made them different to the British. Similar movements happened across the world and in many British colonies such as India, South Africa, and across the Caribbean.

Spearheading the Preservation

Two different organisations spearheaded the campaign to preserve an Irish Ireland:

- ✔ **The Gaelic Athletic Association:** Formed in 1884, this sporting organisation feared that Irish men were becoming weak and effeminate because they were playing British sports such as cricket, soccer, and hockey, and forgetting the traditional manly Irish games of hurling and Gaelic football.

- ✔ **The Gaelic League:** Formed in 1893, the Gaelic League sought to preserve the Irish language. Its leaders argued that without its own language, Irish – often referred to as Gaelic – Ireland could never be a nation. The League's aim was to arrest the spread of the English language and restore Irish as the native tongue.

The Gaelic Athletic Association: Hurling and football

The Gaelic Athletic Association was founded by a school teacher, Michael Cusack, to preserve and cultivate the Irish national sporting pastimes. The Association not only promoted what were called the native games, but also encouraged the use of the Irish language and supported the demands for national freedom.

While the Gaelic Athletic Association was successful in promoting its native games, English sports were still hugely popular. As late as 1900 the game played most often in Ireland was cricket. A decision was made that would profoundly influence the sporting landscape in Ireland: British sports would be banned.

From the 1890s the Gaelic Athletic Association banned its members from playing or even watching what were called the foreign or garrison games (those associated with the British military). These were cricket, soccer, rugby, and hockey. With the support of the nationalist press, who vociferously attacked young Irish men who played such games as unpatriotic, the ban was successful and led to a further upsurge in popularity for the native games.

The Gaelic Athletic Association's ban on foreign games was finally lifted in 1971. However, because of the troubles in Northern Ireland, new rules were introduced that banned members of the British Army or Royal Ulster Constabulary from playing any part in the Association. It also decided that the grounds of the Association should not host foreign games. These were controversial decisions, and in recent years have dominated debates within Irish society. As part of its commitment to the peace process the Association dropped its ban on members of the security forces in 2001, and in 2005 agreed that soccer and rugby could be played at Croke Park.

The sports of the Gaelic Athletic Association are still hugely popular today. The Association's national stadium, Croke Park (named after its founding patron, Archbishop Croke), is the largest in the country. Every September it is full to capacity – 85,000 people – for the hurling and Gaelic football finals. All the counties of Ireland – north and south – dream of winning the All Ireland final, and the players who win the title (all of whom are amateurs) become local heroes.

Michael Cusack, the founder of the Gaelic Athletic Association claimed that the organisation spread across Ireland like a prairie fire. This probably overstates the levels of success that the Association achieved. At the time of its establishment the Association forged a close link with the Catholic Church, and based its club structure around the parish. In principle all parishes had a club and the local priest was the President of the club. In practice, clubs often struggled to establish themselves. It wasn't until the period of the ban, and the promotion of the Association by the press as a patriotic act, that the fire really started to burn. The keys to success though were that the games were good to play and watch, were well organised, and, because of the parish organisation, they forged a real sense of local community that continues to this day.

The Gaelic League: Language and letters

The Gaelic League was the brain child of Eugene O'Downey, a Professor of Irish, and two other academically minded gentlemen, Douglas Hyde and Eoin Mac Neill. Hyde focused everyone's mind in a famous lecture titled 'The necessity of de-anglicising the Irish people'. He argued that English linguistic and cultural forms were taking over, and unless something was done to change things, the Irish, as a culturally distinct people, would disappear forever.

To encourage the work of the League and to spread its message, branches were set up across the country. By 1908 there were 599 separate branches in Ireland, and every county was represented. The League organised speakers to travel the country promoting its work. They published books and plays, and through its branches encouraged people to learn Irish and to take part in events and gatherings that promoted traditional culture. They even encouraged people to wear, whenever possible, Irish-made clothes.

Douglas Hyde was a Protestant, as were many of the members of the Gaelic League. Although the League argued that Ireland was a distinct nation because of its culture, this did not initially equate to demands for political separation from Britain. Hyde always argued that the work of the League was politically neutral and that love of the Irish language and culture was something that could bring all Irish people together – whatever their religion. By the time of the First World War this had changed, and the League became an organisation that saw itself as one that promoted an identity that was Irish and Catholic. This did not mean however that it was closed to Protestants: it also appealed to them as it was a patriotic movement.

Invading America

In 1888 the Association, thinking big, decided to invade America. The aim was to raise money to bring the ancient Irish sporting and cultural festival, Aonach Tailteann, back to life. Unfortunately this wouldn't happen until 1924 (see chapter 21). The aim of the invasion was to play exhibition hurling matches across America and to compete in athletic tournaments to raise money from gate receipts. The whole invasion was a disaster. The Canadian leg of the invasion was cancelled due to snow, and events in America regularly rained off. The plan was audacious and unfortunately the tour lost money. The team ended up being locked in their hotel rooms in New York until a benefactor paid the bills. The failure of the invasion, while leaving America free from Gaelic games, proved that the real home of such indigenous culture was Ireland: these games weren't for export.

Turning back the clock

Those engaged in the cultural revival, for all their good ideas, had a big problem. How to actually implement their ideas and make Ireland Irish? However they may have felt, Ireland, in the late nineteenth century, had a close political, economic, and culture relationship with Britain, the world's largest trading and economic power. They couldn't simply ignore Britain and hope that it would go away. What the Gaelic League and the Gaelic Athletic Association tried to do was to convince people to embrace their own culture, to make them proud to be Irish, and through their various branches and clubs, to let people enjoy themselves in words, songs, music, and play.

Revisiting the country of saints and scholars

As well as promoting Irish Culture amongst the Irish people, the period of the Cultural Revival allowed for the emergence of many of Ireland's most notable artists in the fields of literature, drama, and the arts. Everyone it seemed was an artist, working on their latest poem, play, or painting. The very presence of such high levels of quality work appeared to make real the old adage that Ireland was the country of saints and scholars.

As well as men such as Douglas Hyde and Eoin MacNeill from the leadership of the Gaelic League, the period from the 1880s through to the 1920s witnessed the arrival of such luminaries as the writers W.B. Yeats, James Joyce, Maude Gonne, Oscar Wilde, and Samuel Beckett, the playwrights J.M. Synge and Sean O'Casey and the artists Jack Yeats, William Orpen, and Sean Keating. These people defined Ireland during an age of change. They turned to Ireland – especially the West of the country and its ancient folklore – for their inspiration, and their work still finds an audience today.

Their inspiration

The writers and artists of the Cultural Revival drew their inspiration from Ireland's past. In the search for an authentic representation of this, many of them turned to the West of Ireland for inspiration. The West of Ireland – particularly counties Kerry, Clare, Galway, and Mayo – attracted these arty types as it was seen to be unspoiled. The region had not modernised greatly, and it still contained a large Irish-speaking population who made their living off the land and lived traditional lives. Particularly important were the Aran and Blasket Islands and Connemara, as it was there that oral traditions of folklore and history were dominant. In effect the West was a living museum, full of Irish-speaking people whose past had been passed down to them in oral form from generation to generation. In them, and in the landscape, the writers and artists found a living version of the Ireland that they felt defined the aims of the Cultural Revival.

Why all the fairies?

It always seems as if the writers of the Cultural Revival were obsessed with fairies. Lots of their books and poems feature the little creatures, and there's even a famous cartoon of W. B. Yeats meeting one. But the use of fairies in the literature of the Cultural Revival did have an important point. It gave them a focus for linking together the old traditions of Ireland with the time that they lived in.

In some ways it was a man called Standish O'Grady who started it all. He wrote a book in 1878 called *The History of Ireland*. It dealt not with recent history, but Ireland's ancient past: old sagas, folk tales, and myths. For the readers of his work there was the realisation that what O'Grady had found, and they were reading, were stories about Ireland's ancient Gaelic tradition. The stories dealt with ancient Irish characters – superheroes if you like – who were chivalrous and made old Ireland a better, more heroic place.

Douglas Hyde followed O'Grady into the ring in 1889 when he published a collection of folk stories based on fairy tales and folk lore. These were published in Irish – what was felt by many to be the true language of the Cultural Revival – and drew on the oral memories and traditions of the residents of the West of Ireland. What Hyde brought to life was a world of superstition, mythology, and morality tales that hit a nerve. The traditions and people of the West were seen as romantic and truly Irish. The writers believed in the oral tradition they had discovered and Ireland that was, as one historian has noted, 'miraculously preserved from the contaminating influences of civilisation.'

What the fairies, the ancient legends that inspired them, and the old people who still told the tales gave to the Cultural Revival was great raw material to work with, and a subject matter that was distinctly Irish.

Although the writers who worked during the Cultural Revival were inspirational, and provided Ireland with a unique and distinctive literature, the people involved were mostly from elite Anglo-Irish backgrounds and were Protestants. But, due to their position as members of the gentry, many of them were close to the land. Many of them had estates or properties in the West of Ireland. So while they were distinct from the traditions they wrote about by virtue of their class, they were familiar with them by virtue of living amongst them.

The Literary Revival: Yeats and Others

There are a whole host of writers that can be connected to the Cultural Revival, and many more who were inspired by it. But all that is really needed are the main players. The ones who really drove things along at the end of the nineteenth century, and who, by associating together often, can be seen as the inspirational core for the whole movement.

- **W. B. Yeats (1865–1939).** The giant of the Cultural Revival, and a writer who subsequently developed even finer work after the period of the First World War. Awarded the Nobel Prize for Literature in 1923, he also served in the Irish Senate from 1922–28.

- **Lady Augusta Gregory (1852–1932).** With Yeats she was the guiding light of the Cultural Revival. Famous for her role in establishing the Abbey Theatre and known for her one-act plays such as 'The Gaol Gate' (1906) and 'The Rising of the Moon' (1907).

- **George Russell (1867–1935).** Known by his pen name, AE, Russell spent his life understanding the spirit world. He was a playwright and poet, and helped develop the talents of others.

- **George Moore (1852–1933).** Moore divided his time between London and Dublin, and a writer fascinated by the potential of art and the work of artists. His impact in Ireland was highest at the turn of the century and his *The Untilled Field* was published in Irish (1902) and English (1903).

- **Douglas Hyde (1860–1949).** Famous for his folklore writing, Hyde's greatest impact was as an organiser and scholar. He was founder of the Gaelic League, the first Professor of modern Irish at Trinity College (1909–32), and first President of Ireland (1938–45).

- **John Millington Synge (1871–1909).** Synge had been working in Paris in the 1890s when he met Yeats, who convinced him to travel to the Aran Islands. His works *The Aran Islands* (1907) and *Playboy of the Western World* (1907) capture best his observations of Irish life.

The writers of the Cultural Revival were a small and select group. They knew each other well and often collaborated on their works with others from the group. They drew their inspiration from a wide range of contemporary intellectual fashion, and duly dabbled in occultism, mysticism, magic, and folklore. What they were searching for were new and exciting ways to present literature that was about Ireland, and inspired by things Irish.

The Abbey Theatre

When all the writers started to get together, meeting at various times at gatherings hosted by Lady Gregory at Coole Park, the conversation inevitably moved on from what they were working on, to where it might be staged. While all the writers had conceived and began producing a national literature for Ireland, they had a problem. No national theatre.

It was Yeats and Lady Gregory who really drove the idea of a national theatre along. Initially the idea of a national theatre was delivered at various venues, and the most important fact was the performance of plays with an Irish character. In 1904, six years after its initial foundation, the national theatre idea found a permanent home at the Abbey Theatre. The original structure was destroyed in a fire in the 1940s, and the current theatre opened in 1966.

The first play that was performed under the auspices of a national theatre was Yeats's play *The Countess Cathleen*. Which annoyed a lot of people. The problem was that the play featured Cathleen preparing to sell her soul to the devil to feed the starving Irish (remember, this is only a few decades after the famine). While good theatre, the idea that the good Catholic Irish would ever consider selling their soul was abhorrent, and the critics had a field day.

But as with any art form, controversy is good news. The work that was staged by the national theatre movement was mostly high quality and met a need within people to engage with Irish-inspired plays. The Irish Literary Theatre, as it was called, went from strength to strength.

The plays that were staged mixed those in English with others in Irish, such as Hyde's *The Twisting of the Rope*. It also constantly dealt with the thorny issue of the Irish nation. There had been one in the ancient myths and tales, so could there be one in the future? Yeats certainly thought so. His landmark play, *Cathleen ni Houlihan*, focused on an old woman who represented Ireland. She talked to her audience of those who have assisted her in the past, and might die for her in the future. It struck a chord with the public, and was a very popular play.

The Irish Literary Theatre was renamed the Abbey Theatre in 1904. For the quality and range of work that has been produced there, it is one of the most important places in Irish history. While it was important for allowing the writers of the Cultural Revival a place to stage their work, it also gave them the means to communicate their ideas with the public. It wasn't always a place of consensus, and there were regular controversies over the works that were performed. But that in itself was a sign of its success. It showed that the public was engaging with the debates that were being put forward.

Although the original Abbey Theatre was burnt down – by accident, not by angry critics and crowds – it was rebuilt. The Abbey is still going strong today. Its programme continues to feature work in English and Irish, regularly revisits the work of those writers who inspired it, and showcases emerging new talent. A must-see for the literary or theatrically minded visitor to Ireland.

Playboy riots

John Millington Synge spent a lot of time in the Aran Islands. He revelled in the islanders' use of language and was fascinated by their lifestyle, traditions, and customs as they struggled to make their living off the coast of Ireland. He produced a series of plays based on his observations of the islanders and from others he met in the rural communities of the West of Ireland and in county Wicklow.

Synge was no romantic though. While he admired these rural dwellers, he did not idealise them. In 1903 his play *In the Shadow of the Glen* produced a furore. Its main character was a young woman locked in an empty marriage with an old man in a remote cottage. At the end of the play she runs away with a travelling man rather than stay with her elderly husband. Ireland wasn't ready for such salacious tales. Synge was attacked for suggesting that Irish women could be anything but virtuous. His play was seen as a slur on Irish morals and the strength of the Irish character.

Ireland was a deeply religious country, and in the late nineteenth century the emergent idea of Irish nationalism was being fashioned so that it was linked closely with Catholicism. The Irish were conceived as a people who were devoted to their country and their religion. Depictions of the Irish, such as Synge's, that challenged this view were abhorrent to many.

Synge hit the headlines again in January 1907. His new play, *The Playboy of the Western World* premiered at the Abbey Theatre. The play sparked riots on the opening night that would continue during and after every performance for its entire first week. A pattern that would continue when it toured America in 1911.

Arthur Griffith, the founder of the nationalist party Sinn Fein, wrote that the play was 'a vile and inhuman story told in the foulest language we have ever listened to from a public platform'. So what was the problem? The opponents of the play argued that it depicted the Irish peasantry as violent, immoral, and coarse.

Despite all the arguments, the furore surrounding the play reinforced the central place of the Abbey Theatre at the heart of Irish literary life. *The Playboy of the Western World* also survived all the fuss. It remains one of the most popular and widely performed plays of the Cultural Revival.

A National Style: The Rebirth of Irish Art

Art in all its forms, but particularly painting, was a great Victorian obsession. In Britain artists recreated great historic scenes that demonstrated the nation's glorious past. People also loved landscapes that depicted how beautiful Britain was. All this work was meant to appeal to the emotions, and to make people feel proud, and a bit weepy eyed at how great it was to be British.

The British art establishment was incredibly powerful. All the main training colleges were in Britain. Those in London were seen as particularly cutting-edge, and set the fashions. British artists defined what good art was.

The Painter Laureate: Paul Henry

Although not the only person to paint the Irish landscape, it was Paul Henry, above all, who defined an Irish national style. His paintings of the Conemarra landscape became iconic images of Ireland. They were not only applauded when put on public display, but were also widely used in the 1920s and 1930s by railway companies advertising the delights of holidaying in Ireland. He painted mountains, the sea, piles of turf, and his landmark white cottages and captured an idealised Ireland. His paintings, when they come up for sale, often demand six figure sums. For most of us though, there's always lots of posters and postcards of his work available at a much cheaper price.

In Ireland artists struggled with a basic question. What is Irish Art? Do we, in Ireland, have a national style? If you're feeling Irish, what should you paint to express that?

Like the writers, the artists turned to the West of Ireland for their inspiration. In the people and places of the West they found their national style. Something which was representative of Ireland, and spoke for Ireland.

Lots of Art

There were three very broad categories of Irish art that emerged in the late nineteenth and early twentieth centuries that defined the national style. They were:

- Paintings of the landscape.
- Depictions of peasant people and their lives.
- Sculptures and paintings of the great historic and contemporary figures in Irish life.

All this work often came together in exhibitions that were explicitly designed to showcase Irish art, and was also driven by the teaching at Dublin's Municipal School of Art. From there a group of artists emerged, tight-knit like their literary counterparts, who explicitly set out to create a national art.

The main figures that require attention in the artistic world of this period are:

- **Sir John Lavery (1856–1941).** Inspired by Whistler in his early career, Lavery was a society painter. Born in the north of Ireland he always had an interest in things Irish and this was encouraged by his wife Hazel (whom he painted often and who appeared on the first banknotes of independent Ireland). Lavery is most famous for his paintings of leading political figures.

- ✔ **Sir William Orpen (1871–1931).** Best known as a war artist, Orpen's importance to Ireland was as a teacher at the Dublin Municipal School of Art where he trained people such as Keating and Clarke.

- ✔ **Harry Clarke (1889–1931).** Clarke was the foremost artist in stained glass in Ireland and had an international reputation. With his wife Margaret he travelled to the West of Ireland and was strongly influenced by the mythical tales he heard there.

- ✔ **Sean Keating (1889–1977).** Trained by Orpen, Keating discovered his inspiration in the West of Ireland and painted some of the most stridently nationalist work of the revolutionary period.

- ✔ **Jack Butler Yeats (1871–1957).** Brother of writer W.B. Yeats and one of the most significant Irish painters, Yeats started as a book illustrator and was an important painter of life in the West. During the revolutionary period he painted political scenes, and developed a romantic and emotional style from the 1930s.

Hugh Lane and his famous pictures

All this art was all very well, but in the same way that the writers needed a theatre, so the artists needed a national gallery. There had actually been a national gallery in Dublin for ages, but it was traditional. It displayed the great art of Europe, and had little inclination to embrace Irish art. What the artists needed was someone who wished to embrace their project, and understood the need for a gallery and a collection that was avowedly Irish in content and intent.

Sir Hugh Lane was an art dealer and collector who became interested in Ireland and the Cultural Revival through his aunt, Lady Gregory. He commissioned Irish artists such as Jack Yeats to undertake commissions, and worked closely with others in the Cultural Revival movement to open an art gallery for Irish art. He finally achieved this goal in 1906 when the Dublin Municipal Gallery opened. He gave lots of his own collection to the gallery, and convinced many others to do the same. The gallery was quickly established as one of the most important in Ireland.

Lane also offered to leave the Gallery his collection of French paintings, the so-called Lane bequest, on condition that a permanent gallery was built to house them. Dublin corporation failed to do this, and the paintings controversially went to the National Gallery in London. In 1914 Lane died on board the Lusitania when it was torpedoed by the Germans off the coast of Cork. The issue of the Lane bequest became a source of disagreement between London and Dublin, that was only resolved in 1959. It was agreed that the paintings would be shown alternatively between the two cities. The Lane Gallery is still open in Dublin, and contains, as it was supposed to, a great collection of national art.

When Lane died in 1914, it was rumoured that he also had with him paintings by Monet, Rembrandt, Rubens, and Titian on board the Lusitania. These were supposedly insured for $4 million. But were they ever on board, and what happened to them? The wreck of the Lusitania is now protected by a heritage order, but those who have seen the wreck claim they have seen sealed tubes down there that might contain the pictures. One day we might find out!

Was the Cultural Revival a Success?

So, the books are still read, the plays performed, and the Gaelic Athletic Association going from strength to strength, but did the Cultural Revival matter in the grand scheme of things? How did an Irish person at the turn of the century really relate to a play being staged at the Abbey for a dominantly metropolitan audience?

In other words, how important was Cultural Revival and what kind of impact did it have?

Preserving Irish nationalism

Many historians have argued that the Cultural Revival bridged the gap between the fall of Parnell and the rise of Redmond (see Chapter 19). For a decade Irish nationalism was without a strong leader and lacked political cohesion. Into the void stepped the Cultural Revivalists. They ensured that the Irish people, when lacking political leadership, remained active and engaged with the idea of what it was to be Irish.

The main reasons why the Revival has to be seen as important are:

- ✔ It allowed for the creation of sporting, literary, and theatrical forms that were, by definition, Irish.

- ✔ The revival stemmed the flow of British forms of culture into Ireland.

- ✔ By playing games, reading books, attending the theatre, or using the language, the Revival allowed people to think of themselves as Irish.

- ✔ Although not explicitly political in its aims, the work of the Revival linked the promotion of an indigenous culture with the aspiration for an independent Ireland.

- ✔ The various movements associated with the Revival spurred on many Irish men and women to become activists. Many of the leading figures of the revolutionary period cut their teeth in the organisations such as the Gaelic League and the Gaelic Athletic Association.

Preserving Ireland as an Irish land

The simple question in relation to the cultural revival is 'Did it work?' Clearly the Gaelic League and the Gaelic Athletic Association did have successes. The cultural revival attracted mass memberships, and in both the cultural and sporting arenas their work in the late nineteenth century laid the foundations for a vibrant Irish culture that still exists today. However the clock couldn't be turned back. While the Irish language was preserved it never replaced English as the main vernacular of the Irish people. The influence of Britain was simply too great. Alongside a burgeoning native culture, the Irish continued to be affected by the media, arts, and sports of its near neighbour.

But what the later decades of the nineteenth century had shown was that Ireland could be Irish. This might seem an obvious statement, but an important one. By making people think of themselves as Irish, and treasure their language and heritage, the Cultural Revival ensured that people didn't become British. Ireland would remain distinct, and not simply a geographic unit of Britain which, in its habits, was no different to London or Manchester.

For all its success, the Cultural Revival didn't convince everyone. Many people simply went about their daily lives and remained untouched by everything that was happening. Many unionists and Protestants understood that the Revival was challenging their values, and so ignored it, preferring instead to play cricket, watch plays written by English writers, and dismiss the Irish peasant as backwards rather than noble.

Chapter 21

Fighting Against Britain: The Revolution

. . . .

In This Chapter

▶ The advance of Irish nationalism

▶ Understanding the opposition from unionists

▶ The impact of the First World War

▶ Ireland in revolution

▶ Dividing Ireland

▶ Seeking consensus in the face of civil war

. . . .

As the twentieth century began, Ireland seemed a more peaceful place than it had been in recent decades. Economic reforms and changes to the patterns of land ownership had bought a degree of prosperity to some sections of Irish society, and while the tide of emigration had not halted, the numbers involved were shrinking.

Despite these apparently positive developments, the political and cultural demands for an Ireland that was free from Britain and its influence had not lessened. The political upheavals in London in 1910 (see chapter 18) had placed the Irish politicians in Westminster in a position of primacy and Home Rule seemed a possibility. By 1922 Ireland, or at least part of it, would exist as a separate independent state, but the years leading to that point would see massive political upheavals and loss of life.

Home Rule and a House Divided: Nationalists vs. Unionists

The Home Rule Bill, which created an independent Irish parliament, had been passed by the British parliament in 1912 and was due to be enacted in 1914. Under this bill, Ireland would have its own parliament, but certain big issues, such as foreign policy, would remain in the hands of the parliament in London. Ireland would also remain a full member of the British Empire. This was a form of self-government that worked wholly within the constitutional sphere, and did not create a separate Irish state that was in any way a Republic.

Constitutional nationalism, in the form of John Redmond's Irish Parliamentary Party, was not the only nationalist force in Ireland, however. Other nationalist forces, including such groups as Sinn Fein and the Irish Republican Brotherhood, existed outside of Parliament and pursued their own ends. In addition to the various nationalist groups were the unionists – those who opposed the idea of Home Rule altogether.

This crowded political landscape meant that the pressures on the custodians of constitutional politics were huge. If any concessions were made in the passage of the Home Rule Bill, or if the unionists took military action to prevent the enactment of Home Rule, then a welter of political, and armed, opposition would be unleashed.

In short, Ireland was becoming increasingly restless and difficult to manage. And this situation was happening at the same time that German intentions in Europe were becoming increasingly troublesome.

Sinn Fein et al.: The advanced nationalists

It was clear to many nationalists that the unionist population, those who wished Ireland to remain part of Britain, would not meekly accept Home Rule. Sinn Fein and other nationalist movements that existed outside of parliament understood this and readied themselves for action. The various groups, often referred to as *advanced nationalists,* and their agendas were as follows:

- ✔ **Sinn Fein:** Meaning 'ourselves alone', Sinn Fein had been formed in 1907 by Arthur Griffith. This party offered a more radical reading of the Irish-British relationship. Rather than accepting continued British involvement in Irish affairs and membership of the Empire, as would be enshrined in the Home Rule Bill, Sinn Fein argued for complete and total independence from Britain. Initially the party did not advocate the use of violence to achieve its aims. Sinn Fein was always a fringe political movement until after the Easter Rising of 1916 (see the later section 'Easter Time in Dublin') when it rose to electoral prominence.

- ✔ **Irish Republican Brotherhood (IRB):** The IRB was a secret movement advocating physical force for the purpose of creating an Irish Republic and drawing its inspiration from the Fenians of the nineteenth century. The IRB believed in the use of violence to attain its aims. While ideologically highly committed, the IRB's membership only numbered some 2,000.

- ✔ **The Irish Volunteers:** Formed in 1913 by Eoin MacNeill, the Volunteers were a direct response to the formation of armed groups in Ulster that would oppose Home Rule by force. The Volunteers aim was to guarantee the rights and liberties of Irish people. By the outbreak of the First World War the estimated membership of the Volunteers was 180,000.

- ✔ **The Irish Citizen Army (ICA):** The ICA was formed in 1914 as a socialist worker's army. Although committed to the ultimate creation of a socialist state in Ireland, the ICA acknowledged that, without independence from Britain, the workers' republic it dreamt of could not be achieved.

- ✔ **Cumann na mBan:** Meaning the 'Association of Women', Cumann na mBan emerged from the suffragette struggle. Its aim was to assist in the arming, equipping, and support of Irishmen in the defence of Ireland.

Although the advanced nationalists, with the exception of the Irish Volunteers, lacked mass support from the Irish populace, they were not without funds and resources. Many Irish-Americans believed vehemently in the complete rejection of British rule in Ireland, and were content to fund movements that were dedicated to that goal. American money was used to support the political campaigns of the advanced nationalists, and from 1914, these funds were regularly used to secure arms and ammunition.

The unionists and the Ulster Volunteer Force

Unionists were appalled by the idea of Home Rule for Ireland (see Chapter 18), and believed that their way of life, economic security, and their very safety was under threat from the idea of a nationalist and Catholic dominated Ireland. In 1914 the Ulster Volunteer Force was formed by the unionist leaders Edward Carson and Sir James Craig to defend the union by force if necessary. By 1915 the police estimated that the Force had some 53,000 rifles in its possession and a membership of 100,000. Seen primarily as a force for the defence of unionism, the Ulster Volunteer Force was popular amongst the majority of unionists.

Civil war looms

As the date for the enactment of Home Rule edged ever nearer, it became clear that the unionists would not meekly accept their fate. They would, through the Ulster Volunteer Force, fight against the creation of an independent Ireland. Ranged against the unionists were the various nationalists groups, listed in the preceding section, who would equally take up arms to ensure that Home Rule did become a reality.

Curragh Mutiny

Given the strength of feeling in Ulster against the proposed Home Rule Bill, the British government were awake to the idea that Ulster could erupt in violence once the Bill was enacted. In December 1913, the government made the importation of arms and ammunition illegal, but with little effect. In March 1914, it put the British Army in Ireland, based at the Curragh, on alert in advance of any explosion of unionist rebellion in Ulster.

Aware that many officers would have natural affiliations with the plight of the unionists (many of them were unionists themselves), the commander-in-chief of the Army in Ireland demanded that any officer unwilling to invade Ulster and act against rebellious unionists to restore order must resign. In the event, 130 officers tendered their resignations rather than face the possibility of marching against the unionists. This mutiny of the leading officers in Ireland caused real problems for the government: how could law and order, and the Home Rule Bill, ever be enforced in Ulster if the army refused to be mobilised?

The mood in Ireland at the time was ominously reflected in two speeches in 1914. In January 1914, the Conservative Andrew Bonar Law made clear his belief that Ireland was 'drifting inevitably to civil war' and that Home Rule would be resisted 'by force if necessary'. In July, the king acknowledged that 'the cry of civil war is on the lips of the most responsible and sober-minded of my people'.

Ireland was, in the summer of 1914, undoubtedly on the verge of a major conflict.

Time Out for a World War

For Irish nationalists at least, 1914 should have been a great year. The self government they had so long dreamt of was due to be enacted in September and they would have control over their own affairs. It was clear early on that the party would be dampened by the opposition from unionists; after all, opposition from unionists, especially the formation of the Ulster Volunteer Force, was solid, and it was clear that they would not stand idly by when the Bill was enacted. The forces of nationalism, particularly the Irish Volunteers, were prepared to take up arms against unionist intransigence and would, in all likelihood, be supported by the forces of advanced nationalism who would use any struggle to promote their own agenda.

But then, in August, one month shy of Home Rule being enacted, the Germans gate-crashed the party and the whole thing was called off.

For the British the situation was a complete nightmare. As storm clouds gathered in Europe and a war against Germany became a possibility, they didn't know what would happen in Ireland. Would events there spiral out of control and undermine the war effort, or would the various groups in Ireland postpone their struggles for the greater good?

Achtung, baby! The Germans show up

Turns out that, although a World War is never a good thing, the arrival of the Germans on the scene in the summer of 1914 allowed all the problematic permutations of what might happen in Ireland to be shelved. There was a war to be fought in Europe, and everyone was briefly off the hook.

In all likelihood the outbreak of the First World War prevented a potential civil war in Ireland between unionists and nationalists. The avoidance of such a struggle was desirable, but events during the 1914–18 conflict changed the political landscape in Ireland, and led to the ascendancy of radically minded and non-constitutional forces. If the World War had not happened, the British would have been forced to involve themselves in the support of the Home Rule as it had been drafted in 1912.

The British declaration of war on Germany in August 1914 caused the Home Rule Bill to be suspended until the conflict was over.

Ireland responds

The struggle on the Western Front postponed the struggles in Ireland between unionists and nationalists, but how did the Irish, unionist and nationalist, react to the War against Germany? The positions that the various groups took up were:

- ✔ **The Unionists**, who saw themselves as integral parts of Britain and Empire, fully supported the war effort. The Ulster Volunteer Force became the bedrock of the 36th (Ulster) Division as a unit in the British Army. The 36th were allowed to retain their distinctive unionist identity, and their uniforms featured the recognisable insignia of Ulster.

- ✔ **The nationalists**, led by Redmond, also threw their weight behind the war. Redmond argued that the war against Germany was a struggle for Ireland as much as it was for Britain, and that nationalists should take part to defend their own freedoms. Although the Volunteers, numbering some 170,000, were offered to the British army, they were not granted their own division in the same way as the unionists.

> ✔ **The advanced nationalists**, led by Sinn Fein, opposed the war as an imperial struggle in which Ireland had no part. They called for Irish men to leave the Volunteers and join a new force, the Irish or Sinn Fein Volunteers, whose role would be to defend Ireland in the face of aggression from any nation. By 1915, only 11,000 men had answered that call.

Unlike the rest of Britain, Ireland, whether unionist or nationalist, was never subject to conscription of its men into the armed forces. This meant that all Irishmen who fought in the war, including the thousands that died, were volunteers. The British believed that enforcing conscription in Ireland would be too difficult. When the idea was mooted in the spring of 1918 the chief secretary of Ireland informed the cabinet that they 'might almost as well conscript Germans'. The attempt to introduce conscription in 1918 had profound effects and contributed to the rise of Sinn Fein.

Ireland suffered greatly during the war. As a rough estimate some 35,000 of the 140,000 men who volunteered to fight were killed. For the unionists the sacrifice was most marked on the first day of the Battle of the Somme when the 36th (Ulster) Division went into action. It was decimated by the Germans, and the sacrifice is annually marked in Ulster on 1 July each year.

Easter Time in Dublin: The Failed Rebellion and Its Effects

While everyone's attention was turned to the battles against Germany the advanced nationalists began plotting. A long-held belief in the nationalist tradition was that England's difficulty was Ireland's opportunity. What could be more difficult than a World War?

So in 1915 the IRB began plotting a rebellion against the British. The plan was for a nationwide rebellion by the IRB forces which would lead, in turn, to a popular uprising. The date was set for Easter Sunday 1916.

The enemy of my enemy . . .

Sir Roger Casement was enlisted to gather arms and support for the Rising from Irish allies – who better in a time of War than the Germans who had their own reasons for destabilising Britain by supporting havoc in Ireland? The Germans donated 20,000 rifles and ammunition to the cause. On Good Friday 1916 Casement was delivered to the coast of Kerry by submarine and awaited the delivery of the weapons from the German ship, the *Aud*. The rebellion was under way.

The Proclamation of the Republic

Although the Rebellion failed, the reading of the Proclamation outside the General Post Office was one of its most important moments. Read by Patrick Pearse, the newly appointed President of the Republic, to a small and probably bemused crowd of people, the Proclamation defined the nature of the Irish Republic and gave future nationalists an ideological blueprint.

It declared the 'Irish Republic as a Sovereign Independent State', promised universal suffrage and guaranteed civil and religious liberty for all. The Proclamation also acknowledged the assistance of Ireland's 'gallant allies in Europe' – the Germans – and ensured that everyone involved was guilty of treason.

The British became aware of a strange German ship off the coast of Ireland, and attempted to intercept the *Aud*. Its captain, rather be caught with his cargo, scuttled the ship. The rebellion had suffered its first, and maybe fatal, blow. Despite attempts to call off the rebellion in face of the loss, the decision was made by IRB leaders, such as Patrick Pearse, to go ahead with it on Easter Monday.

Crushing the rebellion

While the citizens of Dublin enjoyed a public holiday and many members of the British forces were at Fairyhouse races, the rebels, a combination of IRB and Irish Citizen Army members, captured, or rather walked into, key buildings across Dublin and declared a Republic in the name of the Irish people.

The British were slow to react, but once they did their answer was swift and brutal. Within a week the rebellion was crushed, much of central Dublin was destroyed and 500 from both sides killed. All the leaders were arrested, and fourteen were executed, including the seven who had signed their names on the Proclamation.

The insurgents of 1916 were led by the IRB, a secret organisation. The British had no clear-cut image of who was leading the Rebellion, and in the aftermath the press began referring to the event as the Sinn Fein Rising. Although this led to many Sinn Fein members and other nationalists being arrested in the wake of the Rebellion, whether involved or not, it fixed the party at the forefront of the public mind as the leaders.

The fallout from the Rebellion

Reflecting on the events of Easter 1916 (refer to the preceding section), the poet W.B. Yeats wrote 'a terrible beauty is born'. He wasn't far wrong.

The Rebellion changed everything. Although the insurgents gained little support during Easter week, the executions and the introduction of martial law to Ireland, the constant sacrifices on the Western front, and the lack of movement on the issue of Home Rule turned the public towards the spirit of revolution.

The executions of the leaders of the Rebellion also created martyrs for the Irish nationalist cause, as did the imprisonment, in British prison camps, of some 3,000 Irish people. Sinn Fein moved quickly to capitalise on the situation and in 1917 fought and won its first parliamentary by-election. Support for Sinn Fein mushroomed. By October 1917 the party had 1,300 clubs across the country with a membership of some 250,000.

What happened next:

- ✔ Sinn Fein kept winning by-elections.

- ✔ Eamon de Valera, the only surviving commander of the 1916 Rebellion, became President of Sinn Fein.

- ✔ In March 1918, John Redmond died and the constitutional Irish Parliamentary party was left in tatters.

- ✔ The British passed, but never enforced, a Conscription Act for Ireland in April 1918. It was opposed by Sinn Fein, the constitutional nationalists, and the Catholic Church.

- ✔ In May 1918 all Sinn Fein leaders were arrested for treasonable activity, and organisations such as the Gaelic League and Cumann na mBan were banned.

- ✔ The First World War ended, and in the 1918 General Election Sinn Fein won 73 of the 105 Irish seats.

Ireland had been transformed. From the heady days of the passing of the Home Rule Bill in 1912, the Irish had been through a Rebellion and a World War that radicalised the situation and left Sinn Fein in the ascendancy.

Bloody Ireland: The War of Independence

With Sinn Fein in power and the Home Rule Bill dead, what would happen next? The unionists were still opposed to any agreement that took them away from Britain, and the British government were just as vehemently opposed to the demands of Sinn Fein for an Irish Republic that had been proclaimed during the Easter Rebellion. For its part, Sinn Fein refused to attend

Westminster, as it did not recognise British rule, and it established its own parliament, Dail Eireann, in Dublin. It organised ministries and courts, raised funds, and declared the Irish Republican Army (IRA) as the defenders of the self-proclaimed state.

Sinn Fein wanted to create the Republic that had been proclaimed in 1916. Clearly neither the British nor the unionists would accept this. A war seemed inevitable. The Irish wanted their freedom, but the arguments of unionists to remain British were equally powerful. Also Britain had to think about its authority across the Empire: If it was seen to be weak in Ireland would it risk rebellion in India or South Africa?

In January 1919 two members of the Royal Irish Constabulary (the Irish police force) were shot dead by members of the IRA. The War of Independence had begun. The struggle between Britain and Ireland would last until the summer of 1921. It was a brutal war between the forces of the British Army and some 3,000 young men and women of the IRA who used guerrilla tactics and were organised as highly mobile flying columns. The catalogue of the war is full of tales of daring and heroic operations, but also wilful murder and terrible cruelty on both sides.

The combatants

The War of Independence was mainly concentrated in the southern half of Ireland. The War had little impact in Ulster, although unionists were deeply suspicious of the nationalist communities and several attacks took place. The War was effectively a struggle between the British and the forces of Irish Republicanism with the unionists remaining on the sidelines.

The British government constantly argued that it was fighting a rebellious mob and that there was no popular support for the IRA or the War. While not a mass popular movement, it is clear that Sinn Fein, and by proxy the policy of fighting the British, did have popular support. Without the assistance of the Irish public, the Irish Republican forces could not have been as effective as they were.

The IRA, the IRB, and Michael Collins

While the IRA fought the War across Ireland, the IRB, which had been rebuilt and reorganised by Michael Collins after 1916, was instrumental in undermining the British security and intelligence system in Ireland. Collins was a brilliant strategist and effectively made Ireland ungovernable. It was a war that the British could never win, but then neither could the Irish Republican forces.

Bloody Sunday

One of the worst days of the War happened on Sunday 21 November. In an attempt to neutralise the British intelligence network, Michael Collins ordered his men to kill the leading figures resident in Dublin. In the event ten men were killed and four injured, one fatally. The killings were a blow to the British. The response was swift and brutal. That afternoon three Irish prisoners held in Dublin Castle were shot dead. Across the city British forces drove into Croke Park where a game of Gaelic football was under way. They opened fire on the players and the crowd, and within minutes fourteen spectators and one player lay dead.

The Black and Tans

The most controversial aspect of the War of Independence was the decision to introduce an additional force to Ireland to supplement the Royal Irish Constabulary. Known as the Black and Tans because of the colour of their uniforms, the force of 8,000 men was recruited mainly from ex-servicemen. They were a ruthless force who sought to defeat the Irish Republican forces and also terrorise the Irish population.

The arrival of the Black and Tans in Ireland brought a sickening new dimension to the War. Each attack or killing by Irish forces was met by a Black and Tan assault on people and property. House burnings, murder, rape, and assault became the weapons of the Black and Tans, and they sought to convince the Irish public that support for the Irish cause was untenable.

The Black and Tans were responsible for some of the most notorious killings of the War. In March 1920 they murdered the Lord Mayor of Cork in front of his family, and in November that year they killed a young Priest, Michael Griffin, in Galway after luring him from his home on a bogus sick call. In December 1920 they also played a part in the wholesale burning of large parts of Cork city centre in response to the killing of eighteen members of British forces by the IRA at Kilmichael. Both sides were guilty of such intimidation. The IRA also terrorised civilians, and attacked sections of the Protestant population.

Truce – Part 1: A divided Ireland

In 1920 the British sought to end the conflict by offering Home Rule parliaments to both Dublin and Belfast. Belfast accepted. The 1920 Government of Ireland Act created a separate parliament in Belfast that would govern over the six counties of Northern Ireland. For unionists this allowed them to remain part of the United Kingdom and the Empire, while also having control of its own affairs.

Dublin, however, in the form of Dail Eireann, refused.

With these events, the British granted the unionists their own parliament in Belfast and created a six-county Northern Ireland. Although the Irish aspiration was a 32-county Republic, the Government of Ireland Act had already created a divided Ireland. In any negotiations, a united Ireland was unlikely to return to the agenda because of unionist opposition to the idea. In all probability the Irish would have to settle for less than they had fought for.

If at first you don't succeed: Truce – Part II

By the spring of 1921 the War of Independence was getting ever more bitter, with more death and destruction. By July 1921, 1,400 people had been killed (624 British military personnel, 552 IRA members, and 200 civilians) and much of the Irish infrastructure was damaged (key buildings such as the Custom House, which was attacked in 1921, took a decade to be rebuilt). Yet neither side was making any headway.

The Irish had to make a decision:

- ✔ Continue fighting the war with little chance of outright victory and ever depleting resources.
- ✔ Enter talks with the British and try to secure the Republic through negotiation.

They chose the latter. When the British Prime Minister offered the Irish another truce in July 1921, work began on finding a permanent solution for Ireland. Preliminary discussions took place during the summer, and the official peace conference began in October.

The Irish were represented at the peace negotiations by five men who carried the authority to act on behalf of Dail Eireann. Although key figures such as Michael Collins and Arthur Griffith were included, de Valera chose to stay in Dublin. The negotiations lasted until December, and the Irish delegation kept Dublin constantly informed on their progress. The main themes of discussion were:

✔ What the future relationship of an independent Ireland would be to the British Crown and Commonwealth.

✔ The question of partition and the future of Northern Ireland.

✔ The right of Britain to retain certain navy ports in Ireland to protect its security needs.

David Lloyd George, Prime Minister, and the British negotiators refused to move on the issue of partition, and Northern Ireland was left out of the agreement. The Treaty that was signed on 6 December 1921 created a new nation, the Irish Free State, which comprised the 26 southern and western counties of Ireland. The new state remained a member of the Commonwealth in line with the Canadian model of dominion status. All members of the new state's parliament would also have to swear an oath of allegiance to the British Crown.

To seal the agreement it had to be ratified by the British and Irish parliaments. In Britain that posed no problems, but in Ireland, war clouds gathered. Again.

Civil War and a Free Ireland

Dail Eireann debated the Treaty during December 1921 and early January 1922. It was a rancorous and bitter debate. While Collins argued that the Treaty was the best deal possible, giving Ireland the scope to achieve freedom and all that it had wished for over seven hundred years, De Valera argued that Ireland had fought the war to create a republic, and anything less was untenable. And so the Dail split, as did the country and even many families. De Valera led the anti-Treaty side with Collins and Griffith leading the pro-Treaty side. The Dail voted on 7 January, 64 in favour of ratifying the Treaty, 57 against.

On 28 June, 1922 the Irish Civil War began. Collins now led the forces of the Irish Free State and had all the machinery of government at his command. The anti-Treaty forces fought the War in the same way the Irish had fought against the British. Fighting was largely restricted to the south-west of the country.

The losses during the War were highly damaging to the future of Ireland:

✔ In August 1922 Arthur Griffith died of a heart attack, and days later Michael Collins was killed in an ambush. Ireland was left without the future leadership skills of two of the political heavyweights who had signed the Treaty and argued in favour of accepting it.

✔ To ensure order in the country the state forces introduced military courts with wide powers. Between September 1922 and April 1923, 77 anti-Treaty personnel were executed. These executions left a bitter legacy and opened the pro-Treaty forces to accusations of cruelty.

✔ By the end of the War 12,000 anti-Treatyites were in prison, 800 Free State troops had been killed, and possibly as many as 5,000 of their opponents. The cost of the war was terrible and demonstrated starkly how bitter the divisions of Civil War were. All these wounds would have to be healed in future decades.

The War ended in April 1923 when de Valera ordered his forces to end the fighting. The Free State forces had won the day, and an independent Ireland had come into being. Freedom had been won at a terrible price, and many believed that a partitioned Ireland that belonged to the Commonwealth wasn't even free.

Chapter 22

One Land, Two Systems: Partition

*I*n December 1921, Britain and Ireland had both agreed to a bold new concept. The six counties of the north-eastern part of the country, Northern Ireland, would remain part of the United Kingdom (as this area was dominated by unionists), while the remaining twenty-six counties would be an independent country. The big question was, would the Irish Free State (which was eventually renamed the Republic of Ireland in 1948) survive on its own?

This chapter explores the years from Partition, examines how the two Irish states fared as they adapted to their changed circumstances, and closes with a look at what happened during the Second World War.

Who Rules What? The Two Irelands

The terms of the Treaty between Ireland and Britain in December 1921 were very precise and clearly defined. They set out who ruled which piece of Ireland and what each side were responsible for.

> ✔ **Northern Ireland:** Northern Ireland was made up of six counties: Antrim, Armagh, Down, Fermanagh, Londonderry, and Tyrone. These were the counties with large unionist and Protestant populations and the ones that wanted to remain part of the United Kingdom. By excluding the counties of Cavan, Monaghan, and Donegal, the unionists ensured that did not include too many counties with nationalist majorities. The politicians in Northern Ireland would run their own affairs through a parliament at Stormont, although Westminster would retain control of all the big issues, such as foreign policy.

✔ **Irish Free State:** The Irish Free State was made up of twenty-six counties, which included all those in the provinces of Leinster, Munster, and Connacht, plus the three counties of Ulster (Cavan, Donegal, and Monaghan) that had majority Catholic populations and had therefore been excluded from Northern Ireland. The parliament of the Irish Free State was called Dail Eireann and was based in Dublin. It had control of its own affairs, although its members did have to swear an oath of allegiance to the British King, and the Free State remained a member of the British Commonwealth. These issues had contributed to the Civil War (see Chapter 21) and would remain contentious right through to the 1930s and 1940s.

There was little love lost between the two Irish states, each remaining deeply suspicious of the other. Many people in Northern Ireland saw the Free State as a Catholic-dominated country that was disloyal to Britain and the Empire. They feared that the long-term intention of the Free State was to create a thirty-two county Irish Republic and destroy unionism in the process. Many in the Free State had the opposing fears. They saw Northern Ireland as a bastion of unionism and Protestantism, and worried that Stormont would use its economic power and close links with Britain to undermine the fledgling state.

Life in Northern Ireland, 1920s and '30s

Northern Ireland during the 1920s and '30s was fraught with problems. While the unionists had got what they wanted in the process of partition – they remained part of the United Kingdom – their economy stagnated in the 1930s, and relationships with the Catholic community were always strained.

Party politics, Unionist-style

While the creation of Northern Ireland had copper-bottomed the relationship between unionists and Britain, the newly formed government in Stormont was concerned about the threat from the IRA (Irish Republican Army; refer to Chapter 21 for information about this nationalist group). The first few years of the 1920s were marked by continual concerns that the nationalist community would rise up against Stormont and try to destabilise Northern Ireland.

The new state of Northern Ireland was born in a climate of sectarian tension – Unionist/Protestant against Nationalist/Catholic. In the years between 1920 and 1922, 557 people were killed in communal violence in Northern Ireland. It was also estimated that during those years up to 11,000 Belfast Catholics had been driven from their jobs and 23,000 forced from their homes.

The violence was so bad that many Catholics decided that they would have a better future in the Irish Free State and left Northern Ireland. Those who stayed bore the brunt of Unionist efforts to eliminate, as much as it could, what it considered to be the nationalist threat. Consider these events:

- ✔ The Stormont government rapidly expanded its police force to control the Catholic population whom they feared would support the IRA. By the end of 1920 some 20,000 men had been enlisted into a new military-style police force – the Ulster Special Constabulary. This force was a constant factor of Northern Irish life until the late 1960s, and was dominated by Protestants.

- ✔ In 1922 and 1923, the levels of discrimination in Northern Ireland were drastically increased by changes in the electoral system. Proportional representation was abandoned, which ensured, given the size of the Protestant community, that unionist candidates would fare better than their nationalist counterparts. Electoral boundaries were also redrawn so that Catholic votes were fragmented and Protestant votes made more effective. The new boundaries further ensured a unionist majority in all elections. The system was referred to as *gerrymandering*, and would be a big issue in the 1960s and the rise of the civil rights movement (see Chapter 23). All these changes ensured that unionist politics didn't fragment and that they were able to achieve their most important goal, at least until the 1960s: the survival of Northern Ireland.

Clearly Northern Ireland from the 1920s was a discriminatory society, and this wasn't fair to the Catholic community. Yet remember that the unionist population felt that it was their right to remain part of the United Kingdom. They saw the Catholic community as alien and a threat. By supporting the interests of Protestants over Catholics – who became marginalised in the process – Stormont ensured, until the 1970s, its own survival.

Economic woes

Northern Ireland depended on a small number of industries for its wealth. The two biggest were shipbuilding and linen manufacturing. Although relatively prosperous in the early 1920s, these traditional industries suffered badly as a result of the world depression from 1929. Unemployment in shipbuilding never fell below 13 per cent, and went as high as 65 per cent in the 1930s. The same was true in the linen industry, where unemployment peaked in 1938 at 56 per cent. Compared to the rest of Britain, Northern Ireland fared badly. In the late 1930s, unemployment in Britain was 13 per cent. In Northern Ireland it was 38 per cent. The situation was bad. The levels of sectarianism in society meant that unemployment was felt hardest by the Catholic population, and the gap between the two groups grew ever bigger.

In the early 1930s the economic downturn, combined with sectarian tensions, led to rioting in Belfast and other parts of Northern Ireland. In July 1935, three weeks of rioting left 13 dead, and many Catholics were driven from their homes.

The troubles in Northern Ireland, which began in the late 1960s, were initially sparked by the social and economic inequality that was evident in society. The roots of the poverty and discrimination that the Catholic community felt in the 1960s were to be found in the way that Northern Ireland was run from the 1920s. It was conceived as a Protestant land for a Protestant people, and the Catholic community always came in second best. The lack of Catholic representation in Northern Ireland was heightened by the initial decision of the nationalist leadership to boycott the new state in the hope that it would wither away. It didn't, and they were left out of the process of shaping Northern Ireland.

For all its problems prior to the Second World War, Northern Ireland had one key success: it survived. It had to make no major concessions to the Free State, and neither did it have to concede anything to its Catholic community. It made it to the late 1930s as it wanted to be: a loyal part of the United Kingdom and Commonwealth.

Building a Free Irish State, 1920s

One of the great joys of having a new country is that you get to do things your way. The government of the Irish Free State had the opportunity to make a new state. They could develop it as they wished, and let the whole world know what it would mean to be Irish in the new Free State. Sounds great, but not that easy to actually do.

First, they had to make decisions on everything involved in running a country: what form of government they would have, whether their police force would be armed or unarmed, what the national anthem would be, what kind of currency they'd use, and so on. If that wasn't enough, because of the Civil War (see Chapter 21), not everyone in Ireland actually agreed with the idea of the Free State, and so controlling that faction became an issue, too. Also, there was the Protestant minority that remained. Many of them remained in the civil service jobs they had previously occupied, landowners stayed on their estates, and the Protestant working class communities of Dublin and Cork carried on in their old jobs.

The first party to govern the newly independent Ireland came from the pro-Treaty side of the Civil War. They organised themselves under the name Cumann na nGaedhal ('the League of the Gaels'), and were led by W.T.

Cosgrave. The opposition from the Civil War period, Sinn Fein, refused to recognise the legitimacy of the new Free State and abstained from parliament. (Many of its leading members were still in prison anyway because of their part in the Civil War.) Effectively, Cumann na nGaedheal ran a one party state, and could get on with the business of government without worrying about a sizeable parliamentary opposition.

Cumann na nGaedheal stayed in office from 1922 to 1932. In that decade they organised the mechanisms of government, law and order, and finance that are essential to any nation. Their main acts were:

✔ Produced the first national constitution in 1922.

✔ Worked within the terms of the Treaty of 1921 and established good working relationships with Britain and the Commonwealth.

✔ Established a functioning civil and legal service (admittedly based on the British model), and an unarmed police force, the Garda Síochána.

✔ Designed postage stamps and a currency for the Irish Free State, and successfully created an identity for the new nation.

Britain was watching what the Irish were doing very carefully. The Irish Free State was one of the first countries (since the Americans) to dare to challenge the British and go their own way. The British were aware of their commitments to Northern Ireland, and didn't want to see the Free State become an unsettled nation. How Ireland coped with independence would set precedents for other nations in the Empire. The British wanted everything to go smoothly.

While state building was a great adventure for the Irish, the reality was far more complex. Not only did they have an internal group, those in Sinn Fein, who disagreed with the very concept of the Free State, but they also had the perceived legacy of centuries of British rule to deal with. And of course the border issue, and the very presence of Northern Ireland in what they considered their country.

Creating an independent Irish identity

At the beginning the leaders of the Free State engaged in many symbolic acts. For a start they painted all the postboxes green. Now that doesn't sound like a big deal, but it was hugely important. It announced to everyone who lived in the Free State that they no longer posted their letters into red British postboxes that would be processed by the Royal Mail. Instead they put their letters into green, Irish postboxes, and their letters would be dealt with by the postal service of the Free State.

In the same vein the Free State began issuing its first postage stamps, and introduced its own coinage and bank-notes. Strangely the coinage, although featuring depictions of Irish animals, was actually designed by an Englishman.

Landmark buildings in Dublin that had been destroyed during the 1916 Rising, the War of Independence, and the Civil War were rebuilt. By the late 1920s the Post Office, Custom House, and Four Courts had all been rebuilt and were open for business again.

Embracing Irish tradition: The Irish Olympics

Clearly making a new nation work is very important. You have to have civil servants, a budget, a functioning economy, and so on, but that's all a bit dull really. How do you make the world sit up and notice that there is a newly independent Ireland in existence?

It had long been argued that one of the things that made Ireland unique was its culture. The move for political independence had been underpinned by an embrace of Irish traditional culture in the late nineteenth century (see Chapter 20). Given the contentious nature of the revolution and the Treaty, one of the few points that most people could agree on was that Irish culture was a good thing. The new government decided to turn to an old idea, repackage it, and use it to announce the Free State to the world.

In the 1880s, members of the Gaelic Athletic Association had argued that an ancient sporting festival – Aonach Tailteann – should be revived. They never found the money then, but the idea hung around. Even during the revolution leading politicians spoke of the revival as a good idea. The Irish parliament, Dail Eireann, had even agreed to give money towards a revival in 1922. Sadly the Civil War got in the way. Finally in 1924, it happened.

The idea of Aonach Tailteann could be traced back to Ireland's ancient past. Such celebrations had been a regular feature of Irish life until the Normans arrived in 1170. The original Aonach Tailteann had been staged during a period of truce, and was a time for celebration. Sporting, artistic, and literary events were staged to demonstrate how talented the Irish were. The function of the revived Aonach Tailteann was the same. The event was held within a year of the ending of the Civil War, and it celebrated the birth of the new nation. It also gave sportsmen and women, artists, and writers an opportunity to show off as they had done centuries before.

Aonach Tailteann opened in the summer of 1924 and ran for two weeks. It was christened in the popular press, the Irish Olympics. It combined competitions in sport, with others in writing, art, music, and dance. All the competitions were open to anyone of Irish birth or heritage, and many athletes who had been at the 1924 Olympic Games in Paris came to Ireland to compete.

Who knew Tarzan was Irish?

One of the most commonly known stories about Aonach Tailteann is that Tarzan won a swimming medal. Well, it's true. The man who would go on to become world-famous for playing Tarzan in twelve motion pictures, actor Johnny Weissmuller, was an Olympic swimmer. He stopped in Ireland on the way back from the 1924 Paris Olympics, and was allowed to compete in the Aoanch Tailteann swimming events. Although the rules only allowed people of Irish birth or heritage to take part, they were ignored for Weissmuller, and Tarzan took home his Tailteann medal.

Dublin was colourfully decorated to welcome competitors and spectators, and a carnival atmosphere was evident in the city. There was a grand opening ceremony and all members of the government, plus a host of invited dignitaries, were in attendance. The Irish Olympics eventually lost money, but in many ways the government were happy. By organising such a large-scale event, they captured the imagination of the press and the public. The staging of Aonach Tailteann was reported in newspapers around the world. Instead of reporting the war in Ireland, the newspapers in America, Britain, Australia, and elsewhere were discussing the impressive spectacle and the success of the new state. Although Ireland has never hosted the Olympic Games, Aonach Tailteann performed the same function as the Olympics do for any host nation: it made the world sit up and take notice.

Staging and competing in sporting events remains an important way for any new nation to announce its arrival on the world stage. In the 1920s the Irish Free State keenly embraced sport as a way of announcing its existence. Not only did they stage Aonach Tailteann in 1924, 1928, and 1932, but they also hosted a motor-racing Grand Prix in Dublin's Phoenix Park in 1929, and had its first Olympic victor, hammer-thrower Pat O'Callaghan, in 1928 (he also won this event at the next Olympic Games in 1932).

Power for the people

In the midst of all the public acts of state building, the Cumann na nGaedehal government had some real issues to deal with. Ireland had entered the twentieth century with a mainly rural economy and was, by European standards, not very modernised. The big challenge for the government was to create an infrastructure that would allow the dream of independence to become a reality through increased living standards.

One of the big gripes had always been that Ireland, during the period of British rule, hadn't developed a modern system of energy supply. Ireland had few natural resources such as coal, and thus generating energy was difficult.

But to progress industrially it would have to develop and use the natural resources it did have.

Prior to the First World War various people had suggested that the answer to the energy problem was to use Ireland's rivers as a source of energy, but no scheme was ever developed. Shortly after the foundation of the state, an Irish engineer, Dr. Thomas A. McLoughlin, submitted proposals for damming the River Shannon and building an electric power station at Ardnacrusha, a few miles from Limerick, which would bring power to cities and towns. It was an audacious plan, but one that the government supported.

The whole plan for the Shannon River was produced by McLoughlin and the German firm Siemens in just six months. The proposed dam on the Shannon, which was completed by 1929, was thirty metres high, and involved the use of 23,000 cubic metres of timber, 2,700 tonnes reinforcing steel for concrete, 66,000 tonnes of cement, 10,250 tonnes of fuel oil, 118,000 tonnes of coal, and 700 tonnes of explosives. It wasn't a job for the light-hearted, and at the time was the largest civil engineering project undertaken anywhere in the world. By 1931 it was producing an amazing 96 per cent of the Irish Free State's electricity.

McLoughlin's plan for getting electricity from the Shannon was an incredible success. The actual construction process fascinated Irish people so much that bus and rail excursions would go and see the works at Ardnacrusha. It was often described by the newspapers of the time as the eighth wonder of the world. When the dam was completed, and electricity started flowing from the Shannon, it was heralded as a major achievement. Not only had such a big project been completed so quickly, but it had apparently modernised Ireland overnight.

While the Shannon dam project was a success, and did provide much of Ireland with electricity, it didn't jump start Irish industry in the ways that had been hoped. Despite various initiatives, the Free State remained, until well after the Second World War, a predominantly agricultural nation. Even though the Shannon dam was producing electricity, many rural parts of the country weren't connected to the grid until the 1940s and 1950s.

Unfinished business: The legacy of Partition

In the arguments over the Treaty that created the Irish Free State, Michael Collins acknowledged that it wasn't the 32-county Republic that people had fought for during the revolution. He argued that the Treaty, and the Free State it gave birth to, allowed Ireland 'the freedom to achieve freedom'. In other words, one of the great hopes for those who had supported the signing of the Treaty between Britain and Ireland was that partition wouldn't be permanent; that is, that some day, Ireland would be reunited. Article 12 of the Treaty had paved the way for a boundary commission to sit, and the Irish hoped that this would change the border in their favour.

The boundary commission finally came together in 1925. In the years between the signing of the Treaty and the boundary commission sitting, unionists had become increasingly hostile to the idea. Rather than take part in a body that they believed intended to shrink Northern Ireland, the unionists refused to send a representative.

In the event, the boundary commission suggested that the border be shortened by 51 miles, and some 31,319 people would end up as citizens of the Free State as a result. The news was leaked to the press, a political crisis followed, and in the end nothing was done. Rather than adjust the border, and risk upsetting everyone, the representatives of Northern Ireland, the Free State, and the British government agreed it would be simpler to leave things alone. They all signed an agreement that Article 12 should be forgotten, and the border should remain fixed as it had been drawn up in 1920.

So, for all of Michael Collins' 'freedom to achieve freedom', the border wasn't up for redrawing. The partition remained a contentious issue, and politicians in the Free State were happy to use it as a propaganda tool. In real terms however, there was never any suggestion after 1925 that the border could be changed.

De Valera and His Happy Maidens: The Free State in the 1930s

The Cumann na nGaedheal government of the Irish Free State spent their first decade in office establishing the workings of the state. They had clear successes, and achieved great acclaim for their vision with projects such as the Shannon Dam. Their real problem was the resentment that lingered after the Civil War.

Sinn Fein had refused to accept the Treaty and had fought against it during the Civil War. They had refused to enter parliament, and worked against Cumann na nGaedheal. By the mid-1920s the government were sick of this kind of opposition from outside parliament and demanded that Sinn Fein take their seats in the Dail.

The history of the first government in the 1920s has been quite contentious. Some historians applaud Cumann na nGaedheal, and argue that they made the best of a difficult situation. They managed to put all the major institutions of state in place, and avoided a renewed flare up of the Civil War. Others argue that the government wasn't aggressive enough, that it worked too closely with the British and didn't create a stridently independent Ireland. One issue of contention was whether Cumann na nGaedheal failed to deliver on the promises of the revolution. Rather than creating a socialist Republic, as suggested in the 1916 proclamation of an Irish Republic, the government of the 1920s was, by its own admission, the most conservative bunch of revolutionaries ever.

Enter the Fianna Fail

The leader of Sinn Fein, Eamon de Valera, decided he had to act. In 1926 he set up a new party, Fianna Fail ('Soldiers of Destiny'). Shortly afterwards they entered the Dail, and genuine two-party politics began in the Free State.

Fianna Fail and Cumann na nGaedheal weren't simply two parties who disagreed with each other in the way of normal politics. Both parties had emerged directly from opposing sides in the Civil War. They deeply distrusted each other. People in each party blamed their opponents for deaths in the Civil War, and remained ideologically opposed to each other over the workings of the Treaty. Throughout the late 1920s and early 1930s there were regular rumours that elected officials were entering the Dail carrying firearms as they were convinced that their personal safety was under threat from the other side.

Despite having opposed the Treaty and staying out of parliament during the early years of the Free State, de Valera and his Fianna Fail party were very popular among those who had opposed the Treaty and the working classes. There was a belief that Cumann na nGaedheal were only acting in the interests of big farmers and landowners. By the time of the 1932 election Fianna Fail were able to win by a minority and form a government.

Given the bitterness between the two parties, it has often been argued that Cumann na nGaedheal would fail to recognise the election result, and would choose to stay in office through the use of force. Instead, they adhered to the rules of democracy and allowed their former Civil War enemies to take power, less than a decade after the ending of that war. Most historians acknowledge that Cumann na nGaedheal acted selflessly in accepting the popular vote and allowing their erstwhile enemies into office. In doing so they stabilised Irish democracy at a time when it could have easily fallen back into a state of war.

Whereas the Free State of Cumann na nGaedheal had operated under the terms of the Treaty, and had co-operated with Britain and its Commonwealth, the agenda of de Valera and Fianna Fail was far more radical. De Valera had a very particular vision for Ireland.

On St Patrick's Day 1943, in one of his most famous and most quoted speeches, de Valera said: 'That Ireland which we dreamed of would be the home of a people who valued material wealth only as a basis for right living, of a people who were satisfied with frugal comfort and devoted their leisure to the things of the spirit – a land whose countryside would be bright with cosy homesteads, whose fields and villages would be joyous with sounds of industry, with the romping of sturdy children, the contests of athletic youths and the laughter of happy maidens.' The speech summed up what de Valera wanted, essentially a self-sufficient, rural, and Catholic Ireland. His vision was radically different to that of Cumann na nGaedheal, which had wanted to work within the terms of the Treaty and follow economic orthodoxy. It was popular though as he stayed in office from 1932 until 1948.

The Free State under de Valera

Once in office de Valera acted quickly. He passed a whole load of legislation aimed at turning back the clock on the Treaty and turning the Irish Free State into the kind of country that he envisaged. He secured a full majority in an election in 1933, and this ensured that he was in office, with a majority, until well after the Second World War.

His main achievements in the 1930s were:

- ✔ **Abolition of the Oath of Allegiance:** This meant that members of the Dail no longer had to swear allegiance to the British Crown.

- ✔ **Getting rid of the post of Governor-General:** This post had been a contentious, albeit symbolic part of the Treaty. The Governor-General had originally been able, in principle, to reserve or deny royal assent to any Dail legislation. By abolishing the post, de Valera meant that all law-making power was fully in the hands of the Irish.

- ✔ **Return of the Treaty ports:** In 1922 it had been agreed that Britain needed to retain control of certain coastal ports in Ireland to protect itself. In 1938 de Valera convinced the British that they no longer needed them, and they were all returned to Ireland.

- ✔ **Debt cancellation:** The Treaty had made the Free State liable for a whole series of monies that were owed to Britain. De Valera disagreed, and after fighting a tariff war with Britain in the 1930s, he secured a scaling down of the debt to a one-off payment of £10 million – a bargain!

What de Valera did effectively, and very controversially, was to rewrite the terms of the Treaty – or at least those parts he objected to. This gave the Free State a greater degree of freedom and control over its own affairs. He didn't withdraw from the Commonwealth however: that step wouldn't be taken until 1948.

The Treaty ports are the best illustration of how de Valera was able to relinquish the hold that Britain had on the Irish state. By getting the ports back in 1938 he ensured that there was no British army or navy presence within the Free State. Most historians argue that this is why Ireland was able to be neutral during the Second World War. If the Treaty ports had still been occupied by British forces they would have been a justifiable target for the Germans. As it was, Ireland could claim neutrality and there was no reason for the Germans to attack.

Fighting over the beef

When de Valera took office in 1932, he had some hard battles ahead of him before he could create the kind of Ireland he wanted. His goal was to free Ireland from its commitments to Britain that had been agreed in 1921. One of de Valera's biggest gripes was the amount of money that the Free State was supposed to pay Britain every year. The British had argued that the purchase of land, by the Irish, in the late nineteenth and earlier twentieth centuries, had been done with money borrowed from London. In the 1920s the Irish government had collected the money from farmers in the form of land annuities, and this money had been passed over to the British.

De Valera thought it was ridiculous that Irish farmers should pay money to Britain for Irish land. So he stopped paying. The British retaliated by placing import duties on a whole raft of Irish goods, especially agricultural imports. De Valera, never one to back down, retaliated by putting import duties on British products. The economic war had begun.

The economic war would last until 1938 when it was finally resolved by a one-off payment from Ireland to Britain to settle the debt. In the meantime the Irish economy suffered. It couldn't replace the British export market, and so the national income dropped. De Valera took cows that couldn't be exported from the big farmers (who voted Cumann na nGaedheal anyway) and distributed the meat to his own supporters for free.

While free beef was great for Fianna Fail voters, de Valera's actions in the early 1930s demonstrated how he mishandled the economy and brought about strong opposition from his detractors which would take shape as the Blueshirt movement.

The battles of the Civil War had only been over for a decade when de Valera took power. While anything he did was bound to create opposition from those who had fought against him in the Civil War, he had to act without destabilising the country. He had to use much of the machinery of the new state – the legal system, the police force, and the army – that he had previously detested to ensure that he stayed in power.

Reaction to de Valera: The Blueshirts

Many people were deeply suspicious of de Valera and Fianna Fail. They worried that the new government would use their power to settle old scores. Many believed that a simple parliamentary opposition in the form of Cumann na nGaedheal wouldn't be up to the job of stopping de Valera. So in the early 1930s, a new organisation, the Army Comrades Association, was formed. The organisation wanted to protect the rights of ex-army officers who feared that their pensions would be under threat from the new government that it had fought against a decade earlier. They decided, in line with similar movements in Europe at the time, to wear a coloured shirt as a uniform. Ireland now had the Blueshirts.

One of de Valera's first acts in power was to dismiss the head of police, General Eoin O'Duffy, as he didn't trust him. The sacking of O'Duffy proved to de Valera's opponents that he couldn't be trusted to act fairly. O'Duffy became a martyr for the anti-de Valera movement, and he was asked to head the Blueshirts.

O'Duffy would take the Blueshirts deeper into the world of European fascism. He adopted various fascist ways of thinking about politics and the economy (such as plans for a corporate state and a restricted electorate) that he borrowed from the Italian Duce, Mussolini, and began acting like a dictator at the head of his movement. He even convinced Cumann na nGaedheal that he was the future. The party disbanded, and reformed, with the Blueshirts at their side as a new party: Fine Gael.

The battles between the Blueshirts and the government became increasingly violent. Blueshirts died in political clashes, and it looked for a time as if the whole situation would turn into civil war again. De Valera held firm and used the full weight of the law against the Blueshirts. By 1935 the movement was in disarray, and O'Duffy quit. By 1936 the Blueshirts were history.

Once O'Duffy was gone and the Blueshirts stood down, Fine Gael continued as the main parliamentary opposition. They formed the government on several occasions in the second half of the twentieth century. Although completely committed to parliamentary democracy, Fine Gael's roots have never been forgotten, and they are still regularly referred to in the Irish media as the Blueshirt party.

Off to Spain

The end of the Blueshirts wasn't the end of O'Duffy. He remained deeply committed to his beliefs. In 1936, when the Spanish Civil War started, he argued that Ireland couldn't stand idly by. He felt that the Irish should join Franco and fight against the forces of communism. Although Ireland was strictly neutral in the Spanish Civil War, O'Duffy put together a force of some 700 men (still kitted out in blue shirts), and led them to Spain to fight for Franco. The whole trip was a disaster. Poorly resourced, and unloved by Franco's military leaders, O'Duffy's brigade saw little action. They returned home after twelve months.

A new Ireland and a new constitution

Having got through the first few years in office, and seen off the opposition, de Valera turned to enacting his real dream for Ireland. The greatest step towards a more concrete sense of independence came in 1937. De Valera didn't like the constitution that had been created in 1922, so he decided to write his own. The new constitution – Bunreacht na hÉireann – which is still in force today contained the following key points:

✔ The title Irish Free State replaced with Eire.

✔ The recognition that the island of Ireland (all 32 counties) was a natural territorial unit, and Northern Ireland an artificial creation.

✔ The British Governor-General to be replaced by a new head of state, the President of Ireland.

✔ Recognition of the special place of Catholicism in the state.

✔ Irish recognised, along with English, as the official language of the state.

The constitution brought to life the kind of Ireland that de Valera had fought for during the revolutionary years (see Chapter 21), but had not been delivered by the 1921 Treaty with Britain. The constitution was very inward-looking and concerned with the internal state of Ireland rather than its place in the contemporary world. De Valera had long argued that Ireland should be self-sufficient and the spirit of the constitution, and the handling of the economy, ensured that the country stagnated until the 1960s. Until the 1960s the Irish economy failed to develop a strong industrial base or entice inward investment into the country. Emigration numbers remained high, and the rate of modernization low.

The 1930s saw the Free State slowly remove itself from its legal obligations to Britain that had been established under the 1921 Treaty. Ireland really came into its own as an independent nation, and was a key member of the League of Nations during the 1930s. De Valera even became President of the Assembly of the League of Nations in 1938 and was involved in many of the discussions that tried to avert World War II.

To Fight or Not to Fight? Ireland and World War II

While Ireland charted its way through the choppy waters of the 1920s and 1930s, the political landscape in Europe was changing rapidly. Democracy appeared to be failing, and fascist regimes came to power in Germany and Italy, while communism strengthened its grip on the east. The start of the Second World War would force Ireland – North and South – to make difficult decisions. But how much choice did the politicians in Belfast and Dublin really have?

Although Northern Ireland had its own parliament in Stormont, it remained part of the United Kingdom, and all foreign policy decisions were made by London. Once Britain decided, in 1939, to go to war against Germany, Northern Ireland was also at war. In the newly named Eire, the decision about the war was their own. Britain could not tell de Valera what to do, and so he elected to go his own way, and declare Eire neutral in the war.

Northern Ireland at War

The Northern Ireland government was totally loyal to Britain and the idea of Commonwealth, and fully supported the war against Germany and its allies. As with the First World War the British decided that conscription would be too politically divisive to be implemented in Northern Ireland. As a result everyone who joined up between 1939 and 1945 from Northern Ireland was a volunteer. Although it was the unionist population who were most enthusiastic about the war, many northern nationalists also joined up.

During the conflict Northern Ireland's shipbuilding industry was of great importance to the war effort. Belfast produced ever greater numbers of ships as the war progressed, and many of its linen factories were turned over to the production of military supplies.

Don't believe all you read in the papers

The Irish newspapers were heavily censored during the war. Although the Irish papers carried war news, the neutrality stance meant that stories about Irish men and women fighting in the war were usually excluded. How though did the press deal with stories of Irish men who had died during the war? As strange as it might seem, a common tactic, especially for naval fighters, was to report that such and such had died in a boating accident in the Mediterranean – as if anyone would take a boating holiday in the middle of the war!

The Germans were well aware of Northern Ireland's contribution to the British war effort, and the strategic importance of the main ports with their access to the Atlantic. As a result Germany bombed Northern Ireland. The worst attacks came in April and May 1941 when 1,000 people were killed and 15,000 people made homeless. During those air-raids fire engines from Eire were driven across the border to assist, and relief centres were established south of the border to help the homeless.

The Irish at Home

The decision made by de Valera that Eire should remain neutral was a popular choice at home, but one that was heavily criticised in Northern Ireland, Britain, and America.

During the war, Eire was neutral in favour of the allies. While taking no part in the war, Eire did make a contribution. Some 250,000 people left Ireland to work in British factories during the war, and 50,000 joined the British forces. Of the 223 airmen who survived crash landings on Irish soil, those who were from the allied side were allowed to go home, while the Germans were interned for the duration of the war. Definitely a case of playing favourites!

There was a major controversy at the end of the war when Hitler killed himself rather than risk capture by the Russians. De Valera, playing out his public neutrality stance to the end, visited the German Embassy in Dublin and passed on his condolences for the loss of their national leader. To many observers it seemed a strange and inappropriate thing to do – in de Valera's mind he was simply being even-handed.

How neutral Eire actually was during the war has been a source of controversy. While many remain critical of the actual decision to stay out of the war, it has been argued that the Irish actually supported the allied war effort. It is difficult to see how Eire could have materially supported the war if it had fought, but its strategic position between Britain and the Atlantic Ocean was of great importance.

Post-War Rebuilding

After the end of the War both Northern Ireland and Eire had to rebuild. Both of them had very different experiences because of their war records.

Northern Ireland continued as a part of Britain, and post-war innovations such as the National Health Service were extended to include the Province. There was a period of rebuilding those parts of Belfast and elsewhere that had been damaged during the war, and industries such as shipbuilding gained short term benefits from restocking the naval and merchant fleets that had been lost in the war. Politically everything continued as before in Northern Ireland. The Protestant and unionist majority continued in control of Stormont, and the Catholic population was left without any say in government (apart from a few local councils) and treated as second-class citizens. All this would lead to a growing sense of disquiet in Northern Irish society that would explode into violence at the end of the 1960s (see Chapter 23).

In Eire the stance of neutrality led to post-war problems. In 1946 Eire had tried to join the United Nations, but their application was vetoed by the Soviet Union. They objected to Eire's friendly wartime relations with the fascist states, and they were excluded from the new global club. It took until 1955 before Ireland was allowed to join in.

Beware Churchill bearing gifts

The British and Americans were particularly keen that Eire join the allies in the war against Germany. They wanted access to Ireland's ports so as to better fight the war in the Atlantic, but they also worried that a neutral Ireland would be easily invaded by the Germans and used as a launching pad for an invasion of Britain. To try and convince Eire to join the war, Churchill approached de Valera in June 1940. He promised to deliver Irish reunification if Eire entered the war. De Valera rejected the offer, believing there was no substance to Churchill's gift. He didn't believe that Eire would benefit from entering the war, and didn't feel that militarily the country was strong enough to take part.

At the end of the war Churchill made his feelings clear. In celebrating the victory in Europe he thanked Northern Ireland for all it had done during the war. He also said that if he had been forced to depend on Mr de Valera Britain could have well perished forever from the earth.

So, at the end of the war Britain and Northern Ireland had come through victorious, but everyone was upset with Eire for not joining in. De Valera rightly argued that having survived the war intact, Eire had achieved much.

By the end of the war, de Valera had been in office for thirteen years. There was an election scheduled for 1949, but the country had seen enough of de Valera and Fianna Fail. A series of problems in the immediate post-war years would further weaken his hold on power. If a new government was formed after the election they would have to do something radical to make an impact after so many years of one party in charge.

The biggest change eventually came in 1948, when an election was called early and Fianna Fail lost. The new government was a coalition led by Fine Gael with John A. Costello at the helm.

The greatest act of the government (which only managed to stay in power for three years before de Valera took over again) was to make Ireland a Republic. In 1948 all the necessary laws were passed, and the country declared as the Republic of Ireland. In many ways the re-branding of Ireland into a Republic was a paper exercise. It did not bring about the Republic dreamt of during 1916, but made the separation of Ireland, North and South, more marked.

The second half of the century would bring yet more changes to Ireland, even though the first half had been exciting enough.

Chapter 23

Troubles Begin Again . . . And Maybe Finish

- -

In This Chapter

▶ The roots of political protest in Northern Ireland

▶ Understanding rising levels of street violence

▶ Political violence and the British response

▶ Difficulties in finding a solution to the troubles

▶ The 1990s peace process and beyond

▶ The Celtic Tiger and after the boom

- -

*I*n the years after the Second World War the Irish Republic and Northern Ireland continued their separate existence. The Republic steadily modernised from the 1960s, and although the aspirations for a united Ireland never disappeared there seemed nothing could be done while the unionist population in Northern Ireland wanted to remain British.

In Northern Ireland things began to change in the 1960s. Unionists had no intention of sharing power with the nationalist and Catholic population, and poverty and discrimination remained a fact of life for many people from that part of the community.

This chapter will show how social changes transformed the situation in Northern Ireland, and led to the rise of a civil rights movement demanding equality for the nationalist and Catholic population. Northern Irish society could not adjust to such rapid changes and violence flared in the late 1960s. For three decades Northern Ireland was the venue for a bitter war between different paramilitary forces and the forces of the British state.

The roots and progress of the peace process will be explained, and the recent dramatic growth of the Irish economy – and its accompanying wealth – will also be explained. For such a short period of time, many things happened.

Troubles in the '60s and '70s

The roots of Northern Ireland's conflict became apparent in the 1950s and 1960s. These were:

- An economic downturn in traditional industries such as shipbuilding weakened the Protestant community's sense of security.

- A belief grew amongst the Catholic community that they were being discriminated against by the unionist government controlling the Stormont parliament.

- Protestants became suspicious that the Catholic population was seeking to take over by promoting a united Ireland with the subsequent domination of the Catholic religion.

- A rising educated Catholic middle-class demanded reform of a political and social system that discriminated against them.

- Concern grew within the British government and civil service that Northern Ireland was a state lacking modernisation and equality.

Then, in 1968, the Northern Ireland Civil Rights Association (NICRA) was formed. It was a movement that demanded equal rights for Catholics in Northern Ireland, and its appearance marked the beginning of a mass movement that would galvanise politics and lead to a series of street demonstrations that gave birth to 30 years of violence.

NICRA and civil rights

Organisations such as NICRA – there were others such as the Campaign for Social Justice – argued that Northern Ireland was a discriminatory state that only served the interests of the Protestant community. Despite attempts at reform by the unionist Prime Minister Terence O'Neill, there was a feeling of too little, too late.

NICRA made a number of demands to make Northern Ireland a fairer society for everyone to live in. These were to:

- Defend the basic freedoms of all citizens including access to housing, jobs, and welfare.

- Protect the religious and political rights of the individuals.

- Highlight all abuses of power.

- Guarantee freedom of speech, assembly, and association.

- Inform the public of their lawful rights.

Burntollet Bridge

Since the summer of 1968 various civil rights marches had ended in violence. In January 1969 a People's Democracy march from Belfast to Derry was ambushed at Burntollet Bridge by loyalist (loyal to Britain) demonstrators. Many people, some estimates put the number at 300, were injured, and there was a feeling that the police had failed to protect the marchers. The whole episode was caught on camera, and the images flashed around the world. When the bloodied and beaten marchers arrived in Derry it sparked another bout of serious rioting.

NICRA's initial demands related specifically to equality for the Catholic population. They were not attempting to destroy or undermine Northern Ireland and break the relationship with Britain.

The violent response

NICRA took to the streets in a series of public marches to promote their cause. These marches met with counter-demonstrations from Protestant and unionist groups that often turned violent. Fearing an escalation in street violence, the Stormont government banned NICRA marches.

In 1968 and 1969 Northern Ireland spiralled towards violence. A civil rights movement that sought social, rather than explicitly political, changes that would threaten the territorial status of Northern Ireland, had been met with a violent response from a Protestant and unionist community who feared their motivations. Riots, arson attacks, and physical assaults became common. The police force was stretched, and did not have the support of the Catholic community. The difficult question was how the situation could be brought under control.

Troops in

On 12 August 1969 a traditional Apprentice Boys parade took place in Derry. Such parades were seen as inflammatory by the Catholic community as they celebrated the victory of Protestant King William over Catholic King James in the seventeenth century. The parade led to intense rioting, and an escalation of sectarian violence in Derry and across Northern Ireland that the police could not contain. In an attempt to restore order the decision was taken, on 15 August 1969, to send British troops onto the streets of Northern Ireland.

Initially, both Protestants and Catholics welcomed the troops because:

✓ The police force, the Royal Ulster Constabulary (RUC) was exhausted and could no longer contain the situation.

✓ There existed a belief amongst the Catholic population that the RUC was no longer a neutral force.

✓ Acts of violence were not restricted to street rioting, but were taking on a sectarian dimension. Many Catholics and Protestants were burnt out of their homes by arsonists from the opposing side.

✓ It was felt, especially amongst Catholics, that the troops would protect Catholics from Protestant rioters, and that they would be politically neutral as they did their job.

The troops did initially calm the situation and violence reduced in intensity for a while. The political situation did not stabilise however. The voice of nationalism became stronger, and their demands for reform louder, with the formation of the Social Democratic and Labour Party (SDLP). At the same time the ruling unionist government began to fracture. While some in the party argued for further social and political reforms that would produce a fairer society, others clung to their belief that unionists had a right to rule Northern Ireland without reference to the Catholic minority.

Violence returned to the streets in 1970 and 1971, and the troops quickly lost the support they had initially received from the Catholic community. Rather than appearing as their protectors, they were rapidly transformed into another force that was seen as enforcing unionist rule.

Enter paramilitary forces

During this period paramilitary forces came into being that would make the violence in Northern Ireland more organised and focused. Both communities developed paramilitary movements. These were:

✓ The Provisional Irish Republican Army (Provisional IRA). Formed in 1970 after splitting from the Official IRA, the Provisional IRA emerged from the streets of Northern Ireland specifically to defend the Catholic community from attack.

✓ The Ulster Volunteer Force (UVF). Formed in 1966, they were sworn to defend Northern Ireland's relationship with Britain in the face of Catholic demands for change.

✓ The Ulster Defence Association (UDA). A more public force than the UVF, with similar aims, the UDA claimed 40,000 members by 1972.

Internment of Catholics

August 1971 witnessed a further upsurge of violence across Northern Ireland. In Derry four days of rioting culminated in two men being shot by the army. The government at Stormont decided to act to calm the situation, and decided that if they took known troublemakers off the streets, the situation would be calmed. On 9 August 1971 the army arrested 342 men, and the process of internment without trial began. Rather than producing calm, internment only inflamed the situation. Those arrested were all from Catholic communities, and the use of the army to arrest suspects reinforced the perception that they were a far from neutral force.

The response to internment was swift and violent. Rioting erupted across Northern Ireland, and in three days 22 people were killed, and 7,000 driven from their homes by sectarian acts of arson. The government at Stormont seemed to have completely lost control. With the failure of government and widespread violence on the streets, more young people, on both sides, were convinced that the only way they could secure their future was by joining and supporting the paramilitaries.

Bloody Sunday

The civil rights movement campaigned against internment which they considered another example of injustice in Northern Ireland. In January 1972 a march was organised in Derry to protest against the ongoing policy of internment. The march was well-attended and was supposed to be a peaceful gathering.

As such protests had often led to rioting, the march was heavily policed by the British army, including the paratroop regiment that were brought to Derry from Belfast for the day. The march ended in terrible bloodshed. The army claimed that they had come under attack from Provisional IRA snipers, and had only returned fire. The marchers contended that the Paratroopers had fired without provocation on unarmed demonstrators. In the event the Paratroopers fired 108 rounds of live ammunition into the crowd, and by the end of the day 13 unarmed protestors were dead.

Bloody Sunday is seen as one of the key events in the history of Northern Ireland, and one of the most contested. Although an initial investigation, the Widgery report, found the army blameless, many argued that they were guilty of firing without provocation. The story of what happened on that day was regularly revisited, and became the subject of a major movie, *Bloody Sunday*, starring James Nesbitt, in 2002. The pressure to discover conclusively what had happened led to the creation of the Saville Inquiry by the British government in 1996. It was such an extensive inquiry that a final report is not expected until 2006.

14 May Days

In the early 1970s there had been an attempt to bring devolved government back to Northern Ireland and end the period of direct rule from London. The new assembly for Northern Ireland was elected to run Northern Ireland in 1973. In an attempt to protect the rights of the minority Catholic population, a Council of Ireland had been suggested. This would allow the Irish Republic a consultative role in the politics of Northern Ireland. For many unionists this was the thin end of the wedge, and would signal the beginning of the end for Northern Ireland. For them, any involvement of the Irish Republic in their affairs was objectionable. In May 1974 the Unionist Worker's Council (an amalgamation of loyalist paramilitary groups and unionist politicians) declared a general strike against the idea of the Council of Ireland. They brought Northern Ireland to a complete standstill. The British government decided they were unwilling to use troops against the strikers, for fear of mass violence and a high death toll, so scrapped the attempt at devolution and reverted to direct rule from London. The strike demonstrated the power of unionism when it was united.

Direct rule from London – again

The killings on Bloody Sunday led to another upsurge in violence and a rapid growth in support for the Provisional IRA. The British government realised that they could no longer support the Stormont government in Northern Ireland. Despite some attempts at reform since the late 1960s, the situation had spiralled out of control, and the two communities were more divided than ever. The decision was taken in March 1972 to suspend the government of Northern Ireland and govern directly from London.

The IRA attacks

In the late 1960s and early 1970s many in the Catholic community in Northern Ireland became completely dissatisfied with the state of affairs there. They felt economically and socially discriminated against and did not believe that the unionist government at Stormont represented their interests. While many supported the initiative of the civil rights movement and nationalist political parties such as the SDLP, the situation did not improve. They felt under attack from loyalist paramilitaries, and had lost faith in the ability of either the RUC or the army to protect them. Instead, many felt that events such as Bloody Sunday simply illustrated the fact that the forces of the state were being used against them.

In such a situation they looked for someone that would protect their interests. In seeking to defend themselves and take action against their attackers, many turned to the Provisional IRA as a force that could serve their interests. The Provisional IRA offered:

- Protection from attacks by loyalist paramilitary and security forces.

- A vehicle for disenfranchised and disillusioned young men and women to take action against their attackers.

- Political arguments linking the problems in Northern Ireland with the unfinished business of 1922 (refer to Chapter 21).

- A belief that Northern Ireland could not be reformed internally, and that only the creation of a reunited 32-county Ireland could give the Catholic community safety and prosperity.

Initially the Provisional IRA was concerned with the defence of the Catholic community, but as the months passed by, they developed a strategy of bombing economic targets in order to destabilise British rule in Northern Ireland. While this was an effective strategy, 1971 witnessed another change in direction. On 6 February 1971 Gunner Harris became the first regular soldier to be killed by the Provisional IRA. The list of legitimate targets was widened to include members of the British Army, and the officers of the RUC.

No one can win

In the 1970s and 1980s killings and bombings were a regular feature of life in Northern Ireland. The forces of the state, the Army and the RUC, had to contend with sustained and organised violence from Republican forces, the Provisional IRA, and a range of different Loyalist paramilitary organisations.

But what did these different groups want and what did they hope to achieve?

- The Provisional IRA believed that a violent struggle would eventually force the British to decide that they should leave Northern Ireland, and that a 32-county Republic would be created as a result.

- The various loyalist paramilitaries were dedicated to the protection of Northern Ireland and its sovereign relationship with Britain. They argued that the use of violence was justified to support the state and to attack its enemies in the Provisional IRA.

- The British worked on the principle that they had to protect the democratic will of the majority in Northern Ireland, namely the unionist population, who wanted to remain as part of Britain. They used the full force of their political, security, and legal systems to try to achieve this.

All these different aims were clearly contradictory, and the upshot was a situation where large numbers of people were killed by the different sides in the conflict.

Enniskillen

To many observers the bombing of the Remembrance Day service in Enniskillen, on 8 November 1987, was one of the worst acts of the whole period of the troubles. The IRA targeted the service, which was taking place at the town's war memorial. Eleven people were killed in the bombing and 63 were injured. The immediate aftermath of the bomb was captured by an amateur camera operator filming on a hand-held video recorder. The pictures were relayed around the world and brought widespread condemnation for the attack. The following day the IRA expressed deep regret for the attack, and Gerry Adams, the leader of Sinn Fein acknowledged that such attacks on civilians undermined the validity of the armed struggle. The father of one victim, Gordon Wilson, who lost his daughter in the attack, won widespread admiration for his statement the day after her death. He said, 'I have lost my daughter and we shall miss her, but I bear no grudge. Dirty sort of talk is not going to bring her back to life. She was a great wee lassie.' The dignity of Wilson's statement, and its impact, are considered the reason why there were no loyalist revenge attacks for the bombing of Enniskillen.

Between 1969 and 1989, 2,761 people were killed as a result of the conflict in Northern Ireland. Of these:

- ✔ 623 were killed by loyalist paramilitaries, namely Catholic civilians (72 per cent), Protestant civilians (18 per cent), other loyalist paramilitaries (5 per cent), republican paramilitaries (3 per cent), and members of the security forces (2 per cent).

- ✔ 1,593 were killed by republican paramilitaries, namely members of the security forces (53 per cent), Protestant civilians (25 per cent), Catholic civilians (12 per cent), other republican paramilitaries (9 per cent), and loyalist paramilitaries (1 per cent).

- ✔ An estimated 150 were killed by members of the security forces.

In an attempt to control the violence the British introduced the Prevention of Terrorism Act in 1974, which allowed suspects to be detained without access to legal representation, and authorised the elite SAS to operate in Northern Ireland against Republicans.

By 31 December 2001 the number of deaths attributed to the Northern Ireland troubles had risen to 3,523 and over 40,000 have been injured.

Clearly such a rate of deaths, and the associated high level of injuries, were a tragedy for Northern Ireland. Such levels of violence meant that Northern

Ireland ceased to be a normal democratic society. All aspects of life, from housing, education, and sport, through to business development, employment, and culture were affected. It was clear that the situation could not go unchecked. But by the end of the 1970s, all attempts at finding a political solution to the troubles had failed. No one would concede their core demands, and an embrace of violence appeared more effective than searching for peace. Stalemate? By the late 1970s the Northern Ireland conflict appeared to many observers to be an intractable problem. While strategies had been used by the British to try to reduce the levels of violence (higher security force numbers on the street, the Prevention of Terrorism Act, and better use of intelligence information) they could not make the paramilitaries disappear. There was also an acknowledgment within British government and military circles that they could never defeat the paramilitaries. If a solution was to be found it would have to be a political one. But how could this be managed when the demands of the nationalists and republicans for self-government and Britain's withdrawal were in complete contrast to the demands of the majority unionist population of Northern Ireland who wanted to remain part of Britain?

It appeared at the end of the 1970s as if a point of stalemate had been reached, and there was no alternative to an ongoing sectarian conflict.

Troubles in the '80s and '90s

The 1980s would see a new upsurge in violence. Events would lead to intense periods of rioting, and for the first time, the numbers killed by loyalist paramilitaries would outstrip the figures of those killed by republicans. The Provisional IRA's campaign of bombing, in Northern Ireland and beyond, would lead to ever larger scale bombs and sustained attacks on the economic infrastructure of Britain. Despite all this, the 1980s witnessed political developments that would sow the seeds of the 1990s peace process.

The hunger strikes

In the early 1970s the British government withdrew special category status from paramilitary prisoners which, until then, had meant that they were not subject to prison rules that applied to ordinary criminals. The paramilitaries, especially the republicans, objected to this. They claimed they were not criminals but prisoners of war and deserved to be treated differently while in prison.

Their demands were:

- ✔ The right to wear their own clothes.
- ✔ No prison work.
- ✔ Freedom of association with other prisoners.
- ✔ Extra recreational facilities.
- ✔ More letters and parcels.

In 1978 republican prisoners refused to wear prison clothes and began wearing only their bed blankets by way of protest. They complained that because of this protest they were regularly attacked by prison staff, and they intensified their campaign. They refused to leave their cells, wash, or use the toilet facilities. This campaign, the *dirty protest*, led the prisoners to live in cells covered with their own excreta and other waste. Despite the campaign, and the sympathy that their plight earned, the government was unmoved. In March 1981 the dirty protest was transformed into a hunger strike.

A group of prisoners began refusing food. As the condition of each prisoner deteriorated, new prisoners would also begin fasting. On 5 May 1981, the first hunger striker, Bobby Sands, died. His funeral was attended by 100,000 people, and the British government was criticised across the world for having done nothing to end the dispute.

Shortly after Bobby Sands began his protest, Frank Maguire, an MP in Northern Ireland, died. Sands, although fasting in prison, stood in the ensuing election, and won the seat. The first hunger striker to die was then not merely a protestor, but a member of the British parliament.

Although Bobby Sands was elected specifically on the prison protest issue, his victory demonstrated to the republican movement that it could win elections. Sinn Fein had always refused to fight in British parliamentary elections. However, if they could win, as Sands had demonstrated, it would make their demands more legitimate as they would have popular electoral support. Through elections, Sinn Fein understood that it could gain a popular mandate for its policies. From the 1980s Sinn Fein fought, and was successful in, a host of national and local elections.

The response to the hunger strikes in Northern Ireland was violent. In the period of the protest 61 people died in violent incidents. Thirty members of the security forces were killed by the Provisional IRA, and seven civilians were killed by plastic bullets that the security forces fired into the crowds during rioting.

By the time the hunger strikes were called off in October 1981, ten hunger strikers had starved themselves to death.

Bombing Britain

The Provisional IRA conducted a long war in Northern Ireland against those they considered their enemies on the ground. They understood however that such attacks, as they became a daily incident, did not grab the headlines in Britain. If they were to succeed in driving the British out, they had to make the people of Britain question why their government supported the rights of the unionist majority. To do this, the Provisional IRA developed a strategy that was designed to sicken the British people into questioning the government. The policy never worked, but it led to a series of spectacular and devastating attacks on Britain, including:

- ✔ 1974: An attack on a coach carrying army personnel in Scotland kills twelve. Bombs in pubs in Guildford and Birmingham kill twenty-four people. The famous London shop Harrods is also bombed, but no one is killed.

- ✔ 1976: A Provisional IRA bomb kills the newly appointed British ambassador to the Irish Republic.

- ✔ 1979: The first cousin of the Queen, Earl Mountbatten, is killed while on holiday off the Irish coast. On the same day 18 British soldiers are killed in Newry.

- ✔ 1982: The Household Cavalry is targeted as it undertakes ceremonial duties in Hyde Park, London. Two cavalrymen and seven horses are killed.

- ✔ 1983: Harrods is again targeted and six people are killed during the Christmas shopping period.

- ✔ 1984: The Conservative party conference in Brighton is attacked, and five killed. Prime Minister Margaret Thatcher escapes.

- ✔ 1989: In an attack on the base of the Royal Marine band at Deal, in Kent, ten bandsmen are killed.

- ✔ 1992: The City of London is targeted. Three are killed and leading finance houses, such as those in the Baltic exchange, are destroyed.

- ✔ 1993: Two bombs planted in litter bins in Warrington explode, killing two children.

- ✔ 1996: Major attacks on economic targets in Manchester and London's docklands destroy shops and offices.

The use of violence in pursuit of political and ideological goals is always a difficult and emotive issue. While in no way did the Provisional IRA tactics lead them to winning their struggle and driving the British out of Northern Ireland, the high and sustained levels of violence kept the situation in the public spotlight, and brought about political talks aimed at a lasting and peaceful settlement to the problems of all communities in Northern Ireland.

From Gibraltar to Milltown Cemetery

In March 1988 three unarmed members of the Provisional IRA were shot dead by members of the SAS in Gibraltar believing that they were about to detonate bombs in the area. The killings were hotly disputed. On 16 March, at the funerals at Milltown Cemetery for the dead, Provisional IRA members were attacked by a loyalist gunman, Michael Stone, and three people were killed. During the West Belfast funeral procession of one of those who had been killed at Milltown, Kevin Brady, a car approached the procession at high speed. Fearing another loyalist attack in the style of Michael Stone, the mourners attacked the car. Its occupants, two off-duty soldiers, were beaten and shot dead. The eight killings, in a period of little more than two weeks, were some of the most disturbing in Northern Ireland, and those at Milltown and West Belfast, were screened live on television and the images shown around the world.

The American angle

As so many Americans claimed Irish roots, the ongoing struggle in Northern Ireland was of great interest to many of them. While physically detached from the conflict on the streets of Northern Ireland, many of them felt that the IRA was fighting a justifiable struggle that would finally expel the British from the island of Ireland.

The largest single group in Northern Ireland that supported the nationalist cause was NORAID (Irish Northern Aid), which was founded in 1971. Its stated aim was to provide humanitarian assistance to political prisoners and their families, although many in the unionist community have argued that it directly funded the activities of the IRA.

At the political level the Northern Ireland conflict has been a constant feature of life in Washington. Democrats with Irish ties, such as Edward Kennedy and the late Tip O'Neill, worked to keep Northern Ireland on the American political agenda. Under the Presidency of Bill Clinton (1993–2001) Northern Ireland, and the associated peace process, became a major government initiative, and Clinton was a key element in driving the process forward.

The annual celebration of St Patrick's Day affords all Irish-Americans the opportunity to embrace their Irishness. The President always welcomes the Irish Taoiseach to the White House, where he is presented with a bowl of shamrock, and many dinners and banquets take place promoting Ireland.

Going political

By the start of the 1990s there was a growing feeling in Northern Ireland that some form of resolution to the troubles had to be found. The difficulty was to find some way in which the demands of the different groups could be reconciled. The main political parties involved were:

- ✓ **SDLP:** the main nationalist party, led by John Hume, who believed that a constitutional resolution was the best way forward. They also argued that the Irish Republic had to be included in any solution.

- ✓ **Sinn Fein:** the leading republican party, Sinn Fein had close ties with the IRA. Led by Gerry Adams, Sinn Fein argued that the British should leave Northern Ireland.

- ✓ **Ulster Unionist Party (UUP):** led by David Trimble, the UUP believed that Northern Ireland should be part of Britain and that the rights of the unionist majority should be respected. However, they also understood that some resolution was required, and that nationalists and republicans who renounced violence should be involved in the governance of Northern Ireland. Until 2005, the UUP was the largest unionist party.

- ✓ **Democratic Unionist Party (DUP):** the DUP has always argued that Northern Ireland is part of Britain and that position is non-negotiable. Led by Ian Paisley, the DUP has consistently argued against Sinn Fein's inclusion in government until the IRA has been disbanded. The DUP has recently become the largest unionist party in Northern Ireland.

Peace Comes Dropping Slow

In 1993, John Hume and Gerry Adams began talks to try to see if they could jump-start some form of peace process. They issued a series of statements aimed at getting all the other parties to join in and start a debate. The British and Irish governments tried to assist the fledgling peace process with a number of joint agreements. The rapid progress of twists and turns in the road to peace included:

- ✓ The Downing Street Declaration, 1993. It stated that Britain no longer had any selfish interest in Northern Ireland, but would protect the will of the majority. The Irish Republic recognised that any Irish self-determination had to have the consent of the majority of the population, including unionists. Both nations committed themselves to peaceful means and the ending of paramilitary violence.

✔ The IRA ceasefire, announced in August 1994, and reciprocated by loyalist paramilitaries two months later.

✔ The Joint Framework document, February 1995. Signed by the British and Irish governments, established a programme for the creation of new cross-border institutions and a new government for Northern Ireland.

✔ November 1995 saw a visit by President Clinton to Northern Ireland to bolster the peace process, and the direct involvement of Senator George Mitchell as head of an international body to oversee decommissioning of paramilitary weapons.

✔ By January 1996 the IRA believed that the process was stalling and that Sinn Fein were being denied entry to talks. They ended their ceasefire and major explosions were detonated in London.

✔ During 1996 talks continued between the two governments and the major parties in Northern Ireland. The DUP refused to attend, and Sinn Fein were excluded because of their close links with the IRA.

✔ In May 1997, Tony Blair was elected Prime Minister in Britain, and immediately authorised talks with Sinn Fein to see how they could be brought into the peace process.

✔ The IRA announced, in July 1997, the resumption of their ceasefire.

The road to peace in the 1990s was long and hard. The difficulty was to get all the parties involved, and to resolve the issue of the paramilitaries and how they could be turned away from violence. The decommissioning of IRA weapons, and whether this should take place before any talks, was a stumbling block. Also, the refusal of the DUP to join any talks meant that there was a vocal opposition to the process.

Getting everyone to talk

In the summer of 1997 all-party talks on the future of Northern Ireland began. The DUP still stayed away, but Sinn Fein took their place at the table for the first time. To by-pass the tricky topic of decommissioning, an Independent International Commission on Decommissioning was formed that would oversee the destruction of weapons by the paramilitary forces.

The talks were tense, and various parties very uneasy about progress. At various times parties with paramilitary associations, such as Sinn Fein, were excluded for a period of weeks because of renewed acts of violence. To instil confidence in the whole process, bodies such as the Parades Commission were established to judge on the routes of contentious marches in Northern Ireland, and in January 1998, Tony Blair announced a new investigation into the events of Bloody Sunday.

Drumcree and the Parades Issue

The Orange Order, which was founded in 1795, is a Protestant fraternal organisation and is most famous for its parades that celebrate the victory of Protestant King William over Catholic King James at the Battle of the Boyne in 1690. The parades are a long-standing feature of life in Northern Ireland, but have always been contentious. Many Catholics objected to the parades passing through their neighbourhoods and the sectarian supremacy that they associated with such displays. One of the most contentious parades during the years of the peace process was that at Drumcree. The Catholic residents of the Garvaghy Road objected to the parade passing through their neighbourhood, and staged a sit-down protest to block the parade in 1995. The standoff lasted three days and led to riots across Northern Ireland. In 1996 the parade was initially ordered to be rerouted, but was sent down the Garvaghy Road after a standoff between Orangemen and troops. The parade has remained contentious ever since, although since 1998 its route has been changed by the Parades Commission. Four Catholic deaths in the surrounding area were attributed to loyalist paramilitaries supporting the Orange Order stand between 1995 and 1998.

By April 1998 things had reached crisis point. There was a deadline of 9 April for an agreement, and it was unclear for several hours that a deal could be done. On 10 April 1998, Good Friday, it was announced that the Belfast Agreement had been signed. It was endorsed by the majority of Northern Ireland's political parties, and promised a bright new future for everyone.

Good Friday, New Northern Ireland?

The Belfast Agreement created the following mechanisms to allow Northern Ireland to move away from its troubled history:

- ✔ A Northern Ireland Assembly with legislative powers.
- ✔ A power-sharing formula that would allow the main parties to nominate ministers.
- ✔ A North-South Ministerial Council that allowed for cross-border co-operation.
- ✔ The release of all paramilitary prisoners from organisations observing the ceasefire.
- ✔ A two-year target for paramilitary decommissioning.
- ✔ Reform of the Royal Ulster Constabulary.
- ✔ The demilitarisation of British army bases in Northern Ireland.

Nobel prizes

The Troubles in Northern Ireland have led directly to the awarding of two separate Nobel Peace Prizes. The first was awarded in 1977 to Betty Williams and Mairead Corrigan, the founders of the Northern Ireland Peace movement. They had come together in response to the death of Corrigan's niece and nephews, who were killed when the Army shot dead a member of the Provisional IRA, whose car then ran into them. The women staged a series of rallies across Ireland and Britain demanding peace in Northern Ireland. The second award was made in 1998 to John Hume of the SDLP and David Trimble of the Ulster Unionist Party for their role in the peace talks that led to the signing of the Belfast Agreement (which is also often referred to as the Good Friday Agreement; the day on which it was signed).

The Agreement initially got off to a great start when it was ratified by large majorities in referenda that were held in Northern Ireland and the Irish Republic. After that however, the deal was plagued with problems. Although there were initial acts of IRA decommissioning, they were not enough to satisfy unionist critics.

The police force was reformed, and the Police Service of Northern Ireland brought into being in 2001. However, the new force failed to gain the support of many nationalists and criticisms remained in some quarters that policing in Northern Ireland was still not serving both sides of the community.

The Assembly has sat at various times, but has now spent more months in a state of collapse than it has sitting. With a steady polarisation of politics between Sinn Fein and the DUP, a division that was reinforced in the 2005 British general election, the successful implementation of the agreement looks a long way off. Since becoming the largest unionist party, the DUP has constantly argued that the whole agreement should be renegotiated. In 2005 Northern Ireland was still ruled directly from London, and the Assembly was still suspended awaiting the renewed political negotiations that will allow it to reconvene.

The IRA standing down?

One of the main aims of the whole peace process was to remove the paramilitaries from the streets. It was argued that while such organisations, whether republican or loyalist, existed there could be no development of a peaceful democratic society.

It is clear that many involved in the different paramilitary organisations have embraced the peace process and do want to create a peaceful Northern

Ireland. However, there is much suspicion. Many people, on either side, were wary of the motives of the paramilitaries as they moved into the political sphere.

While the number of deaths, bombings, and attacks has reduced significantly, there is a feeling that the work of the paramilitaries is ongoing. Both sides have engaged in punishment beatings, and there is a constant suspicion that some have been involved in criminal activity.

The Impact of 9/11

The attacks on America in 2001 had a profound effect on the politics of Northern Ireland. Whereas the IRA had found some support in the United States for their struggle, the announcement of a worldwide war on terror after 9/11 altered the status of the IRA. In August 2001 three Irishmen were arrested in Colombia on suspicion of training the Revolutionary Armed Forces of the country's Marxist rebels. Although originally acquitted, the Irishmen were found guilty after an appeal court reversed the earlier verdict. While on bail, the men fled Colombia, and re-entered the Irish Republic in 2005. In the context of American foreign policy after 9/11 the Colombian-Irish link was troubling. The Irishmen were identified as either Sinn Fein or IRA members and, if the charges were true, their presence in Colombia represented part of the American-defined network of terror. The changing global politics after 9/11 have meant that the IRA is viewed with suspicion in America, and there has been great pressure on the IRA to move quickly into the political arena.

Sinn Fein and the DUP were seen, during the early years of the peace process, as being at the extremes in nationalism and unionism respectively. So while the IRA had done what it had been asked in 2005, and ended its war, the biggest challenge was to get these two parties, so long opposed to each other, working together in government. This was something that could simply not have been imagined a few years earlier.

After the 2005 announcement that the IRA was standing down, the way was clear for Sinn Fein and the DUP to try to form a government. The Northern Irish parties, plus the British and Irish governments, came together in October 2006, at St Andrew's in Scotland, and agreed a new road map for the future. This led to fresh elections for the Northern Ireland Assembly in March 2007. The two biggest parties were Sinn Fein and the DUP, and they formed a government. The Reverend Doctor Ian Paisley was First Minister, and Martin McGuinness his Deputy First Minister. Such was the impact of these two adversaries working well together on the public stage, that the media christened them the 'chuckle brothers'.

The confidence in the lasting nature of the peace was such that the British Army fully withdrew from Northern Ireland in July 2007. While relations between Sinn Fein and the DUP have been far from easy, they have worked through the major issues, such as policing, and agreed to compromise. At the end of the first decade of the twenty-first century, Northern Ireland is governing itself through its Assembly, and while threats to the peace remain in the form of dissident republicans, the North is now beginning to leave the troubles behind it.

The IRA made a major move on the decommissioning front in October 2003 and began putting weapons beyond use, but this was not the complete end to the armed struggle that unionists wished to see. In July 2005, the IRA formally announced the end of its armed campaign, and stated that it would pursue exclusively peaceful means. While Gerry Adams called the move a 'courageous and confident initiative' and Tony Blair said it was a 'step of unparalleled magnitude', the unionists were less convinced. They stated that they would not allow entry of Sinn Fein into government and the restoration of government in Northern Ireland until they had seen evidence of complete decommissioning.

The Celtic Tiger

For most of its existence, the Irish Republic had been a relatively poor, under-modernised nation. Although joining the European Union in 1973 bolstered the Irish economy, the 1980s saw another period of downturn and high levels of emigration. In the 1980s the Irish unemployment rate was 18 per cent. In the 1990s the Irish Republic underwent a staggering period of economic growth and became one of the fastest growing economies in Europe.

In 1994 economist and broadcaster, David McWilliams, drew analogies between the situation in Ireland and what had happened in countries such as Hong Kong and South Korea a decade earlier, and coined the phrase *the Celtic Tiger*. This shorthand way of describing the boom in Ireland became a popular term for summing up what was happening in the country.

As well as all the economic modernisation, Ireland also underwent many social changes. For the first time since the famine of the mid-nineteenth century emigration stopped. People began turning away from the Church, and began demanding more liberal attitudes towards divorce and abortion. With higher disposable incomes, the Irish also became big consumers, and city centres, especially Dublin, were transformed by the opening of an endless array of restaurants, bars, and nightclubs.

Ireland gets rich

From being the poor man of Europe in the 1980s, Ireland became the rich man. Between 1991 and 2003 its economy grew by an amazing 6.8 per cent per year, and Irish living standards became amongst the highest in Europe.

The Irish are famous for having emigrated to the four corners of the world. That trend continued well into the 1980s, but since the advent of the Celtic Tiger, outward emigration has largely stopped. What has begun happening, for the first time ever, is that large numbers of immigrants have begun arriving in Ireland. Immigrants from African and Eastern European nations have arrived in Ireland seeking to benefit from the wealth of the country. While there have been many positive aspects to this inward movement of people, there has also been a rise in racism among many sectors of the Irish population.

Ireland got rich by having a very low corporate tax rate, and by encouraging a whole series of multinational companies to locate in the country. Ireland was particularly successful in attracting high technology companies, and is now one of the biggest producers of computers in Europe. It also helped that Irish workers were relatively cheap to employ, but very highly skilled.

The success soon became apparent. During the 1990s the property market soared, consumer spending boomed, and by 2005 unemployment was a mere 4.2 per cent. As the government was apparently careful to use its new found wealth to cut public debt, it has also been able to invest money in major renewal projects such as the Luas tramway system in Dublin.

While many people in Ireland got rich during the Celtic Tiger years, there were still areas of high social deprivation in the country. In some of the Dublin city suburbs crime rates and drug use remained high, as did the levels of poverty and unemployment. Schemes were in place to try to equalise the spread of wealth throughout the country, but it's clear that not everyone benefited from the Celtic Tiger.

Being Irish is trendy

With the boom happening, and the Irish leading the way in economic and cultural innovation, Ireland became one of the trendiest places on the planet. It was seen as a cool place to go on holiday, and especially to enjoy Dublin's nightlife. Out of Ireland in the 1990s also came Riverdance, U2, a decent Irish soccer team, and renewed interest in traditional music and art forms. Ireland really was, and remains, the place to be.

The boom goes boom

It all looked so good for Ireland during the early 2000s. The economy boomed, peace came to Northern Ireland, and for the first time ever, other people wanted to come and live in the country.

In a globalised world, all economies are linked. While Ireland had done well for a time, it wasn't immune to any downturn that might begin elsewhere. The key question for Ireland, if any global downturn began, was how would its impact be felt?

Nationalisation, NAMA and others

Once the Fianna Fail government realised that the Irish banks were over-extended in late 2008 (for 'over-extended' read 'bankrupt'), it tried to calm everybody down by guaranteeing all the money that the banks owed and what was invested in them. Unfortunately it didn't calm anybody down, and the government had to begin pumping billions of euro into the Irish banks to convince the financial markets that all was well. This meant that the majority of the Irish banks were nationalised, and their huge debts owned by the Irish people. It's one thing saving a banking system, but protecting private investors – in other words property speculators –

was seen as something else. But Fianna Fail, who had benefitted so much from the support of these individuals during the good times, did just that. NAMA, the National Asset Management Agency, came into being in April 2009. It took all the bad debts owned by the banks, the ones the property speculators had racked up, and took them into government ownership. Bottom line, the Irish state, which was in a pretty bad way as tax income had reduced dramatically, bailed out the banks and the property developers, and passed the debts onto the people. At the end of 2010, there is only one other country in the world, with as much state-owned debt as Ireland.

To make the boom happen, the Irish government had done some smart things, like attracting lots of inward investment. It had also done some very silly things. First, the government had never properly regulated its banking system. Second, it believed, as many commentators did, that the foundations of Ireland's economic prosperity were solid, and that the good times would continue. Wrong! When the sub-prime mortgage crisis affected the United States, and Lehman Brothers Bank crashed, the Irish were still whistling away to themselves.

In 2008, Irish unemployment started to creep up, businesses started going bankrupt, and the amount of money in the government coffers started to reduce significantly. So much of the wealth had been built on property speculation, that once this began slowing up, so did the government's tax revenue.

By September 2008, Ireland was in recession, But that was only the start. The banks suddenly realised, as did the property investors, builders, and home owners, that the property they owned was not worth what they had paid for it. For most people this meant struggling to pay the mortgage, but for an elite band of property developers who had borrowed billions of euro from the banks, it meant default.

The outsiders arrive

After having got itself into such a mess, and owing a lot of people, nations and financial institutions a lot of money, Ireland was not the most popular country in the world. There were fears that the size of Ireland's debt, and its potential inability to pay it off, would lead to other European countries defaulting, and worse of all, might signal the end of the Euro. Something had to be done.

So, who you gonna call? After spending a few months denying Ireland was over extended, the Fianna Fail government finally made the call. In November 2010, it was acknowledged that the International Monetary Fund (IMF) and the European Union were going to come to Dublin and look at the books. Having looked at the books, the IMF didn't particularly like what they saw. They agreed that Ireland needed to borrow some €85 million to ensure its survival. The people of Ireland were less than delighted and protests followed.

Ireland has a long history of emigration. When things get tough at home, it's time to go. Sadly for the generation born in the 1980s, who grew to adulthood during the Celtic Tiger years (and who forgot about poverty and emigration), there was suddenly no boom, and not many jobs. By the end of 2010, Irish unemployment had risen to 14 per cent, and the tide of emigration began again. In 2009, 60,000 people left Ireland, and the following year the figure was over 120,000. While the bars in Dublin, Cork and Galway close down for lack of custom, the Irish bars of Boston, Chicago, New York, Sydney, Melbourne and elsewhere, are doing better business than they have in years. Ireland, once more, is a country of tears, and a land of emigration.

Any Good Points?

Given the rapid collapse in Irish fortunes, it's often hard to see any bright spots. True, the Irish Republic is massively in debt, its people are emigrating, and social services have been savaged as a way of saving money. But, in spite of the problems, the peace process in Northern Ireland has held good, and shared government between two old enemies appears to be working. Also, the Irish seem to have gone back to what they really do excel at: literature. While the Irish Republic has been, and even in the downturn, continues to be good at attracting new technology companies to the country (Facebook, E Bay, Google and others continue to invest in Ireland), it's writing that they do best. The 2000s saw the emergence of a new wave of Irish writers, who have won global acclaim, and who often write, not simply of the Irish condition, but of contemporary and global themes. So in the gloom, it's the artists that might shape the future of the country, and shine a light on what it means to be Irish. So make sure to read, if you haven't already, the works of those much applauded Irish writers including Colm Toibin, Anne Enright, Joseph O'Connor, Colum McCann, Claire Keegan and Kevin Barry.

Part VII
The Part of Tens

The 5th Wave   By Rich Tennant

"Let me ask you a question. Are you planning to kiss the Blarney Stone, or ask for its hand in marriage?"

In this part . . .

This part gives you a whole load of information about Ireland and things Irish. It's the kind of knowledge that makes you look smart, well-informed, and a bit of a know-it-all. Everyone thinks they know something about Ireland. With these lists you can know ten of the very most important and essential facts. Some may be quirky but they are entertaining too.

These lists tell you what the main turning points were in Irish history, which are the greatest Irish documents, and what the most important things are that the Irish have given to the world. You'll also find a list of places that you must see if you decide to visit Ireland, and for the biographically minded amongst you, a brief insight into the lives of ten Irish people who should be much better known. Clearly these choices are mine, and you might think I've got it all wrong. Don't worry about that though – you can make up your own list if you want!

Chapter 24

Ten Top Turning Points

*1*n every national history there are always those key moments that changed everything. Ireland has had lots of them, so getting the list down to ten is a bit of a challenge.

What's included here are those events that really did have an impact on Ireland, and made everyone sit up and take notice.

The Arrival of Christianity

Although it's too simplistic to say that all of Ireland's problems have been caused by religion, it's clearly an important part of the nation's history. Prior to the arrival of Christianity Ireland had been seen by many people in Europe as an untamed backwater, full of wild tribes who were devoted to an uncivilised way of life. Clearly that overstates the case, but with the arrival of St Patrick in Ireland came Christianity (skip to Chapter 4). Patrick and his followers had a long and hard job establishing the Church in Ireland, but the fact that they did is hugely important. While the rest of Europe slipped into the chaos of the Dark Ages, Ireland shone out as a beacon of Christian learning and civility. It was because Ireland was immune to the Dark Ages, and its monasteries were so highly skilled, that the country was able to send missions out to Europe and subsequently re-establish Christianity on the continent.

The Normans Arriving

Ireland wasn't all peace and tranquillity before the Normans landed in 1169, but at least the country had avoided (with the exception of the passing Vikings) a major invasion. Once the Normans sailed in, the future of Ireland was changed forever. Britain was not only geographically next door, but once the Normans were in place, it was politically involved with the future of Ireland. So, perhaps the biggest turning point of all in some ways: Ireland's isolation ends and 700 years of fun and games begin (jump to Part II).

The Reformation

Back to religion! The first turning point saw Christianity arrive, and the one Church served Ireland very well for a few centuries. The problems started in Britain when Henry VIII decided he didn't like his wife anymore. Divorce followed and Henry felt the displeasure of the Roman Catholic Church in full. Rather than knuckle down and reach an agreement with Rome, Henry set up his own Church, and suddenly there were two religions (see Chapter 11). The state religion for Britain and Ireland was the new one, Protestantism, while the Irish clung to the old one, Catholicism. The battle between the two Churches and their followers kept everyone busy in Ireland, and the history of the place is scarred with the multitude of deaths caused by religious division. If only Henry had stayed with his wife.

The Battle of the Boyne

Clearly the battle between Catholic and Protestant was never going to be an easy one, and the real problems came when members of the British royal family couldn't stay faithful to the Protestant Church. When James II wanted to inherit the Crown all kinds of people got upset because he was a Catholic. Those who wanted to stay loyal to the Protestant Church invited King William of Orange over from Holland to contest the future of the Crown. William won his famous battle at the Boyne in 1690 and about 1,500 men died in the fighting (head to Chapter 14). What it meant in absolute terms was that the final hope that the Irish might see a Catholic King was gone, and the Protestants celebrated. They still do celebrate the battle every 12 July.

Wolfe Tone's Rebellion

The British had always distrusted the Irish and were always wary of plots against the power of their authority in Ireland. Although there had been lots of different plots and various fights over the years, 1798 stands out as one of the most serious challenges to British rule, and one that changed Ireland. Wolfe Tone believed in the idea of an Irish Republic, but invited the French along to help him fight for it. To British minds the French were the mortal enemy and had recently done the unspeakable during the French Revolution – lopped the head off the monarch. Wolfe Tone's rebellion got squashed, and to make sure that Ireland was more carefully managed the Act of Union was brought in (see Chapter 15).

Famine and Emigration

The Irish Famine of 1845–51 was one of the worst disasters to befall any country. It led to an estimated million deaths as a result of starvation and illness and started a tide of emigration that took decades to stop. It's a big turning point for two main reasons. First, it made many Irish people hate the British as they felt the Famine had been made worse by London's mismanagement of the whole episode. Second, it took the Irish across the world in their hundreds of thousands and created the huge, and massively important, Irish diaspora (check out Chapter 18).

The Cultural Revival

Ireland's very well known for all its poets and dramatists. Obviously the country always had them, and still has them today, but the golden age was definitely the last few decades of the nineteenth century (see Chapter 20). During that period the Irish were becoming increasingly vocal in their demands for some form of independence. However, many leading thinkers and activists warned them that independence in name was no good if they had forgotten how to be Irish. What they argued was that Ireland was increasingly being influenced by British customs and habits, and that they needed to recover traditional Irish forms of art, sport, and culture. The Cultural Revival was born, and gave us some of the great literary, dramatic, and artistic work of the period. It's also important as it underpinned the political movement for Home Rule and made people feel and think Irish.

The Revolution

When Ireland was offered Home Rule in 1912 everyone thought that the future was bright. The First World War intervened however, and Home Rule was forgotten. Into the chaos of the time came various political and armed organisations who wanted to win Ireland's total freedom by force. The period from the Easter Rising of 1916, through the War of Independence (1919–21) and culminating with the Civil War (1922–23) is known as the Revolutionary period (head to Chapter 21). It's a key time in Irish history as it led to the expulsion of Britain from southern Ireland and the partition of the country between Northern Ireland and the twenty six counties of the Free State (later Irish Republic).

Joining the European Union

The Irish Republic always seemed content to go its own way in the years immediately following the Second World War, but all that changed in the 1960s. Ireland became increasingly modern, and realised that the new economic structures put in place by the European Union would be very important to the future. Ireland finally joined the European family of nations at its second attempt in 1973, and has been a keen supporter of the whole enterprise ever since. Membership in its own right could be seen as a key turning point as it placed Ireland in the heart of Europe. The key legacy of membership, or so most people would argue, is that being part of Europe laid the foundation stones for the economic prosperity that arrived in Ireland in the 1990s in the form of the Celtic Tiger.

The Good Friday Agreement

The Troubles in Northern Ireland had been seen by many observers as difficult, if not impossible to solve. The death toll in the period from the late 1960s and into the 1990s gave little encouragement to those who wanted a peaceful solution. In the 1990s however, the political climate changed, and there seemed to be a momentum behind a search for peace. The signing of the Good Friday Agreement in 1998 was a major step in ending the Troubles once and for all. It hasn't been plain sailing since the Agreement was signed, and there are still tremendous difficulties and disagreements in Northern Ireland (see Chapter 23). However, the Good Friday Agreement was a key point in turning Northern Ireland away from conflict and towards a lasting peace.

Chapter 25

Ten Major Documents

In This Chapter

▶ Legal and political documents

▶ Literary and historical works

▶ Religious manuscripts

▶ One ditty

*T*he Irish have always been famous across the world for their literary culture. From ancient times to the modern period, the Irish have always been busy scribbling away. What's listed here is a personal take on the major contribution that the Irish have made through their writing. But go and check out any library, anthology, or history book to read about lots of other neat documents the Irish have written.

Confession of St Patrick, 450

St Patrick was a key figure in the history of Ireland (see Chapter 4), and the Confession is one of his, and Ireland's, most important written texts. Basically the Confession functions as Patrick's autobiography. It tells of his early life, how he found God, and why he decided that it was his mission to bring Christianity to the Irish. Most experts accept that the Confession is a genuine document and can be attributed to Patrick. That means it's only one of two works that have been identified as having been written by the man himself.

The Book of Kells, 800

Now housed in Trinity College, Dublin, and one of Ireland's most visited tourist attractions, the Book of Kells is one of the most lavishly decorated and important illuminated manuscripts that survives. Basically it's the four gospels of the Bible written in Latin. But it's so much more than that. It shows the excellence of the work that was produced by the highly skilled monks who lived in the monasteries of the period. It's absolutely staggering in its detail and beauty, and a testament to the abilities of the men that put it together. It has long been seen as one of Ireland's most important and religious books.

History of Ireland, 1634

Written by Geoffrey Keating, the *History of Ireland* was produced as a text in Irish under the title *Foras Feasa ar Éirinn*. It traces the history of Ireland from the creation of the world through to the arrival of the Normans. Produced originally in manuscript form the work was translated into English and Latin within a year of its initial completion. So far as the seventeenth century had best sellers, Keating's work was it. Keating's work was a key text in the creation of an Irish sense of identity, and was central in linking the idea of an Irish nation to its ancient history as a strong and successful kingdom.

Pairlement Chloinne Tomáis, 17th Century

Written by an unknown author, *Pairlement Chloinne Tomáis*, is an important example of early satirical writing in Irish. The text was a contemporary satire that attacked those Catholics who had benefited from seventeenth century land reforms, and who were viewed as having become British rather than staying true to their Irishness. The text satirises the attempts of Tomáis to speak English, which he does terribly, and the respect that his annihilation of the foreign tongue wins him from his neighbours. *Pairlement Chloinne Tomáis* is available in an English translation these days, and is well worth looking at to understand how the Irish felt about people who deserted their native culture.

The Irish Rebellion, 1646

The violence in Ireland during 1641 (see Chapter 14) frightened Protestants to their very core. Sir John Temple's book, first published in 1646, claimed that 500,000 Protestants had been killed in the first two months of the rebellion. It was propagandist reporting, but it sold well. The importance of the book is not simply its excessive description of the events of 1641, but how the book was used in subsequent decades. Every time the Catholics of Ireland stirred against the Protestant community, out came Temple's book to show everyone how bad it could get. The Jacobite threats of 1713, 1714, 1724, and 1746 all saw new editions of Temple's book rushed into the shops.

The Necessity for De-Anglicising Ireland, 1892

On 25 November 1892, Douglas Hyde delivered a lecture entitled *The Necessity for De-Anglicising Ireland*. It is one of the most important documents in the Irish cultural revival, and set out the case for the recovery of a traditional Irish identity. Hyde's lecture is very important for its clarity of argument, but also because it makes clear that while Ireland might fight for her political freedom, she had to be aware of the need to be culturally distinct. The lecture is seen as one of the most important turning points in the production of Irish culture in the late nineteenth century and is still regularly discussed today.

Proclamation of the Irish Republic, 1916

Probably one of the most important documents in the history of Irish Republicanism, the Proclamation was read out to a bemused Dublin public on the first day of the Easter Rising in 1916: You can see it in the National Museum in Dublin. It had been written by Patrick Pearse and James Connolly, and covered only one sheet of paper. Only a thousand copies of the Proclamation were produced, but it is important for its content. The Proclamation outlined what kind of country an Irish Republic would be, and combined contemporary thinking from Irish nationalist circles with that of socialism. Recently an original copy of the Proclamation sold at auction for €360,000!

Bunreacht na hEireann, 1937

The Irish Constitution was published in 1937 and, with a few amendments, is still in force today. It was written mainly by Eamon de Valera (see Chapter 22), and set out his vision for the way in which Ireland should be governed. In its entirety the document contains fifty different articles and covers everything from the place of the Church in Irish life to the way the different institutions of government function. Without it the Irish Republic wouldn't exist in its current form.

Ulysses, 1922

Written by James Joyce, *Ulysses* regularly tops the lists of the most important works ever produced in the English language. It is based on the events of 16 June, 1904, in Dublin, through the eyes of the main character, Leopold Bloom. It took Joyce seven years to write, but the book has had real staying power. Every year, on 16 June, people come from around the world to Dublin so that they can retrace Bloom's journey around the city. The book has been made into a film, reprinted in many different languages, and has a large and devoted following. Many people equally see the whole thing as unreadable!

Teenage Kicks, 1978

Accepting that it's not strictly a document, *Teenage Kicks* still stands as one of the great Irish works. A pop song of the 1970s, *Teenage Kicks* was written by John O'Neill and performed by the Undertones, a group that had come together in Derry in 1976. Although not a literary masterpiece, the song personifies the energy of the popular music that emerged from Ireland during the period of the Troubles. It's a simple tale, but with its Irish and punk background, a song that you can't help singing along to.

Chapter 26

Ten Things the Irish Have Given the World

In This Chapter

▶ Contributions to military and medical science

▶ Ideas to make life more pleasant for people and animals

▶ Outlandish characters, from mythical creatures to American presidents

The Irish are recognised everywhere as a highly inventive and cultural people. For a small nation, they've punched well above their weight and made a huge contribution to the world we live in today. Earlier chapters in this book discuss lots of good things the Irish have given the world, such as Guinness. This chapter is devoted to those good things that haven't been dealt with yet. Bottom line – without the Irish, things just wouldn't be the same.

Irish Coffee

Wherever you go in the world, somewhere on the restaurant menu seems to be lurking the Irish (or sometimes Gaelic) coffee. Rather than being a drink steeped in a long and ancient tradition, the appearance of the first Irish coffee only happened in 1943. The drink is attributed to a man called Joe Sheridan, a barman working at the airport terminal restaurant in Foynes (from where flying boats used to depart from Ireland). The drink is a mix of coffee, sugar, and Irish whiskey, over which is poured a tablespoon of double cream. Added properly, the cream floats on top of the coffee, and the whole mix looks like a glass of Guinness. Although not the fashionable drink it once was, it is, nonetheless, a major Irish contribution to the culinary world!

The Abominable Snowman

Strange though it seems for a country that rarely sees any significant snowfall, it was the Irish who gave the world the greatest legend of the Himalayas. In 1921 a man from Tullamore, County Offaly, Charles Howard-Bury, was sent to map out the Himalayas, and figure out a route to the top of Everest. Prior to Howard-Bury's expedition, no European had been within forty miles of the world's highest mountain, let alone climbed it. The man from Tullamore did his job, and he mapped out a practical route by which Everest might be climbed (although it would actually take another 32 years before anyone managed that feat). While in the Himalayan foothills, Howard-Bury spotted in the snow some big footprints he couldn't explain. In a dispatch to the *Times* of London, he not only described the footprints, but attributed them to a large creature, the likes of which the world had never seen before. The Abominable Snowman had been born, and the Irish were responsible for a major contribution to the world of mythical creatures.

The Pneumatic Tyre

In the late nineteenth century, riding a bike was a fairly brutal experience. Solid tyres meant that every bump in the road could be felt, and broken wheels were a common and time-consuming irritant. Enter John Boyd Dunlop. Although born in Scotland, Dunlop had relocated to Belfast where he worked as a veterinary surgeon. His son, a bike fanatic, complained how uncomfortable life was on two wheels, so good old Dad, a part-time inventor, set to work. The result, in 1889, was the pneumatic tyre. The new air-filled tyre was such a success that a local bike racer, William Hume, asked to be allowed to use them. It was a revelation, and at a competition in Belfast, he raced to victory. An entrepreneur, Harvey du Cros, spotted the potential for the tyre, and went into business with Dunlop. Within the year the first Dunlop factory opened in Dublin, and the pneumatic tyre revolutionised bike riding. So thanks to Mr Dunlop for making life on a bike so much more comfortable.

Wind

Okay, so the Irish didn't give the world wind, but they were responsible for letting us all know how windy it actually is. Sir Francis Beaufort was born in Navan, County Meath, in 1774, and like many men of his time left home while still in his teens for a life on the ocean wave. He served in the British navy through the French Revolutionary and Napoleonic Wars, but was really fascinated about how life at sea could be made safer. He travelled the world mapping the oceans, and developed a system – the Beaufort scale – by which wind velocities could be measured. It made sailing for all much safer and meant that the world knew just how windy it was. Not content with one major contribution, Beaufort also proved, when no one was sure, that screw propellers were more efficient for steam ships than paddles, and invented a semaphore system for rapid communication. But it was his wind that he left behind for all of us.

Presidents of the United States of America

We all know that the Irish made a huge contribution to America, and that the numbers of people there who claim Irish descent run into the millions. But it was in the top job that the Irish really made their impact. Of all the Presidents to-date, at least a third, and some argue nearly half, had Irish roots. The first was Andrew Jackson. President from 1829–37, Jackson was conceived in Ireland, but born in America to parents from Boneybefore, County Antrim. Jackson is important because he sets the trend: most American Presidents with an Irish heritage are drawn from an Ulster Presbyterian background (eleven of them to-date), and not, as you might expect, from an Irish Catholic one. Since Jackson, there has been James Knox Polk, James Buchanan, Andrew Johnson, Ulysses Simpson Grant, Chester Alan Arthur, Grover Cleveland, Benjamin Harrison, William McKinley, Theodore Roosevelt, Woodrow Wilson, John Fitzgerald Kennedy (the most famous Irish President of them all – and the only Catholic in the list), and Ronald Reagan. More recently genealogists also worked hard to prove that Bill Clinton had Irish roots, and that George W Bush was a descendant of Strongbow (see Chapter 6).

Shorthand Writing

Not so popular now we all have computers, but several generations of office managers and their secretaries would have been lost without shorthand. Those bizarre squiggles and shapes that allowed dictation to be taken at speed were the brainchild of John Gregg from County Monaghan. Gregg's form of shorthand was most popular in America and was based on a phonetic system. It was adapted for use in languages other than English, and Gregg spent much of his life improving the system he had first dreamt up. At its peak, the Gregg system was essential to business life in America and was seen as so necessary that it was a standard feature on the school curriculum. People who excelled with the Gregg system could take notes at an average of 270 words per minute. Catering for everyone, the Gregg system of shorthand was eventually adapted so that left-handed people could use it.

The Submarine

Although the submarine was invented in America, it was an Irishman who gave the world a safe way of journeying underwater. John Holland was born in 1841 in County Clare. His first job was as a teacher for the Christian Brothers, but ill-health and financial insecurity forced him to emigrate to America in 1874. Once in America, Holland was taken by news of a Navy submarine design contest. He wanted to take part but lacked funds. Fortunately for him, his brother was Fenian, and people in that organisation were quite taken with the idea of something they could use to attack British ships. In 1881, Holland duly revealed his first submarine, the Fenian Ram. It was a three-man submarine that could dive to a depth of forty-five feet underwater. Having paid for it, the Fenians felt the submarine was theirs and stole it. They had one serious problem though; only Holland knew how it worked. So Holland and the Fenians parted company. In 1888 his next and Fenian-free submarine Holland IV won the Navy design competition, and he was on his way. He formed his own company, which sadly failed, and he eventually sold his patents. The American Navy continued developing his technology and the submarine entered military service.

Love of Animals

The Irish are known over the world for their horses, and they have always had a close relationship to animals because of their rural existence. Yet it was an Irishman who was central in the establishment of the first group to protect animals from cruelty. The Society for the Protection of Cruelty to Animals, the predecessor of societies across the world that protect animals, wouldn't have happened without Richard Martin, otherwise known as Humanity Dick.

Martin was born in 1754 to a family of wealthy Galway merchants. He was elected a Member of Parliament for Galway and lobbied extensively to stop cruelty to animals. He successfully introduced a bill to Parliament in 1822 to grant sheep and cattle protection from maltreatment. Martin was also a well-known duellist in Ireland and once fought one against the famed Fighting Fitzgerald for the honour of a wolfhound that had been shot by Fitzgerald. It was always animals that Martin defended. He was well-known in London for arresting people he felt were maltreating their animals and once famously brought a donkey to court as a witness in a trial against its cruel owner. Eccentric he may have been, but Humanity Dick was a friend of the animals.

The Hypodermic Syringe

Where would we be without the hypodermic syringe? Much loved by doctors and nurses and feared by almost everyone else, the hypodermic syringe is one of the most common surgical instruments in the world. The hollow needle was invented in Dublin, at the Meath Hospital, by Francis Rynd in 1845 as a way of introducing fluids into the body of the patient. He published his results in the journal *Dublin Medical Press,* and the idea was taken up around the world. The first injection into a live patient was carried out by Rynd on 12 March, 1845: it isn't recorded whether the patient screamed or not.

The Ejector Seat

Not many of us will ever have any reason to use an ejector seat, but the tale behind its invention probably strikes a chord with everyone. Sir James Martin was born in Crossgar, County Down in 1893. He was an engineer who, by the young age of 29, had set up his own business, the Martin Baker aircraft company. The company originally made aircraft, but during the Second World War began working on a system that would safely eject a pilot from a plane. The inspiration for the ejector seat allegedly came to Martin when he was stuck next to a nagging woman on a flight with no means of escape. He applied the idea of firing your seat away from undesirable fellow passengers to the problem of pilot safety, and the ejector seat was born. The first model was shown to the military in 1946, and in that year the first successful ejection from a moving plane was made. By 2003 the Martin Baker ejector seat had saved the lives of 7,000 pilots around the world.

Chapter 27

Ten Great Irish Places to Visit

. . . .

In This Chapter

▶ Sites to see for history buffs

▶ Wondrous natural formations and vistas

▶ Places to go for food

. . . .

Bookshops are full of guide books that will direct you around Ireland. Some are for the luxury traveller, others for people with a small budget and a backpack. Whether you are in Ireland for a few days or spending longer looking around, you'll find the list here helpful. It outlines some of the best places, the quirky places, and the stunningly beautiful places.

Cobh

Even the most diehard resident of Cobh would never claim that it was a beautiful place, but it's still well worth a visit as so much happened there. Cobh is about 15 miles away from the city of Cork and is the most important port in Ireland. It was named Queenstown in 1849 to honour a visit made there by Queen Victoria, and renamed Cobh after Independence in 1922. Its initial fame stems from its role as the largest departure point for Irish emigrants in the nineteenth century. The story of those emigrants, and the history of Cobh, is now told at the Heritage Centre on the harbour front. It's a great museum, and brings to life what Cobh was once like. The town was also the last port of call for the *Titanic* before she argued with an iceberg, and the place where the victims of the passenger ship *Lusitania*, torpedoed by a German submarine at the height of the First World War, were brought ashore in 1915. The sinking of the *Lusitania*, in which 1,198 people died, is commemorated in the town where most of the dead from the tragedy are buried.

Dingle Peninsula and the Blasket Islands

One of the great drives (fully signposted from Tralee) in Ireland is around the Dingle Peninsula in County Kerry. While it can get busy in summer, it's still a great place to visit. The landscape is breathtaking, as are the views of the

Atlantic Ocean. There are many ancient remains in the area, including the Iron Age cliff top fort at Dunbeg. At the tip of the peninsula, you can look out to the Blasket Islands, and an excellent Visitors' Centre introduces you to life as it once was on the islands. In Dingle itself, you'll find a bustling town full of shops and restaurants and Ireland's most famous dolphin, Fungy, who regularly appears for the benefit of tourists in the Bay. To understand the appeal, history, beauty, and fascination of the West of Ireland in one day, this is the drive to take.

Irish National Stud and Museum

One of the great Irish contributions to the world has been its horses, especially its racehorses. Not only have Irish horses won every major race in the world, over jumps or on the flat, but the Irish bloodline has been essential to horse breeding across the world. Horse breeding and the associated stud fees are a sizable proportion of the annual income of the Irish state. The best way of understanding the stud business and its importance to Ireland is to visit the National Stud and Museum in Kildare. You get to see lots of working stallions and their offspring, as well as have an opportunity to walk round a beautiful piece of open countryside within an hour's drive of Dublin. You also get to see the skeleton of the famous racehorse Arkle and, if you really want to know, learn how insemination works in horses.

Giants Causeway

Probably Northern Ireland's most famous landmark, and much beloved by the compilers of tourist literature, the Giants Causeway was formed some 55 million years ago. The volcanic eruptions that took place formed tall hexagonal columns that are tightly packed in a honeycomb formation, some rising as high as 12 metres. The Causeway features in legend as the place where Finn Mac Cool, the giant of ancient fable, used the rocks as stepping stones to cross to nearby Scotland (see Chapter 3). Nearby is also the famous Old Bushmills Distillery for those who want to understand Ireland's rich past as a whiskey-distilling country.

Derry

The history of conflict in Ireland is long and complex. One place where much of the action was regularly played out across the centuries was Derry. Its seventeenth-century walls are still intact and serve as a reminder of the Siege of Derry and the Protestant success in keeping out the opposing Catholic army.

This is still celebrated every year in August. The Apprentice Boys of Derry – a Protestant society – march around the city walls in celebration of the historic victories. More recently, the Northern Ireland troubles scarred Derry very badly. The Bogside, the Catholic area of town, was a no-go area for the security forces in the late 1960s and early 1970s, when the nationalist community took control of the area. It was known by the name Free Derry, and was adorned by murals that initially worked as territorial markers. Derry was also the scene of Bloody Sunday in 1972, and the deaths of thirteen civilians are commemorated in the Bogside by a succession of contemporary murals. To understand the history of communal strife in Ireland, a visit to Derry is a must as the historic and more contemporary signs of conflict are still there to be seen.

Kinsale

Famed as the site where a Spanish force occupied a piece of Ireland in 1601–02, Kinsale was also the location for disagreements over James II's succession to the throne that led to French forces harbouring there. Primarily a harbour town, Kinsale occupies a fine location and is worth the trip for the history and the location. The primary reason for any trip to Kinsale however should always be the same though: food. Kinsale is probably Ireland's leading culinary centre and is packed with excellent restaurants and bars, and some of Ireland's best chefs, who serve food sourced with local ingredients. It's a good place to indulge your hunger at anytime of the year, but really comes into its own during the first week of October when the Kinsale Gourmet Festival is held. Go there hungry and come away full of great food.

Croke Park

The headquarters of the Gaelic Athletic Association, Croke Park in Dublin, is the home of Irish sport. Games of hurling and Gaelic football can be seen there most Sundays during the championship season which runs from late April to mid-September. Even if you've never seen these Irish games before, go along. Apart from the finals, tickets are never a problem, and the atmosphere is great. All the players are amateur, and there is a real sense of community about a day in Croke Park. Someone sitting around you will be able to explain the rules to you, tell you how great their team is, and explore with you every slight that their opponents for the day have ever given to their own county. The referee will also be marked out as a man of upstanding character, fair-mindedness, and reason (or maybe not). If you can't make it on a match day, be sure to visit the excellent museum at the ground, which traces the history of the Gaelic Athletic Association and also allows you to try your hand at some basic hurling and Gaelic football skills.

Knock Shrine

In 1879 the silent apparition of the Virgin Mary, St Joseph, and St John the Evangelist to 15 people made Knock, in County Mayo, the foremost pilgrimage site in the whole of Ireland. Two subsequent Church Commissions of Enquiry, in 1879 and 1936, accepted the testimony of the witnesses, and Knock's place in Irish history was assured. Today over one million pilgrims visit Knock every year. Knock's place at the heart of the Catholic Church in Ireland was underpinned in 1979 when Pope John Paul II gave a Mass there, and again shortly afterwards when Mother Teresa visited. Even if you're not Catholic, a visit to Knock is worthwhile just to see the size and scale of the place, and the nearby shops full of Catholic paraphernalia make for interesting browsing.

Natural History Museum, Dublin

Most countries have a National History Museum, and Ireland is no exception. But whereas such museums in other places have been modernised and updated, the Natural History Museum in Dublin's Merrion Square is frozen in time. Apart from being renovated, the museum is a classic example of what the Victorians would have seen on a day out. It's more nineteenth century than twenty-first. The museum contains two million specimens of natural life in Ireland and from throughout the world. Opened in 1792, the organisers of the museum spent years killing it, stuffing it, and putting it on display for your pleasure. So if you want to see everything from the biggest shark ever caught off the Irish coast, to the smallest parasite found in the stomach of a dog, then this is the place for you. It's a testament to the collecting mania of the Victorians and their eye for presentation. It's kind of gross, but worth a visit for that reason alone.

Croagh Patrick

Just south of Clew Bay in County Mayo lies Croagh Patrick, a mountain of some 764 metres. If nothing else it's a beautiful place, and climbing the peak allows you a great view of the Mayo coastline, Clew Bay, and the scores of tiny islands in the Bay. What makes Croagh Patrick interesting is that it is the place where St Patrick is supposed to have spent four days in solitary prayer. For more than 1,500 years one of Ireland's great annual pilgrimages has taken place at Croagh Patrick, when thousands (many barefoot) retrace St Patrick's footsteps, and complete penitentiary rites at the stations, on the journey to the summit. Once at the summit, the climbers celebrate Mass at a small oratory that was built there in 1905. The pilgrimage takes place on the Sunday following the last Friday in July. Many Catholics make the climb, but it has also now become an annual ritual for many other people as they simply want to take part in a major annual national happening. If you are in the area, and don't fancy the climb, then see the nearby Famine Ship that memorialises the loss of life from starvation and disease, or else catch a boat across to Clare Island in the Bay, take a pint, and watch the best sunset in the West of Ireland.

Chapter 28

Ten Irish People Who Should Be Better Known

In This Chapter

▶ Scoundrels and murderers

▶ Athletes, artists, and adventurers

▶ One mighty fine bovine

*I*t's relatively easy to start making a list of well-known Irish people, and if the list starts including people of Irish descent, then the whole thing gets completely out of control. What's far more interesting is to consider those people who lived fascinating lives, made a contribution (good and bad) to the age they lived in, and that the rest of us have duly completely forgotten. So let's hear it for the unsung Irish who really should be better known by all.

Lady Betty

I did say that not everyone had done good things with their lives, and Lady Betty certainly gets into the bad category. She was born in County Kerry, but lived in County Roscommon during the second half of the eighteenth century where she ran a lodging house. More interested in money than the well-being of her customers, Lady Betty murdered one of her guests for the contents of his wallet. Not only was she arrested for her crime, but poor old Lady Betty's victim was actually her son, who had returned home after a long period travelling. Found guilty, Lady Betty was sentenced to be hanged. Her fellow condemned were members of the Whiteboy movement (rural troublemakers). As the Whiteboys were much feared, the hangman decided not to turn up for work. Spotting her chance of liberty and with no work experience in the particular field, Lady Betty offered to act as the public executioner. On her first day in the job she hanged twenty-five people (not bad for a beginner) and was employed by the state as public executioner for Connacht until her death. Nobody liked her much though, and she did have to live her life inside Roscommon Jail for her own protection.

Big Bertha

Yes, the list did say people who should be better known, and although not strictly a person, Big Bertha lived such a life that she deserves to be included here. Bertha was born in 1963 and finally passed onto the great pasture in the sky in 1993. Not a long life you might say, but for a cow it was a world record. Big Bertha was a droimeann, a white-backed cow, and belonged to Jerome O'Leary of Blackwater Bridge, County Kerry. Not only did she hold the record for being the oldest cow in the world, an achievement in itself that is worthy of recognition, but she was also the most prolific cow in the world. During her long life she produced 39 calves – another world record. So, while not a person, Bertha held two world records. As most of us never hold even one, Big Bertha deserves her place in the list.

Christian 'Kit' Davies

Kit Davies had a stable upbringing. She was born in 1667 to a prosperous brewing family in Dublin and, when she was still young, inherited her aunt's inn. All looked even better for Kit when, at twenty-one, she married Richard Welsh. But then he disappeared. It took a year for Richard to make contact and explain himself, and the excuse was a good one. He had been forced to join the army and was fighting for England in the wars in Flanders. Not one to let a good man get away, Kit took matters into her own hands. She passed herself off as a man and joined the army herself so she could look for her husband. She spent four years fighting in the war, and it took until 1706, when she was wounded at the Battle of Ramilles, until her true sex was discovered. She was a celebrity, and while the army retired her from active service, she followed her husband as a butler and provided troops with food and comfort. Sadly for Kit, her husband was killed in action in 1710. She quickly married again (a man from her former regiment), but he too got killed. Too old for the army life, Kit was granted an ex-serviceman's pension, and with her third husband, was given a place in the Chelsea Pensioners' Hospital in London. When she died in 1739 she was buried with military honours.

Tomás Ó Criomhthainn

Tomás was born shortly after the end of the famine on the Blasket Islands. He made his living as a farmer and fisherman and lived a subsistence lifestyle. Tomás was a great listener and grew up surrounded by the folk tales and oral histories of his relatives and fellow islanders. Encouraged by people who visited the Blasket Islands to hear his stories, all spoken in his native Irish, Tomás began recording them in the written form. Tomás produced an island journal, *Allagar na hInise* in 1928, and his most famous work, an autobiography, *An Toileánach* a year later. Tomás deserves all the credit for bringing his stories to life and making them available to a wider audience. Without him, other Blasket writers such as Peig Sayers and Muiris Ó Súileabháin might never have emerged. With the removal of the remaining population from the Blasket Islands in 1953, and the demise of a way of life, Tomás's work stands as a permanent testament to the community that made their living off the coast of Ireland.

Thomas 'Buck' Whaley

There are many ways to making a living, and Whaley, although an active politician, tried his best to provide for himself by gambling. Born in 1766, Whaley started his gambling conventionally and tried his luck with cards. He played often and for high stakes, but in Paris it all unravelled. He kept losing and was forced to leave the city in the face of mounting debts and many angry people who were demanding their money. Allegedly he lost £14,000 in one evening. On his return to Dublin, Whaley discovered that it wasn't conventional gambling and betting that could bring fame and fortune, but outrageous wagers. In 1788 he took on a £15,000 bet that he could walk from Dublin to Jerusalem and back within two years. He made it back to Dublin within 18 months and won the bet. Whaley was to attempt his most daring feat at the height of the French Revolution when he hatched a plan to rescue Louis XVI from the guillotine. Sadly for the French King, Whaley lost his nerve and Louis lost his head. In 1785 Whaley successfully got himself elected as an MP but fell foul of everybody by first taking bribes to vote for the Act of Union and then taking more bribes to vote against it. After a life disgracefully lived, Whaley died of rheumatic fever in 1800.

Monsignor Hugh O'Flaherty

There are many Irish priests who are famous, and many more that deserve some recognition, but Hugh O'Flaherty's achievements deserve greater recognition. O'Flaherty was born in Cahirciveen, County Kerry, in 1898 and completed his studies for the priesthood in Rome. During the Second World War, O'Flaherty used the Vatican and other Church property as a hiding place for Jews who were under risk from deportation to the concentration camps. He then used an extensive series of contacts that he had built up to ensure that these people and many allied servicemen caught in enemy territory made their escape from Italy to safe or neutral countries. By the end of the War, it was reckoned that O'Flaherty, or the Pimpernel of the Vatican as he had become known, had saved 4,000 lives. Israel honoured O'Flaherty by naming him as one of the 'Righteous Gentiles', the highest award that can be given by the state to non-Jews.

George Barrington

Born in Maynooth, County Kildare, in 1755, Barrington became a hugely popular figure during his lifetime and was immortalised in ballads and fiction. He made his name as a pickpocket. He was successful because he was well-dressed and had impeccable manners. Barrington was no street urchin, but a gentleman who simply couldn't be equated with his crime. His favoured victims were from the social elite and well-to-do: theatre-goers, patrons of race-courses, promenaders, and aristocrats. As a result of his audacious crimes, he became a regular feature in the newspapers of the time and was known as the 'Prince of Pickpockets'. He served several jail sentences, but there were always influential sponsors available who would assure the authorities of his good character and get him released early. In 1790 his luck ran out, and he was caught trying to steal a gold watch at Enfield racecourse. He was sentenced to seven years transportation and landed in Australia in 1791. Once there, he underwent a change of character. He found religion, was pardoned, and made superintendent of prisoners. He became well-known in Australia and was regularly referred to by the authorities as a model of reform. His lasting legacy was a series of books about life in New South Wales, although his life as a celebrity pickpocket makes for more interesting reading.

Sir Leopold McClintock

Not many people get places named after them, but Sir Leopold managed it in his own lifetime. Born in Dundalk, County Louth, in 1819, McClintock made his name as an Arctic explorer. In 1851 the ship he was on board, the Assistance, got frozen in by the ice and McClintock undertook a sledge journey of 1,290 kilometres – a feat that no one had ever managed before. From then on, McClintock was back in the Arctic most years. In 1852 he mapped the west coast of Prince Patrick Island, travelling 1,950 kilometres in 105 days by sledge. The reward was geographical infamy: Cape Leopold McClintock was named after him. He was promoted as a result of his Arctic explorations and took command of the frigate *Doris* in the Mediterranean. Although a sunnier posting, it was only a stepping stone towards his eventual promotion to the rank of vice-admiral. The real legacy of McClintock, despite a small barren part of the Arctic that is named after him, is the sledge. Without his work during all those miles pulling one about the frozen wastes, they wouldn't work as well as they do as he constantly improved their design. Remember him next time you take one out for a ride on a snowy day.

Lola Montez

Born as Elizabeth Gilbert, Lola lived life to the full. She was born at Grange, County Sligo, in 1821 and at 16 eloped with a 30-year-old army officer. The couple moved to India, but the relationship was doomed. On the return home, Lola began an adulterous affair with a minor noble that scandalised society. She was publicly branded an adulteress and so reinvented herself as Lola, a noble Spanish dancer. She began touring Europe performing her Spanish dance act and appeared regularly in the major royal courts of the time. Her career was hampered by one simple fact: She wasn't actually a very good dancer. Her beauty saved the day for her, and in 1846 she became the mistress of Ludwig I, King of Bavaria, who liked dancing and Spanish things and never clued onto the fact that Lola was from Sligo.

Rather than enjoy her new life, Lola interfered in the affairs of state and the entire Bavarian cabinet resigned in protest at her being given citizenship in 1847. Things went from bad to worse when, in 1848, she was attacked by an enraged mob who wanted to assassinate her for her interference in Bavarian life. This was the end for Ludwig, and he left her. She moved on to London, and married a 21-year-old soldier from a rich family. She forgot to tell anyone that husband number one was still alive in India and that they were still married, and she was prosecuted for bigamy. Moving to America, she reinvented herself once again, this time as a lecturer talking about fashion, beauty, and strong-minded women in history. The lecturing made her rich, as the public liked her and adored her life story. What a life, and like her lecture topic, what a strong-minded woman.

Mary McMullen

Nowadays sports people are well-known because their feats are quickly transmitted around the world by television. Not so in the eighteenth century. In those days you had to be really good to capture the public imagination. Born in 1764, Mary left Ireland for England and became an expert at the fashionable sport of the period – pedestrianism (or walking for money). McMullen's favourite feat was to walk 148 kilometres in under 24 hours (don't try this at home). She achieved fame as Mrs McMullen or the Female Pedestrian. She completed all her walks in full respectable Victorian women's dress which wouldn't have helped at all and was still walking for money in front of crowds into her 60s. It is recorded that she was watched by crowds of 6,000 people in 1826, when she completed two 148-kilometre walks within four days. She may not have had the million pound sponsorship package, and certainly no modern training shoes, but McMullen was a true athlete pioneer.

Index

• J •

• K •

• *O* •

FOR DUMMIES®

Making Everything Easier! ™

UK editions

BUSINESS

978-0-470-97626-5

978-0-470-97211-3

978-0-470-71119-4

Asperger's Syndrome For Dummies
978-0-470-66087-4

Boosting Self-Esteem For Dummies
978-0-470-74193-1

British Sign Language
For Dummies
978-0-470-69477-0

Coaching with NLP For Dummies
978-0-470-97226-7

Cricket For Dummies
978-0-470-03454-5

Diabetes For Dummies, 3rd Edition
978-0-470-97711-8

REFERENCE

978-0-470-68637-9

978-0-470-97450-6

978-0-470-74535-9

English Grammar For Dummies
978-0-470-05752-0

Flirting For Dummies
978-0-470-74259-4

Football For Dummies
978-0-470-68837-3

IBS For Dummies
978-0-470-51737-6

Improving Your Relationship
For Dummies
978-0-470-68472-6

Lean Six Sigma For Dummies
978-0-470-75626-3

HOBBIES

978-0-470-69960-7

978-0-470-68641-6

978-0-470-68178-7

Life Coaching For Dummies,
2nd Edition
978-0-470-66554-1

Management For Dummies,
2nd Edition
978-0-470-97769-9

Nutrition For Dummies, 2nd Edition
978-0-470-97276-2

Available wherever books are sold. For more information or to order direct go to www.wiley.com or call +44 (0) 1243 843291

30093 (p1)

FOR DUMMIES

A world of resources to help you grow

UK editions

SELF-HELP

978-0-470-66541-1

978-0-470-66543-5

978-0-470-66086-7

Origami Kit For Dummies
978-0-470-75857-1

Overcoming Depression For Dummies
978-0-470-69430-5

Positive Psychology For Dummies
978-0-470-72136-0

PRINCE2 For Dummies, 2009 Edition
978-0-470-71025-8

Psychometric Tests For Dummies
978-0-470-75366-8

Raising Happy Children
For Dummies
978-0-470-05978-4

STUDENTS

978-0-470-68820-5

978-0-470-74711-7

978-0-470-74290-7

Reading the Financial Pages
For Dummies
978-0-470-71432-4

Sage 50 Accounts For Dummies
978-0-470-71558-1

Self-Hypnosis For Dummies
978-0-470-66073-7

Starting a Business For Dummies,
2nd Edition
978-0-470-51806-9

Study Skills For Dummies
978-0-470-74047-7

Teaching English as a Foreign Language
For Dummies
978-0-470-74576-2

HISTORY

978-0-470-68792-5

978-0-470-74783-4

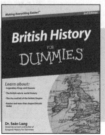

978-0-470-97819-1

Teaching Skills For Dummies
978-0-470-74084-2

Time Management For Dummies
978-0-470-77765-7

Training Your Brain For Dummies
978-0-470-97449-0

Work-Life Balance For Dummies
978-0-470-71380-8

**Available wherever books are sold. For more information or to order direct go to www.wiley.com
or call +44 (0) 1243 843291**

24940 (p2)

FOR DUMMIES®

The easy way to get more done and have more fun

LANGUAGES

Spanish For Dummies

978-0-470-68815-1
UK Edition

French For Dummies

978-1-118-00464-7

German For Dummies

978-0-470-90101-4

MUSIC

Guitar All-in-One For Dummies

978-0-470-48133-2

Guitar Chords For Dummies

978-0-470-66603-6
Lay-flat, UK Edition

DJing For Dummies

978-0-470-66372-1
UK Edition

SCIENCE & MATHS

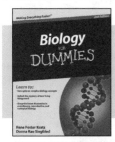

Biology For Dummies

978-0-470-59875-7

Algebra I For Dummies

978-0-470-55964-2

Genetics For Dummies

978-0-470-55174-5

FOR DUMMIES®

Helping you expand your horizons and achieve your potential

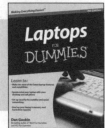

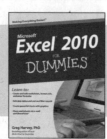